CHINOOKAN PEOPLES

of the

LOWER COLUMBIA

CHINOOKAN PEOPLES

of the

LOWER COLUMBIA

ROBERT T. BOYD,
KENNETH M. AMES, AND
TONY A. JOHNSON,

Editors

UNIVERSITY OF WASHINGTON PRESS
Seattle and London

© 2013 by the University of Washington Press
Composition by Integrated Composition Systems,
    Spokane, Washington
Design by Thomas Eykemans

Printed and bound in the United States of America
17 16 15 14 13   5 4 3 2 1

University of Washington Press
PO Box 50096, Seattle, WA 98145, USA
www.washington.edu/uwpress

Library of Congress Cataloging-in-Publication Data
Chinookan peoples of the lower Columbia / Robert T. Boyd,
Kenneth M. Ames, and Tony A. Johnson, editors. — First edition.
    pages   cm
    Includes bibliographical references and index.
    ISBN 978-0-295-99279-2 (cloth : alk. paper)
1. Chinookan Indians—Lower Columbia River Watershed (Or. and
Wash.)—History.   2. Chinookan Indians—Lower Columbia River
Watershed (Or. and Wash.)—Social life and customs.   3. Lower
Columbia River Watershed (Or. and Wash.)—History.   4. Lower
Columbia River Watershed (Or. and Wash.)—Social life and customs.
I. Boyd, Robert T.
    E99.C58C55   2013
    979.5'4—dc23   2013015931

The paper used in this publication is acid-free and meets the minimum
requirements of American National Standard for Information Sciences—
Permanence of Paper for Printed Library Materials.

Website: http://www.anthropology.pdx.edu/chinookanpeoples.php
Cover image: *Canoe, Columbia River,* watercolor attributed to Edward
Belcher, 1841. Courtesy Rare Books and Special Collections, University
of British Columbia Library, Belcher Fonds File 1, List 32, Vancouver, B.C.

CONTENTS

PART I. THE CHINOOKAN WORLD

Illustrations follow pages 145 and 306

MAPS, TABLES, AND ONLINE MATERIALS

ONLINE MATERIALS
(www.anthropology.pdx.edu/chinookanpeoples.php)

PREFACE

BEFORE the Columbia, there was *ímał;* before Astoria, Longview, and Portland, there were *qíq'ayaqilxam, qániak, gáłap'uλx,* and *gałáq'map;* before Oregonians and Washingtonians, there were Chinooks, Skilloots, Multnomahs, Clackamas, and Shahalas. It was a different world.

When Euro-American peoples arrived over two centuries ago, the Lower Columbia River was home to a thriving culture, with towns, houses, transportation, gardens, and literatures, all analogous to, but very different from, our own. Chinookan culture does not fit the picture many have of American Indians, or even of Northwest Coast Indians. Researchers who have studied Chinookan culture and the descendants of the Chinookan people themselves know this. But this knowledge is not general. One purpose of this book is to share with the contemporary inhabitants of Chinookan lands, and beyond, what we know and are finding out about this fascinating, antecedent culture.

Expect the unexpected in this book. Some Chinookans lived in outsized plankhouses that were occupied for centuries. Political "tribes" did not exist. The populations of some wild plants were managed, without being planted. Salmon was not the "staple" food that it has always been assumed to be. There was direct canoe contact as far north as Cape Flattery and east to the Columbia Gorge, and trade networks that extended even farther. Lower Columbia peoples had an orally transmitted literature with poetic and dramatic conventions and stories that were the equivalent of early European myths and sagas. Lower Columbia art, though sharing a few elements with North Coast art, was fundamentally and stylistically unique. There was no "church," and spirit relations were expressed through individuals. For a people classified as hunter-gatherers, Chinookans had relatively dense populations, and the decline in their numbers came not from warfare, but epidemic disease. The contemporary Chinook Tribe, unlike most tribes that have survived in the Northwest

Native American community, has (as of this writing) no formal recognition from the US government.

Another purpose of this book is to introduce readers to contemporary Lower Columbia Chinookans. Despite the devastating diseases, depopulation, and culture loss of the early contact era, Lower Chinookans—descendants of the people the first Euro-American explorers and settlers met—still live on the lower river. Chinook people below Longview, Washington, belong to the nonrecognized Chinook Tribe or are enrolled with federally recognized tribes at Shoalwater and Quinault. The Portland Basin peoples—Cascades, Clackamas, Multnomah—are mostly enrolled in the Confederated Tribes of the Grand Ronde, though through the vagaries of treaty-making and extensive intermarriage, many (particularly Cascades) are enrolled at Yakama, Warm Springs, and Cowlitz.

LANGUAGES AND CULTURES

The name "Chinook" (pronounced with the "ch" as in "chin" not "shin") is from *c'inúk*, the Lower Chehalis name for a village on Baker Bay, in the Columbia River estuary, and for its inhabitants. Early Euro-Americans adopted the name for the people who lived around the mouth of the Columbia and in time extended it to include all those who spoke the languages that are now recognized as members of the Chinookan language family.

In the early 19th century, Lower Chinook was the language of the people who lived near the mouth of the Columbia River, the Chinook to the north and the Clatsop to the south. Upper Chinook consisted of a chain of dialects spoken by people on both sides of the Columbia upriver as far as Five Mile Rapids, above The Dalles. The dialect spoken the farthest downriver (regarded by some as a separate language) was Kathlamet (Hymes 1955). Kathlamet may or may not have included Skilloot, which was spoken between Oak Point and the Kalama River but became extinct before it could be recorded. Next upriver, in the Portland Basin, were the Multnomah, whose speech was never sufficiently recorded but was presumably intermediate between Kathlamet and Kiksht. Kiksht was spoken by the Clackamas, the Cascades, and the upriver people—the White Salmon, Hood River, Wasco, and Wishram (Thompson and Kinkade 1990:41). It is the only Chinookan language still spoken today. There is a degree of correspondence between the divisions of the Chinookan family and vegetation zones within Chinookan territory. Chinook should not be confused with Chinuk Wawa (also called Chinook

Jargon), a form of pidgin Chinook that developed on the Lower Columbia at or before the beginning of contact with Europeans.

Since the late 19th century, anthropologists have divided North America into what they call "culture areas," geographic regions whose peoples share major features of culture. The Chinookans west of the Cascade Mountains shared plankhouses, dugout canoes, dependence on fishing, and beliefs about social stratification with peoples along the coast from southeast Alaska to northwest California, all of whom are part of the Northwest Coast culture area. The Chinookans east of the Cascade Mountains sometimes have been placed with peoples of the Upper Columbia and Upper Fraser Rivers in what is known as the Plateau culture area, perhaps because of culture traits linked to their inland environment; in other classifications, they have been placed in the Northwest Coast, perhaps simply because they are Chinookans. In this book, we deal with the Chinookans who inhabited the Columbia from its mouth up to and including The Cascades rapids. A relatively unpopulated area separated The Cascades and the Hood River–White Salmon people, who are usually placed in the Plateau culture area.

Through the mid-20th century, some anthropologists tried to distinguish divisions and subdivisions of culture areas by defining clusters of culture traits. This method placed many adjacent peoples into different culture areas and subareas, ignoring intimate social ties among them (Suttles 1990). Chinookans—as well as most of their neighbors—participated in a much larger social network, known as the Greater Lower Columbia.

THEMES IN CHINOOKAN RESEARCH

Three broad themes are important in the study of Chinookan culture: the concept of complex hunter-gatherers, different from the small-scale hunting-gathering peoples who have been the subject of so many anthropological ethnographies; regional social networks, which were prevalent in many parts of the world where there were no overarching political institutions; and the process of making tribes, whereby traditional organizing principles evolved through contact with white government into forms that were better suited to deal with a dominant political entity.

In 1966, Wayne Suttles gave a paper at the "Man the Hunter" symposium at the University of Chicago. The 75 anthropologists who attended that conference had done fieldwork among surviving or recently acculturated hunting-gathering cultures, including African Bushmen and Pygmies, Asian Veddas and Andaman Islanders, Australian Aborigines, and many North and South American Indian peoples who had one thing in common in their recent past—they did not practice (*stricto sensu*) "agriculture." Instead of planting crops, they hunted wild animals and gathered wild plants. This mode of getting food was assumed to limit the development, the so-called complexity, of their cultures. Most of these peoples were nomadic or semi-nomadic, had material cultures limited to what they could carry or construct easily, lived in family-based social units with no political superstructures, and practiced forms of animism.

Suttles was in an unusual position among the other experts at the conference. "His people"—the Straits Salish of Washington—like almost all other Native peoples of Washington–Oregon–British Columbia, were socially and economically more complex than the others who were being discussed. Even though the Straits Salish were nonagricultural, they were like agriculturalists in many aspects of their culture. The grand old man of cultural categorization, George Peter Murdock, did not include Northwest Coast Indians among his roster of living and recent hunter-gatherers and sniffed that "the Indians of the North Pacific coast seem to me to fall well beyond the range of cultural variation of any known hunting and gathering people" (Suttles 1968:15). Suttles's paper, "Coping with Abundance: Subsistence on the Northwest Coast," now an anthropological classic, elaborated:

> The Northwest coast refutes many seemingly easy generalizations about people without horticulture or herds. Here were people with permanent houses in villages of more than a thousand; social stratification, including a hereditary caste of slaves and ranked nobility; specialization in several kinds of hunting and fishing, crafts, and curing; social units larger than villages; elaborate ceremonies; and one of the world's great art styles. The area appears to have been matched in population density, among food-gathering areas, by only two or three areas adjacent to it. . . . These features of Northwest coast culture and demography are generally thought to have been made possible, or even inevitably produced, by the richness of the subsistence techniques of its peoples. Perhaps, then, the study of Northwest Coast [subsistence] can offer some guidance in estimating the possibilities of cultural development under comparable conditions in prehistoric times. (56)

Suttles was speaking about all Northwest Coast peoples, of course, and some of his statements fit better with those cultures to the north of the

Columbia River. But most ring true for the Chinookans as well, and some (such as population size) even more so. Drawing from his archaeological studies on the North Coast, the Plateau, and especially the Chinookan villages at Cathlapotle and Meier, Kenneth Ames has added to and elaborated on Suttles's list of traits that define Northwest Coast complex hunter-gatherers: they had food surpluses and sophisticated processing and storage methods, they had household economies and regional exchange, and they utilized a diverse range of wild foods and "manipulated their environments to increase productivity" (Ames and Maschner 1999:25–27).

From archaeological work in the last few decades, we now know that complex hunter-gatherers were common during the last 12 thousand years of human history. In fact, the old evolutionary assumption that plant domestication/agriculture preceded and was necessary for the development of many types of cultural complexity is no longer tenable. Well-documented historic and archaeological examples of complex hunter-gatherers beyond the Northwest Coast include the peoples of the Plateau culture area (Prentiss and Kuijt 2004), the Chumash Indians of the Santa Barbara Channel (Arnold 2001; Gamble 2008), Calusa of Florida (Widmer 1988; Marquardt 2001), the Jomon of Japan (Habu 2004), and the Natufians of the Levant (Schwartz and Akkermans 2003). Complex hunter-gatherer societies may have been typical of the more recent human past, and their diversity and richness are intellectually invigorating. Studying Chinookan culture may shed light on the lifestyles of many of our ancestors, as well as point out the diverse ways in which human cultures can express themselves.

Lower Chinookan peoples also were the focal culture in a large regional social network of a type that was probably common among so-called stateless societies around the world. Yvonne Hajda (1984) called the regional network centered on the Lower Chinook the Greater Lower Columbia. Throughout Native Oregon and Washington, most social relations occurred within the context of kin systems—maximally extended families. Senior males were considered leaders, but with no power to coerce their relatives, only the ability to guide by example and influence. Because there was a social preference for marrying outside one's family and village, which were often the same, people established networks of in-laws over sometimes broad geographic areas. It was these kinship networks that formed the core of the broader interactive region that Hajda defined.

Traditionally, anthropologists defined the Northwest Coast culture area by a list of shared culture traits. South of British Columbia, common culture traits included salmon as a staple food, the First Salmon ceremony, and complex fishing techniques; multifamily rectangular plankhouses and temporary dwellings, with winter villages and summer dispersal; bilateral kinship and extended families, loosely defined social classes, and slaves as property and rank-wealth status; horn bowls, wooden dishes, bent boxes, twined basketry, and an absence of pottery or masonry. The origins of the culture area approach were in turn-of-the-century museum exhibits, where cultures were grouped and distinctive artifacts displayed in limited spaces. In the mid-1900s, anthropologists cumulated "culture element" lists and produced statistically significant categories (e.g., Kroeber 1939; Driver 1961; Jorgensen 1980), but all these endeavors were static. There was no room for process, and that is what Hajda's model provided.

The Greater Lower Columbia included all Native cultures between the central Washington and central Oregon Coasts and all the Lower Columbia River drainage to just above The Cascades. The core area corresponds to the Lower Chinookan territory that is the focus of this book, but other members of the ecumene include Alsea and Tillamook on the Oregon Coast; Lower Chehalis and Quinault on the Washington Coast; two small Athapascan enclaves (Clatskanie and Kwalhioqua); and peoples of two important Lower Columbia tributaries, Cowlitz (Salishan) and Tualatin (Kalapuyan).

Using largely ethnohistorical data, Hajda (1984:123–32) defined the region by network linkages and distinctive culture traits. The network links included, first and foremost, documented marriages between groups but also food trades, conflicts, resource collecting, and visiting—nearly 80 all told, which fell into certain patterns. Her sample could be expanded greatly today, given the publication of new primary documents such as the *Annals of Astoria* (McDougall 1999). Hajda also looked at key culture traits/markers, including hairstyle (loose), dentalia through the nasal septum, women's dress (usually fringed cedar bark), four or five dugout canoe types, above-ground "burials" (usually in canoes), gabled plankhouses, and "Chinook style" head flattening. The last trait, interestingly, seems to have been the clearest diagnostic of the Greater Lower Columbia. People who had flattened heads were potential marriage partners, and all resided within the Greater Lower Columbia; by contrast, those without flat heads were either slaves (usually obtained from alien groups) or, quite literally, outsiders.

Other regional networks in the Northwest include Wayne Suttles's Coast Salish continuum, which consisted of overlapping networks of those who married, those who potlatched, those who participated in other ceremonial activities, and so on (Elmendorf 1971; Suttles 1987). There was also a regional network on the Columbia Plateau, defined by linkages (Anastasio 1972) and significant (in this case archaeological) traits (Hayden and Schulting 1997). Another clear region was on the north coast of British Columbia, where matrilineal kin structures circumscribed marriage patterns and labrets (lip plugs) symbolized membership (Suttles 1990:13). Given what we know from the Northwest, more research into regional systems could be very productive.

Early explorers and traders recognized this commonality of interaction and culture. Fault lines are different today, of course, but there is a shared cultural heritage among all the peoples of the Greater Lower Columbia: Chinook, Tillamook, Quinault, Cowlitz, Clackamas, Cascades, and so on are more alike than they are different.

The postcontact history of the Lower Chinookan peoples also serves as a prime example of what contemporary historians like to call "making tribes." Anthropologists term the study of group identity "ethnicity" and the process of group formation "ethnogenesis." In both disciplines, research involves (internally) the study of group markers and symbols and (externally) the dialectic/tension on boundaries that set one group off from another. Two classic studies in ethnicity/ethnogenesis in anthropology are Frederic Barth's *Ethnic Groups and Boundaries* (1969) and Edmund Leach's *Political Systems of Highland Burma* (1964), both of which demonstrate the continually evolving, fluid nature of ethnic and national groups. Among historians, two books in the "making tribes" genre, which emphasize the interaction between Native American groups and the US government, deal with the evolution of contemporary Northwest tribes: Alexandra Harmon's *Indians in the Making* (1998) on Puget Sound tribes and Andrew Fisher's *Shadow Tribe* (2010) on the mid-Columbia (Sahaptin) River people. The processes these authors describe are similar to what Lower Columbia Chinookans experienced.

In a region where people traditionally self-identified by family, extended family, and village or village cluster, how did "tribes"—with clear territorial claims and rules of membership, chiefs, councils, and other political institutions—arise and become prevalent? Lower Chinookan postcontact history has been one of constant change and frequent turmoil. Even before recorded face-to-face contact with Euro-Americans began in 1792 and again in the 1830s, Chinookans suffered severely from the effects of contact. Smallpox and malaria decimated populations, weakened traditional social structures, caused the loss of specialized knowledge, and produced considerable village regrouping and consolidation. Shortly after the epidemics ended, white settlers moved in, and within little more than a decade Lower Columbia Native Americans became a minority in their own homelands.

With the expansion of US territorial and federal government into the Northwest, Native Americans were subordinated to a new set of institutions. Much more rapidly than elsewhere in North America, treaties were made and reservations were established. The change that resulted from direct white contact from 1831 to 1856 was as revolutionary as it had been from epidemics during the preceding half century.

In the more than 160 years that Chinookans and other Lower Columbia peoples have been subject to US territorial, state, and federal laws, their experiences have mirrored those of other Native American peoples brought under US dominion, though with differences arising from local conditions. Traditional groups have sometimes been removed, sometimes remained in place, sometimes broken apart, sometimes kept more-or-less intact, almost always in response to governmental actions. This is where "making tribes" comes into play. The contours and membership of tribal groups respond to governmental institutions and edicts. During the first round of treaty-making on the Lower Columbia in 1851, groups were defined and leaders anointed by the signing of the treaties. The process was repeated, but with differences in the second treaty round, in 1853–55. Lower Chinook people refused to sign the Chehalis treaty and mostly stayed put, while upriver Chinookans were included in other treaties and removed to multiethnic reservations. At Grand Ronde, Warm Springs, and Yakama, Chinookans became minorities within minorities; they were subjected to cultural leveling, married into and integrated with coresident peoples, and assumed new identities as residents/ enrollees of their reservation communities.

Indians were not US citizens until 1924, and Indian groups were treated as dependent sovereign nations—hence, the legal need for treaties. During the 20th century, federal regulations became more specific in what they expected of Indian groups, recognized or not. The Indian Reorganization Act of 1934 encouraged tribes to select chiefs, form councils, compile tribal rolls, and put in place other Anglo-American ideas and institutions. Native groups began to deal with the US government through legal structures, first the US Court of Claims (1946–78) and then the federal recognition process (since 1978). Lower Columbia peoples, mirroring what has happened elsewhere in the US, have been affected by this process. Skilloots and Multnomahs lost their distinctive identities following the 1830s epidemics, while Kathlamet and Wahkiacum descendants are now part of the Chinook Tribe. Clackamas and Cascades are largely enrolled members of multitribal confederations, while Lower Chinook people have differentially affiliated with recognized tribes/reservations or stayed with their own unrecognized tribal organization.

This is the variable fate of the Lower Chinookan people: some lost early in the contact period, others redefined and affiliated with different groups, and some maintained their group integrity and identity, despite assimilative pressures and the changing policies of the federal government. This book documents the Lower Chinookan peoples' journey from then to now. As Indian people like to say, "We are still here."

ROBERT T. BOYD
January 2013

The section on "Languages and Cultures"
was written by Wayne Suttles.

ACKNOWLEDGMENTS

CHINOOKAN *Peoples of the Lower Columbia* has been a true collaboration among the editors; there is no senior author here. We have held innumerable meetings and split the editing and guidance of contributors' chapters according to our own research interests. Among our many authors, three in particular have done more than their share and deserve special mention: linguist and anthropologist Henry Zenk provided italicized standard spellings of Chinookan words and names appearing throughout the volume (symbols and standardization follow Jacobs 1958–59); ethnohistorian/cultural anthropologist Yvonne Hajda served as a third reader for several chapters; and archaeologist Liz Sobel coauthored three chapters. We are thankful for the enthusiasm and spirit of the University of Washington Press acquisitions editor, Marianne Keddington-Lang, whose support was very welcome in the final years of this project. We also want to thank Mary Anderson, the associate director of the press, for her support, and Julidta Tarver, who encouraged the project in its early years and generously agreed to proofread the book. The editors also want to thank all the contributors for their forbearance in dealing with what at times may have seemed like incessant editing and patience during the many years it took for this volume to become reality.

We also wish to express our appreciation of the volume participants and the others who contributed funds to cover the costs of the book's visuals. The nonvolume fund contributors are Pamela Amoss, Alison Stenger, and Willamette Cultural Resources Associates.

We are grateful for the help and input of the Chinook Tribe, the Cultural Resources Department of the Confederated Tribes of Grand Ronde, and, above all, the Chinookan and neighboring peoples of the Greater Lower Columbia, whose cumulated wisdom constitutes the bone, muscle, and soul of all that is said here.

Two of our contributors, the "elders" Wayne Suttles and Dell Hymes, did not live long enough to see final publication. To them, and to the many generations of Chinookan people who came before, we dedicate this book.

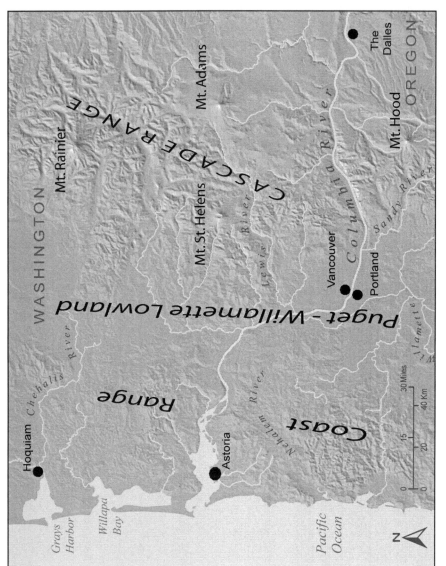

MAP 1. Environmental zones of the Lower Columbia River region

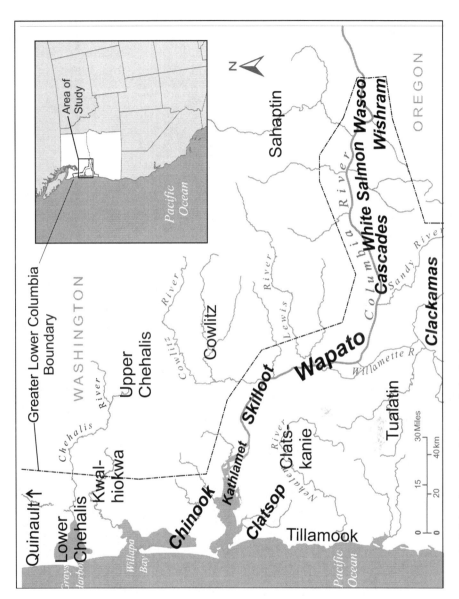

MAP 2. Tribal distribution on the Lower Columbia River

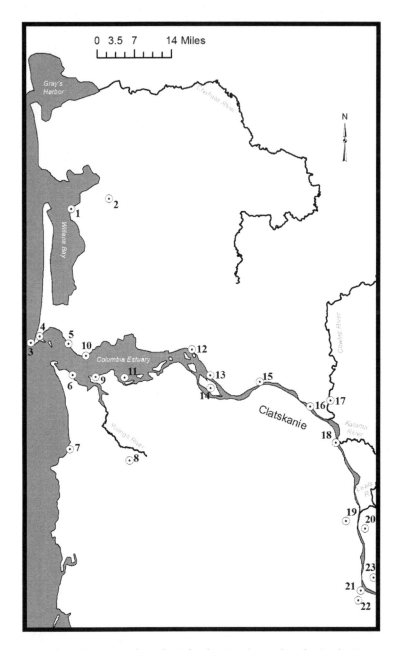

MAP 3. Modern place-names from the Columbia River's mouth to the Cowlitz River. Key: 1. Bay Center; 2. South Bend; 3. Peacock Spit; 4. Cape Disappointment; 5. Chinook; 6. Tansy Point; 7. Seaside; 8. Saddle Mountain; 9. Astoria; 10. Point Ellice; 11. Cathlamet Bay; 12. Skamokawa; 13. Cathlamet; 14. Puget Island; 15. Oak Point; 16. Mount Coffin; 17. Kelso; 18. Coffin Point; 19. Scappoose Bay; 20. Ridgefield National Wildlife Refuge; 21. Columbia Slough; 22. Smith and Bybee Lakes. (Map prepared by David Harrelson and Volker Mell and used courtesy of Confederated Tribes of Grand Ronde.)

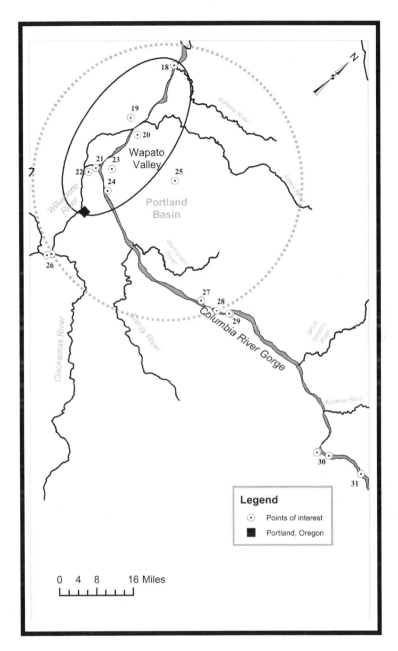

MAP 4. Modern place-names from the Cowlitz River to The Dalles. Key: 18. Coffin
Point; 19. Scappoose Bay; 20. Ridgefield National Wildlife Refuge; 21. Columbia Slough;
22. Smith and Bybee Lakes; 23. Vancouver Lake; 24. Fort Vancouver National Historical
Site; 25. Battle Ground Lake; 26.West Linn and Willamette Falls; 27. Beacon Rock;
28. Bonneville Dam; 29. Cascade Locks and Bonneville Landslide; 30. The Dalles,
The Dalles Dam, and Wascopam; 31. Celilo Falls. (Map prepared by David Harrelson
and Volker Mell and used courtesy of Confederated Tribes of Grand Ronde.)

CHINOOKAN PEOPLES

of the

LOWER COLUMBIA

First Salmon Ceremony, Astoria, Oregon, 2007. (Courtesy of Kenneth M. Ames, photographer)

A baby boy was born to proud Chinook parents. The baby was put to its mother's breast. Grandparents and the baby's siblings were brought to see him. A Chinook cradle had been made with a carving of a strong spirit to look after him. Images of canoe paddles were placed on that cradle to remind him of his past and future. The young boy was placed in the cradle and slept and ate there. Another grandmother, the placenta, was taken by the father into the woods. Deep enough not to be disturbed, but in a place where he could return when he felt the need. A young tree, tall and strong, was located in a good place along the creek. A hole was dug among the roots. Five long dentalia, saved for the purpose, were unwrapped. Grandmother was turned over in the fashion of his ancestors and placed carefully in the hole. With the gift of dentalia and words spoken in Chinook, much was placed there. A knowledge that the boy would grow tall and strong and live a long life with the help of that tree. A thank you to the grandmother for taking care of the boy, and an understanding that by ritualized treatment of the grandmother she would help bring a child of a different sex the next time.

The boy's limbs were pulled and rubbed to make them straight and strong. Chinook lullabies sent him off to sleep. Only good words were said to him, and he was reminded how much he was wanted here, all to make sure he did not go back to the place he came from, a place called Sunrise. The parents knew that all babies miss Sunrise and their acquaintances there. That special care paid off, and he chose to stay with them. Later, when he learned to speak, he told of the people he knew and what he had done there.

A few years passed, and his hair was long. He was handsome, and he had grown strong. He would be strong in the canoe, and he already had a paddle. He was a good runner, and he loved to shoot his bow. His family was proud of that boy, and he had the name of his grandfather.

His mother was pregnant again. She took off her necklaces and bracelets, went quickly through the doors, and never looked at an animal being butchered or at snakes. She followed the many taboos of her ancestors and gave birth to the girl baby they both knew they would have.

The boy was born in 2005 and the girl in 2010. They, like their three older siblings, are Chinookans of the Lower Columbia River.

THE CHINOOK PEOPLE TODAY

Tony A. Johnson

W HERE are the great Chinooks of the Columbia River today? To the casual observer it may appear that we are gone completely. Even those educated in such matters have made assumptions and statements that have led them to that conclusion. Even some who have done best by us, recording our ancestors' knowledge in great detail, have done us an injustice by claiming that their informants "proved to be the last survivors of the Chinook" (Boas 1894:6). This claim of having known or worked with the last Chinook or the last Clatsop led to our community being largely ignored by generations of ethnographers and linguists. But there was still much to study and to learn from us. An indigenous heartbeat continues to beat in the chests of Native residents of the Lower Columbia River, and we have continued to hold much to ourselves for the benefit of our children. Gary C. Johnson, Chinook tribal chairman from 2000 to 2006, made this clear in a 2002 interview:

> We need people to know the Chinook story and what happened, and the
> difficulties that our families have faced over all the years. I would really like
> them to know the Chinook people and the elders who have lived tradition-
> ally and tried to maintain the culture. They're a strong people, a soft-spoken
> people, just really a caring people . . . they opened their arms and helped
> the newcomers to the area and they continue to act that way. If we need
> something from those people, they always come through for us, and getting
> to know the way our people were, and still are, is very important. It's also
> important, too, that the story is told about what happened to the land, how
> people in my father's generation, my grandmother's generation, were taken
> and sent to Indian schools and the government policy was clearly stated.
> You know, kill the Indian, save the child. And it was really tough times for
> people to live through, and to try to maintain their culture and try to main-
> tain their family connections. Those stories need to be told so people under-
> stand. Some of our families have a tough time today, and it's because of what

parents and grandparents and great grandparents have gone through, and that's one of the reasons it's really important to be able to offer the housing, the health care, the education, those kinds of things, and build our tribal community.

The Chinook Indian Tribe/Chinook Nation is a politically united community of people who descend primarily from the five westernmost groups of Chinookan-speaking people: Lower Chinook, Clatsop, Willapa, Wahkiakum, and Kathlamet. These formerly independent tribes were always associated with one another, but only since the late 1800s have they formed a united community. The political entity that arose from this was named by its members the Chinook Indian Tribe/Chinook Nation (hereafter referred to as the Chinook Tribe). The tribe has had several main towns of residence that have maintained strong connections and traditional alliances through time.

Members of our community, like those in most confederated environments, identify themselves with one group or another within the Chinook Tribe. People will proudly claim "I am Wahkiakum" or "I am Clatsop and Kathlamet." A community anecdote concerning the birth of Chinook elder Herbert Frank illustrates this point. When Frank was born, his grandfather Samuel Millet entered the room and asked his daughter Emma Luscier, "What's the baby?" She replied, "This is a Wahkiakum." This impressed Sam, who said, "My father he came back, his [the baby's name] will be my father's name" (Harrington 1942–43; Antone Luscier, personal communication, 1997).

Our community members are in many cases mixed to varying degrees with the local non-Native population and neighboring tribes. Through relationships with the federal and state government, neighboring tribes, and our own community, however, we maintain a distinct identity in southwest Washington and northwest Oregon.

It is essential to mention the Shoalwater Bay Indian Tribe, the only group of downriver Chinookans that currently have a formal government-to-government relationship with the United States. The one-square-mile Shoalwater Reservation was established by a presidential executive order on September 22, 1866, for what were called miscellaneous "Indian purposes." The reservation has been occupied primarily by Lower Chinook, Lower Chehalis, and Clatsop people. It exists today in the northwestern corner of Willapa Bay and is closely related to the Chinook Tribe, especially the Chinook community at Bay Center, Washington.

At the time of earliest contact with Europeans, foreign diseases had already diminished the Chinooks. Despite this, we gained great fame as a people of strength, technological prowess, and economic savvy. We have and continue to be greatly misunderstood. We are simultaneously looked to for the knowledge of our ancestors and told that we are not a tribe by the very federal government that bears a trust responsibility to us.

The Chinook Tribe and individual members have maintained ongoing and consistent relationships with the United States government, the State of Washington, local governments, and the governments of other tribes. Despite this, we have found ourselves in the position of having to prove our identity in the course of struggling to maintain rights to land, hunting, fishing, and other issues of significance. The Chinook Tribe today is involved in a legal process that is termed "federal acknowledgement," which is nothing less than a fight for survival. We Chinook who were raised in and closely connected to the homeland of the Chinook people consider it to be self-evident who we are. In addition to being instilled with the values and history of the Chinook people, the communities surrounding the Chinooks have always treated us as Native Americans.

In the recent past, the Chinook people were relegated to out-of-the-way places, and it is in such communities that we live today—communities like Bay Center, Altoona, and South Bend, Washington, and Astoria, Clatsop Plains, and Seaside, Oregon. The largest and most distinctively Chinookan of these communities in recent times has been Bay Center, which has been home to many prominent individuals from all corners of the Chinook Tribe's original homelands. Some of the representative families and their original affiliations are the Pickernells, Hyasmans, Olivers, and Hawks from the Lower Chinook; the Salakies, Cultees, and Jacksons from the Clatsop; the Georges and Charleys from the Willapa; the Elliots, Goodells, and Eros from the Wahkiakum; and the Mallets and Talltriches from the Kathlamet.

Non-Native residents of Willapa Bay have consistently referred to Bay Center as the "reservation." Ross Neilson, who served as auditor of Pacific County from 1934 to 1941 and as treasurer from 1942 to 1973, had ample opportunity to get to know the residents of the region. He testified: "Long before South Bend or Raymond was organized, Bay Center was a reservation for Chinook Indians with status about the same as Tokeland's Shoalwater Reservation" (Beckham 1987:105). He believed this for good reason. Not only was there a large population of Chinook tribal members in this community, but many of those members lived on Indian trust land at Bay Center. Throughout Chinook territory, individuals and families had parcels of land held in trust by the federal government, including the house where Gary and LeRoy Johnson were raised in South Bend. It is important to remember that the Shoalwater Reservation was originally established for all Indians on Willapa Bay and that many of the current members of the Chinook Tribe were associated with it in an earlier time as well.

Prior to the mid-1800s, we maintained a much different relationship with the newly arrived Europeans and Americans. Until that time, the Chinook had been the majority population in the area and the source of most of the economy and labor for non-Native enterprises. We were not discounted or taken lightly. Many Chinooks who had survived the earlier epidemics temporarily prospered from these relationships.

Then, with the growing numbers of overland settlers and continuing disease, we became more like observers of our own history, as we lost control over much that was important to us. We were removed from our village sites, the graves of our people, and our fishing and hunting sites, many of which had been occupied by our people from the beginning of human existence in the Pacific Northwest. Many of those who had relied on our help and participation felt for our situation, but by then there was an infrastructure that enabled newcomers to bypass us. We simply came to be in the way.

In addition to disease, the newcomers brought alcohol, which was a significant problem in Chinook families and communities. According to our elders, drowning was not a common occurrence long ago. We were and are a water people, who according to custom washed twice a day in the cold water of our local streams, ponds, and rivers. After alcohol was introduced, however, a great number of our people were lost to alcohol-related drowning. This is remembered, along with the epidemics, as a reason for our rapid decline in population.

Early places of refuge for Chinooks retreating from the influx of non-Natives into our country were remote locations that newcomers did not immediately consider to be valuable. A place like Goose Point, the primary early Chinook community in Bay Center, was simply a swamp where cedar planks were laid down during the winter to allow access from house to house. The Pillar Rock area was another such location. There was no road there until 1947, and the Chinooks could remain secluded while still finding work in the fishing industry. Chinook fishing families still call these areas home.

In many ways, the Chinooks have been driven off the Columbia River. Chinooks continue to reside in Columbia River communities such as Cathlamet, Naselle, Astoria, and Ilwaco, but the only area on the river that maintained, until recently, a distinct Chinook identity was the Pillar Rock/ Altoona/Dahlia area. Sadly, as property values increase in these areas, the number of Chinook families that can afford to reside there typically decreases.

Another example of such a remote location is Long Island in southern Willapa Bay. In earlier times, Long Island was a site of villages, a stopping point for Chinooks as they traveled and a destination for people visiting or looking for specific resources. It is still a place of power, a sacred site. Chinook oral history tells us of a time when the people had been removed from much of their land. Disease had taken most of them, and they were simply moving from place to place and with the seasons where work or resources allowed. During this time, an epidemic, perhaps the last real epidemic in our homeland, threatened to take the remaining Chinooks. It hit many Chinook communities, including the village at Goose Point. Many Chinook families were on Long Island at the time, and the disease never crossed over to infect them, and there are Chinooks today who have this fact to thank for their ancestors' survival. Chinooks continued to reside on Long Island in varying numbers, although later they had to move from the island, as from so many other places.

The five tribes associated with the Chinook Tribe today, as well as others, signed treaties at Tansy Point, near Astoria, Oregon, in 1851. The treaties were signed in good faith by our ancestors and by Superintendent Anson Dart, who was empowered by the federal government to do so. It was our understanding that these were legal documents, and the Chinook peoples acted accordingly. When these treaties were taken to Washington, DC, for ratification, however, the US Senate refused them, apparently because they were too generous to us. While not exceptional, the treaties allowed the tribes to maintain land in their traditional homeland near the graves of their ancestors, an important consideration. They also allowed for access to goods, the abiliy to build, cash payments, and use of resources. It was an important time for our people.

In 1855, we were again asked to participate in treaty negotiations, this time with Washington Territorial Governor Isaac Stevens. The Lower Columbia River people who participated in the negotiations, conducted on the Chehalis River in Grays Harbor, Washington, were disappointed to learn that the government hoped to move us north to the Olympic Peninsula. Our ancestors feared that they would be moved to the land of the Quinault, who were considered traditional enemies. This fact, combined with our unwillingness to leave the villages and graves of our ancestors, made our ancestors, as well as those of the Chehalis Tribe, unwilling to sign the treaty. The following year, Governor Stevens completed treaty negotiations in Olympia with the Quinault and Quileute Tribes. Quinault had been the only group agreeable to the terms of the 1855 Chehalis River treaty negotiations. The resulting Treaty of Olympia created the present-day Quinault Indian Reservation.

On January 14, 1861, a significant group of non-Natives living on the Lower Columbia expressed their concern with our plight in a letter to the federal government:

MEMORIAL OF CITIZENS OF OREGON AND WASHINGTON ASKING FOR RELIEF FOR SUNDRY INDIAN TRIBES

January 14, 1861

TO THE COMMISSIONER OF INDIAN AFFAIRS

TO THE HONORABLE THE CONGRESS OF THE UNITED STATES:

Your Petitioners, citizens of the State of Oregon and Territory Washington respectfully report:

That in the year 1851 the then superintendent of Indian Affairs assisted by agents and sub-agents by authority and direction of the President of the United States negotiated a treaty on Clatsop Plains in Oregon with the Indians residing on the Lower Columbia and on the coast near the mouth of said river, consisting mainly of Chinook, Clatsop and Tilla-mooks, whereby the government undertook to pay said Indians large sums of money and property to relinquish their lands to the white settlers which treaty was never ratified. Under the act, Congress donated lands to settlers. All the lands of these Indians capable of being occupied or used by them including the villages, gardens and fishing have been taken and they have been driven away or are liable to be driven away by the white owners and cannot build a hut or draw a net without the white man's permission.

During all the wars and troubles with other tribes which have cost the government many millions of dollars, these Indians have remained peace-able and have not engaged in hostilities or caused alarm to the settlers or expense to the government, but on the contrary have sometimes saved the lives and often contributed to the safety and comfort of persons wrecked upon their shores or otherwise cast upon their hospitality, and this not-withstanding the whites were daily incroaching [sic] upon and driving them from their homes under the authority of Congress until at last they have not an acre of uninhabited land remaining.

These Indians are reduced in numbers at least half since the said treaty but the survivors have not, and neither have your petitioners, abandoned the hope that the government will yet do them justice and thus avoid the odious imputation of filching from these long-suffering and friendly tribes the right which was purchased so dearly from their warlike and trouble-some neighbors. Your petitioners therefore pray that an appropriation may be made to compensate the tribes and remnants of tribes which were included with aforesaid treaty for their lands so taken by Congress and donated to white settlers and as these Indians are not of one tribe and have no organization or acknowledged head, they further pray that some person or persons residing in the district and acquainted with the Indians may be appointed under proper safeguards to distribute among them the goods or moneys so appropriated. (Oregon Territory, 1821–68)

Among the long and impressive list of signers of this petition were William Strong, Robert Shortess, Job Lamley, John Brown, and B. F. Olney. After the failure to ratify our treaties, we simply tried to survive. At about the same time, we suffered an even greater injustice, one that we consider wholly illegal. In February 1864, US Secretary of State John P. Usher took all Chinookan lands according to the "Schedule of Indian Land Cessions." It is our opinion that the secretary of state did not have legal authority to write a title for our land.

Chinook tribal members have had varying degrees of success integrating with mainstream society. Some of the skills handed down within our community were immediately marketable as our communities changed with the influx of non-Natives. One such skill was that of the bar pilot. The Columbia River Bar is the only river entrance in the United States that requires a bar pilot, and many were Chinook tribal members who had learned the intricacies of the Columbia River through a lifetime of experience and generations of knowledge.

Fishing has always been an important part of our community. Traditional fishing camps and fishing gatherings, however, came under increasing scrutiny by non-Natives during the early 1900s. The competition for fish and a general disregard for Native Americans led to a well-remembered confrontation that exemplifies our experiences during this period. During the fishing season of 1928–29, a Chinook fishing crew under the direction of Chief

George Charley was confronted while fishing on our traditional fishing lands at Peacock Spit at the mouth of the Columbia River. The US military arrived with the intention of removing us. Antone Luscier remembered that they arrived with fixed bayonets and that all the Indians had were "oars and fists" (1996, personal communication). This was a rare moment when the Chinooks fought, and the military, apparently unwilling to shoot our people, was driven back toward Chinook, Washington. Our crew continued to fish. It is remembered, though, that in subsequent years those who wished us removed simply arrived at fishing sites before we did.

As traditional fishing spots were being removed from our control and we were increasingly unable to fish unmolested, hunger began to be an issue for our people. Sam Pickernell told of times when he would go "gathering" with his grandmother (2001, personal communication). The gathering referred to going to the town of Chinook at low tide, where they had received permission to collect discarded fish heads and parts under a salmon cannery. Despite these things, the tribe maintained its strong connection to the water. Members modernized their gear as time went on, and they are an important part of the local fishing fleet today. In addition to salmon fishing, our members fish for sturgeon and crab and grow oysters and dig clams of all types. George Lagergren's (2002) memories of his early days fishing are typical:

> when I was a young boy I started gillnetting. . . . I'd take a couple, two, three weeks off during the fishing season, and I'd make enough money to buy my clothes and what I needed for my own. And so that's the way we survived. We lived mostly on common foods like fish, smoked fish, we always had a smoke house going because there was fish running in all of these streams just about year round.

Until only recently, our members were able to fish and hunt as any other Indians could in the state of Washington. Our members were issued Blue Cards identifying them as Chinook Indians and granting them the right to fish and hunt as such. This right has been taken away from us, causing great disruption to the traditional lifestyle of many of our members. Most were forced to quit fishing with their Blue Cards in the 1980s, although a few fished with them into the 1990s.

Not only men found work in the fishing industry. Martha Stephans, an elder from the Pillar Rock region, was known for her skills in net mending, and she served as a mender for local fishermen for most of her life. Other women have found work in local canneries and processing plants, and tribal members like Peggy Disney of Bay Center started their own shellfish and fish-buying businesses.

Families continue to enjoy hunting and fishing. Without treaty rights to fish, however, the tribe has been forced to find ways to supplement members' needs for salmon. One solution is an arrangement between local state fish hatcheries and the Chinook Tribe to provide excess salmon. This has become a way for members to stock freezers, smokehouses, and pantries with fish for the winter and to provide food for gatherings and ceremonies.

Even though these fish are a welcome addition to tribal members' increasingly modern diets, many are concerned about the effect of hatcheries on our streams and rivers. Hatcheries and the policies of state governments have been detrimental to the wild salmon of our area, and many runs of wild salmon have become extinct. George Lagergren (2002) says about the Nemah River: "In those days, you see, there was a run of Chinook Salmon that came in about the first part of July. There was a really beautiful nice Chinook salmon that came in at that time, but they're gone now. There's none of those left that I have seen."

Another example of the adverse effect of modern policy is the fate of chum or dog salmon, a favorite smoking fish for our people. According to oral history, the State of Washington, believing that dog salmon is a low-quality fish, put hog wire across many of our streams in an effort to eliminate them from those tributaries. Then a nonnative variety of silver salmon from the Satsop River system was introduced to these waters.

The First Salmon ceremony is of great importance to us. This and other ceremonies have been maintained by individual families or in the minds of elders. The Chinook Tribe has made an effort to reinvigorate the ceremony with a closed community gathering held each year at Chinook Point. The organizers of the ceremony work to maintain the protocols established in our mythology and adhered to by our ancestors for that place on the north bank near the mouth of the Columbia River. This is a direct attempt by the Chinook Tribe to strengthen the fish runs on the Columbia River, the tribe's relationship with those fish, and our culture generally.

Our people's mythology speaks to different time periods in our history. There are the myth days when animals and other things lived much like people do today. There was the time when our world was being changed to prepare it for the people who would be coming, and there are stories of real people and their lives. We are fortunate that ethnographers and linguists worked with our elders to record many of these stories. Beatrice Disney (2002), a Chinook elder, remembers her grandmother Rosa Taltrich-Pickernell as a storyteller: "She used to tell us stories about how the raccoon got his mask and things like that, and us kids would just sit around her chair just fascinated by the stories she would tell." We are fortunate that our elders have preserved many stories that have not otherwise been recorded. Surely much of our oral history was lost with the epidemics, but we are grateful to have those things that have come down to us today. The Chinook Tribe holds an annual storytelling gathering at the end of each winter to celebrate this knowledge and tradition.

Another essential tradition is the giving and receiving of names. The Chinook Tribe continues to remember the necessary elements of this tradition, and many members are working to continue this practice. Current Tribal Chairman Ray Gardner (2002) says of receiving his name:

one of the things that is important to me is . . . my Indian name I was given [it] by my great aunt and it's "Makwat." . . . I was given that when I was four years old, and the translation of that is 'the ghost that walks on water' and what that is, is the real slow-moving fog that lays right on top of the water and moves very slow.

There is also an effort to maintain a traditional relationship with the environment and to preserve traditional subsistence and material culture. Many families speak of the history of migrating from place to place for various activities, from digging roots to gathering bark. Spring is a fondly remembered time for many of our members, especially for the salmonberry shoots and other fresh greens available then. These activities are still practiced today, and tribal youth and elders alike are still compelled by gathering.

Basket making is an art that has survived through our difficult times and is experiencing a resurgence today. Elders like Milly Lagergren and Beatrice Disney, both deceased, were well known for continuing their great Aunt Bessie Pickernell's style of basketry. Their children and grandchildren carry on this tradition, as do other members of her family and the community. Others are working to perpetuate other traditional basketry types. Baskets from our elders continue to be passed down, used, and cherished.

Mismanagement of resources and invasive species are making it increasingly difficult to find many of the resources necessary to perpetuate our culture. Spartina, a nonnative marsh grass, is choking out many of our favorite patches of sweetgrass or saltwater sedge, used in basketry. Stands of cedar, especially old-growth cedar, are becoming difficult to find. Cedar bark from young trees and the wood of large old-growth trees are essential for much of our material culture.

One of the best-known and important uses of old-growth cedar by the Chinook people is the making of canoes. It is said that in the past there were as many canoes as there were people in Chinook territory. They were essential to our old people, and in many ways it could be said that canoes were treated like family members. They were our primary mode of transportation and today are a primary mode of revitalizing our culture. George Lagergren (2002) remembered:

> I grew up on the Middle and South Nemah River. We had a little twelve foot canoe, and me and my brother [Fred] spent a lot of time in that little canoe. We'd leave the house and we'd go down the river on the outgoing tide and we'd go and get our clams or oysters. From the Middle Nemah we'd go down and into the lower part of the bay, and then we'd go west and go clear around to the little old village that we called Sunshine. We watched the tides you see as we traveled, because we could make short cuts from one part of the bay to the other, according to the tides, and then on the tide, then we'd go back around and then when we start up the river again we'd hit the incoming tide, and that helped us. We had two paddles, he had one and I had the other one, and we'd paddle that little canoe everywhere.

Although only a few of our elders' canoes have survived, they also carved model canoes, many of which are in museum collections and in the homes of our community. Based on models, the few surviving originals, and recollections of the elders, tribal members are carving a new generation of canoes. Since 2000, the Chinook Tribe has built, named, and launched six Chinook-style canoes, from 11 to 36 feet long.

More broadly, watercraft-building skills have been passed down through generations of Chinooks. Some tribal members became master builders of modern fishing boats. Joseph "Josie" George (1871–1945) had been a canoe maker in childhood but updated his skills and applied them to modern boat-building. It is a source of pride today to own a Josie George boat.

For many years, the Chinook Tribe has held the Chinook Indian Summer

Festival in Bay Center. The festival has become more and more focused on a paddle event, which opens "the traditional water highway" between Bay Center and the Shoalwater Bay Reservation. The Bay Center–Georgetown Paddle alternates each year with a canoe trip between the two communities and has become an important event uniting the two closely related communities.

The Chinook Tribe participates annually in Tribal Journeys and has traveled thousands of miles in their community canoes. Tribal Journeys is a yearly gathering of the Pacific Northwest canoe nations where a host community invites guests to travel by canoe to their aboriginal area to participate in a week-long potlatch. This revitalization of the potlatch system in the Pacific Northwest results in over a hundred canoes arriving on the beaches of the host tribe.

It is often said that language is the key to culture. By the 1850s, local Chinookan dialects were giving way to Lower Chehalis, Tillamook, and Chinuk Wawa, but they were known by some individuals until about the 1940s. There are individuals who still remember something of the old languages, but the last fluent elder speakers of Lower Chehalis and Chinuk Wawa died in the 2000s. The home language of Chinook tribal member and former council member Phillip Hawks was Lower Chehalis; he did not speak English until entering school in Bay Center. Chinuk Wawa has recently undergone a revival with several individuals learning it from elder first-language speakers. Because of the long time span in which language shift took place in our community, much cultural knowledge passed from one language to another, ending up in myths and anecdotes preserved in English and Chinuk Wawa.

Traditional religion is respected in the tribal community today, and even those who do not practice it do not ignore the taboos associated with it. Winter dancing, for example, is important within the community, as is traditional cold-water and sweat bathing. Individuals with strong power are remembered for that reason, and these sensibilities continue to be encouraged. Goose Point, Bay Center, has been the home of two Shaker churches. While there is no Shaker church today in Chinook Indian country, it is still considered a religion of the community, and numerous community members consider themselves practicing Shakers.

The lifestyle of Chinooks today is in some ways reminiscent of the longhouse living of our ancestors. Chinooks have tended to live in family groups in corners of otherwise American communities. These have been places where community members have taken care of each other and where traditional stories and family histories were preserved. Sometimes these stories were preserved in unusual ways. Myrtle Woodcock (1899–1973), a Chinook elder who is well remembered, rewrote many traditional and historical stories into poetry. She required her children and other Native youth in the neighborhood to memorize the poems so they would not be forgotten.

Despite not having a reservation, the Chinook community was subject to the same "kill the Indian save the child" policies as other Native Americans were. It is remembered that wagons would arrive in the Pillar Rock area to take the Indian children to the boarding school at Chemawa, near Salem, Oregon. Wagons also arrived in the north part of the bay, at Bay Center and the Shoalwater Bay Reservation, to take tribal youth to Cushman, near Tacoma, Washington. Chinook children were taken at very young ages to these schools, and returning home for holidays or other events was a privilege that was not typically granted to new students. Our oldest elders never spoke of their time in these schools, so negative were their experiences there. Ray Gardner (2002) says of his family's experiences:

> when I was young they used to talk about how they would try and get together and speak in their own language [at Indian boarding school] they were punished, and, after they got caught more times, then they actually separated them even within the school to try and keep them from even having the ability to associate with each other.

In later times, some boarding school experiences were better, and today some elders speak fondly of their time attending them.

The Chinook community of the early 1900s was profoundly influenced by the government's Allotment in Severalty policy. While individuals were allotted land by preference on their own reservations, the lack of sufficient land elsewhere led to granting allotments to Makah, Quileute, Hoh, Chehalis, Cowlitz, Shoalwater, and Chinook individuals on the Quinault Reservation, which had a large land base. The Chinooks, with a relatively large population and no reservation, ended up receiving over 50 percent of the allotments created at Quinault. Vital to our case for federal acknowledgment is the fact that the Supreme Court of the United States in *Halbert v. United States* (283 US 753[1931]) confirmed Chinook individuals' rights to allotments on the Quinault Reservation. The result of the case was that the Chinooks became the majority landholders on the reservation and held affiliated treaty rights. As it happens, individuals must be members of federally recognized tribes to receive allotments.

The current constitution of the Chinook Tribe, written in 1951, specifies criteria for membership in the tribe, which is based on descent from three rolls—the Roblin Roll of 1919, the Annuity Payment Roll of 1914, and the McChesney Roll of 1906. When viewed together, they identify the surviving members of the five westernmost bands of Chinooks. The majority of Chinook tribal members reside within the boundaries of our traditional homelands. The tribe has adopted an elected representative form of government, with a nine-member council and a committee structure focused on enrollment, culture, communications, business, health, and fish and wildlife. Tribal offices are in Bay Center, Washington, although meetings are held annually in locations throughout our traditional homelands as a way of honoring each of the five ancestral tribes of our community. To an outsider, perhaps the government is the most obvious feature of the Chinook Tribe, although it would be a rare Chinook today who would identify that as the most important part of our identity.

In discussing the Chinook today, we would be remiss not to mention other Chinookan people of the Columbia River. The great nations of the Chinook people consisted of linguistically and ethnically related groups who lived from the mouth of the Columbia River to the Five-Mile Rapids area east of The Dalles, Oregon. The easternmost Chinookans, the speakers of the Kiksht dialects, the Wasco, the Wishram, the Dog (Hood) Rivers, the Cascades, and others are still with us as well.

The north and south shores of the Columbia River were not always boundaries for Chinookan communities. European concepts used in treaty negotiations and later the division of the Oregon Territory, using the Columbia River as one of the boundaries, divided Chinookan-speaking people in ways wholly contrary to traditional sensibilities. Through these non-Chinookan sensibilities the Wishram and Cascades people were attached to the Yakama Reservation in Washington, while the Wasco and Dog River people were attached to the Warm Springs Reservation in Oregon. In both cases, Chinookans were placed on reservations with majority Sahaptin-speaking people, becoming minorities in the communities to which they were removed. These are the only Chinookans who have maintained unsevered treaty relationships with the US government. They have maintained a distinct identity within these communities through their spirituality, their songs and dances, their mythology, and their language.

This wealth of knowledge, like that in most Native communities, is in danger of being lost, and there are many individuals who should be commended for their efforts to preserve this history. The middle river Chinooks, the Multnomahs, the Clackamas, the Tumwaters, and others are likewise still with us. There are a great number of people from these areas who identify themselves as Chinookan, primarily the Lower Willamette River peoples of the Grand Ronde Reservation. The Cascades, Tumwaters (Willamette Falls), and Clackamas were parties to the Willamette Valley Treaty, which helped establish the Confederated Tribes of Grand Ronde (see ch. 15 in this volume). These Chinookans, along with more than 20 other bands of people attached to the Grand Ronde Reservation, had their trust relationship with the federal government terminated in 1954. In response to this blow, they organized to regain their status, and did so in 1983. The Chinookan people of the Grand Ronde are working to maintain their connections to the past. One of the primary connections for Columbia River Chinookans at Grand Ronde is the persistence of the community language, Chinuk Wawa.

The Chinook Tribe is a long-standing member of Native organizations, including the Small Tribes of Western Washington, the Western Washington Indian Employment and Education Training Program, the Affiliated Tribes of Northwest Indians, the National Congress of American Indians, and the Southwest Washington Inter-tribal Health Alliance. For nearly two decades, the tribe received Administration for Native American funding through the federal government.

Our situation as a so-called unrecognized tribe is not unique. There are many tribes in similar situations throughout the United States. Some tribes were terminated by the federal government, while others, like the Chinook, were simply neglected. Numerous tribes, like those in western Oregon, gained or regained their status as recognized tribes through acts of Congress. A new process within the Bureau of Indian Affairs was created that was intended to provide a timely and fair process for tribes to gain recognition. This process, administered by the Office of Federal Acknowledgment, reflects the BIA's concern that Congress lacks the knowledge to decide who, in fact, is Indian.

The Chinook Tribe was an early petitioner under this process and persisted in its bid for recognition from 1978 until 2002. In January 2001, during the presidency of Bill Clinton, the *Federal Register* published the BIA's opinion that the Chinook Indian Tribe/Chinook Nation was a tribe. On the 89th day of the 90-day comment period, the Quinault Tribe, fearing the ramifications of Chinook recognition, filed negative comments.

Chinook tribal status had been in place for approximately 18 months when the tribe was notified that its status had been revoked, primarily because of internal BIA politics and the Quinault Tribe's intervention. Unbelievably, Chairman Gary Johnson was notified of the revocation on July 5, 2002, while he was in Washington, DC, for the national kickoff of the Lewis and Clark Bicentennial. Despite this, both before and after the decision, Chinooks contributed in major ways to the Bicentennial, hosting a four-day Chinook Nation Commemoration, creating several museum exhibits, and participating in events at the White House and across the nation. The federal government gave us grant money so that we, the people who had helped save Meriwether Lewis and William Clark, could tell our story.

The Chinook Tribe hopes to clarify our status for a number of reasons. Many consider formal recognition to be the only way to guarantee our existence as a cohesive community into the future. It is essential for economic development, the establishment of a land base, the preservation of our culture, the reinstatement of fishing and hunting rights, the ability to repatriate our ancestors' bones and sacred items from museum collections, and the ability to better care for our community's health and well-being.

The history of the Chinook Tribe in postcontact times is but a blink of an eye. Many non-Chinooks feel that injustices occurred so long ago that they should just be forgotten. We know, however, that we are just a few generations away from the time when we were the only people who resided in this country, and we continue to live with the consequences of two hundred years of American history. An important teaching of our people is that it takes as long to fix a problem as it took to make it. We know that our positive actions now will affect the future of our children and grandchildren.

The members, and especially elders, of the Chinook Tribe must be thanked for their contributions to our understanding of our history. While written by one individual member, this information belongs to the Chinook Indian Community.

At a potlatch hosted by the Swinomish people in 2011 our Chinook Canoe Family was on the floor. The hosts called several representatives from our family. Then they called for the oldest and youngest members who traveled to Swinomish with us. The youngest person at that time was our daughter. We carried her forward to accept her gift, a beautiful hat woven of cedar bark.

Their calling her to the floor required an announcement: they had pierced her ears! Not literally, of course—she was not yet one year old—but a descen-

dant of chiefs who hopes to inherit that rank has to have their ears pierced when they are brought out in that way to a community for the first time. This is a Chinook teaching.

Ears were pierced for many reasons, and they recorded the story of a person's life. My father's great-great grandmother, Tonwah, was the first of his ancestors on that side of the family to have a photo taken of her. That picture shows the evidence of a remarkable life. A life recorded as holes pushed into ears.

Our daughter, her siblings, her relatives, and all Chinooks have a lot of room left on these ears.

PART I

The Chinookan World

ONE

ENVIRONMENT AND ARCHAEOLOGY
OF THE LOWER COLUMBIA

Elizabeth A. Sobel, Kenneth M. Ames, and Robert J. Losey

T HE Columbia is the great river of the American West. The interplay of river, ocean, mountains, and climate produced a rich and productive but dynamic environment, and people have lived in and adjusted to this environment for at least 12,000 years. The fourth largest river in North America, the Columbia is exceeded in water volume only by the Mississippi, St. Lawrence, and Mackenzie Rivers. Its source is in British Columbia, on the west slope of the Canadian Rockies. Between there and where it enters the Pacific Ocean, the Columbia flows 1,268 miles (2,040 kilometers), winds through four mountain ranges, descends 2,657 feet (810 meters), drains 257,993 square miles (668,200 square kilometers), generates more hydroelectric power than any other waterway in North America, and historically has supported more salmon than just about any other North American river (Roberge 1985:11–16; Schwantes 1989:12).

The Lower Columbia generally refers to the river's final 196-mile (315-kilometer) run from the western edge of the Columbia Plateau to the Pacific Ocean. The Lower Columbia begins at The Dalles, a constricted portion of the river channel also called Five Mile Rapids or the Long Narrows. From there to the Pacific, the river flows through four distinct physiographic provinces—Cascade Range, Willamette-Puget Lowland, Coastal Uplands, and Outer Coast.

Below The Dalles, the Columbia cuts 75 miles (120 kilometers) westward through the Cascade Mountains, which extend north from California though Oregon and Washington to British Columbia. At 14,436 feet (4,400 meters), Mount Rainier is the highest peak and is visible from the Columbia River on a clear day; other high stratovolcanoes visible from the Lower Columbia are Mount Adams, Mount St. Helens, Mount Hood, and Mount Jefferson. Lower peaks in the Cascade Range are generally 3,000–6,500 feet (914–1,981 meters) high. Rainfall is heavy on the Cascades' western slopes, averaging as much as 98 inches (250 centimeters) annually. Dense forests are dominated by Douglas-fir (*Pseudotsuga menziesii*), western red cedar (*Thuja plicata*), and western hemlock (*Tsuga heterophylla*) (Avery 1961:23; Orr et al. 1992:141–48; Schwantes 1989:7–14).

The Columbia River Gorge, where the river passes through the Cascade Range, was created some two million years ago and is defined by steep basaltic walls up to 3,900 feet (1,200 meters) high. The Gorge formerly contained a waterfall and a series of rapids that early Euro-American travelers called the Cascade Rapids, now submerged beneath Bonneville Dam. Tides affect Columbia River water levels as far east as Bonneville Dam, 186 miles (300 kilometers) from the sea. As the only near-sea-level passage through the Cascade Mountains, the Gorge is extremely windy and wet and occasionally very cold, particularly during winter periods when winds push into the Gorge from the east. Moist coastal air moves eastward through the Gorge and upward, over the mountains, generating roughly 71 inches (180 centimeters) of precipitation annually (Orr et al. 1992:153–55; USGS 2008).

After leaving the Gorge, the Columbia takes its 53–mile (85–kilometer) course through the Portland Basin, called the Wapato Valley and Columbian Valley by Meriwether Lewis and William Clark. This lowland—which contains the cities of Portland and Gresham, Oregon, and Vancouver, Washington—is part of the larger Puget-Willamette Lowland, an alluvial plain some 137 miles (220 kilometers) in length and 18 miles (30 kilometers) in average width. The lowland runs south from Puget Sound to southwest Oregon, flanked on the east by the Cascade Range and on the west by the Coast Range. The Puget-Willamette Lowland is humid with a long growing season, high biodiversity, and high biomass. Historically, this biologically rich landscape encompassed multiple habitats, including wetlands, riparian forests, oak woodland savannas, and meadows. The adjoining foothills bore coniferous forest. The Columbia's course through the Wapato Valley is broad and slow, weaving through swampy bottomlands, winding among islands, and diverging into numerous sloughs (Ames and Sobel 2009:2; Hajda 1984:51–55; Orr et al. 1992:203–4; Schwantes 1989:7–14).

Departing the Wapato Valley, the river flows 62 miles (100 kilometers) through the Coast Range. In Oregon, the crest of the Coast Range averages

1,500 feet (460 meters) in elevation, and some peaks rise more than 4,000 feet (1,200 meters); in Washington, the Willapa Hills have rounded peaks generally less than 200 feet (60 meters) in elevation. The coastal mountains have mild winters, cool summers, and thick vegetation dominated by Douglas-fir, red cedar, and western hemlock (Livingston 1969:1–3; Orr et al. 1992:167–80; Schwantes 1989:7–14). As the Columbia River flows through the Coast Range, it enters its estuary and becomes exceptionally broad, flowing through flat, sandy plains and reaching its maximum width of 9 miles (15 kilometers) about 12 miles (20 kilometers) before reaching the Pacific Ocean.

The river mouth is almost 4 miles (6 kilometers) wide between Cape Adams on the south and Cape Disappointment on the north. The Columbia's broad entrance, where heavy fogs are typical, prevented European and US explorers from detecting the mouth of the river until 1792, 17 years after the first maritime explorations of the Pacific Northwest; the expeditions that sailed by the river's mouth during those years thought it was simply a bay (Hajda 1984:35–46; Ruby and Brown 1976:24–58). The Columbia's mouth is not only large but also exceedingly rough, and entry into the river is treacherous. Since European arrival in 1792, hundreds of individuals have died and some two thousand vessels have sunk trying to cross the river mouth. It is the third most dangerous river entrance on earth and the only US entrance requiring river bar pilots (Dietrich 1995:97).

Most of these environmental features were in place well before European contact. The Columbia Plateau is 17 million years old, and the Cascade Mountains are 2 million years old. Over the past 20 thousand years, the Lower Columbia River area was significantly modified by geological processes, including glacial activity during the Late Pleistocene or Ice Age. Between 19 and 12.5 thousand years ago, glacial Lake Missoula in eastern Montana repeatedly breached ice dams, generating a series of catastrophic floods across eastern Washington and the Lower Columbia River Basin. Carrying ice, huge boulders, and tons of debris, the so-called Missoula Floods scoured eastern Washington and then entered the Columbia River about 81 miles (130 kilometers) east of The Dalles. The floods steepened the walls of the Columbia River Gorge and deposited huge volumes of gravel and other sediments in the Wapato Valley (Orr et al. 1992:209–14).

The most recent large-scale geological events affecting the Lower Columbia are the Cascade Landslides in the Gorge. The latest of these, the Bonneville Landslide, occurred between AD 1400 and AD 1500, and its debris formed a natural dam that temporarily blocked the Columbia. The river

Years AD/BC	Region	Estuary	Wapato Valley
AD 1850	Early	Early	Early
AD 1750	Modern	Modern	Modern
AD 1500	Late	Ilwaco 1	Multnomah
AD 1000	Pacific		Phase
AD 500			
AD 1		Ilwaco2	Merrybell
BC 500	Middle		Phase
1000	Pacific		
1500		Sea Island	
2000		Phase	
2500	Early		????
3000	Pacific		
3500			
4000			
4500		????	
5000			
5500			
6000			
6500		Young's River	????
7000	Archaic	Complex	
7500			
8000			
8500			
9000		????	
9500			
10000			
10500		????	????
11000			
11500	Clovis/Stemmed Pts		
12000	????		
12500	Paisley Cave		

FIGURE 1.1. Archaeological cultural phases for the Greater Lower Columbia River

eventually breached or eroded the dam, possibly causing a significant flood event downstream. Landslide debris on the floor of the river created The Cascades (O'Conner 2004; Pringle et al. 2002; Schuster and Pringle 2002; Bourdeau 2001).

Massive earthquakes have affected the Columbia every 500 years, on average, for at least 3,500 years, the last in 1700 (Jacoby et al. 1997; Losey 2002; Satake et al. 1996; Yamaguchi et al. 1997). Each earthquake triggered a tsunami

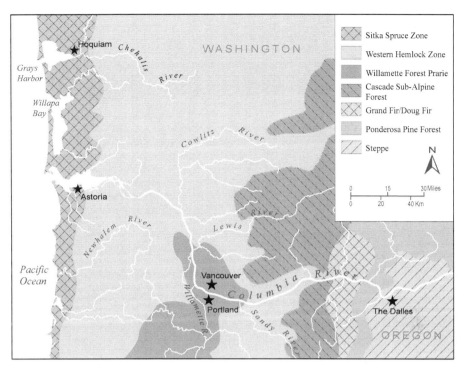

MAP 1.1. Lower Columbia River vegetation

and caused long stretches of the Pacific Coast to abruptly sink below sea level and undergo major flooding (Atwater 1987, 1992; Atwater and Yamaguchi 1991; Darienzo and Peterson 1990, 1995; Shennan et al. 1996, 1998), reconfiguring shorelines throughout the Lower Columbia area (Minor and Grant 1996; Peterson et al. 2000).

The climate and biota of the Lower Columbia also have changed over time. Paleoecological data record these changes during the last 11 thousand years, when humans first entered the region. The most relevant data are from three sites, at Taylor Lake and Lost Lake on the northern Oregon Coast and at Battle Ground Lake in Washington, southwest of Mount St. Helens (Long et al. 2007). During the Early Holocene (from about 10,000 to 7,000 BP), the climate was warmer and drier than it is today, especially during summers. West of the Coast Range, forests were dominated by Douglas-fir, as they are today, but Early Holocene forests were more open and contained more fire-tolerant species. East of the Coast Range, the Wapato Valley was characterized by open oak (*Quercus*) savanna (Walsh et al. 2008).

In the Middle Holocene, after about 6700 BP, the climate became cooler, with more effective moisture. West of the Coast Range, a relatively modern forest took over, with Douglas-fir still dominating but species such as Sitka spruce (*Picea sitchensis*), western hemlock, and western red cedar present. East of the Coast Range, the oak savanna declined, replaced at Battle Ground Lake by Douglas-fir and western red cedar (Walsh et al. 2008). Oak savanna did not entirely disappear, however, and was common in the Willamette Valley during the 18th and 19th centuries, partly because of human impacts on the landscape (Boyd 1999a).

In the Late Holocene, over the past two thousand years, climactic changes led to a warmer, dry period from about AD 850 to AD 1250 (the Medieval Climatic Anomaly) and the subsequent cooler wetter period from AD 1450 to AD 1850 (the Little Ice Age). These shifts affected local vegetation and fire regimes (Long et al. 2007; Walsh et al. 2008), but impacts on humans in the region are less clear.

CULTURE
Earliest Occupants (before 11,500 BC)

There is no archaeological evidence on or near the Lower Columbia River that tells us about the region's earliest people. We know that humans were present in the Americas by 11,500 BC (Goebel et al. 2008), so we assume they also were present along the Columbia River by then. There is controversial evidence for an earlier human presence in the Americas—for example, remains from the Monte Verde site in southern Chile that may date to as early as 12,500 BC (Dillehay 1997). In 2008, human feces dating to about 12,300 BC were found at the Paisley Cave site in central Oregon, fairly close to the Columbia River (Gilbert et al. 2008).

Biological evidence, including modern and ancient DNA, shows that modern Native Americans descend from ancient Asian populations that migrated into the Americas. These people probably traveled from Siberia to Alaska by way of Beringia, which stretches between Alaska and Siberia and is now the floor of the Bering Sea. Beringia is often called a land bridge, but it may have been as much as 1,118 miles (1,800 kilometers) wide and included interior Siberia and Alaska. Early migrants may have walked across Beringia into Alaska where, until perhaps 14 thousand years ago, glaciers blocked their way southward into the rest of North America. Alternatively, they may have traveled by boat along the southern coast of Beringia, in which case their way southward along the North American coastline would have been blocked by glaciers until perhaps 16 thousand years ago. The coastal migration hypothesis, then, allows for human arrival in the Americas some one thousand to two thousand years earlier than the inland migration hypothesis (Ames and Maschner 1999; Goebel et al. 2008; Roosevelt 2000; Roosevelt et al. 1996; Stone 2003). If the first Americans did move southward along the North American coastline, then the Columbia River was the first available route into the continental interior.

Paleoindian Period (11,500 BC–10,500 BC)

The Paleoindian period is the earliest established period of human habitation in the Americas. The only widespread and well-documented early Paleoindian material culture in North America is the Clovis complex, best known for its Clovis points, which probably functioned as knives and spear tips. Archaeologists typically date Clovis sites to the period between 11,500 and 10,800 BC (Goebel et al. 2008), but the Clovis complex may date to a briefer span of fewer than 400 years, between 11,200 and 10,800 BC (Waters and Stafford 2007). Archaeologists have interpreted Clovis sites as evidence of a highly mobile hunting-gathering people with a subsistence economy centered on megafauna (very large mammals), but recent analyses indicate that at least some peoples in that period did not focus on megafauna and had more sedentary land-use patterns (Collins 2007:59–87; Goebel et al. 2008; Kornfeld 2007; Byers and Ugan 2005; Cannon and Meltzer 2004). Clearly, Paleoindian economies and societies were more diverse than researchers once thought.

The Pacific Northwest has yielded only a scattering of Paleoindian sites, all of them Clovis sites. Along the Lower Columbia River and throughout Washington and Oregon, Clovis sites include mainly flaked stone artifacts (Ames and Maschner 1999:65–66; Croes et al. 2007; Matson and Coupland 1995:66–67; Pettigrew 1990:518–21). All known Clovis sites in the Columbia River region were found on the ground surface or in disturbed subsurface contexts, with one exception: an undisturbed cache of Clovis artifacts from the East Wenatchee site (also known as the Richey-Roberts site) in Washington (Ames and Maschner 1999:65–66; Gramly 1993; Matson and Coupland 1995:66–67). The cache contained some of the largest known Clovis points and a number of bone rods that may have had ceremonial significance (Ames et al. 1998:103). The lack of sites suggests that the region was thinly inhabited during the Paleoindian period, the inhabitants generally did not use Clovis technologies, or both.

Archaic Period (10,500–4,400 BC)

The low density of known Early Archaic (10,500–7,000 BC) sites in the Pacific Northwest and the near absence of storage features and house remains imply that people lived in small, mobile groups and built lightweight houses. Early Archaic remains from the Northwest interior have been assigned to the Windust phase, during which people likely preferred wetlands and used resources that included bison, elk, deer, antelope, rabbits, and fish. Windust points— stemmed, lanceolate flaked stone tools—probably served as spear points, atlatl dart points, or knives. Although no plant remains have been recovered, we assume that Early Archaic peoples used plants as food and raw materials (Ames et al. 1998:103–8). Early Archaic remains are uncommon on the Northwest Coast. Known coastal sites indicate an economy that involved a mix of deep-sea resources, such as halibut; wetland (intertidal, estuary, and river) resources, including shellfish, salmon, flounder, eulachon, seal, sea lion, and beaver; and terrestrial resources, including elk and deer.

The Lower Columbia River area contains only one sizable Early Archaic deposit, dating from about 7,300 BC to 6,000 BC (Butler 1993; Butler and O'Conner 2004). The Windust phase component at the Five Mile Rapids site is located beside an eddy at the upstream end of the Columbia River Gorge, an excellent place for harvesting salmon. In the 1950s, University of Oregon archaeologists under the direction of Luther Cressman excavated some 150 to 200 thousand salmon vertebrae and a range of artifacts, but no apparent fishing gear, from the Windust component (Cressman et al. 1960). In the 1990s, Butler (1993; Butler and O'Conner 2004) re-excavated portions of the site and confirmed that the abundant salmon bones were of cultural— not natural—origin. By the end of the Early Archaic period along the Lower Columbia River, therefore, subsistence economics included riverine resources and, in some cases, may have targeted salmon. In the Lower Columbia River Valley, Early Archaic remains are limited to a number of Windust points found as far downriver as the Wapato Valley (Portland Basin) and possibly some Windust-like points found near the mouth of the Columbia (Ames and Maschner 1999:125; Minor 1984).

Much like their predecessors, Late Archaic (7,000 BC–4,400 BC) peoples across the Northwest lived in small, mobile groups and used a variety of terrestrial, wetland, and marine resources (Ames and Maschner 1999:123–27). The sites in the area are scattered through the Cascade Mountains and foothills, on plateaus in the Wapato Valley, and on the Columbia River floodplain. Most appear to represent short-term habitations or "camps." Flaked stone tools from these sites reflect a shift from the stemmed, lanceolate points of the preceding period to smaller leaf-shaped points, often called Cascade points. Late Archaic remains also include large leaf-shaped bifaces, such as those found near the mouth of the Columbia at the Youngs River Complex.

Pacific Period (4400 BC–AD 1750)

Pacific Northwest Native cultures developed into their historic form during the Pacific period. Significant changes include the appearance of a subsistence economy based on storing large volumes of food; increased population density, sedentism, and household and community size; escalated warfare; development of canoe-based land-use patterns; more institutionalized social status differences; management of natural resources and landscapes; and a suite of changes relating to European and Euro-American influence.

The few Early Pacific sites (4400 BC–1800 BC) along the Lower Columbia are located mainly in the uplands overlooking the floodplain. The dearth of sites is likely due to the region's dynamic geological history, which probably destroyed or submerged many sites, as well as the relative paucity of professional archaeology in the area. On the Northwest Coast generally, Early Pacific remains are more abundant and reflect more intensive subsistence strategies than in preceding periods. This pattern is apparent in areas bordering the Lower Columbia, where people exploited tubers in the Willamette Valley and shellfish on the Oregon Coast (Ames and Maschner 1999:89, 107–8, 137–39; Minor 1991).

Along the Lower Columbia River, sites from the Middle Pacific (1800 BC–AD 200/500) are more abundant than sites from any preceding period. Around the river's mouth and the adjacent coastline, Middle Pacific remains are assigned to the Sea Island phase (Minor 1983), which includes the oldest known shell midden remains (Connolly 1992; Minor 1983, fig. 4) and the oldest known plankhouse remains (800 BC–AD 300) in the region, at the Palmrose site in Seaside, Oregon. Residents at the Palmrose site likely used a range of saltwater, freshwater, and terrestrial habitats in a pattern typical of historic Northwest Coast economies. Palmrose also contains antler objects with carvings resembling designs on later Columbia River artifacts, evidence of the development of the Chinookan Art Style (Ames and Maschner 1999:159, 237; Connolly 1992:97–102; Matson and Coupland 1995:228–29; see also ch. 10 in this volume).

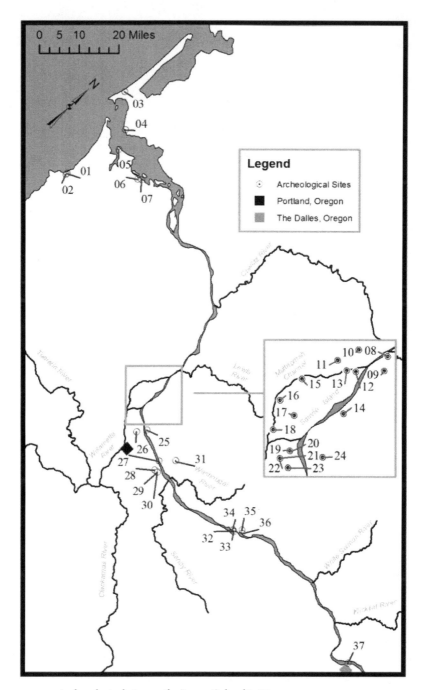

MAP 1.2. Archaeological sites on the Lower Columbia River

In the Wapato Valley, Middle Pacific remains are assigned to the Merrybell phase (Pettigrew 1981). Here, the oldest known Middle Pacific sites postdate 600 BC, and most postdate AD 1. Multiple Middle Pacific sites in the Wapato Valley contain remains of houses; the most fully excavated is the Kersting site, which contains several rectangular structures dating to about AD 1 (Jermann et al. 1975). Middle Pacific sites in the Wapato Valley generally lack preserved plant and animal remains, but we can infer that the inhabitants focused on wetland and riverine environments (Pettigrew 1981, 1990).

The Late Pacific (AD 200/400–AD 1750) has been more fully studied than other periods of Lower Columbia prehistory. Traditional Chinookan culture was firmly established by the early centuries of the Late Pacific period. Late Pacific sites in the Wapato Valley and Columbia Gorge are included in the Multnomah phase, while those along the mouth of the Columbia River and the adjacent coastline are included in the Ilwaco phase. Late Pacific sites contain smaller flaked stone points, widely interpreted as arrow points (Pettigrew 1990). The prevalence of these small points and the rarity of larger points indicate the use of bow-and-arrow and the abandonment of atlatl technology.

Large-scale excavations of Late Pacific sites have focused on residential sites in the Wapato Valley and Columbia River Gorge (e.g., Ames et al. 1999) and to a lesser extent along Willapa Bay (Kidd 1967; Shaw 1977). Similarities among these sites suggest that by the Late Pacific material culture had become relatively uniform throughout the Lower Columbia region.

Key to map 1.2:
1. 35CLT13 (Avenue Q)
2. 35CLT47 (Palmrose)
3. 45PC35 (Fishing Rocks)
4. 45PC105 (Station Camp)
5. Fort Astoria
6. 35CLT34 (Indian Point)
7. 35CLT33 (Eddy's Point)
8. 45CLO1 (Cathlapotle)
9. 45CLO4 (Wapato Portage)
10. 35COO3 (Cathlacump)
11. 35COO5 (Meier)
12. 35COO7 (Pumphouse)
13. 35CO34 (Ede)
14. 45CL21 (Kersting)
15. 35MUO1 (Cholick)
16. 35MUO6 (Lyons)
17. 35MUO9 (Merrybell)
18. 35MUO4 (Sunken Village)
19. 35MU112 (Wild Bee)
20. 35MU105 (Columbia Slough)
21. 35MU44 (St. Johns)
22. 35MU46 (St. Johns)
23. 35MU117
24. 45CL31 (Old Channel Complex)
25. Fort Vancouver
26. 35MU119
27. 45CLO6 (Fisher's Landing)
28. 35MU57 (Broken Tops)
29. 35MU29 (Spada)
30. 35MU32 (Spada)
31. 45CL406
32. 45SA12
33. 45SA13
34. 45SA19
35. 45SAO5
36. 45SA11 (Clah-Cleh-Lah)
37. 35WSO4 (Five Mile Rapids)

Modern Period (AD 1750–Present)

Before AD 1792, Western and Asian influences reached the Lower Columbia in the form of ship wreckage, horses, disease, and European manufactures (Hajda 1984; Ruby and Brown 1976; see ch. 5 in this volume). Direct contact between Europeans and Lower Columbia Natives began in 1792 with visits by maritime fur traders and occasional exploring parties, including the Lewis and Clark Expedition in 1805–6. The continental fur trade in the Lower Columbia began in 1811 with the establishment of Fort Astoria at the mouth of the river and expanded in 1824 with the construction upriver of Fort Vancouver.

Many European trade items—glass beads and metal bracelets, for example—operated as prestige goods within the Native sphere (Ames 1995; Sobel 2004). European goods were significant for their mechanical or utilitarian functions, and items such as European gunflints and flaked glass projectile points have been recovered from Native trash middens (Ames et al. 2011; Wilson et al. 2009). Projectile points made of glass, cut iron, chipped porcelain, and melted lead are examples of indigenous technological innovation using European trade goods (Ames et al. 2011; Banach 2002; Ozbun 2008; Sobel 2004).

Four extensively excavated contact-era sites—Middle Village at the mouth of the Columbia, Meier and Cathlapotle in the Wapato Valley, and Clahclellah at The Cascades—contain evidence from the fur-trade era. Cathlapotle and Clahclellah show substantial differences between residential units in their access to European manufactures (Sobel 2004). Meier residents were minimally involved in trade with Europeans, and Middle Village residents were heavily involved. Cathlapotle residents fell in between (Ames et al. 2011). Middle Village may have been a Native trade depot, as the deposits are rich in a range of trade goods that is absent or rare upstream and there is a lack of evidence for many domestic and food-getting activities (Wilson et al. 2009). Despite participation in the fur-trade economy, Native material culture and technology in the region remained quite stable, with a continued emphasis on plant and animal products and stone raw materials until the 1840s or later (Ames et al. 2011; Sobel 2004).

As they had during the Pacific period, multifamily households operated as basic social, political, economic, and demographic units. Competition among households for control over trade with Europeans and household production of goods sought by fur traders likely increased, as did the wealth and prestige stemming from that control (Sobel 2004, 2006, 2012). At Cathlapotle, for example, postcontact deposits contain a markedly high quantity of scrapers, probably used to process elk hides sought by fur traders visiting the Lower Columbia during the Early Modern period (Ames et al. 2011; Smith 2006).

Several archaeological studies have examined the effects of Euro-Americans on Native subsistence. Analyses of Cathlapotle mammalian faunal remains show stability between precontact and postcontact deposits in mammal consumption (Harpole 2006; Zehr 2002), though Butler's (2000b) study of faunal remains from a suite of Columbia River sites indicates a postcontact increase in Native consumption of mammals and large-bodied fish. This shift could reflect Native depopulation due to epidemics of introduced diseases and a consequent decrease in competition for preferred animal foods.

Studies at Meier and Cathlapotle detected possible postcontact shifts in household organization, suggested by changes in the sizes and locations of hearths (Gardner-O'Kearney 2010). The bone and antler tool assemblages from these sites also yielded evidence of technological responses to contact (Fuld 2011). Archaeological and ethnohistoric data have been used to argue that some Kathlamets persisted as a local group in the Columbia River estuary into the 1850s (Minor and Burgess 2009).

CURRENT ARCHAEOLOGICAL ISSUES

A fundamental problem in the archaeology of the Lower Columbia River is that we do not yet have a strong grasp of the times and places of major cultural and social developments. Archaeological coverage of the Lower Columbia is geographically sparse and temporally spotty. While the earliest radiocarbon date for the region dates to almost 6,600 years ago, only 28 dates (8.5 percent) of some 330 fall between 6,600 and 2,500 years ago; the remainder fall between 2,500 years ago and the present. As a result, we are especially ignorant of human habitation in the Lower Columbia prior to 2,500 years ago.

Most professional archaeology in the Lower Columbia complies with cultural resource preservation laws, which is restricted mainly to locations affected by federal projects. Compliance archaeology is necessarily limited, since it was primarily designed to ascertain how proposed development projects would affect archaeological sites. Answering archaeological research questions is secondary, and compliance projects rarely involve long-term or large-scale excavations. Gaps in our knowledge of Columbia River culture also result from the deterioration of archaeological sites before they are systematically studied.

The region's dynamic geological history also creates archaeological gaps. The sea-level rise from about 16 to 2 thousand years ago affected environments at the mouth of the Columbia and farther inland (Losey 2003); in Portland, the Columbia River rose 100–230 feet (Peterson et al. 2011). The resulting changes in water level and sedimentation likely inundated early human habitation sites, eroded some, and buried others so deep that archaeologists have not found them (Ames and Maschner 1999:51; Peterson et al. 2011; Pettigrew 1990:519). Melting Pleistocene glaciers also caused the massive Missoula Floods, which between 19,000 and 12,500 years ago would have pulverized, eroded, and buried sites along the Columbia River (Waitt 1980). During the Holocene, multiple earthquakes and their attendant tsunamis caused subsidence of some shoreline areas on the coast, burying the archaeological record and submerging it below sea level, where it is difficult to detect and study (Losey 2007; Minor and Grant 1996). At least some of these quakes caused landslides in the Columbia River Gorge (Pettigrew 1990:523–25).

An additional problem limiting our study of Lower Columbia peoples during the postcontact period is that traditional views of this time period privilege historical and ethnographic records over archaeological data. The historical and ethnographic records were produced mainly by Europeans, and so reflect European colonial attitudes. Researchers (e.g., Sobel 2012) have just begun to use archaeological data as an independent, empirical line of evidence to identify and correct these Eurocentric biases.

The resulting gaps in our knowledge leave us actively working to answer a number of major questions:

What was the nature of the earliest human occupation in the region? Evidence from other parts of North America suggests that early populations throughout the continent were small, thinly scattered, and highly mobile. In the Lower Columbia area, when did human habitation begin, and how did it compare to early human occupations elsewhere in the Americas?

When and why did recent economic, social, and political patterns develop? We think these patterns developed during the Middle Pacific period. To more conclusively answer this question, we must answer related questions: When and why did Native populations achieve their historic size and density? When and why did the storage and processing of large volumes of food, including salmon, become economic and social mainstays? When and why did people begin organizing themselves into large corporate households? How did

Lower Columbia peoples become the nexus of a large-scale exchange system? How did their technologies evolve over time? How does all this relate to the development of economic, social, and political systems?

What role did Lower Columbia River people play in the broader cultural history of the Pacific Northwest and western North America over past millennia? The Columbia River was a major trade and travel route, and its residents interacted extensively with other groups. How did the relationship of the Lower Columbia to the broader region unfold?

How have European and Euro-American contact and colonization affected indigenous culture and society? European and Euro-American colonization was relatively early and intense in the Lower Columbia compared to surrounding regions. How did this colonization influence Native society, economy, politics, and religion? How and why did Native peoples maintain practices and beliefs in the wake of colonization? What are the ongoing consequences of early white-Native interaction?

Human Relationships with the Natural Environment

Environmental conditions posed challenges to Native people of the Lower Columbia. Some environmental changes seem to have constrained human opportunities, whereas others expanded them. Rising sea levels created productive estuaries, small landslides formed rapids and falls that became prime fishing locations, and climatic shifts created forests rich in culturally important plant species. Native peoples did not live in an untouched wilderness but modified their environments in intentional and unintentional ways.

The intentional modifications to natural environments included burning areas to increase yields and improve game forage (e.g., Boyd 1999a). When Euro-Americans arrived in the Lower Columbia region, the dominant habitat of the Willamette and Wapato Valleys was oak grassland, a parklike environment that later attracted thousands of Oregon Trail pioneers. Scholars debate the origin and extent of Native burning. Research on contact-era anthropogenic burning carries an implicit assumption that deliberate burning began several millennia ago and had major impacts (e.g., Boyd 1999a), but others suggest that it began recently and had little effect on the ecosystem (e.g., Whitlock and Knox 2002). A more nuanced model of Native burning based on pollen records indicates that anthropogenic burning may have begun in the Middle Holocene and that it was localized, which means it could appear in some paleoenvironmental records but not in others (Walsh 2008).

The impact of harvesting on animal and fish stocks is also controversial. Some researchers suggest that Native peoples overharvested large animals and as a result had to spend more time and effort finding, harvesting, and processing smaller fish and game (Butler 2000a; Martin and Szuter 1999a; Laliberte and Ripple 2003; but see Lyman and Wolverton 2002). In this scenario, people's efforts to feed themselves became less efficient over time, particularly in areas with large human populations. But the most comprehensive study to date of archaeological fish and animal remains from the last several thousand years in the Columbia River area found no evidence of over-exploitation (Butler and Campbell 2004).

Native responses to changing sea levels and coastal geomorphology have been examined at several sites in the Seaside area, on the coast just south of the Columbia River. At the Palmrose and Avenue Q sites, a shellfish-rich bay was present 3,500 years ago (Connolly 1992, 1995; Losey in prep.; Losey and Power 2005); but as sea level rise slowed four to five thousand years ago, deposition outpaced erosion and Columbia River sand nearly filled in the Seaside estuary, reducing its size and shellfish productivity and causing a decrease in Native shellfish harvesting. The history of Native shellfish harvesting elsewhere near the mouth of the Columbia River is related to landscape changes of this kind.

Archaeologists and others have also explored the effects of earthquakes and tsunamis on the Lower Columbia. The earthquakes with the most potential to affect Native peoples were those generated by the Cascadia Subduction Zone, an offshore area where the continental and Juan de Fuca tectonic plates meet. Roughly every 5 hundred years for at least the last 10 thousand years, massive earthquakes generated tsunamis that raced both eastward toward the North American coastline and westward into the Pacific. The earthquakes caused the coastline to sink in relation to sea level (Atwater 1987; Atwater et al. 2005; Atwater and Hemphill-Haley 1996).

Oral traditions of groups who lived in the Cascadia Subduction Zone recall earthquakes and tsunamis, particularly the most recent in AD 1700 (Carver 1998; Hutchinson and McMillan 1997; Losey 2002; Ludwin et al. 2005). Some low-lying villages were probably flooded and destroyed, while others were permanently submerged and rendered uninhabitable. Significant population loss likely occurred, and any number of political and social changes might have followed in the wake of such losses (Losey 2007; Losey et al. 2000; Minor and Grant 1996). Food resources, including salmon that spawn in small streams near the ocean and shallow-water shellfish, must have been damaged by surging tsunami waters and erosion, but it is unclear how long such environmental changes persisted (Losey 2005). Farther inland, earthquakes may have generated landslides, blocking rivers and fish runs and producing food shortages. In the decades and centuries after earthquakes, some estuaries were deepened and widened, perhaps becoming more productive over the long term. Native oral traditions sometimes depict earthquakes and associated submergence of the coast as beneficial and link them to the transformation of coastal prairies into saltwater bays and lagoons that became important places for harvesting fish and other subsistence resources (Carver 1998; Kroeber 1976).

The Bonneville Landslide, which occurred between about AD 1400 and AD 1500, was the most recent environmental phenomenon to have significant repercussions on Native settlement and subsistence. Chinookan oral tradition recalls a "Bridge of the Gods" that crossed the Columbia River and fell with the Bonneville Landslide (e.g., Clark 1953; Bunnell 1933). Debris initially blocked the Columbia River, and one theory proposes that the river suddenly breached the blockage, causing a catastrophic flood that destroyed downstream settlements, particularly in the Portland Basin (Pettigrew 1990). Alternatively, the blockage gradually eroded away without causing catastrophic flooding and obliterating towns (Bourdeau 2001). Whether sudden or gradual, much of the landslide debris ultimately eroded away, and the remainder created The Cascades of the Columbia, one of the river's most productive fisheries.

The Bonneville Landslide also may have affected Native fisheries by impeding salmon migration upstream over the short term. Although it probably took only a few months for the Columbia to breach the landslide blockage, clearing enough debris for salmon to make their way upstream took longer (O'Conner 2004). Much landslide debris was redeposited in the Wapato Valley, where it remains, causing a rise in upstream water levels. Some researchers speculate that by raising water levels the debris greatly improved fish passage over Celilo Falls (Condon 1969; O'Conner 2004). If so, the implications for Native subsistence are profound. The huge salmon runs of Celilo Falls and the intensive Native fishing of these runs might have developed since the Bonneville Landslide.

Preservation and Public Education

Our ability to continue learning about the past through archaeology depends on the preservation of archaeological remains. Along the Lower Columbia

River, this means limiting the impacts of development and relic hunting on archaeological sites. Since the Lower Columbia River traverses federal, state, county, city, and private lands, a patchwork of laws and regulations govern archaeological sites along the river (King 2004). Federal laws and regulations are relatively strong, Washington and Oregon state laws are comparatively weak, and county and municipal laws are weaker or nonexistent (with the exception of Clark County, Washington). Consequently, the preservation of archaeological sites on nonfederal lands along the Columbia often depends on the activism of tribes, residents, and archaeologists. Some sites are saved, but many are lost.

Relic hunting also causes the destruction of archaeological sites. Often referred to as "pot hunting," "collecting," and "looting," relic hunting is the unprofessional and often illegal collection or other disturbance of materials at archaeological sites. Relic hunting irrevocably damages a site, decreasing or destroying its structure and content and diminishing its potential to yield information through systematic archaeological study (Clewlow et al. 1971; Hollowell-Zimmer 2003; LaBelle 2003:115–27; Neusius and Gross 2007:615–17; Sheets 1973).

Relic hunting has substantially damaged archaeological sites along the Lower Columbia, and pothunters may have taken hundreds of thousands of artifacts from The Dalles area alone (Butler 2007:627). In recent years, tribes have established cultural committees, developed archaeological programs, and hired archaeologists; and an increasing number of Native people are now working as archaeologists. Native involvement is further facilitated by federal and state agencies' consultation with tribes prior to the initiation of projects that might affect archaeological remains. As a result, archaeologists and Natives increasingly collaborate to preserve archaeological sites along the Lower Columbia.

Archaeological site preservation has also been enhanced through heightened public awareness. The Oregon Archaeological Society, for example, is comprised of avocational archaeologists committed to protecting archaeological sites along the Columbia and working with professionals to study them. Interpretive facilities that educate the public about Lower Columbia archaeology and heritage include the Chinookan plankhouse at the Ridgefield National Wildlife Refuge, the Columbia Gorge Discovery Center, the Columbia Gorge Interpretive Center Museum, the Yakama Nation Museum, the Museum at Warm Springs, Fort Vancouver National Historic Site, Fort Clatsop Lewis & Clark National Historical Park, Horsethief Lake State Park, and a number of historical societies and local museums. Several agencies organize public presentations, develop websites, and produce publications promoting the preservation of Lower Columbia archaeological sites (e.g., Daehnke and Funk 2005). Nevertheless, more public outreach and activism is needed for the long-term preservation of the archaeological resources of the Lower Columbia River.

TWO

CULTURAL GEOGRAPHY
OF THE LOWER COLUMBIA

David V. Ellis

> Coyote was coming. He came to Gōt'át (*gut'át*). There he met a heavy surf.
> He was afraid that he might be drifted away and went up into the spruce
> trees. He stayed there a long time. Then he took some sand and threw it
> upon that surf: "This shall be a prairie and no surf. The future generations
> shall walk on this prairie." Thus Clatsop became a prairie. The surf became
> a prairie. (Boas 1894:101)

In this tale from the Myth Age, the time before people came to the land,
Coyote appears to have come to the Pacific Coast for the first time, where he
transforms the surf to land. He goes fishing on Neacoxie Creek and then to
the Columbia River, first at Clatsop and then on the Chinook side of the river.
At each location, Coyote has to learn the rules on how to fish for and process
the salmon. Coyote declares that the rules apply not only to him but also "the
Indians shall always do this way. Thus shall be the taboos for all generations
of Indians" (Boas 1894:105). Through this story, in which Coyote is both
learner and creator, listeners learn how the land was transformed to provide
for future generations and that those benefits are theirs only if they act
responsibly.

The land of the Lower Columbia was populated by many figures like
Coyote—Blue Jay, Robin, Crow, Raven, Panther, Salmon, and others. Later
came men and women, some named, some nameless. Few are portrayed as
creators of the landscape, but their stories contribute to the sense of place,
time, and identity that defines Chinookan geography.

The conventional approach to cultural geography frames relationships between human groups and their natural environment in terms of human uses of the land and its resources, as well how landscape elements such as terrain, vegetation, and hydrology shape human use. Since the turn of the 21st century, there has been a significant reconceptualization of this approach, especially concerning the cultural geography of the Native peoples of the Pacific Northwest. This new perspective—termed "landscape ethnoecology" (Johnson 2010a; Johnson and Hunn 2010) or simply "place" (Thornton 2008)—expands the concept of landscape to include an understanding of how land helps define a "sense of being" for Native peoples (Thornton 2008:3). Interactions between human populations and their land are complex, defined by both material and symbolic relationships, dynamic in time and space, and reflecting individual and cultural landscapes. One important element of landscape ethnoecology addresses the meaning of the land through an examination of place-names and terms for landscape features, or ecotopes (Fowler 2010; Hunn 2010; Hunn and Meilleur 2010; Johnson 2010a, 2010b; Thornton 2008).

The decimation of Native peoples of the Lower Columbia due to disease and their subsequent displacement from their land have resulted in the loss or fragmentation of much traditional knowledge. The ethnohistoric and ethnographic data for the Lower Columbia River generally dates to the 19th century and reflects the biases of Euro-American observers and the interests of ethnographers of that era. It has not been considered possible, therefore, to undertake a comprehensive and systematic study for the Lower Columbia such as that conducted among peoples whose cultural continuity is relatively unbroken—for example, the Yakama (Hunn 1990, 2010); the Kaska, Gitksan, and Gwich'in (Johnson 2010a, 2010b); the Tlingit (Thornton 2008); and the Sto:lo (Carlson and McHalsie 2001). The Lower Columbia record is best captured through the corpus of myth texts collected between the 1890s and 1950s.

I have sought to define the Chinookan homeland, with an emphasis on land as "home," and to present what we know about both the perceived and the observed landscape. The perceived landscape attempts to represent how the Chinookans saw the river valley as captured in the texts and other accounts (Boas 1894, 1901; Jacobs 1958–59; Lyman 1900). The observed landscape reflects a Euro-American perspective, the landscape as seen by Meriwether Lewis and William Clark and a generation of fur traders and explorers, whose views reflect perspectives on the natural and cultural worlds of Enlightenment science and Europeans and Americans of the late 18th and the early 19th centuries. This landscape also includes the constructions and reconstructions of the archaeologists who have sought to understand the relationships between precontact peoples and the land through the physical remains of past use, a perspective that is explicitly empirical. The observed landscape, therefore, is primarily descriptive, a relatively straightforward picture of the land, the river, the camps and villages, and the people moving among them.

THE PERCEIVED LANDSCAPE

The Chinookan landscape shaped and was shaped by how people saw the land around them. This perception was a complex tapestry that reflected spiritual, mythic, and historical associations, as well as the location of resources that sustained families and enhanced the wealth of those with high status. Places along or in the river might be where spiritual powers were found, where Coyote and Blue Jay encountered other mythical beings, where battles between chiefs had taken place. The remains of abandoned villages and places where ancestors lived added to the stories.

Three sets of texts collected in the late 1800s and early 1900s give us a sense of how Chinookans saw the land in which they lived. *Chinook Texts* (Boas 1894) and *Kathlamet Texts* (Boas 1901) address the lower river from the area around Rainier, Oregon, to the mouth of the Columbia. *Clackamas Chinook Texts* (Jacobs 1958–59) provides glimpses of middle river Clackamas lands. Franz Boas's source was Charles Cultee (*q'ə́ltí*), of Clatsop and Kathlamet heritage; Melville Jacobs's source was Victoria Howard, who was Clackamas and Molala. Edward Sapir's *Wishram Texts* (1909b) addresses lands farther upstream along the Columbia. These texts stretch back to the Myth Age, when Coyote (it¡ā'lapas *it'álapas*), Blue Jay (iq¡ē'sqēs *iq'ísqis*), Salmon (iguā'nat *igʷánat*), Grizzly Woman (*wakícimani*), and other mythical beings inhabited the Chinookan territory and "the people" were animals, often with extraordinary powers. There are also tales of people in the less distant past and some that tell of the world after Euro-American contact.

The Columbia River links most of the stories, rarely absent but rarely named, and its dominance of the landscape is taken for granted. There is no eponymous figure River, nor is there any common image of the river. The upriver Wishram had a specific term for the Columbia (*wí-maɬ*), according to Sapir (1909b:5), but the same term meant simply '(big) river' to other Upper Chinook speakers (e.g., Jacobs 1958–59). It is unclear if the Chinookans on the lower river had a specific term for the Columbia. Boas translates ē'maʟ (*í-maɬ*) as both 'river' and 'bay', but he sometimes translates ʟtcuq (*ɬ-čuq* 'water') as 'river'. Boas (1904:138) lists -'maʟ (-mał) as a noun-stem for 'bay', 'sea', and 'river'. Only in the tale of "The Four Cousins" (Boas 1894:216–22) does he translate a word-ē´maʟē (í-mał-i)-as 'Columbia River'.

The Columbia is the highway along which people and beings move to places both real and unreal. At times the river facilitates contacts; at other times it is a barrier. "Monsters" may dwell in the river, but the river is primarily the source of fish—lampreys, sturgeon, and, most important, salmon—which define much of traditional and modern Chinookan culture. The Pacific Ocean and Willapa Bay were of equal importance—Willapa Bay for shellfish, sea mammals, and fish and the ocean for fish, shellfish, seabirds, and that rare treat, beached whales.

Although the river weaves its way through many of the stories, much of the action takes place on land. To try to capture a sense of how Chinookans saw the land, I pulled a sample of Chinookan terms for landscape features from the texts. There are limits to using this approach. One difficulty is that Boas and Jacobs were not always consistent in how they translated some terms. For example, Boas usually translates mā´ʟxôlē (máłxʷəli) as 'inland' but sometimes as 'forest'. To some extent, translations of terms were driven by context. Furthermore, establishing equivalency between Chinookan and English terms is fraught with peril, given that there are no living Native speakers of Lower Chinook and only a handful of living Native speakers of Kiksht (Wasco speakers at the Warm Springs Reservation and Wishram speakers at the Yakama Reservation) with whom English translations could be verified or refined. Contemporary speakers of Chinuk Wawa, the indigenous pidgin-creole language of the Lower Columbia, can shed some light on these issues.

This equivalency issue on landscape features is a difficult one. Some landscape features, such as 'island,' appear to be relatively easy to define—that is, both English and Native speakers are likely to agree on what constitutes an island—but other terms are more challenging. Boas routinely translates tEm²ā´ēma (təmʔáima, Lower Chinook) and tEmqā´emaX (təmqáimax, Kathlamet) as 'prairies'. But what is meant by 'prairie'? Ask even a native English speaker to describe the difference among 'prairie', 'meadow', and 'grassland'. The Chinookan perceived landscape might also be captured in tales such as the account of Coyote creating Clatsop Plains. In the Clatsop story of Salmon (igʷánat) (Boas 1894:60–87), igʷánat wins the niece of a chief and then flees with her as they are pursued by the chief's people. To slow their pursuers, igʷánat creates a series of five bays, although he is ultimately unsuccessful and is killed. In another Chinook story, a young man demands that his grandmother fetch him water. Worn out by his demands, the grandmother goes a short distance and urinates in five buckets. When her grandson asks where the water comes from, "she named a new creek for each bucket." The story names only one of those creeks, the "upper fork of Bear Creek," which may be Bear River, a tributary of Willapa Bay (Boas 1894:120). In the "Myth of the Elk," a young man, his dog, and Crow destroy a monster, cut up its skin, and throw away the pieces: "the large pieces became large prairies, the small pieces became small prairies" (Boas 1901:58–66).

References to places that we can tie to geographical space are scattered in the texts. Because many of the stories are associated with the Myth Age, it is not surprising that villages and places mentioned in the tales are neither named nor located other than on the river or the ocean. Some of the stories were associated with places known to contemporary audiences but unspecified in the stories themselves; and while some tales do name villages and places, their locations can no longer be identified. Most of the villages we know about are not mentioned by name in any of the Chinookan texts. One can question if this is an indication that no stories were associated with those settlements or that such tales were unknown to q'ɔltí or Mrs. Howard. Most likely it was just not possible to record a lifetime of knowledge in the limited time that scholars worked with these informants.

In addition to named (Table S2.1, online supplemental materials) and known villages, the texts mention other places that provide a sense of the cultural landscapes with which the different groups were familiar. References to the ocean and Willapa Bay, the harvesting of beached whales, and the gathering of shellfish are most common in *Chinook Texts*, but the story of the GiLā́unaLX (*giɬáunaƛx?*) demonstrates knowledge of upriver people at modern Rainier and on the Cowlitz River (Boas 1894:223–33). *Kathlamet Texts* demonstrates the greatest familiarity with the Lower Columbia, but in the "Myth of Salmon" (Boas 1901:50–53) an encounter with people who had been upriver (ikḗcatck *ikíšaćk* 'The Cascades') concludes that "future generations shall always need five days to get to the Cascades." *Kathlamet Texts* also mentions Willapa Bay, the modern Scappoose area, and the Wā́kʲanasîsi (*wák'anasisi*) village opposite the mouth of the Willamette River (Boas 1901:216–20). It also includes the story of a young woman who violates the prohibition of menstruating women gathering roots at a prairie on Saddle Mountain (Suwalalā́xôst *suwalaláxust*) and is carried off by Thunderbird (Boas 1901:221–24).

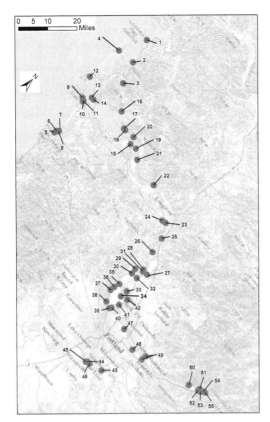

Chinook (for local Salish *c'inúk, činúk*ʷ)

12. *wíitčutk*   14. *qíq'ayaqilxam*
13. *c'inúk (činúk*ʷ)   (Salish *k*ʷ*acámc'*)

'Downstreamers' (*itgíg*ʷ*alatkš*) and associated groups

15. *gałámat*   21. *gałia?išáłxix*
16. *wáqaiqam*   22. *giłáxaniak*
17. *čak*ʷ*ayálxam*   (Salish *squlut-*?)
18. *łálgalk*   23. *qašiámišti*
19. *tǝnǝs-íli?i* (Chinuk 24. *kłágulaq*
    Wawa name)   25. *gałák'alama*
20. *gałiášgǝnǝmaxix*   26. Cathlahaws

Wapato Valley

27. *gáłap'uλx*   36. Claninata
28. *náiaguguix*   37. *gałánaq*ʷ*aix*
29. *łáqst'ax*   38. Cathlacom-
30. *gałáq'map*   mahtup
31. sqǝ́pus   39. *nimáłx*ʷ*inix*
32. namúitk   40. *gałáwakšin*
33. Clannahquah   41. *gałák'anasisi*
34. *máłnumax*   (*wák'anasisi*)
35. Cathlanaminimin   42. Shoto

43. 'Those of Clackamas River' (*giłáq'imaš*)

Willamette Falls

44. *giłáwiwalamt* (*łáwiwala, wálamt*)
45. *čaká·wa* (Molala name)
46. *k'ášxǝkš(ix)*

'Upstreamers' (*šáxlatkš*)

47, 50-51, 54. *gałałála* (*łałála, wałála*)
48. *ničáq*ʷ*li*   53. *sk'mániak*
49. *gaławašúx*ʷ*al*   55. *gaławáyaxix*
52. *qixayagílxam*

MAP 2.1. Best documented Chinookan villages (Lewis and Clark 1990; Hodge 1971; Farrand ca. 1905; Curtis ca. 1910a, 1910b; Hajda 1984; Jacobs 1929–30; Ray 1938; Harrington 1942; Silverstein 1990; French and French 1998); see online version for detail, including additional villages and sources.

Willapa Bay (mixed Chinookan-Salishan).

1. *giłaλ'pílqs*   3. *gitłálilam*
2. *nímax*ʷ   4. *giłápšuyi*

Clatsop (*tłác'ǝp*)

5. *nakut'át*   9. *tłác'ǝp* (*niák'ilaki*)
6. *nikánikǝm*   10. *kunúpi*
7. *niáxaqši*   11. *naiáaqštawi*
8. *niák'iwanqi*

In *Clackamas Chinook Texts*, Mrs. Howard exhibits the greatest familiarity with the area around Willamette Falls (*ikíšačk*, a term that was both a place-name and a reference to a major falls or rapids). One of her stories about winter hunger takes place at a village at Willamette Falls, *k'ašxə́kšix*, "the place where they died of hunger" (Jacobs 1958–59:462–66). But she also tells the story of two beings that become rocks in the Columbia River near present-day Hood River, "Coyote Went around the Land" (Jacobs 1958–59:80–105) and the story of two brothers on a excursion to the coast to hunt seals, "Seal Took Them to the Ocean" (Jacobs 1958–59:207–26). Her tales depict the mountains as dangerous places, occupied by Grizzlies and Mountain Cannibals, but she also recalls spending summer in the mountains as a girl and young woman (Jacobs 1958–59:489–90, 536–37).

In this homeland, the worlds of the living and the dead, the ordinary and the extraordinary, were not separate. In the story of Blue Jay and his sister Iō'i, she is married to a ghost. During the day, the ghosts are bones, while at night the ghosts take form and become people (Boas 1894:161–71). In a Kathlamet tale, two young men hunting seals on the Columbia encounter a war party at night, not realizing that ghosts comprise the party. One young man joins the ghosts in their raid. He is struck by an arrow and appears to survive, but he dies suddenly the next morning after returning to his village (Boas 1901:182–86). In one Chinook story, Blue Jay marries a chief's dead daughter and then travels to the land of "the supernatural beings" (tiō'ʟEma *tiúɬəma*) to restore his bride to life; in another, a man visits the country of the supernatural beings to answer challenges by his father-in-law (Boas 1894:22–36, 153–60).

This overlap or intersection of the material and mythical worlds is found in other stories as well. In "The Four Cousins," the cousins stay at Mythtown (Ikʲaniyi'lXam *ik'ani-ílxam*) at the southern end of Shoalwater Bay on their way to Chehalis. In "The Brothers" (Boas 1901:175–81), four brothers provide only salmon tails as food for their youngest brother, a food normally fed to slaves. Shamed, the youngest brother becomes a supernatural being (iō'ʟEma[x] *iúɬəma[x]*). The older brothers burn their house, and people who sweep the burned remains of the house will be able to see *iúɬəmax*. The house was reported to be at Nagiō'na, the location of which remains unknown (Boas 1901:181).

It was not just the land, the river, and the ocean that formed the cultural landscape. In ancient times, people lived in the sky and were sometimes visited by those below. In the Kathlamet "Myth of the Southwest Winds," the sky people become stars (Boas 1901:67–71); they were part of the past by historical times, but they could still be seen at night.

Resources

The Columbia, its tributary rivers and creeks, Willapa Bay, and the coastal areas around Seaside provided numerous locations for taking salmon, steelhead, sturgeon, and eulachon; gathering shellfish; and hunting seals and sea lions. On the floodplain were ponds and lakes full of wapato and waterfowl; grasslands and riparian woodlands where deer, elk, and smaller mammals could be taken; and a variety of plants, including brushy areas with hazel, crabapple, lowland berries, and thickets of wild rose. There was both food and the raw materials for making medicines, tools, and goods such as clothing, mats, baskets, fishing nets, and bows and arrows. The floodplain and upland forests offered cedar, Douglas-fir, cottonwood, ash, willow, and alder for firewood and for building houses and manufacturing canoes. The Kathlamet story of Robin and Salmon-berry (Boas 1901:118–28) and the Clackamas tale of Black Bear and Grizzly Woman and their sons (Jacobs 1958–59:143–56) describe how Salmon-berry and Grizzly Woman encounter different types of trees and define the uses of their woods.

Some of these resources were open to all friendly folk, but many were under the control of families and villages, and some resource areas were "owned" by individuals or families. In one Chinook text (Boas 1894:88–91), a gull finds tracks of another person on the beach for several days, which angers him because he had inherited the beach. The trespasser is a raven who the gull kills because he has been fishing from his beach. Most resources were not owned in the Euro-American sense of the word; families and villages only held the rights to harvest the resources. Men and women were expected to marry outside their home villages, so many families had kin ties to at least two villages. These connections provided rights of access to the resource areas of the home villages of both spouses and could be extended to the home villages of parents, grandparents, and more remote ancestors. Chiefs, with multiple wives, had even more extensive kinship networks. It is likely that rights of access had to be regularly exercised to be maintained over time, which gave more advantages to chiefs who were better able to marshal the means to travel and gather resources.

The Cycle of the Seasons

Recapturing a sense of Chinookan seasonal patterns is challenging when relying on historical records. Euro-American explorers and fur traders rarely ventured far from the major rivers, and those who wrote about their experiences in the first decades of contact were men who were interacting primarily with chiefs and chiefly families. We thus have a relatively good picture of the activities that were dominated by men—hunting and fishing—and a very poor picture of women's activities, especially those that could not be readily observed from the rivers, such as gathering plants. This male bias is partially offset by the information gathered from Emma Luscier and Victoria Howard. What we can weave from these fragments is an incomplete tapestry, rich images in some portions, faint images in others, and all of it riddled with holes.

Some feel for the ebb and flow of the seasons is captured in the Chinookan texts. In the Kathlamet "Myth of the Salmon" (Boas 1901:50–53), the eponymous Salmon (*igᵂánat*) arrives at the river in the spring. As he moves upriver, he encounters relatives—Ē'qalpō (*íqalpu*) 'skunk-cabbage', ALEmqᵢā'emax (*aɬəmq'áimax*) 'small wapato', Atsqᵢemē'mîx· (*acq'imímix*) 'large wapato', IpᵢE'nxaLX (*ip'ə́nxaɬx*) 'rush root', and Tqanā'pcupcū (*tqanápšupšu*), an unidentified root—who report that they have kept the people alive while waiting for Salmon to come.

For the Clackamas Chinookans, Coyote defined the seasons for some resources: "Whatever their (appropriate) month, then fish of various kinds will be there. Whatever their (right) month, their eels will be there, (also) sturgeon, trout, suckers (and all the other water creatures)" (Jacobs 1958–59:29–30). In "Coyote Makes Everything Good," Coyote describes the sequence of the seasons and their resources: camas and salmon in the early spring and roots and wild carrot later in the spring, followed by grouse, quail, "mudfish," chub, trout, eel, and sturgeon. Wild strawberries appeared in late spring and then blackberries, raspberries, huckleberries, serviceberries, crabapples, and chokecherries through the summer and into the fall (Jacobs 1958–59:75–80). In another Clackamas myth, Coyote instructs the people about how to take dog salmon in the winter (Jacobs 1958–59:102).

In late fall and early winter, Chinookans reoccupied or reestablished the villages that were the centers of social, economic, and political life. "Meanwhile," wrote Gabriel Franchère (1967) in October 1811, "the season had come when the Indians left the seashore [at the mouth of the Columbia] and retired into the woods to establish their winter quarters along the brooks and rivers" (59). In late October 1792, William Broughton (Vancouver 1984:747, 749) reported that the Chinook and Clatsop villages were deserted.

Some residents, especially those in the Wapato Valley (Portland Basin), may have spent most of the year in the village, but many families would have shifted to seasonal camps, occasionally returning to the home village to store foods dried for winter consumption or raw materials to be made into finished goods before leaving for another camp. As the fall rains increased and the weather grew cold, winter houses were reconstructed—wall planks were sometimes taken down in the spring and stored or used for building more temporary shelters at summer camps—or families took up their house quarters again. Each family and household did their best to accumulate enough dried fish, roots, berries, nuts, and other foods to see them through the winter.

Winter was primarily the season of repairing and making tools, weaving mats and baskets, carving bowls, and assembling wooden chests. It was also the season of telling stories, singing songs, and gathering for the guardian spirit dances. Even today, many stories can be told only in the winter. There were few sources of fresh food during winter—fishing for winter steelhead; hunting deer, elk, bear, and waterfowl; gathering shellfish; and possibly trapping smaller furbearers. A whale might be beached on the coast, providing a rare treat.

Another contribution to the winter stores came in late January or early February with the winter eulachon run. Sturgeon, seals, and sea lions pursued the eulachon up the river and, in turn, were pursued by Chinookan fishers and hunters. The most important fishing areas extended from Oak Point upriver to the upper end of the Wapato Valley. Chinookans near the mouth of the river and the estuary could travel up the Columbia to fish—if they had the necessary kin ties—or trade for fresh or dried eulachon. This opportunity was limited, however, to those who had the means to travel or had goods to trade. Others had to rely on the generosity of chiefs or more affluent relatives to share the midwinter bounty.

The end of the eulachon runs marked the beginning of the hardest time of the year, when fish were scarce in the river, land mammals were lean, and few plants were ready to be harvested. Mrs. Howard referred to late winter as "She Is Going," a time when much is promised but nothing delivered (Jacobs 1958–59:534, 656n504). Fur traders reported that late winter could be a time of famine, especially for poorer Chinookans. In March 1814, Alexander

Henry (1992), at Fort George, observed: "About this season of the year their stock of dried Salmon &c being all exhausted, they are generally short of provisions. The only supply they can get is going up the River, and purchasing Sturgeon and Smelt from the Natives above, but few have the means to do this. It is therefore customary about this time to feed upon roots of various kinds" (703).

Winter hunger is a recurring theme in Chinookan stories, especially when an unexpected heavy snowfall traps people. Both the Kathlamet and the Clackamas had a tale of a bad winter caused by a misbehaving boy (Boas 1901:216–20; Jacobs 1958–59:455–57). In the Kathlamet account, the starving villagers are saved by their chief, who gets past the snow around the village and brings back fresh food. A similar Clackamas tale of a rescuing chief follows the story of the misbehaving boy but is not presented as a related event (Jacobs 1958–59:458–66). In the tale of "The GiLā'unaLX" (a group or village near the mouth of the Columbia), a guardian spirit establishes the smelt runs to keep the people from starving when all they have to eat is skunk cabbage and rush roots (Boas 1894:223–33). In "The Spirit of Hunger," Walō' *walú* 'Hunger' is a supernatural being whose appearance in a village named Iqē'lgap¡ē *iqílgap'i* leads to famine. Eventually, a young man fights with Walō' and takes away her mat, which is filled with the bones of animals and the shells of shellfish. When the food debris is emptied into water (the sea? the Columbia?), people are again successful in hunting, fishing, and gathering shellfish (Boas 1901:207–15).

The shoots of camas, a major plant resource for all Chinookans, could be gathered in March as winter waned. "Wild carrot" (possibly *Lomatium* spp.), another early spring food, could be obtained only through trade with the upriver Wasco-Wishram, who gathered it on the dry plateaus of the Columbia Basin. As spring advanced, more fresh foods were added to the larder as people hunted or trapped grouse and quail and fished for "mudfish," chub, and trout (Jacobs 1958–59:77–78).

Families moved out of their winter homes to seasonal camps. Fishing camps were strung out along the river, and women set up camps across the floodplain prairies to harvest early camas and other plants. Upland prairies close to the river—such as those in what is now Clark County, Washington— were favored locations for gathering camas, although it is uncertain to what extent Chinookans moved to these grasslands and how much they relied on trade with inland groups such as the Klikatat and Cowlitz.

Hundreds, perhaps thousands, of Chinookans moved during the spring from the lower river and the Columbia River Gorge to the Wapato Valley to establish a seasonal residence. Some families may have moved into the winter houses of their resident kin, while others built brush or mat shelters in villages or where resources could be readily harvested. At Willamette Falls, a major gathering place, visitors could trade for salmon from the local villagers (who did not allow outsiders to fish at the falls) and gather eels from the rocks (eating eels was taboo for the residents). Such gatherings were favored places and times for socializing, trading, settling disputes, and arranging marriages.

The abandonment of the winter villages probably accelerated in late spring with the spring freshets on the Columbia River. These floods usually peaked in late May and early June but could occur well into July. Traveling upriver in late July 1811, David Thompson (1994:158) reported that "all the lower Lands are overflowed & no campment can be found." For Chinookans, however, the floods were only a temporary disturbance; for a few weeks, villages might be inundated and families moved to camps on higher ground.

The spring chinook run began in late March or early April and extended until the spring freshets in late May and early June, when the major harvest began using dipnets at Willamette Falls and The Cascades (Martin 2006:102–3, 157–58). Coinciding with the later part of the spring chinook run was the late spring run of lamprey. The vast numbers of salmon and lamprey drew seals and sea lions up the Columbia and into the lower Willamette River.

Spring also appears to have been the beginning of the oyster season in Willapa Bay, which peaked during the summer. James Swan (1972) wrote:

> The weather was now propitious for prosecuting the oyster-fishery, and hundreds of Indians came to the [Willapa] Bay from Chenook and the tribes at the north. Some of the Indians came as far as the region round Puget Sound. . . . These Indians, during the summer months, resort to Shoal-water [Willapa] Bay to procure clams and crabs for their own eating, and oysters to sell to whites. (59)

Summer was the time of greatest movement, as families shifted between the camas fields and summer fishing camps, at times returning to the winter village to cache provisions or reconnoiter before moving to another summer camp. In late summer and early fall, families focused on gathering sufficient stores to see them through the winter. The fall chinook run was harvested primarily for drying rather than immediate consumption; fall chinook were leaner, and the drier weather facilitated preserving the fish. Women focused on collecting and drying wapato. Camas was also harvested in the fall (Swan 1972:90), and some families moved into the neighboring hills and mountains to collect nuts and berries and to hunt deer and elk. Salalberry cakes were prepared and dried for personal consumption and trade. With the onset of the winter rains, families began to return to their winter homes. They settled in, looking forward to the season of telling stories and hoping they had enough food stored to make it to spring.

THE CONSTRUCTED LANDSCAPE

Lewis and Clark referred to 25 individual villages or other settlements during their travels through the Wapato Valley and reported that the Clackamas inhabited 11 villages on the Clackamas River. Members of the expedition appear to have seen or visited only 16 of the villages; local Indians reported the remainder to them. A few of the settlements were observed on the expedition's seaward voyage in November 1805 and were never mentioned again. Three were apparently abandoned villages, and others were single houses along the river that the explorers may not have considered villages. Other than the settlements referenced in passing, most were given names that Lewis and Clark believed were the Native names for the villages. No names were obtained for the 11 individual "Clark-a-mus" (Clackamas) villages.

What constituted a village for both Euro-Americans and Chinookans can be difficult to grasp. The term was used by the first Euro-Americans in the region to explore the Columbia River, and it has continued to be widely used in both the popular and professional literature. But what is the meaning of the Lower Chinook and Kathlamet word ē'lXam *ílxam* (and the Clackamas and Wishram word *wílxam*), which has been uniformly translated as 'village' or 'town' (Jacobs 1958–59; Sapir 1909b)? Boas translated the Kathlamet and Lower Chinook terms—tê'lXam, tê'lx·Em (*tílxam*) as 'the people', as did Jacobs and Sapir the Kiksht term *idə́lxam*—indicating a relationship between the terms for town/village and people. Boas (1904:129) noted that the Lower Chinook terms for people and town were derived from a stem ēlx (*-ilx*), which meant 'land' or 'country'. For most English speakers, the words "village" and "town" convey much more than simply the physical structures and organization of a human settlement. Despite these conceptual or linguistic challenges, the use of these terms appears to refer to settlements that were named, were regularly occupied by a group of people, involved the construction of substantial dwellings, and were centers of social, economic, and political life.

Not all of the villages were occupied at the same time. Some were seasonal settlements, some were occupied year-round, and others may have been the homes of a few families for short periods of time. The appearance and disappearance of villages from the historical accounts suggest that some of the settlements were short-lived. Some may have been occupied for a generation or two, abandoned, and then reoccupied years later. Others were occupied for centuries.

Many of the villages were along the banks of the Columbia River, especially around the mouths of major tributaries. Settlements were clustered at The Cascades, at Willamette Falls, along the lower Clackamas River, along Multnomah Channel, on the river's estuary, and around Willapa Bay (Hajda 1984:81). A few villages were away from the river on bodies of water such as Scappoose Bay and Vancouver Lake. Villages were also along some of the smaller streams, primarily the sloughs that meandered across the floodplain. All of the known Chinookan villages were located along waterways or on bodies of water that were connected directly or indirectly with the Columbia. The only stretch of the river that apparently lacked settlements was from the Lower Cascades to the Sandy River. Water access to and from the Columbia—the great highway of the region—appears to have been critical in the locations of these settlements.

Being near important fishing locations and expanses of river bottoms was also important in determining where villages were situated. Proximity to important shellfish locations appears to have influenced the placement of settlements on Willapa Bay. The largest concentration of villages on the Lower Columbia was on and around Sauvie Island, where the island and the mainland offered the greatest expanse of floodplain on the lower river. Access to wood for houses and firewood was also important. In the Columbia River Gorge, winter villages appear to have been located on the north side of the river for better protection from the winter winds and better exposure to the sun.

Lewis and Clark and a few other early observers provided population estimates for the villages, but we do not know their sources of information, especially for the villages they never saw. There are at least two sets of estimates, substantially different from each other and prepared at different times. Boyd and Hajda (1987) hypothesize that one estimate reflects fall village populations and a second the spring populations. The spring population is almost triple the winter population estimate. This difference and other information suggest that large numbers of people moved into the Wapato Valley in the spring to take advantage of the seasonal bounty of resources. There are references to fall visitors as well, evidence of shifts in residence that probably occurred throughout the year, except in winter.

So we know that village populations were far from static. If Lewis and Clark's population estimates are accurate, then village populations swelled in the spring with hundreds of seasonal visitors, at least in the Wapato Valley. Some visitors may have moved temporarily into existing households, staying with friends and relatives. Others probably set up temporary shelters, such as the 24 houses of bark and straw at Ne-er-cho-ki-oo, near today's Portland International Airport. On April 9, 1806, at Wah-Cleh-lah (*wałála*) at The Cascades, Lewis observed residents in the process of moving from their winter village to their spring settlements: "14 houses remain entire but are at this time but thinly inhabited, nine others appear to have been lately removed, and the traces of ten or twelve others of ancient date were to be seen in the rear of their present village" (Lewis and Clark 1990:97).

The Chinookan villages described in the early 1800s ranged in size from one to 28 houses. More permanent Chinookan houses had a framework of wooden posts and rafters to which wide, split-cedar planks were attached to form the walls and roof (Franchère 1967:114; Lewis and Clark 1990:218–21, 1991:27; Ross 2000:111–12; Strong 1906:12–13). Houses occupied for shorter periods of time had walls and roofs of bark slabs or perhaps the small houses "thached with Straw, and covered with bark" that Lewis observed around the more permanent cedar-plank house at Ne-er-cho-ki-oo (Lewis and Clark 1990:17).

Smaller villages may have consisted of one large house or a row of houses facing the river or a stream. Larger villages may have had more than one line of houses. In the Chinook story of Ōkulá'm (*ukulám*), Thunderer's son-in-law visits a large town that has five rows of houses (Boas 1894:35); the Clatsop village of Liă'menaʟuctē (*łiáminałušti?*) also had five rows of houses (Boas 1901:236). Middle Village near the mouth of the Columbia River had multiple "blocks." Around these more formal rows might be other houses, less linear in orientation—women's menstrual huts and the sweat lodges, "of which they make frequent uce both in sickness and in health and at all seasons of the year" (Lewis and Clark 1991:33). Alexander Henry (1992) described a village at Oak Point as "one range of Eight houses measuring 120 paces in length and eight other detached Houses of about 15 paces each in length, all on a parallel with the River" (677). All of the Chinookan tales reference chiefs or headmen and their houses, but only the Clackamas stories (e.g., "The Basket Ogress Took the Child") describe the location of the headmen's house as at the center of the village (Jacobs 1958–59:388). In some Clackamas stories (e.g., "Gíckux igíckux and his Older Brother"), the central characters live in houses at the end of the village (Jacobs 1958–59:315). Many contemporary Chinooks believe that rank was predetermined in village structure, with poorest individuals to the east (often Mouse in myths) and the chief(s) farthest west.

Each village probably had a core household or several households that changed little over long periods of time. Some residents may have been more transient, staying for a few seasons or a few years but relocating when kin ties allowed them to shift to another village that offered better resources or a more generous or powerful chief. Households and villages might grow too large for available resources, leading to the creation of new households or villages. Interpersonal conflicts might also lead to individuals or families moving to another village or establishing a new settlement. The extensive network of kin ties among Chinookans made it relatively easy for an individual or a family to move if conditions in the resident village became disagreeable.

Temporary camps were established along the river during the fishing season and were most common along the river below the Wapato Valley and at The Cascades. Euro-Americans rarely described them in detail but simply noted that there were one or two "lodges," "huts," or "tents" (e.g., Henry 1992:665, 674; Lewis and Clark 1991:13). Ross (1956), for example, described people at seasonal camps building "large square sheds, for the purpose of drying and curing their fish, roots, and berries" (112).

Burial grounds were another cultural presence on the landscape. Mount Coffin, for example, was on the north side of the river a short distance above the mouth of the Cowlitz River, and Coffin Rock is an island just downriver from modern Goble, Oregon (Franchère 1967:47–48; Henry 1992:642; Lewis and Clark 1990:27–28; Parker 1967:143, 155; Ross 2000:118; Vancouver 1984:754–55). Islands were common locations for burials, and Lewis and Clark and later fur traders and missionaries mentioned burial islands in upper Cathlamet Bay, at Willamette Falls, and near modern Skamania, Washington (Henry 1992:658; Lewis and Clark 1988:358–59, 1991:9; Parker 1967:136). Broughton (Vancouver 1984:749) described three elaborate canoe burials near a Clatsop village. Remote hillsides were also common burial locations.

The Lower Columbia River possesses one of the richest archaeological records in the Pacific Northwest. While there are hundreds of recorded archaeological sites in the Lower Columbia region, most are poorly reported and are known only from surface artifacts or exposures in streambanks. Relatively few excavations allow us to determine when the sites were occupied and how people used them.

Minor (1983) undertook extensive archaeological, ethnographic, and ethnohistoric research around the mouth of the Columbia River, including archaeological sites on the coast, on the Columbia River estuary, and in the interior. His settlement model indicates that the Chinook had summer villages on the river's estuary and that winter villages were on the lower reaches of tributary streams that offered access to fall salmon runs and shelter from storms. Both winter and summer villages provided excellent access to a considerable variety of habitats and resources, so moves to short-term camps were tied to specific resources. Those living closest to the coast made greater use of marine resources, especially shellfish, while those living farther upriver made greater use of interior resources such as game. Minor found that the archaeological data indicate that there had been little change in these patterns for at least three thousand years.

In the Wapato Valley, archaeologists have proposed contrasting models of settlement and resource use. Based on data from archaeological sites around Vancouver Lake, Dunnell et al. (1973) proposed a pattern of regular seasonal shifts between major and minor settlements and camps. These seasonal movements were necessary to provide better access to resources. Their model was similar to Minor's, with summer and winter villages on the Columbia River floodplain and more short-term camps on the floodplain and in neighboring uplands. The winter villages, they concluded, occupied permanent locations, while the summer settlements were smaller and their locations more likely to change. Seasonal camps were more ephemeral and might be occupied only a few times before being abandoned.

A decade later, Saleeby (1983) used data from animal remains at archaeological sites on Sauvie Island and the adjacent mainland across the Vancouver Lake area to revisit the Dunnell et al. (1973) model. She concluded that the distribution of archaeological sites around Vancouver Lake could easily be explained by minor seasonal shifts in the locations of villages. The winter villages were not abandoned in the summer, but activities associated with the village were moved very short distances, resulting in what now appear to be different occupations. The faunal remains from the sites on and around Sauvie Island indicate year-round occupation, and all the resources needed to support a village throughout the year could easily be obtained within a day's travel from any particular village. Seasonal shifts in residence, therefore, were unnecessary. Saleeby is also clear that year-round occupation of villages was possible only in the Portland Basin due to the unusual abundance of resources in the area, especially wapato.

More recently, O'Rourke (2005) analyzed the distribution of archaeological sites in the Portland Basin to develop a predictive model of where sites are found. Focusing on environmental variables and making minimal use of ethnographic and ethnohistoric data, she found that proximity to water and elevation were the most important variables influencing the locations of archaeological sites, with proximity to navigable water being the most critical. Location along or very near the Columbia and Willamette Rivers was key for village sites and was so important that the occupants were willing to accept the occasional flood as a small price to pay for living along a major waterway.

Data from the Cathlapotle site at the confluence of the Columbia, Lewis, and Lake Rivers, a major village site occupied for almost four hundred years and visited by Lewis and Clark in the spring of 1806, indicates that settlement was subject to infrequent flooding (Ames and Maschner 1999:63). The Columbia's spring freshets could result in major inundation on the floodplain, but such floods were rare and might last only a few weeks. Relocating a village to higher ground for a short period might have been considered annoying rather than devastating.

The only comprehensive settlement model developed from archaeological data developed for the upriver Chinookan territory (the Columbia River Gorge) is that proposed by Minor et al. (1989). Based on fieldwork on the Lower and Middle Cascades, they hypothesize a pattern of seasonal shifts in settlements (255–59). Summer settlements were situated along the Columbia in good fishing locations, with winter settlements situated in more sheltered areas away from the river. Some fishing sites continued to be used through the winter to provide fish to the winter villages.

Minor and his colleagues (1989:257–59) argue, however, that this pattern reflects occupation of the Cascades area by non-Chinookan groups with cultural ties to the Columbia Plateau to the east. By the time of Euro-American contact, this pattern had changed with summer settlements at the Cascades by Chinookan peoples whose winter villages were downriver at the western end of the Gorge or in the Portland Basin. The ethnohistoric record for The Cascades suggests a more complex pattern, however, with some Chinookan winter villages at The Cascades and some Chinookans moving up the Columbia from Portland Basin villages for summer fishing. Alexander Henry's account (1992:646–56) of a punitive expedition by the North West Company against Indians at The Cascades in January 1814 clearly indicates that the villages at The Cascades were Chinookan villages.

Some 19th-century descriptions (Landerholm 1956:89, 167–68; Lewis and Clark 1990:483, 1991:38, 40, 57, 96–97, 99) indicate that at least some groups—most notably the "Watlala" *watála* at The Cascades—moved to the Portland Basin during the summer months and established settlements on the south bank of the Columbia between the Sandy and Willamette Rivers; *watála* winter villages were at The Cascades. Not all of the Gorge groups made this seasonal move, however, and some may have lived in the Gorge year-round.

"THEIR HOUSE WAS FULL OF MEAT AND TALLOW"

Two landscape threads weave their way through the texts and the archaeological data. The first is the Columbia River, a defining feature of the constructed landscape that played—and continues to play—the central role in the Chinookan landscape. The Pacific Ocean and Willapa Bay for the Clatsop and Chinook proper and Willamette Falls for the Clackamas helped shape that landscape, but the river unquestionably dominates as a recurring element in the stories and as a defining element for the archaeological record. The river and the land were bound together as the source of all the people needed for survival. Together, they framed how Chinookans saw themselves and the world. For them, there was no separation of the natural and the cultural worlds. The landscape was a whole, where all the elements combined to define a physical existence and a mythical, spiritual, and metaphysical presence.

The river and the land offered food, the second landscape thread. Whether in the accounts of Blue Jay and Coyote or the first Indians or the Indians of the not-too-distant past, mythical beings and humans devoted much of their time to fishing, hunting, and gathering shellfish and plants, as well as preparing and consuming food. Competition for food resources is often the focus of the stories.

The fear of hunger is evident in many accounts, and Euro-Americans occasionally noted apparent starvation in late winter. While camped opposite the mouth of the Sandy River in early April 1806, Lewis was told by Indians traveling down the river from The Cascades "that their relations at that place were much streightened at that place for the want of food; that they had consumed their winter store of dryed fish and that those of the present season had not yet arrived" (Lewis and Clark 1991:49). As Vibert (1997:163–204) documented in the Columbia Plateau, Euro-American accounts of starvation tend to be exaggerated and often reflect a bias against diets rich in fish and plant foods. The same bias may be reflected in accounts of conditions on the Lower Columbia. Still, the Chinookan stories of winter hunger and its devastating effects clearly demonstrate that fear of hunger and starvation was important in the lives of people. That fear was not unique to Chinookans but was found among Native people all along the Northwest Coast (Boyd 1990:136; Cove 1978; Suttles 1968:58–59).

The Lower Columbia landscape may have been seen primarily as a source of food. Coyote created the Clatsop Plains to provide the people with a prairie where they could gather roots, improved a falls, populated the water with good things, and noted the nearby presence of camas and berries (Jacobs 1958–59:80–105). This perceived landscape would have included the availability of food resources in both space and time. Integrated with this basic subsistence perspective were social perspectives. Resources were not always predictable or abundant; they were more likely to come to those who were clever and vigilant to the requirements of strict taboos and to those who honored their obligations to share with kin and neighbors when they were successful. When food was abundant, when the house was full, lives were in balance.

This thread is harder to find in the archaeological record. Possibly the best evidence for the concern for food is in the storage pits that occupy the floors of the houses at the Meier, Cathlapotle, and Clahclellah archaeological sites (Ames et al. 2008). Families and households accumulated a precious supply of provisions to sustain themselves through the winter; and, for chiefly families, their influence and prestige might be determined by their ability to support others through hard times. Hunger and starvation threatened both lives and the social order.

Finally, the perceived landscape has always been inhabited by a history that includes events and personages of the ancient and more recent past, some of which left physical reminders that provide information to us today. That history adds a dimension to the landscape that was unseen by the first Euro-American observers.

This mosaic of river and land, prairie and woodland, lakes and ocean, mountains and sky, and all the cultural memories constitute the cultural geography of the Lower Columbia Chinookans. On that foundation, Chinookans built a cosmopolitan and vibrant culture. Their descendants today continue to make it a Chinookan landscape.

THREE

ETHNOBIOLOGY: NONFISHING SUBSISTENCE AND PRODUCTION

D. Ann Trieu Gahr

O UR knowledge of Chinookan ethnobiology—the science of understanding the relationships between people and the living world—
derives from five primary sources: historic documents, ethnographies, Chinookan oral texts, archaeological reports, and contemporary
Chinookan family lore. The historic documents, which date from the 1790s
through the 19th century, include journals, memoirs, ships logs, legal proceedings, surveys, and other publications produced in the interests of colonialism. Most early visitors came as members of exploring or trading parties
on behalf of empire-building nations. Some recorded descriptions of the
landscapes, flora, fauna, and people they encountered, and a few collected
plant and animal specimens. The most famous of the journals were written
by members of the Lewis and Clark Expedition in 1805–6. Later 19th-century
scientific societies and institutions underwrote botanizing and zoological
expeditions that contributed to the knowledge of the region (McKelvey 1991).

Even though ethnographic research along the Lower Columbia River was
primarily motivated by salvage ethnography and none was devoted to ethnobiology, details can be gleaned from the ethnographies, especially the texts
or collections of oral history and myth that Franz Boas recorded from
Charles Cultee (Chinook/Kathlamet) and that Melville Jacobs recorded from
Victoria Howard (Clackamas). Peripheral detail on the Chinookan people of
the Wapato Valley area is found in Henry Zenk's (1976) study of subsistence
and ethnobiology of the neighboring Tualatin, a Kalapuya group. Ethnographic studies of neighboring coastal groups, including the Nehalem Tillamook (Jacobs 2003, 1990; Harrington 1942–43; Ray 1938), provide data on the

Chinook along the coast. It is also useful to look at subsistence information on the linguistically affiliated Upper Chinook from the eastern periphery of the Chinookan area, who are commonly linked culturally to the peoples of the Plateau (e.g., Adams 1958; Boyd 1996; French 1961, 1999; French and French 1998; Sapir 1909b; Spier and Sapir 1930).

While an interest in Chinookan material culture motivated the collection of artifacts and relics beginning with the first Euro-American settlement of the area, an archaeological perspective on ethnobiology is relatively recent. Until the 1980s, researchers inferred plant and animal resource use from stone and bone artifacts such as projectile points, clubs, net sinkers and gauges, bone harpoon points, bowls, choppers, knives, wedges, mauls, mallets, abraders, adzes, and mat creasers (e.g., Minor 1983; Pettigrew 1990; Strong 1959). Direct evidence was restricted to fortuitous finds of plant and animal remains in screens or recovered in situ during excavation. The first zooarchaeological study on the Lower Columbia was of faunal remains from six Portland Basin sites (Saleeby 1983); others date from the first decade of the 2000s (Baker 2007; Butler et al. 2009; Lyman 1994b, 2003a; Zehr 2002). Systematic recovery of plant remains as a major part of archaeological research began with the 1994 Cathlapotle (45CL1) excavations (Trieu 2004b), and Darby's (1996, 2005) study of wapato use in the Portland Basin was the first to investigate a major Lower Columbia food resource. Most archaeobotanical information remains tucked away in appendices to excavation reports.

RESOURCE DIVERSITY VERSUS FOCAL RESOURCES

For the Chinookan peoples, access to a diversity of resources was a hallmark of well-being and wealth (Boas 1894, 1901; Jacobs 1958–59; Sapir 1909b). Available resources included over 86 taxa of shellfish, fowl, and mammals used for meat and more than 27 species of fruit, 3 different nuts and seeds, 12 species of greens, and over 35 species of root foods. Resources used in technology show a similar diversity, with over 118 taxa identified, reflecting a deep knowledge of the physical properties of wood, fiber, skins, horn, bone, and stone (Tables S3.1, S3.2, online).

Visitors who dined with Chinookan families consistently described their hosts' warm hospitality and the generous meals served (e.g., Douglas 1959:149; Lewis and Clark 1988:348, 357, 1990:118, 120, 1991:18; Swan 1972:168, 264–65; Townsend 1999:190). Meals usually featured fresh fish or meat, accompanied by local, seasonally available vegetables, fruits, and greens, as well as smoked and dried foods. Imported foods provided additional variety (Hajda 1984; see also ch. 7 in this volume). William Clark described such a meal one December day at a Clatsop village:

> was invited to a lodge by a young Chief was treated great Politeness, we had new mats to Set on, and himself and wife produced for us to eate, fish, Lickorish [shore lupine, *Lupinus littoralis*], & black roots [edible thistle, *Cirsium edule*], on neet Small mats, and Cramberries [*Vaccinium oxycoccos*] & Sackacomey berris [kinnikinnik, *Arctostaphylos uva-ursi*], in bowls made of horn, Supe made of a kind of bread made of berries [cf. salal, *Gaultheria shallon*] common to this Countrey which they gave me in a neet wooden trencher, with a Cockle Shell to eate it with. (Lewis and Clark 1990:118)

Diverse diets provide stability in the food resource base (Turner 1996:284) and incorporate essential nutrients that are related to lower infant mortality rates and longer life spans (e.g., Hockett and Haws 2003).

In addition to the emphasis on resource diversity, there was a strong reliance on cultural keystone species—that is, resources that play a key role by materially supporting cultures and becoming intertwined with cultural traditions and narratives (Cristancho and Vining 2004; Garibaldi and Turner 2004). Criteria to identify a cultural keystone species vary, but those identified by Garibaldi and Turner (2004) are most relevant to the Lower Columbia: intensity and multiplicity of use; linguistic indicators such as specialized terminology and/or names, that is, months or seasons or places; role in narratives, ceremonies, or symbolism; unique position or irreplaceability in culture; and role as a trade item.

Using these criteria, several sources of food and technological resources emerge as keystone species. Salmon was a major resource, but so were the cervids (elk and deer), seals, sea lions, and sturgeon. Among plants, berries, wapato, camas, and western red cedar qualify as keystone species. Other plants such as bracken fern, Oregon white oak, and maple appear to have played a more dominant role than the historical documents indicate, perhaps in earlier times and in more restricted locales.

Cervids (Elk and Deer)

From the mouth of the Columbia to The Cascades, elk and deer were a focus of intense use (Boas 1894, 1901; Drucker 1933–54; Jacobs 1958–59; Sapir 1909b;

Spier and Sapir 1930), and deer and elk bone dominate the mammalian faunal assemblages of Lower Columbia archaeological sites (e.g., Croes et al. 2007, 2009; Lyman 1994b, 2003a, 2005; Minor et al. 1989; Saleeby 1983; Wilson et al. 2009; Zehr 2002). Even in coastal sites where marine resources were abundant, such as Palmrose (35CLT47) and Par-Tee (35CLT20), cervids represent a significant proportion of mammalian resources (Colton 2002). Meat was eaten fresh or roasted, boiled, and smoke-dried into jerky. Both elk and deer were major sources of high-quality protein, along with iron, phosphorus, zinc, and selenium, and venison was a rich in riboflavin and niacin (USDA 2005). In addition, people found technological uses for all parts of the elk and deer, including skin, head, antlers, brain, bladder, and bones.

People hunted elk and deer individually and in groups. Individual hunters often acquired their skills through a guardian spirit (e.g., Boas 1894:234–37, 264–65, 1901:221–24; Sapir 1909b:257–59). John Wacheno, a Clackamas, described a dance that lasted three to five nights given when a boy killed his first deer (Drucker 1933–54:27–28). When hunting as a group, sometimes the best hunter served as leader and animals were driven to a point where bowmen could shoot them (Ray 1938:116). Dogs were also used to drive or flush deer or elk (Boyd 1996:69; Drucker 1933–54:4; Lewis and Clark 1990:274, 318). Wacheno recalled wolves chasing deer and elk into the river, where people clubbed them (Drucker 1933–54:4), and Lewis and Clark described large pitfalls for taking elk (1990:206).

In the Cascade Mountains, large-scale hunting was undertaken in the winter using pitfall traps and when snow slowed the deer's movement and facilitated tracking (Boyd 1996:59; Spier and Sapir 1930:180–82). Missionaries at Wascopam noted large quantities of deer taken in winter, in one case 20 to 30 per day by a single hunter; in another account, hunters from several villages were observed with eight to ten canoes filled with venison (Boyd 1996:59). Farther downriver, elk and deer hunting was associated with late summer and early fall, when people went into the mountains for hunting and berrying (Jacobs 1958–59:489–90). In the Kathlamet texts, Cultee reported that in August hunters at Saddle Mountain drove elk over a precipice, with 30 to 60 elk taken at a time (Boas 1894:221–24). Despite such mass harvests, however, a hunting ethic dictated taking only the number of animals that were needed (Sapir 1909b:259).

There were no large-game alternatives to the cervids, which were an important source of meat, fat, marrow, and other byproducts, especially hides. Evidence of trade of elk and deer meat between Chinookan groups is scarce, though Curtis (1970) noted that the Wishrams traded for venison from the Klikatats in the Columbia River Gorge. Meat trade with Euro-Americans was frequent (e.g., Franchère 1967; McDougall 1999; Lewis and Clark 1988, 1990), and dressed hides and items such as clamons (elkskin armor) were a major trade item (Ruby and Brown 1976:59–72) during the late 18th and early 19th centuries. Cameron Smith's (2006) research on lithic tools at the Cathlapotle and Meier (35CO5) sites highlights the importance of terrestrial game hunting, and Sobel's (2006) analyses of obsidian use at Cathlapotle link it to the contact-era export of elk hides and perhaps clamons.

Berries

Throughout the Northwest, several varieties of blueberries, huckleberries, raspberries, cranberries, and salalberries have always been a primary fruit source for Native peoples. It also appears that elderberries were important (Losey et al. 2003). Archaeological evidence for berries has been found in many sites throughout the region (Lepofsky 2004), including along the Lower Columbia River at Cathlapotle (Stenholm 1999), Meier (Trieu 2000), and 45PC106 (Wilson et al. 2009). Berries were unique in Chinookan culture as a resource that was mass processed and stored for winter as well as traded. They were a nutritionally important source of fiber; vitamins C, E (alpha tocopherol), and K riboflavin; and manganese (Keely et al. 1982; Kuhnlein 1989; USDA 2012).

In narrative texts, women are often described as the berry pickers, and numerous references in historical documents record the importance of berries. The richest ethnographic evidence is from the easternmost Chinookan peoples. Mabel Teio of the Wishram related a tradition shared with other Plateau peoples, the Feasts of Rejoicing: "when a little girl was big enough to pick huckleberries to make iunáyExix̱ (*iunáyǝx̱ix*) (a huckleberry-load; a package of dried huckleberries of standard measure), the old women were called, and it was given to them. This gave her good luck in picking berries and made her a rapid picker" (Spier and Sapir 1930:261–62). First Fruits ceremonies were practiced in most Oregon Coast societies (Barnett 1937), and Emma Luscier of the Lower Chinook mentioned the presence of First Fruits and First Roots ceremonies (Ray 1942:133). The Chinook may have practiced a simple ritual such as the one Clara Pearson of the adjacent Tillamook described, where girls gave their first picked berries or roots to elders (Jacobs 2003:215).

Throughout the Northwest, traditions of First Fruits and First Roots ceremonies occur at the same time as the First Salmon ceremony (Gunther 1928). Regardless of whether berries were included in ceremonial rituals, however, among all Chinookan peoples and their neighbors berry season was associated with a special time in the summer and fall when families went to higher elevations (Boas 1901:231–35; Jacobs 1958–59:143–56, 282; Spier and Sapir 1930:182). August to September was huckleberry time, missionaries at Wascopam reported, and the mission was vacated as people went to the mountains for four to six weeks of berrying and hunting (Boyd 1996:55). The Upper Chinook calendrical term for September, itgaxałágwax ákułmin (*itgaxałágʷax ákʷłmin*), translates as 'her huckleberry-patch moon' or 'the month for huckleberrying' (Spier and Sapir 1930:208). Clara Pearson of the Nehalem Tillamook identified seven seasons, three of which were named for berry plant resources, "time of salmonberry sprouts," "salmon berry time," and "salal berry time" (Jacobs 2003:80). To the north, the Quinault seasonal calendar included times for picking salmonberry sprouts, salmonberries, and elderberries (Olson 1936).

In addition to being eaten fresh, berries were mass processed. They were dried, preserved in oil, and dried into cakes or loaves, using quantities of from 6 to 15 pounds (Franchère 1967:106–7; Jacobs 1958–59:489–90; Lewis and Clark 1990:237, 239, 297; Swan 1972:89). The stored berry loaves were crumbled and mixed with cold water until thick, as described in William Clark's meal, while elderberries were steamed in earth ovens (Gunther 1973; Ray 1938:129). The remains of hundreds of berry-drying trenches have been recorded in the Cascade Mountains in southern Washington (Mack and McClure 2002). The harvest and production of berries were substantial enough to make them a trade item (e.g., Boyd 1996; Douglas 1959:102; Lewis and Clark 1988:347, 371, 1990:74, 133; 1991:99–100; Mack and McClure 2002), and the size of the standard berry baskets also indicates trade (Spier and Sapir 1930:261). Good quality berry patches were associated with burned-over places, and many Northwest Coast ethnographies report that berry patches were regularly burned to enhance productivity (Deur and Turner 2005; French 1999; Jacobs 2003:80; Mack and McClure 2002). Berry patches also were part of the resource ownership system throughout the Northwest (Turner et al. 2005).

Wapato

Wapato, an aquatic plant that produces tubers, stands out as a staple resource in the historic documents, and it meets the definition of a keystone resource, especially in the Wapato Valley. The tubers, which early explorers often compared to potatoes, store well and were easily prepared for eating by roasting them in hot ashes (Lewis and Clark 1990:74; Ray 1938:129). A good source of protein, carbohydrates, thiamine, riboflavin, phosphorus, potassium, iron, and magnesium (Kuhnlein and Turner 1991:360), wapato was harvested primarily between September and May, with a hiatus in harvesting during the high water in winter (Darby 1996). The Tualatin seasonal round indicates that wapato harvest time occurred from the end of September through October (Zenk 1976:40). In the Kathlamet texts, a wapato myth character plays a leading role to ward off seasonal hunger among Salmon's people while Salmon is away (Boas 1901:150).

Remains of wapato have been identified in archaeological sites all along the Columbia, including three in the Wapato Valley: at Cathlapotle, Meier, and St. John's (Trieu 2005); on the estuary at Station Camp (Wilson et al. 2009); and at The Cascades Clahclellah site (45SA11) (Minor et al. 1989). The tuber appears to have been a primary resource for intensive production that may have supported the high populations that lived on the Lower Columbia (Darby 2005). Melissa Darby has identified five intensification strategies associated with wapato:

Resource ownership. Darby infers ownership of wapato plots based on ethnographic analogy and historical documents. Using the better-documented ethnography of the Katzie of the Lower Fraser River as analogy, she notes that land tenure involved wapato and cranberry resource areas (Darby 2005:206–7; Turner et al. 2005:156–57). Cultee's Chinook rendition of "Robin's Myth" contains a tantalizing account of ownership, in which Robin and Blue Jay cure a choking duck and in payment receive the rights to two sides of a lake, where they dig two canoeloads of wapato (Boas 1894:149–52).

Settlement patterns. Of 30 documented Chinookan towns and villages in the Wapato Valley, all were in close proximity to wapato habitat (Darby 2005:211). Seasonal migrations there correlated with wapato harvest times.

Trade and exchange. Historical documents record a thriving wapato trade to Euro-Americans and among Chinookan groups (e.g., Darby 1996, 2005; McDougall 1999).

Specialized harvesting tools. Small shovel-nosed canoes were used to gather large quantities of tubers (Darby 2005:209).

Control of predators. Wapato is a favored food of waterfowl, muskrats, and beaver (Darby 2005:212), and the high proportion of muskrat bone from Meier may indicate killing for predator management as well as for pelts. The Meier avian assemblage also contains an array of waterfowl, including dabbling ducks and swans (Frederick 2009), which eat wapato. Smaller faunal assemblages—such as Sunken Village (35MU4) (Croes et al. 2009), Station Camp (Wilson et al. 2009), Cholick (35MU1) (Saleeby 1983), and Pumphouse (35CO7) (Saleeby 1983)—include ducks and swans as well as beaver and muskrat. Darby (2005) focuses on the central role of wapato by identifying these animal species as predators. In fact, wapato may have been seen as beneficial because it attracted desired animal resources in a concentrated area and thus created favorable conditions for capture.

Camas

Camas, a lilaceous prairie species, is frequently mentioned as a major food resource (e.g., Boyd and Hajda 1987) and may fit the criteria of a keystone resource. Camas bulbs were mass processed by cooking them in a pit oven from two to five days and then pressing them into large loaves that were dried and stored (e.g., Douglas 1959:105; Swan 1972:91). Wacheno reported that camas was not processed into cakes but left whole, "like figs," and then boiled to eat (Drucker 1933–54:5). Nutritionally, camas bulbs have a high carbohydrate value and are a good source of thiamine and riboflavin (Turner and Kuhnlein 1983).

Camas was harvested from late spring to summer (Douglas 1959:105; Tolmie 1963:189), although harvest time on Willapa Bay was said to be from August to September (Swan 1972:89). Tualatin also sometimes harvested camas in the fall, although late spring and summer were the primary harvest seasons (Zenk 1976:54). The Tillamook, who lived just south of the coastal Chinookan groups, identified June and July as camas harvest months (Jacobs 2003:80). Chinookan linguistic evidence places camas activity in the spring, and Wacheno named a spring month in Clackamas Chinook as wɔlícnan nūLmīn (*walíšnan nuλmin?*) "'brings up camas'—'May'" (Drucker 1933–54:42). This calendar name corresponds to a calendar name obtained from an elderly Clackamas woman living with the Wishram, who identified April as camas time, walícnan (*walíšnan*) (Spier and Sapir 1930:209).

Ray (1938) wrote that "the extent to which camas was used is uncertain," although among groups that had "access to camas it is very fully used" (119). This ambiguity is well founded. Camas is described in several historical documents for the Chinookan area and listed as a food item, often with a brief description of earth ovens and cooking methods (Douglas 1959:56; Franchère 1967; Hinds 1836–42:107; Lewis and Clark 1988, 1990, 1991; Scouler 1905; Tolmie 1963:171; Kane 1971a). In oral narratives and ethnographies, camas is referred to more frequently than wapato (Boas 1894, 1901; Drucker 1933–54; Jacobs 1958–59; Ray 1938; Spier and Sapir 1930). In the historical documents as a whole, however, this pattern is reversed and wapato is referred to many more times than camas is. It is possible, as Ray stated, that camas was used primarily by groups that had access to it. James Swan, who lived at Willapa Bay and provided a detailed explanation of camas harvesting and earth-oven cooking, declared that it was his favorite vegetable next to fried bananas (Swan 1972:90–91).

Contemporary Chinookan consultants believed that camas was most likely imported from upriver (Gill 1985:12). Archaeologically, camas has been identified at Station Camp (Wilson et al. 2009) and in three Wapato Valley archaeological sites: Cathlapotle (Stenholm 1999), Meier (Trieu 2000), and St. John's (Trieu 2005). At Cathlapotle, small earth ovens and other features yielded a relatively large number of camas bulbs (N=ca. 48) that archaeobotanist Nancy Stenholm (1999) favorably compared with camas processing sites in the Calispell Valley, north of Spokane, Washington.

Western Red Cedar

The use of western red cedar by Northwest Coast peoples is legendary (Suttles and Lane 1990:24). It had primacy in a variety of technological applications, from houses, canoes, and clothing to medicine and fire tinder. Cedar also was used to create ceremonial items such as head rings (Boas 1894:89, 155). A specialized vocabulary referred to manufactured items from cedar. In Chinook, for example, tE′cgan (tɔ́-šgan, plural noun) refers to cedar planks, ʟʹuēʹluʟ (ɬ-ʔuílul?) to cedar bark, and ēʹcgan (í-šgan, singular noun) to the tree or a bole (Boas 1894, 1901).

No other species could fill the role of western red cedar. The wood is soft enough to work with stone tools; the straight grain lends itself to splitting, making it ideal for house planks; and it is permeated with decay-inhibiting organic compounds (Trieu 2005). There is no documentation of the trade of cedar wood as a raw material in the Lower Columbia, but manufactured items such as canoes (Boas 1901:126) were traded among groups. Below the Wapato Valley, women wore short skirts of shredded and wound cedar bark, and cedar-bark and cedar-root hats were a trade item with Euro-Americans (e.g., Douglas 1959:138; Lewis and Clark 1990:221, 1996:198).

Cedar wood and inner bark have been identified in several sites along the Lower Columbia, including Meier, Cathlapotle, and St. John's (Trieu 2000, 2005). At the St. John's site, a folded bundle of cedar inner bark that resembles a basket weaver's prepared materials was recovered in association with copper beads strung with stinging nettle fiber. The copper beads had preserved in the patina the impressions of beargrass (*Xerophyllum tenax*) leaves, another highly valued basketry material.

OTHER SIGNIFICANT RESOURCES

Other Chinookan resources that do not meet all the qualifications of a keystone resource but that may have been more important in the past or in certain ecological zones include seals, sea lions, sturgeon, clams, bracken fern, lupine, and oak.

Bracken firm rhizomes were used among all western Washington groups except the Chinook (Gunther 1972:14). Evidence from north of the Chinookan area strongly linked luxuriant growth of bracken and other prairie plants to fire management of prairies (Norton 1979a), and bracken fern was one of the 11 native plants tended in family-owned plots among the Coast Salish (Suttles 2005). It is not clear how important bracken fern was among the Chinookans. Although John Minto (1900:311) recalled seeing women and girls in the vicinity of Cathlamet Point collecting bracken fern fiddleheads and preparing to steam them in an earth oven, most sources refer to the rhizome. Lewis and Clark (1990:224, 228) described eating bracken fern root, which they thought tasted like wheat dough. According to Emma Luscier, dried bracken roots were mixed with fish eggs (Ray 1938:129), and John Wacheno stated that women cooked, peeled, and then ground the root using a mano and metate (Drucker 1933–54:5). Whether Chinookan groups made bracken fern "bread" is not clear.

Bracken emerges as even more important in the Chinook and Kathlamet oral narratives. It was stored and traded for salmon (Boas 1901:226, 1894:231), and Emma Luscier recalled that her father Sam Millet was instructed by his guardian spirit, a gray owl, to eat a few bracken fern roots. Bracken fern was symbolically linked to snakes (Ray 1938:79). Charles Cultee associated bracken fern with both snakes and supernatural powers, explaining the connection to the supernatural as a deterrent against overharvesting bracken fern by not taking the largest rhizomes (Boas 1901: 225–30, 228).

Archaeobotanical evidence from three sites in the Wapato Valley—St. John's, Meier, and Cathlapotle—argues for a closer examination of bracken as a key resource. Remains include a significant amount of unidentified fragmented, charred parenchyma tissue that resembles fern rhizome. At the Olympic Peninsula Hoko River wet site (dating from about 100 BC to AD 200), fern rhizomes appeared to have been the remnants of processing, and their presence was linked to stone bowls and grinding stones recovered in the dry deposits (Croes in Lepofsky 2004). In New Zealand, where the Maori had a tradition of using bracken fern, starch-grain analysis has been a productive line of evidence (Horrocks et al. 2004; McGlone et al. 2005), but Lower Columbia archaeobotanical research has not yet included it. Bracken fern is a good source of carbohydrates, phosphorous, magnesium, iron, zinc, and copper (Brand-Miller 2010).

Oregon white oak is another plant resource that may have been overlooked as an important resource (Norton 1979a:187). Early visitors to the Lower Columbia often described oak trees as growing in groves or orchard-like settings (e.g., Boyd 1996; Douglas 1959; Franchère 1967; Lewis and Clark 1988, 1990; Swan 1972; Townsend 1999; Vancouver 1984). Both the wood and acorns were used, with oak wood serving a number of technological uses in addition to being a highly regarded fuel (Jacobs 1958–59:143–56). Archaeobotanical evidence from Meier and Cathlapotle demonstrates the use of oak as fuelwood in the Wapato Valley (Trieu 2000).

Ethnographic evidence for acorn use is widespread. In western Washington, the Chehalis, Cowlitz, Klallam, and Squaxin ate acorns (Gunther 1973:27), as did Plateau groups such as the Klikatat, Tenino, Umatilla, Kittitas, Wenatchie, and Sanpoil (Ray 1942:136). Groups along the Oregon Coast used acorns (Barnett 1937:166), and they also were a commodity on the eastern fringe of the Chinookan area (Boyd 1996:56; Lewis and Clark 1988:317, 1991:99–100; Spier and Sapir 1930:185). The Wishram had standard-sized baskets, the agúlulix (*agúlulix*), for storing and trading acorns (Spier and Sapir 1930:185).

The acorns produced by Oregon white oak are highly nutritious, and their low tannin content requires minimal processsing. As a high energy source, they yield more than 500 calories per 100 grams and are an excellent source of fat, mega-6 fatty acids, carbohydrates, and protein, as well as vitamins and minerals, thiamine, niacin, vitamin B6, folate, iron, magnesium, copper, and manganese (USDA 2012). Acorns ripen in the fall, and September was wak!núwi (wak'núwi), or acorn month, in the Clackamas Chinook calendar (Spier and Sapir 1930:209). Mabel Teio of Wishram reported that acorn harvest time was November, after the acorns had fallen from the trees (Spier and Sapir 1930:184).

Descriptions of processing vary. The two most detailed, for the Clackamas by Wacheno (Drucker 1933–54:40) and among the Wasco-Wishram (Boyd 1996:56; Spier and Sapir 1930:184–85), involve first steam-roasting acorns in a pit oven, then burying them in pits packed with a pleasant-smelling blue mud. In Wacheno's method, white-fir twigs were mixed with the clay used to pack the pits (Drucker 1933–54:40). Sahaptins leached the acorns by burying them in an aromatic mud and then roasting them in a pit oven (Hunn 1990:183). Emma Luscier reported that "acorns were buried in the mud for leaching before being used" (Ray 1938:130). The Tualatins used both methods (Zenk 1976:61), and the Chehalis and Cowlitz buried acorns in mud all winter to leach them (Gunther 1973:28). After leaching, the softened shells were removed (Spier and Sapir 1930:185), or they were sometimes pounded and mixed with steelhead oil. The Chehalis and Squaxins simply roasted acorns over the fire, and the Klallams ate them without any preparation (Gunther 1973:28). An often-cited acorn preparation is Paul Kane's (1971a) description of "Chinook olives," which involved digging a bushel-sized pit by the house entry door, filling it with acorns, capping it with dirt, and then using it as a repository for urine to "cure" the acorns. It was, he said, "the greatest of delicacies" (33). The narratives, however, invariably place acorn pits away from houses near water sources (Boas 1901:142–54; Jacobs 1958–59:423–30; Ray 1938:148–51).

Despite this evidence, the ethnographies and historical documents are unclear as to the role of acorns in people's diets, and the question remains as to whether they were a staple food resource. Mrs. Luscier tersely stated that "acorns were fairly extensively used" and that with the "exception of acorn" nuts and seeds "were little used" (Ray 1938:123, 129–30). Wacheno reported that both men and women harvested acorns and that large quantities were put up for winter (Drucker 1933–54:40). Three accounts in the Chinookan texts of Raccoon stealing his grandmother's acorns describe five large caches stored by the river. His punishment for stealing was severe, pointing to the value of the acorns (Boas 1901:142–54; Jacobs 1958–59:423–30; Ray 1938:148–51). Among the Wishram, however, acorns were said to be more like a snack than a staple (Spier and Sapir 1930:185). Acorn use among the Tualatins ceased by the mid-19th century, when people were removed to the Grand Ronde Reservation (Zenk 1976:60), and decline in the use of acorns as a major staple may have occurred among Chinook people as well.

The answer to the question of the role of acorns in Chinookan diet may well rest in the archaeological record. At Meier and Cathlapotle, the remains of charred acorns are ubiquitous (Trieu 2000), although they are rare at the St. John's site (Trieu 2005). The best evidence for intensive acorn processing comes from recent archaeological investigations at the Sunken Village, where investigators have mapped over 100 acorn leaching-pit features along a 125–meter stretch of the Multnomah Channel (Croes et al. 2009; Mathews 2007, 2009). The pits, marked with branches or stakes from western hemlock boughs, represent the largest archaeologically investigated food-processing facility on the Lower Columbia, and for that reason alone the role of acorns in Chinookan subsistence must be examined. The Sunken Village acorn pits have attracted the interest of Japanese archaeologists because of their striking similarity to nut-processing pits found in western Japan (Matsui 2009:2–3), dating as early as the Incipient Jomon period (11,300+/-300 BP) (Habu 2004).

CONCLUSIONS

While studying subsistence is critical to understanding a society, human relationships with the living world are multifaceted and complex. Pharmacology, the ritual use of plant and animal resources, and other relationships with plants and animals such as taboos, tutelaries, and pets are also significant, and more research is needed in these fields if we are to better understand the Chinookan worldview.

Focusing on nonfishing plant and animal resources gives us a mostly terrestrial view of Chinookan ethnobiology, providing an opportunity to turn from the emphasis on fish (especially salmon) in Chinookan subsistence to other parts of the subsistence economy, such as plant resources, cervids, shellfish, and aquatic mammals. Such studies complement Virginia Butler's work on Lower Columbia archaeological fish remains, an investigation of the role that side channel or backwater fishes may have played in local subsistence economies (see ch. 4 in this volume). Another research trend involves the role that resources used for technology may have played in the economy, such as the large-scale processing of western red cedar for houses, canoes, and basketry.

For Chinookan peoples, having a diverse range of resources was a key to well-being, but studying focal resources—those resources with high cultural salience that fill a unique economic niche and are often processed and stored in high volumes—is critical to understanding their economy. While Garibaldi and Turner (2004) explicitly recognize that cultural keystone species vary over time and in specific locales, their criteria are difficult to operationalize beyond the past 200 years, a relatively narrow span of time. Nevertheless, these criteria do have the potential to highlight overlooked resources.

Beyond gaining an accurate portrayal of Chinookan lifeways, understanding the dynamics of the Chinookan subsistence economy has a bearing on perennial issues in Northwest Coast history in particular and on models of human social evolution in general. In anthropological academic circles, peoples of the Northwest Coast have long been regarded as unique for having developed a complex, multitiered social system without agriculture. Research over the past three decades, however, has revealed that the Pacific Northwest is not unusual in this way. In Australia (Lourandos 1997), Japan (Habu 2004), the Levant (Bar-Yosef 1998), South America (Scheinsohn 2003), and elsewhere in North America (Sassaman 2004), a variety of socially complex societies developed that were supported by economies where domesticated plants and animals played little or no role.

One question that is still being explored is how Northwest Coast subsistence systems supported towns and villages without agriculture. The answer has long centered on the intensive harvesting of salmon (e.g., Fladmark 1975; Matson 1992; Schalk 1981), but scholars (Ames and Marshall 1981) have suggested that plant resources are also key to understanding the role of food production in Northwest Coast traditional economies. The initial research was targeted at overturning the perception that peoples of the Northwest Coast did not cultivate plants (Deur 2002; Deur and Turner 2005). Part of the process of refuting longstanding misconceptions has been gaining a better understanding of cultivation and plant resource management (Lepofsky et al. 2005; Peacock and Turner 2000; Smith 2005; Turner and Peacock 2005). Nancy Turner and her students (Turner and Peacock 2005) have illuminated a wide repertoire of plant-management practices, including selective harvesting, tilling, transplanting, broadcast sowing, weeding, pruning, burning, and fertilizing. Many researchers and observers have overlooked these practices, expecting to see instead a familiar form of agriculture dominated by plants with significant phenotypical changes, such as seen in annual cereal crop plants. This revised view of cultivation has required looking beyond isolated plant species to the tended, gardenlike landscapes found throughout the Northwest Coast.

Except for Darby's (1996, 2005) work on wapato, Chinookan data on plant resource management have offered little to this discussion, although there are some hints of plant resource management. The Clackamas Chinook texts, for example, correlate burning with higher production of berries and camas (Jacobs 1958–59:143, 156–66), and prairie landscapes often are described in the historical documents in gardenlike terms (e.g., Douglas 1959:105–14; Franchère 1967:49–50; Lewis and Clark 1991:55; Tolmie 1963:171). Many non-fish resources—deer, elk, camas, bracken fern, and oak—are part of Northwest Coast prairie or oak savannah ecosystems. To the north and south of the Chinookan area, these ecosystems were maintained through fire management (e.g., Boyd 1999a; Leopold and Boyd 1999; Norton 1979a; Norton et al. 1999; Turner 1999). Camas, bracken fern, and oak all appear to be more prevalent in the Chinookan oral texts than in the historical documents, and we can hypothesize that these resources were probably more important in the past than in the colonial period.

A change in the subsistence economy just before contact may be due to the role of population size on food production systems. Before contact, peoples of the Lower Columbia had some of the highest population densities in North America (Ames and Maschner 1999:26). As Boyd (1999b) has concluded, however, "the Indian populations of the lower Columbia suffered more from the effects of introduced diseases than those of any other subregion of the Northwest Coast culture area" (232). Smallpox epidemics began as early as the 1780s, a generation before the Lewis and Clark Expedition. Food resources such as bracken fern and acorn require significant labor to prepare and may have assumed a lower profile in people's diet after contact. The Tualatin Kalapuyas, for example, indicated that acorns were a more important resource before the reservation period, when larger populations lived in prime oak savannah habitat (Zenk 1976:60). Patterns of use of other food resources occurred around the contact period. Fish remains in Wapato Valley archaeological sites show a general shift after contact toward larger-bodied fish such as sturgeon and salmon and a decline in the use of smaller-bodied fishes. Likewise, white-tailed deer populations rebounded after contact, followed by the near extinction of the species because of Euro-American land-use practices. These data point to the possibility of Chinookan management and enhancement of prairie habitat, most likely by fire regimes that kept deer populations stable despite centuries of human predation (Lyman 2006).

Another factor that may have led to changes in the subsistence economy was Chinookan peoples' entrance into global trade during the late 17th and early 18th centuries, which may have resulted in the less intensive use and management of prairie habitats. Furthering our understanding of Chinookan land management practices will require a multidisciplinary approach (see Lepofsky et. al. 2005) that integrates archaeology, paleoethnobotany, zooarchaeology, and historical ecology in addition to renewed attention to the oral texts, especially the Chinookan narratives.

There is another forward-looking and pragmatic component to this research. Traditional ecological knowledge (TEK) is a body of knowledge built up over generations of experience with plants, animals, and ecosystems. Northwest Coast indigenous peoples hold in common cultural values that guide their relationships to the land and water and the plants and animals that share these places with them. TEK has three interwoven dimensions: worldview, strategies for sustainable living, and exchange of knowledge (Turner 1996). Challenging expectations that this knowledge was lost during the early contact era, researchers are finding that TEK was often retained in the details of recipes and remedies, family hunting and fishing practices, and oral traditions (e.g., Anderson 1997; Burton et al. 2007; Cullis-Suzuki et al. 2006; Gottesfeld 1994; Mack and McClure 2002; Thornton 1998; Turner 2005). Rediscovering TEK is an important aspect of cultural heritage recovery and education programs (e.g., Adams 1958; Gill 1985; Sobel and Cotter 2008; Thompson 2004, 2005, 2007).

Increasingly, TEK guides the work of restoration ecologists, wildlife managers, conservation biologists, land-use planners, land stewards, and others concerned with developing improved relationships with local environments. Works such as *Ecologies of the Heart* (Anderson 1996), *Sacred Ecology* (Berkes 2008), and *The Earth's Blanket* (Turner 2005) have introduced ethnobiology and traditional ecological knowledge to a wide audience. Applications of such knowledge have been made to projects that are restoring salmon fisheries (Langdon 2006), pacific lamprey (Close et al. 2001; Close et al. 2002; Peterson 2006), beargrass (Shebitz 2005), huckleberries (Senos et al. 2006), and wapato (Garibaldi and Turner 2004). In other instances, archaeological evidence is playing a role in understanding ecosystem dynamics such as aboriginal hunting and land-management patterns, climate change, habitat loss, and sea otter recovery (Ecotrust 2001), Columbia white-tailed deer (Lyman 2006; Lyman and Wolverton 2002), mountain beaver (Lyman and Zehr 2003), sooty shearwaters (Bovy 2007), and Columbia River and Great Basin fishes (Butler 2004; Butler and Delacourte 2004). A clear understanding of Chinookan ethnobiology has the potential not only to add to our knowledge of Chinookan peoples and their culture but also to deepen our understanding and appreciation of the histories of the plants and animals that inhabit the Lower Columbia River estuary.

FOUR

ABORIGINAL FISHERIES OF THE LOWER COLUMBIA RIVER

Virginia L. Butler and Michael A. Martin

S ALMON has an iconic status in the Pacific Northwest, and both scholars and the general public traditionally have viewed it as the dietary
staple of Northwest Coast Native people. Early 20th-century anthropologists named the Pacific Northwest the Salmon Area to highlight the
primacy of this resource to Native economy and ways of life (Wissler 1917).
Later 20th-century anthropologists theorized that the complex Native cultures seen at European contact—characterized by large population size, hier-
archical social organization, and elaborate art—were made possible largely
by the catching and storing of large quantities of salmon (e.g., Matson 1992).

Scholars have challenged this salmoncentric view on several fronts. First,
analysis of ethnographic records has highlighted the diversity of resources
used (Suttles 1990; Moss 1993), including the important role of plants (Deur
and Turner 2005; see ch. 3 in this volume). In a recent test of the hypothesis
that increasing salmon use was a driving mechanism for the development of
cultural complexity, Butler and Campbell (2004) reviewed zooarchaeological
records from multiple south-central Northwest Coast sites. While salmon
remains were the most ubiquitous fish taxon and the dominant fish in about
half the assemblages, other species (flounder, herring, and sculpin) dominated almost half. There was no evidence that salmon use increased in tan-
dem with increasing cultural complexity.

Recent analysis of ethnohistorical accounts (Martin 2006) and fish
remains from Lower Columbia River archaeological sites (e.g., Butler 2002a,
2005; Frederick 2007; Wigen 2009) offer an opportunity to evaluate the
salmoncentric paradigm in this region of the Northwest Coast. The Colum-

bia River system is known for its once-spectacular salmon runs. Before late 19th-century declines caused by overfishing and habitat destruction, 10 to 16 million salmon and trout representing six species migrated into the Columbia between March and October on their way to spawning grounds (NWPPC 1986). Given the vastness of the resource, there has been a tendency to assume that salmon was the *sine qua non* of indigenous peoples' way of life in the Columbia and elsewhere in the Pacific Northwest (e.g., Saleeby 1983; Lichatowich 1999; Beckham 2006; see also Hunn 1990).

The Lower Columbia River is here defined as the 230–kilometer (140–mile) section between the mouth and The Cascades, a large set of rapids now drowned by waters behind Bonneville Dam. We draw on two kinds of records to document aboriginal fisheries: 19th-century eyewitness accounts, mainly by explorers and fur traders, provide details on the types of fishes, the season and location of fisheries, and methods of capture and preparation (Table S4.1 online); and archaeological records, mainly from fish bones and teeth left by aboriginal fish harvesting and food preparation at villages and campsites, help document which fish were used at various times and places (Table S4.2 online). While archaeological records lack the detail found in historical records, they provide a much longer history of fisheries and are an independent record for fish use and human adaptations overall.

Together, the records show a complex picture of Columbia River fisheries. While salmon are prominently featured in 19th-century records, the capture, preservation, and trade in sturgeon and eulachon are also a critical part of the fisheries. During spring, the fisheries tended to target sturgeon over the spring chinook. The archaeological record also shows that salmon, sturgeon, and eulachon were heavily used and also the importance of minnow, sucker, and perhaps even stickleback, all of which are almost ignored in 19th-century accounts. These last fishes would have been most prominent in backwater areas of the Columbia River floodplain, a vast seasonally flooded wetland that represented an extremely productive resource patch with fish and other resources.

NINETEENTH-CENTURY ACCOUNTS

Most native fish species for the Lower Columbia reported in the current literature (Farr and Ward 1993; Wydoski and Whitney 2003) were part of the Native American fishery. Eyewitness accounts by explorers and natural historians (Lewis and Clark, Townsend, Douglas, Scouler, Wilkes), fur traders

(McDougall, Franchère, Stuart, Henry), and settlers (Swan) provide extremely useful details on traditional fishing between 1800 and 1855 as well as a starting point for interpreting the archaeological record of fish use (see Table S4.1). Epidemic diseases in the late 18th century and again in the 1830s reduced lower-river Indian populations by as much as 90 percent, which resulted in the loss of much traditional knowledge of fish and fishing. Thus the historic and archaeological records are especially valuable for showing the richness and complexity of fishing practices of Chinookan people.

The historical records have limitations, however. First, most were written during a time of dramatic change in people's lives on the lower river. Population losses would have affected social organization, tribal territories, access to fishing areas, production of fishing gear, and other aspects of life. Thus 19th-century practices may not reflect those of even a few decades earlier, much less several centuries. Also, many accounts are from fur-trade agents engaged in buying fish from Indians to provision their posts. The fish purchased were those that could be taken in and preserved and that were compatible with Euro-American tastes. The accounts were written through the filter of the Euro-American worldview that obviously carried certain prejudices, and most reports were made by visitors who were in the area only part of a year or who traveled in limited areas. Identifying fish species in 19th-century accounts can also be challenging (see Martin 2006). Recognizing these potential problems and biases, we have taken a critical approach in analyzing the records, seeking multiple, independent records for practices. We also view the short summaries below as hypotheses that can be investigated rather than as definitive accounts.

Salmonidae

The Columbia River is home to multiple species in the Salmonidae family, including anadromous runs of salmon and trout in the genus *Oncorhynchus* and nonmigratory forms of whitefish (*Prosopium*) and trout (*Salvelinus*). Species of *Oncorhynchus* were the most important food resource in the family, which includes chinook salmon (*O. tshawytscha*); coho salmon (*O. kisutch*); chum salmon (*O. keta*); sockeye salmon (*O. nerka*); pink salmon (*O. gorbuscha*), in limited numbers; steelhead trout (*O. mykiss*); and cutthroat trout (*O. clarki*). Except for some steelhead, adults in the genus die after spawning. Young salmon emerge from spawning sites and, depending on the species, spend from a few weeks to more than a year in freshwater before migrating to sea, where they live between two and seven years before returning to their natal stream to spawn and repeat the life cycle.

Until the declines in the 19th and 20th centuries, chinook salmon were far and away the most important salmon species to Columbia River commercial fisheries because of their abundance and size—in excess of 1 meter (3.2 feet) long and 6 kilograms (13.2 pounds). Columbia River chinook have three main runs: the spring run enters the Columbia from February to June; the summer run travels through the lower river from June through August; and the fall run lasts from mid-August through October (Fulton 1968, 1970). Most fish in the spring and summer runs do not spawn in lower-river tributaries but migrate through the main stem en route to distant upper-system spawning areas. An important exception is a portion of the spring run that ascends the Willamette River over Willamette Falls, which is passable only in high water associated with spring snowmelt. In contrast to the spring-summer runs, several populations of fall chinook migrate into and spawn in several Lower Columbia tributary rivers and streams—for example, Youngs River, Clatskanie, and numerous tributaries of the Cowlitz and Kalama Rivers (Martin 2006). Fish that make up the spring-summer run in the lower river are less reproductively mature than fall-run fish and have a fresher appearance and higher fat content.

Euro-American accounts of chinook salmon fishing on the lower river mention taking fish at two natural constrictions: Willamette Falls (for the spring run) and The Cascades (for all the runs). The fishery began as soon as the spring run arrived at both falls, varying yearly from early April to early May (Martin 2006) and continuing at The Cascades until October. Native Americans constructed elaborate wooden fishing platforms and walkways adjacent to and over narrow channels through which migrating salmon had to pass; at The Cascades, some channels were constructed by aligning boulders and rocks in rows as much as 15 meters (50 feet) long (Wilkes 1845:380). Fishermen scooped up fish using hoop nets that were about 1.2 meters (4 feet) in diameter mounted on a pole about 9 meters (30 feet) long (e.g., Wilkes 1845), and snagged them with gaffs (long poles with hooks fixed to the end). The productivity of this fishery was enormous. At Willamette Falls in 1841, it was estimated that one person could catch 20 large fish in an hour (Wilkes 1845:345).

Eyewitness accounts of chinook salmon fishing downstream of the falls using seines is less common. The description of beach seining for salmon in Baker Bay at the mouth of the Columbia in the late 1850s is the most detailed

(Swan 1972:137). Extremely large nets—30–180 meters (100–600 feet) long and 2–5 meters (7–16 feet) deep—made from spruce root or grass were deployed by several people working between the shore and in a canoe offshore. Floats tied to the net margin were made from cedar, and the base of the net was held down by notched round pebbles weighing less than .5 kilograms (1.3 pounds). Other observers simply mention that seines were used for salmon fishing (Martin 2006). One challenge to seining would be the net damage caused by trees and branches resting on the channel bed or shoreline; such debris would have been extremely common before flood-control measures were in place on the river. Upriver of The Cascades, seining occurred over sand or water-worn cobbles, free of sharp bedrock (Douglas 1959). The high costs associated with the manufacture and maintenance of nets may have limited their use, especially relative to fishing at the falls.

Historic accounts do not mention the construction and use of weirs to capture salmon or other fish on lower-river tributaries and streams, which is striking considering that weirs were used to capture salmon in Puget Sound rivers (Suttles and Lane 1990:489) and commonly used elsewhere on the Northwest Coast. Moss (2012:323–38) reports over 1,300 remains of ancient weirs from Oregon to Alaska. Archaeologists Gary Wessen and Richard Daugherty (1983) found remains of a weir on the south bank of Vancouver Lake, though freshwater fish and not salmon were the likely target. In 1841, the Wilkes Expedition described a weir on the Chehalis River, a drainage system north of the Columbia (Martin 2006).

Several accounts mention that chinook salmon were speared from canoes or in shallows from shore, using hooks or harpoon heads fitted on the end of a long pole. In some variations, the spear portion would be tied to the pole by a cord that would detach when the fish was struck, and the fish would be hauled in by the cord; in other cases, fish would simply be stabbed and hauled into the canoe. The spear fishery tended to target the fall-run fish that were migrating into lower-river tributaries to spawn. Fish were relatively concentrated and accessible at tributary mouths, allowing for a very productive fishery. In 1811, for example, a single fisherman from Chinook Village on Baker Bay was observed spearing 120 salmon in one morning (McDougall 1999:56).

According to 19th-century accounts, fish caught in the spring-summer run on the lower river were mainly consumed fresh and were not smoked or dried, whereas the fall-run fish were smoked. This practice was probably due to several factors. Fish in the spring-summer run contained much more fat than those in the fall run (Schalk 1986), and the timing of the spring-summer runs coincided with periods of higher rainfall and cooler weather; both conditions made it more difficult to preserve earlier running fish than later arrivals. Three eyewitness accounts indicate that the flesh from fall-run chinook was preserved inside residences, where fish were hung by the rafters and cured by the smoke and heat from hearth fires (Townsend 1999:256; Corney 1965:46; Swan 1972:111). An 1853 account describes fish being butchered and processed for storage at a camp on the Naselle River, apart from residences. This practice included separate curing of heads and tails, with the main part of the body sliced thinly and dried. Three other accounts note the production of dried salmon. Describing practices below Fort Vancouver (Work 1824) in 1824 and in 1853 at the mouth (Swan 1972:111), observers noted that dried or roasted salmon was finely broken up, pounded, and pressed into baskets and that oil and berries were added to the mixture. The third account, from 1836, noted that Indians produced pemmican from dried salmon, but we do not know the location (Parker 1967). Overall, though, there was much less salmon preservation on the Lower Columbia than in the arid regions upriver of The Cascades. No 19th-century accounts refer to the elaborate and extensive sets of drying racks such as at The Dalles. In fact, large quantities of dried chinook salmon were shipped downriver from The Dalles area for trade with lower-river Native people and fur traders (McDougall 1999:178, 188).

Salmonids other than chinook are mentioned less frequently in 19th-century accounts. Chum (or dog) salmon, which migrate into the Columbia from October through December, was noted by several observers, although usually for its local abundance in streams. Like fall-run chinook, chum enter freshwater ripe and ready to spawn, mainly in tributaries below The Cascades (Fulton 1970). With limited fat, chum salmon were smoked and stored (Stuart 1935:8). Several Euro-American visitors complained about chum as a food source; David Douglas (1959:239–40), for example, noted that it was lean like pine bark. Fish that were described as "small salmon" and "salmon trout" or "white salmon trout" may represent coho salmon and steelhead, but assignment of taxa to species is difficult (Butler 2004). Regardless of the taxon, their use was relatively minor. None of the 19th-century accounts appear to refer to fishing for either sockeye or pink salmon. While pink salmon was probably not abundant in the Columbia (based on commercial fishery records), the river supported large numbers of coho and sockeye salmon, and their limited mention in 19th-century accounts is surprising. There is also no mention in the accounts of capturing and using other resident salmonids, including whitefish or bulltrout.

Sturgeon

The northeast Pacific and Pacific Slope drainages are home to two species of sturgeon: white sturgeon (*Acipenser transmontanus*) and green sturgeon (*A. medirostris*). White sturgeon, which is more abundant than green sturgeon in the Columbia system, grow to about 6 meters (20 feet) and weigh about 580 kilograms (1,200 pounds), while green sturgeon are smaller, at about 2 meters (6 feet) and 160 kilograms (350 pounds) (Parsley et al. 1993; Wydoski and Whitney 2003). White sturgeon can live for as many as 100 years and they mature late, after 10 years, making them highly susceptible to overfishing (Rieman and Beamesderfer 1990). Both species migrate in and out of marine waters. Green sturgeon are mainly found in the estuary below river mile 38, while white sturgeon are found along the entire main stem to the headwaters of the Columbia and Snake River systems. Multiple 19th-century accounts indicate that Euro-Americans were familiar with both species but that they preferred the taste of white sturgeon.

Although white sturgeon were available throughout the year, particularly large numbers were taken from February to April, when the fish collected to prey on spawning runs of eulachon (*Thaleichthys pacificus*). Native Americans caught large quantities of sturgeon, including some to sell to fur traders. Between February and April 1813, for example, traders purchased at least 300 large fish to supply Fort Astoria, and the fort head suggested that the winter sturgeon fishery was sufficient to support 50 to 60 men for four months. During midsummer, fur traders purchased smaller quantities of white sturgeon from the fishery in Baker Bay (McDougall 1999).

Sturgeon were captured using hook and line, net, gaff, or spear. At least some sturgeon angling was configured as a set line, where a series of baited hooks on leaders or secondary lines spaced at about 3.7 meters (12 feet) apart was attached to the main line. Fishers fixed a line to the shore using a large rock weighing 7–8 kilograms (15–16 pounds) and stretched the line away from shore using a float anchored to the river bottom with another rock (Franchère 1967). Individual fish were netted in a funnel-shaped net, 1.5–2 meters (5–6 feet) wide, 3–4 meters (10–12 feet) long, with a white lure at the end. Two men in a canoe, holding lines connected to the net, drew the net along the channel bottom. When they felt movement in the net, the fishermen closed it, trapping the fish (Franchère 1967:112–13). In the Baker Bay summer fishery, fishers speared sturgeon from a canoe with a single toggle harpoon. One eyewitness reported that this method was used by specialists who had the knowledge to locate the fish and the strength to land it without tipping over the canoe (Swan 1972). Finally, sturgeon may have been collected on the beach or in nearshore shallows. In fall 1805, a local Indian told William Clark that beached sturgeon and other fish were obtained in this way (Lewis and Clark 1990:121).

People on the lower river prepared and sold fish fresh and smoke-cured. For smoke-curing, a sturgeon was sliced into large pieces and suspended from rafters in houses. Ten to 12 pieces were sold in "bales." On April 19, 1812, Duncan McDougall (1999) purchased 10 to 12 bales for Fort Astoria, which he hoped would last until the salmon arrived in May.

Eulachon

Eulachon, also known as candlefish or smelt, is distributed from northern California to the Bering Sea. A relatively small, short-lived (~3 years), anadromous species—about .14–.20 meters (5–8 inches) long—eulachon live most of their lives in inshore marine waters. Adults migrate in dense schools short distances up rivers to spawn in winter and early spring (Wydoski and Whitney 2003); about a month after eggs are laid, larvae hatch and drift downstream to saltwater to begin the cycle again. At one time, the Columbia River had the largest run of all eulachon rivers (Biological Review Team 2008). Prime spawning areas included the lower reaches of the Sandy, Lewis, Kalama, and Cowlitz Rivers and limited sections of the Columbia's main stem. Peak times for the run were in February and March (Wydoski and Whitney 2003), but fish were noted entering the river as early as December and as late as April.

Historical records suggest that annual run size was variable, both overall and in particular tributaries. The Cowlitz River, for example, once supported a large commercial eulachon fishery; over 3 million pounds were recorded in 1932 alone (Smith and Saalfeld 1955). Hudson's Bay Company reports, however, record runs that were absent or limited in the Cowlitz River between 1835 and the 1850s (Hinrichsen 1998), and eulachon did not spawn in the river in eight years between 1910 and 1954 (Smith and Saalfeld 1955). A compilation of commercial fishery landings between 1888 and 2008 also shows highly variable harvest levels (Biological Review Team 2008), which provides a crude measure of variability in the run. According to George Suckley's (1860b) account on the southern end of Vancouver Island, eulachon "are very abundant in certain seasons, but nearly always a season of abundance is followed by three or four years of scarcity. Further northward they are constantly abundant" (348). The causes of the fluctuation are not clear, although changing ocean conditions are thought to contribute (Biological Review Team 2008). Overall, eulachon may not have been a dependable resource in particular locations.

Lower Columbia River Indians captured eulachon using either a rake or a scoop net. Alexander Henry (1992) described the rake as a "pole about 10 feet long and two inches thick, on one side of which was fixed a range of small, sharp bones like teeth, about one inch long, one-fourth of an inch asunder, the range of teeth extending six feet up the blade" (683). Fish were impaled on the "teeth" as the rake was swept back and forth in the water. In both 1806 and 1812, large quantities of eulachon reportedly were taken with "scooping" nets (Lewis and Clark 1990:346; Stuart 1935).

Fish were consumed fresh, but most descriptions refer to smoke-curing. In 1806, Meriwether Lewis wrote: "the natives run a small stick through their gills and hang them in the smoke of their lodges, or kindle a small fire under them for the purposes of drying them. they need no previous preparation of guting &c and will cure within 24 hours" (Lewis and Clark 1990:378). At Cathlapotle (45CL1) on the Lewis River, he saw large quantities of eulachon strung on small sticks, arranged in large sheets, and hung suspended by poles in the roofs of houses (Lewis and Clark 1991:27).

Native people of the Lower Columbia apparently did not render eulachon for oil, a common practice of First Nations people in coastal British Columbia, where the oil is a prized item in trade and community events (Swan 1880). Across all 19th-century accounts, only missionary Samuel Parker (1967), who visited Fort Vancouver in 1835–36, refers to eulachon oil. Given the lack of corroboration from other accounts, it is unlikely that oil was produced in the region.

Almost all historic accounts between 1804 and 1813 highlight the eulachon fishery, its abundance, and its value to Native Americans and Euro-Americans involved in the fur trade. The fishery was strongly seasonal, targeting upriver migrating adults moving into spawning grounds of lower rivers during the late winter-early spring. Observers reported seeing "immense numbers" (Stuart 1935:30), "Great quantities" (Lewis and Clark 1990:346), and "many canoes" (McDougall 1999:72) of eulachon being transported. Actual quantities of fish caught and traded can be estimated from 1810s fur-trade accounts, which report the purchase of dried eulachon by the "fathom," a six-foot length of fish strung head to tail. In 1813, one agent purchased 353 fathoms from Native fishermen (McDougall 1999), about three tons of fresh fish (Martin 2006).

Lamprey

While at least three species of lamprey (sometimes known as eel) are found in the Pacific Northwest (Smith and Butler 2008), the Pacific lamprey (*Entosphenus tridentata*) is the largest (lengths of .75 meters [2.5 feet]) and most commonly recognized and was likely the species most sought by Native people of the Lower Columbia. The Pacific lamprey has a complex life history, reaching adulthood in ocean waters and then migrating into freshwater between April and June to spawn. Eggs are laid in stream gravels; larvae emerge, leave the nest, and then burrow into silt/mud, where they spend four to six years before migrating out to sea to mature before returning to freshwater to repeat the cycle.

Lamprey were not traded to Euro-Americans, although three 19th-century observers commented on the fish. In June 1845, Charles Wilkes (1845a:346) noted large numbers of lamprey ascending Willamette Falls, but no one was fishing for them. Others reported that lamprey were smoked and stored in Native American camps. In April 1834, Dr. John Townsend (1999:210) saw lamprey in an Indian lodge near the confluence of the Willamette and Clackamas Rivers, downstream from Willamette Falls; he reported thousands of lamprey were being smoke-cured in lodges on Hamilton Island near The Cascades in July. In 1812, Robert Stuart (1935) mentioned lamprey but did not include a location.

Key aspects of the lamprey's biology and ethnographic accounts from the Upper Columbia (Close et al. 2004) suggest that the fish were likely intercepted during their late spring and summer spawning migration. They are not fast swimmers and tend to mass at waterfalls, where the steep gradient and current reduce their upstream travel speed. To ascend the falls, lamprey crawl up rock surfaces, using their suckerlike disc mouths to adhere to the rock face, and then slowly creep up and over the walls. Native fishers picked lamprey off the surfaces by hand or using a hook (Close et al. 2004). It is likely that fishers used similar approaches on the lower river.

Miscellaneous Fish

Nineteenth-century accounts note the taking and trade of a few mainly saltwater fish that enter and sometimes reside in the lower river near the mouth, such as flatfish—for example, starry flounder (*Platichthys stellatus*, Pleuronectidae), surfperch (Embiotocidae), and herring (*Clupea pallasii*) (Martin 2006).

The absence of a herring fishery is especially notable. Herring are common in the lower river (Monaco et al. 1990); fish spawn within 55 kilometers (88 miles) of the mouth (Lassuy and Moran 1989). In the 1850s, Swan (1972:27) observed a herring fishery in Willapa Bay, but not in Baker Bay or other places nearby. A reference to *Clupea* by John Scouler (1905), based on a fish that Indian children had caught near Fort Vancouver in 1825, is suspect, as the description and position of the teeth suggest the fish is a cyprinid (minnow family).

Resident freshwater fishes, including multiple species of minnow—northern pikeminnow (*Ptychocheilus oregonensis*), peamouth chub (*Mylocheilus caurinus*), chiselmouth (*Acrocheilus alutaceus*), and dace (*Rhinichthys* sp.)—and largescale sucker (*Catostomus macrocheilus*), are abundant in the lower river and backwater lakes and channels. Both minnows and suckers prefer relatively warm, slow-moving water. Suckers are mainly herbivores, grazing on algae and aquatic vegetation, while minnows tend to be more carnivorous, consuming a variety of invertebrates and fish species. Minnows are commonly thought to be very small fish, when in fact body size varies between large species such as the northern pikeminnow, which can reach more than .5 meter (1.6 feet) long and weigh over 10 kilograms (22 pounds), to medium-sized fish such as the chiselmouth and the peamouth chub, typically attaining 30 centimeters (1 foot), to small dace and shiners (*Richardsonius* sp.), which reach .1 meter (4 inches) in length. Largescale suckers can weigh as much as 3 kilograms (6 pounds).

These fishes are scarcely mentioned in 19th-century accounts, yet their remains are abundant in archaeological sites. One certain reference was made by a member of the Wilkes Expedition (1845:366), who observed a sucker at Willamette Falls in June 1841. On May 11, 1825, at about 10 kilometers (6 miles) below Fort Vancouver, John Scouler (1905) saw "Indians drawing their net ashore and among the variety of fish it contained I selected two species of *Cyprinus*" (175). A few observers mentioned the taking of "small fishes" that could include at least some of the minnow-sucker species. Lewis and Clark (1990:211) noted that small fishes were taken in spring and summer with a scoop net. In 1818, Corney (1965:153) reported that in summer Chinookan people "catch sturgeon, and salmon, and a variety of small fish." On May 22, 1833, HBC trader William Tolmie (1963) encountered a group of Indians on a Columbia River tributary (perhaps the Cowlitz River) traveling to Willamette Falls for the spring salmon fishery. "They subsist," he wrote, "at this season [on succulent stems] & on small fish" (186). Minnows and suckers spawn during late spring and early summer, and adults congregate in the shallows of streams and lakes, spending several days to several weeks on the spawning grounds, when they would have been most concentrated and easiest to catch.

While the lower-river ethnohistoric sources are ambiguous on minnow and sucker fisheries, these fishes have always been important in upriver Plateau fisheries (Hunn 1990; Hewes 1998; Post 1938). Many of the species were taken with specialized gear during the spring before migratory salmon runs arrived (Hunn et al. 1998). Sahaptin speakers have an intimate knowledge of local fish, including names for suckers and a variety of minnow (Hunn 1980). Sucker seem to have been especially revered, with several Plateau groups having rituals associated with its seasonal arrival in late spring (Post 1938), much like the First Salmon ceremony.

Another fish well represented in archaeological deposits is the threespine stickleback (*Gasterosteus aculeatus*), a small-bodied (~.11 meters [4 inches] long), spiny species that is the only member of its family found in Pacific Slope drainages from southeast Alaska to Mexico (Lee et al. 1980). Stickleback are usually found close to the bottom in rivers, lakes, and streams, commonly in association with aquatic vegetation. They can occur in large schools, and fishery researchers have netted hundreds in one net haul (e.g., Hinton et al. 1990). Over 60 nonhuman predators (including coho and some other salmonids, minnow, sturgeon, waterfowl, and mammals) consume stickleback (Reimchen 1994), which introduces some ambiguity in interpreting their role in human subsistence.

Summary

The ethnohistorical accounts highlight several things. First, the fisheries were highly seasonal and localized. Beginning in February and continuing through early April, Native fishers targeted eulachon, the earliest species to migrate into the river system. Sturgeon moved in to prey on eulachon, and fishers took advantage of the food chain and harvested sturgeon, too, which continued until May (and into the summer in some areas). The persistent use of sturgeon in the spring, despite the arrival of the spring salmon run in March, is noteworthy. Native fishers did not take salmon when the fish first entered the Columbia but waited until the runs arrived at Willamette Falls and The Cascades, from early April until early May. Information from these two areas may have signaled the presence of abundant fish and initiated the use of beach seines on the lower river.

Over the summer and fall, fishers continued to harvest salmon at The Cascades and began to target runs in lower tributaries in the autumn, using seines and harpoons rather than weirs. The primary sturgeon fishery was between Oak Point and Fort Vancouver, overlapping the main eulachon fishing areas. Willamette Falls and The Cascades were prime areas for the spring chinook salmon run, and eyewitness accounts of the preservation of sturgeon and eulachon (as flesh, not for oil) are as frequent as those for salmon. Salmon storage focused on the fall chinook run. In some years and in some tributaries, the eulachon run was much reduced, suggesting the fish would not have been a dependable resource.

THE ARCHAEOLOGICAL RECORD

While archaeological fish-bone records lack the rich detail of ethnohistory, they give us a way to trace the use of fish back thousands of years. They also provide a record of fisheries just before and during the time of Euro-American record keeping, providing a cross-check on ethnohistoric accounts. Like ethnohistory, archaeological records have limitations. For example, most of the archaeological fish records are from the Portland Basin, since most archaeology and faunal analyses have focused there, so our look back in time draws mainly from this section of the river. Also, what bones we have to study are affected by such factors as bone preservation and how bones are collected at archaeological sites, identified to fish type, and then tabulated in the laboratory.

We reviewed all fish faunal records reported in archaeological sites from The Cascades to the mouth of the Columbia (see Table S4.2). Faunal records were summarized at the most minute taxonomic level allowed by published records, such as species or genus, but most quantitative comparisons use family-level groupings (see Table S4.3). Remains of salmon and sturgeon generally can only be identified to the family level (Salmonidae, Acipenseridae); many of the remains from minnows and suckers cannot be distinguished from each other, so we used a joint family category (Cyprinidae/Catostomidae). To quantify fish representation, we used the number of identified specimens (NISP), which is the tally of the complete bones or bone fragments identified to a given taxon (species, genus, family). Bone fragmentation can affect this measure, but similarity in bone preservation among sites suggests that this factor is minor, with a few exceptions. Sampling, particularly the size of the mesh used during field excavation and lab work, greatly affects the kinds and abundance of fish types recovered. When large mesh screens are used—6.4 millimeters (.25 inch)—the remains of fish like salmon and sturgeon tend to dominate; tiny fishes such as eulachon and stickleback are mainly retrieved in 1- and 2-millimeter mesh screens. Because Columbia River sites have been sampled using various mesh sizes, we needed to control for this factor by only comparing assemblages recovered with the same mesh size (for detail on the methods used, see Appendix, online).

The chronology for human occupation on the floodplain is short, with most site deposits dating to the last 800 years. We assigned faunal records to one of a four-part chronology based on radiocarbon dates and artifact types unique to particular time periods: Merrybell, 600 BC–AD 200; Multnomah 1, AD 200–1250; Multnomah 2, AD 1250–1750; and Multnomah 3, AD 1750–1835 (Pettigrew 1981). The presence of Euro-American trade goods, for example, was used to define postcontact occupations (here set at AD 1750). Several sites cannot be included in temporal comparisons, given stratigraphic mixing and limited attention to separating out time units. Only a handful of sites have deposits dating before and after Euro-American contact, making it difficult to track change across that important period of time.

Results

The 29 archaeological sites in the study area that report fish remains are clustered in three main areas: 4 at the river's mouth, 20 in the Portland Basin, and 5 at The Cascades (see Table S4.3). More sites than these have been excavated in the region, but fish remains have been consistently studied only since 1995. As elsewhere in Northwest Coast archaeological sites (Butler and Campbell 2004), the frequency of fish remains far exceeds that of mammal or bird remains at most sites, highlighting the importance of fish to the diet of lower-river peoples.

Fish faunal records from the region show that sturgeon, eulachon, and salmonids are common. Salmonid remains are rarely identified as to species, but their size indicates they are mainly from anadromous forms of *Oncorhynchus* and species such as chinook, coho, steelhead, chum, and sockeye (e.g., Butler 2002a, 2005). The archaeological records also contain year-round freshwater residents—two species of sucker, six species of minnow, sculpin [Cottidae], stickleback, and sandroller (*Percopsis transmontana*)—and several mainly saltwater fish taxa that enter the lower estuary—herring, shark, surfperch, flatfish, rockfish (*Sebastes* sp.), and Pacific jack mackerel (*Tra-*

churus symmetricus). The only taxon mentioned in 19th-century accounts that is missing from the archaeological record is lamprey. Because this fish lacks true bones and teeth, its absence must be partly linked to preservation. Still, lamprey have toothlike structures made of keratin (much like fingernail) on their oral disk, and lamprey remains are found in stomach contents of predatory fishes and birds. Perhaps with better knowledge of anatomy and analysis of fine screen samples, their remains will be found in the future (Smith and Butler 2008).

Using the fish bone record to study past fisheries assumes that fish remains truly reflect human activities, which may not be the case. Of particular concern is the origin of the small and extremely abundant remains of fish such as stickleback and eulachon that may have arrived as stomach contents of predators that were caught by people. Sturgeon and northern pikeminnow prey heavily on small fish, and several mammal species found in project sites—such as black bear (*Ursus americanus*), river otter (*Lontra canadensis*), and harbor seal (*Phoca vitulina*) (Saleeby 1983; Lyman 2008)—eat fish. Because humans build fires and cook food, we began our evaluation of the origin of the small fish by comparing the frequency of burned bone across fish taxa in three project sites that had been sampled using 1– or 2–millimeter mesh (Butler 2000b, 2002a, 2005).

In all three sites, the proportion of burning is much less for eulachon and stickleback than for sturgeon, salmon, and minnow-sucker (Table 4.1). At Cathlapotle and St. Johns (35MU44/46), 5 percent or less of stickleback and eulachon remains had been burned, whereas between 17 and 57 percent of the large fish remains are burned. At 35MU117, more of the small fish remains had been burned than at the other sites, yet the frequency is still between half and six times less than for the larger taxa. We could argue, then, that people did not fish for and use stickleback and eulachon, but there are other explanations. The burning data could be interpreted to mean that people simply processed and disposed of large and small fish in different ways. It also may be that since burning makes bone more brittle (Stiner et al. 1995), burned remains of eulachon and stickleback are more susceptible to disintegration than burned bones of larger fish.

Eulachon was a regular part of 19th-century aboriginal fishing and likely was part of earlier fisheries. Stickleback may have been fished or may have been part of the by-catch in a backwater netting strategy. While stickleback is not mentioned in any Columbia River ethnohistoric documents, it is a traditional food and source of dog food in the Yukon-Kuskokwim Delta of

TABLE 4.1. Proportion (% NISP) of burned bone by fish family group and site, based on 2 mm or 1 mm mesh samples

FISH FAMILY	CATHLAPOTLE (45CL1)	ST. JOHNS (35MU44/56)	35MU117
Salmonid	43.5	56.6	24.7
Sturgeon	27.4	12.2	88.3
Minnow-Sucker	23.4	17.6	56.5
Eulachon	2.0	0.2	13.6
Stickleback	0.3	5.5	12.5
Total NISP	2,475	2,501	1,956

southwest Alaska (Alex Nick, US Fish and Wildlife Service, personal communication to Butler, July 2003). Jones (2006) reports that Iñupiat people of northwest Alaska eat stickleback "in times of need or catch them for dog food when nothing bigger is available. They are very fat, so as they cook the oil rises to the top and looks good enough to eat. They can be dipped out in quantity at certain times in some places" (267).

Rigorously interpreting the role of these species in past economies is difficult, and more research on this topic is sorely needed. Based on the large quantity of eulachon and stickleback remains recovered from 25 liters of bulk samples at St. Johns, Butler (2005) projected that over a half million remains each of eulachon and stickleback were present in the entire excavated sample, which was only a small fraction of the site deposits. At Cathlapotle, just a single soil sample provided about 2,000 stickleback bones, representing 430 individual fish (Butler 2002b). These small but superabundant fish represent a potentially enormous source of protein for humans or their dogs that could have been obtained through targeted fisheries or incidental by-catch.

To evaluate the importance of salmon in Lower Columbia fisheries, determine whether fisheries changed over time, and examine spatial trends in fish use along the river, we focused on remains from 13 sites, two of which (Pumphouse and Cathlapotle) were divided into two time units, for a total of 15 assemblages. Thirteen of the 15 assemblages are from the Portland Basin, and two are from the river mouth.

Many of the same fish taxa are present at the sites (Table 4.2). Of the large fish taxa, salmon is present in all 15 assemblages, while minnow and sucker

TABLE 4.2. Ubiquity (frequency of occurrence) of fish taxa in Lower
Columbia River assemblages (excludes assemblages ≤ 50 NISP and those
with unknown recovery or analytic methods)

FISH TAXA	UBIQUITY
15 assemblages, all mesh sizes	
Salmon and Trout (Salmonidae)	15
Sturgeon (*Acipenser* sp.)	13
Sucker (Catostomidae)	14
Minnow (Cyprinidae)	14
Pacific Sandroller (*Percopsis transmontana*)	2
Right-eyed Flounder (Pleuronectidae)	2
Rockfish (*Sebastes* sp.)	2
Pacific Jack Mackerel (*Trachurus symmetricus*)	2
Herring (*Clupea pallasii*)	1
Shark (Elasmobranch)	1
Surfperch (Embiotocidae)	1
8 assemblages (1 or 2 mm mesh)	
Eulachon (*Thaleichthys pacificus*)	6
Stickleback (*Gasterosteus aculeatus*)	8

are found in all but one assemblage and sturgeon is present in all but two.
For the eight assemblages sampled using 1- or 2-millimeter mesh, stickleback is present in all eight, while eulachon is found in six. Thus, many fish
taxa are widespread throughout the 15 assemblages. Several species associated
with marine waters and the lower estuary—herring, shark, surfperch, flounder (including starry flounder), and rockfish—are present only at sites at the
river's mouth, at Indian Point (35CLT34) and Station Camp (45PC106). Pacific
jack mackerel and sandroller were recorded in only two assemblages. Jack
mackerel is primarily a marine fish, known to enter the lower river as far as
Astoria, so its presence at Indian Point is not surprising (Minor et al. 2008).
Its presence at Meier (35CO5), however, 120 kilometers (75 miles) upriver,
suggests that the fish was traded or transported there by village occupants
(Frederick 2007). The identification of tui chub (*Gila bicolor*) at Cathlapotle
and Meier is noteworthy. This species has been found in eastern Washington

TABLE 4.3. Rank-order abundance (frequency of assemblages in which taxon is ranked highest) in Lower Columbia River assemblages (excludes assemblages with ≤ 50 NISP and unknown recovery or analytic methods)

SAMPLE TYPE*	FISH FAMILY	ABUNDANCE	
>6.4 mm. mesh			
8 assemblages	Salmonid	2	
	Sturgeon	2	
	Minnow-Sucker	4	
>3.2 mm mesh			
5 assemblages	Salmonid	1	
	Sturgeon	1	
	Minnow-Sucker	3	
>2 mm mesh			
3 assemblages	Salmonid	1	
	Sturgeon		
	Minnow-Sucker	1	
	Eulachon	1	
	Stickleback		
>1 mm mesh			(exclude stickleback)
7 assemblages	Salmonid	1	(2)
	Sturgeon		
	Minnow-Sucker		(4)
	Eulachon		(1)
	Stickleback	6	

* Site assemblages were subdivided by time unit and mesh size. For sites sampled using nested screens (e.g., 6.4 and 3.2 mm or 2 and 1 mm), comparisons are not completely independent of each other (e.g., the >3.2 mm mesh sample includes remains from 6.4 and 3.2 mm mesh).

(Wydoski and Whitney 2003), and the remains in the Lower Columbia may reflect trade.

When assemblages are compared based on rank-order abundance, min-now-sucker is the most abundant fish type in most assemblages, including the 1–millimeter mesh samples when stickleback is excluded (see Table 4.3).

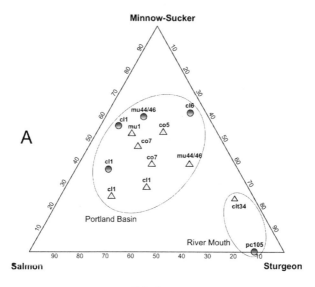

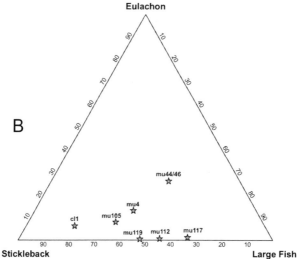

FIGURE 4.1. Ternary plot showing proportional representation of three taxa (Figure by Gunnar Johnson)

Note: Points falling in the central part of the triangle indicate similar proportional representation and a fairly even fishery; those values falling inside the corners indicate dominance of a particular taxon. A) 6.4 mm mesh (triangle), > 3.2 mm mesh (closed circle) minnow-sucker, salmon, and sturgeon. Subareas of Lower Columbia distinguished mainly in sturgeon representation. B) 1 mm mesh samples, eulachon, stickleback and "large fish" (salmon, sturgeon, minnow-sucker) representation. All sites are in the Portland Basin.

Sturgeon and salmon are most abundant in a few assemblages, but overall the records highlight the prominence of minnow-sucker. Furthermore, remains of sucker tend to be much more common than remains of minnow. At St. Johns and Indian Point, sucker remains are over twice as common as those of minnow. The primary species of sucker present in the lower river and in regional archaeological sites is the largescale sucker, so this species must have been important in lower-river fisheries.

Site records for the large mesh samples also show that the Portland Basin supported a relatively generalized fishery in contrast to the river mouth, as shown in the ternary graph (Figure 4.1A), which plots percent frequencies of the three main fish types (salmon, minnow-sucker, sturgeon) along independent axes, from 0–100 percent. Portland Basin sites again are dominated by minnow-sucker, but sturgeon, salmon, or both represent between 15 and 50 percent of site assemblages, suggesting that all the larger fish were important fisheries. The two sites at the mouth indicate a specialized sturgeon fishery, with Station Camp (the remains of a Chinookan village on Baker Bay across the river channel from Astoria) mainly represented by sturgeon remains. The village was occupied exclusively during the fur-trade era (Wilson et al. 2009), and it seems likely that it functioned in part as a processing site for the sturgeon trade. Sturgeon also dominates the Indian Point assemblage; the timing of occupation spans the last several hundred years, so records cannot be linked directly to the fur trade.

A ternary plot for the >1-millimeter mesh samples (Figure 4.1B), all from the Portland Basin sites, highlights the prominence of stickleback and large fish (= salmon, sturgeon, minnow-sucker combined) and the relative scarcity of eulachon. The St. Johns site is represented by close to 30 percent eulachon, but eulachon is represented by few or no remains in three nearby assemblages (35MU119, 35MU117, 35MU112). All of these sites are located on backwater channels near what is now the Columbia Slough and Smith-Bybee Lakes, which are characterized by slow-warm water not typical of eulachon spawning habitat. Eulachon likely was caught elsewhere and transported to the villages and camps by canoe.

Finally, we looked to see if there were any patterned changes in fish use possibly associated with changes in environmental conditions that might improve conditions for some fish over others or in the cultural system such as increase in population, development of new technologies, and changes in settlement pattern. We plotted the relative frequency of the main taxa within each assemblage by time period. The record from the 6.4-millimeter mesh

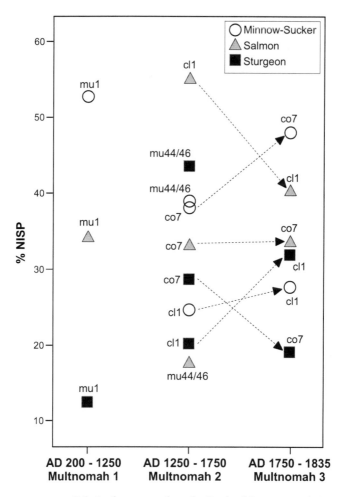

FIGURE 4.2. Relative frequency of taxa by Portland Basin site and time period in 6.4–mm mesh samples (see Map 1.2 for key to sites; figure by Gunnar Johnson). Dashed lines connect site assemblages from two time periods.

screens shows no trends at all (Figure 4.2; not shown, similar lack of patterning with 3.2–millimeter mesh samples); and the frequency of salmon, sturgeon, and minnow-sucker varies as much between sites in a given time period as it does between time periods. At the same time, the >1–millimeter mesh samples show a directional change in representation of eulachon and stickleback, namely increase in both over time (Figure 4.3). Eulachon is extremely uncommon in sites dating to the earliest two time intervals and then shows

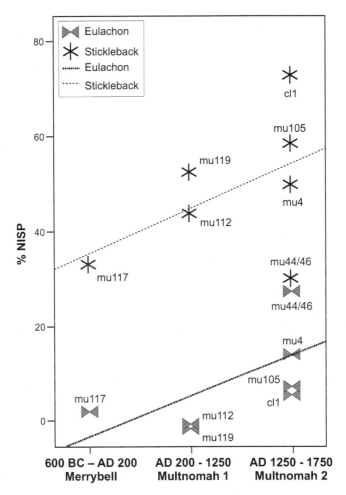

FIGURE 4.3. Relative frequency of small fish taxa by Portland Basin site and time period, >1 mm samples (see Map 1.2 for key to sites; figure by Gunnar Johnson). Best-fit regression line drawn for each taxon.

higher representation in Multnomah 2 (AD 1250–1750). Stickleback frequency also increases over time (except with St. Johns, in Multnomah 2).

Discussion

There is no question that Lower Columbia Indians relied on a great mix of fishes, including seasonal migrants (sturgeon, salmon, eulachon) and year-round residents (several species of minnow and sucker and possibly stickleback). Given the small number of well-dated assemblages, it was difficult to discover if salmon use increased over time, in line with arguments that increased salmon use contributed to the development of cultural complexity. On the one hand, the variation within time periods overwhelms any temporal trend for the relatively large-bodied fishes (minnow-sucker, sturgeon, salmon). On the other, the records from fine-mesh screening show an increasing proportion of eulachon and stickleback. Putting aside questions about cultural origins for a moment, these records suggest that lower-river people increasingly exploited these small fish, which provide lower return (calories/unit effort) than larger fish (e.g., Broughton 1994; Ugan 2005). This trend is a classic example of resource intensification, wherein human populations increase their use of local, lower-ranked resources to accommodate increasing populations that have to make use of such resources because of actual or per capita declines in higher-ranked resources (Cohen 1981). More sampling of fine-mesh samples from well-dated contexts is needed, but the results are provocative.

Both 19th-century eyewitness accounts and archaeological records show important areas of overlap and contrast. Both types of records highlight the salmon, sturgeon, and eulachon fisheries, which extend back at least 2,900 years (Butler 2000b; Ellis 2000). There is a major discrepancy, however, between ethnohistorical and archaeological records regarding the use of minnow-sucker, which is prominent in archaeological samples from the Portland Basin but not explicitly documented by Euro-Americans. Two main hypotheses explain this discrepancy. One relates to sampling bias, namely, that these resident fish species were prominent in the early 19th-century Lower Columbia fishery in some locations but that Euro-Americans simply did not observe them. Most eyewitness accounts date before the 1830s, and most observers were traveling on the main channel of the river, recording activities downstream of the Portland Basin. Most of the archaeological sites are located off the main river channel, on or near backwater lakes and distributary channels, places that 19th-century travelers may have visited only rarely. Some support for the sampling bias hypothesis can be drawn from the mid-Columbia, where 19th-century observers also scarcely mentioned the minnow-sucker fishery. Our understanding of the importance of these fisheries comes from 20th-century Native informants (Hunn 1990), not ethnohistory.

Another hypothesis suggests that fishing for minnow and sucker became less common after Euro-American contact. This hypothesis draws on logic from foraging models, which suggest that return rate (calories/unit effort) for the backwater fishes is lower than that for salmon and sturgeon (Butler

2000a). Lower-river people may have made increasing use of such "lower-ranked" resources as human populations grew and filled the landscape in the centuries before contact. With human population growth and competition for food resources, there would have been fewer sturgeon, salmon, and other higher-ranked resources available for human consumption, forcing people to increase their use of lower-ranked resources. Conditions would drastically change with the arrival of Euro-Americans, especially because of disease and the great decline in Indian populations. Foraging theory would predict that human populations would shift their fishery toward higher-ranked resources, as there would be reduced predation on and competition for them. In turn, fishing for lower-ranked fishes would diminish.

While the second hypothesis is appealing, it has flaws. It assumes that minnow and sucker would be lower-ranked foods relative to fishes such as salmon and sturgeon. This assumption may not be correct, especially if one takes into account the potential productivity of the Columbia River floodplain, where minnow and sucker would have been abundant and accessible. Prior to the major changes in the hydrology of the Columbia (dam construction, dikes, draining projects), the productivity of the floodplain in the Portland Basin may have been enormous. During the spring floods, sturgeon, minnow, sucker, and other fish would get swept into the backwater areas, becoming stranded and relatively easy to procure. The biomass of all resident fish in a given area of Vancouver Lake (the largest lake in the Portland Basin), for example, was over 10 times that in the Columbia River (Knutzen and Cardwell 1984). The fishes occupying the lower-river floodplain today are dominated by nonnative fishes such as carp (*Cyprinus carpio*), bass (*Micropterus* sp.), sunfish (*Lepomis* sp.), and crappie (*Pomoxis* sp.) (Butler 2004), so biomass estimates are undoubtedly affected by such changes to the local ecology. Nevertheless, it is reasonable to hypothesize the high productivity of the backwater habitat—especially if one considers the range of other resources occurring there that were important to Native peoples, including wapato (*Sagittaria latifolia*) and aquatic mammals such as beaver (*Castor canadensis*) and muskrat (*Ondatra zibethicus*).

Research in other parts of North America highlights the resource potential of backwater environments. Analysis of thousand-year-old fish bones from an archaeological site in the marshy backwaters of the lower Sacramento River shows that Native peoples favored resident freshwater fishes over salmon and sturgeon even though those fishes were common in the river system prior to 19th-century losses (Schulz and Simons 1973). Ethnographic sources (McKern, in Schulz and Simons 1973) describe families of Patwin Indians who specialized in obtaining fish from sloughs and lakes. The relatively high productivity of seasonally flooded backwater areas of the Lower Mississippi River Archaic tradition is another example (e.g., Fagan 2005; Limp and Reidhead 1979).

At least for now, we think that the limited attention that Euro-Americans gave this fishery may be related to sampling and that the use of the backwater truly did decline over the 19th century, especially after the 1830s, the time of major malaria outbreaks. During this period of population loss and social upheaval, Native American populations ceased to occupy and to seasonally use backwater areas, which also happened to be prime habitat for *Anopheles*-carrying mosquito.

CONCLUSIONS

The indigenous fishery on the Lower Columbia targeted virtually all native fish species in the river. Salmon (mainly chinook) was important to aboriginal subsistence, but other fishes were, too. Anthropologists have given salmon a primary role in explaining cultural complexity, despite growing evidence that Native American lifeways and cultural adaptations were highly variable across the Pacific Northwest (e.g., Monks 2007; McMillan et al. 2008). We are not sure why this salmon paradigm is so deeply rooted in our collective psyche, but the sooner we shake it off, the sooner we will develop conceptual frameworks that take us closer to understanding indigenous lifeways and adaptations, in all their myriad forms.

Nineteenth-century Native fishers used a range of strategies and tactics to acquire and process fish, including the gear used to catch and transport fish; the social organization necessary to produce and maintain gear; and work parties to intercept fish at particular locations and times, process it for storage or immediate use, and transport it to villages for consumption or trade. Fishers took advantage of seasonal spikes in the numbers of spawning salmon and eulachon and caught predators like sturgeon that moved in for the eulachon. Large quantities of salmon, sturgeon, and eulachon were preserved and traded. Some gear allowed for the mass capture of eulachon and salmon, and sturgeon were netted, hooked, and speared from canoes. Eyewitness accounts especially highlight the productivity of the salmon fisheries at Willamette Falls and The Cascades, where fishers took advantage of the natural geological constrictions that slowed and directed fish movement and built elaborate wooden platforms and stone channels that increased access to migrating fish.

Archaeological records already tell us that salmon, eulachon, sturgeon, and several species of minnow and sucker were part of the lower-river fisheries as far back as 2,900 years ago. To put these bone records into a fuller context of fishing strategies, however, requires additional analytic frameworks and analysis. We need to more systematically examine the link between fishing-related artifacts (e.g., bone points, so-called net weights) and fish species to document capture methods. Such knowledge would inform us about the economic and social context of fish capture and use and tell us how they changed over time and varied by environment. Studying distributions of fish remains and associated artifacts and features within sites will help us further understand the social context of animal resource use (e.g., Huelsbeck 1994; Grier 2006). We also need to investigate how to archaeologically recognize fish processing and storage (e.g., Hoffman et al. 2000; Smith et al. 2011), given the implications of food storage on economic and social matters. Identifying the salmonid species represented in archaeological sites would be worthwhile, using ancient DNA analysis (Yang et al. 2004). Salmonid species are highly variable in their life history, run times, food values, and ease of preserving, and lumping salmon and trout remains into one category keeps us from learning how lower-river people used each species. We need to collect bulk samples for fine-mesh screening to retain remains of very small fish such as eulachon and stickleback. Stickleback remains have also been recovered in Fraser River sites (e.g., Casteel 1976), so this question extends beyond the Columbia River.

Lower-river Native peoples had an extraordinarily rich and complex fishery, extending back several thousand years. Future work will add even more to our understanding of the enduring relationships between people and fishes on the Lower Columbia River.

FIVE

LOWER COLUMBIA TRADE
AND EXCHANGE SYSTEMS

Yvonne Hajda and Elizabeth A. Sobel

ROM about 10 thousand years ago into the early historic period, Lower Columbia peoples participated in far-reaching exchange networks. Archaeological remains and historical documents are imperfect sources of information about the trade (here used interchangeably with the term "exchange"), as each has inherent biases. The archaeological record is biased by preservation factors: the remains of durable trade goods such as glass beads and obsidian often preserve archaeologically, while the remains of perishable trade goods such as Hudson's Bay Company blankets and bison hides rarely preserve. The documents that make up the historical record are biased by a different set of factors, including writers' experiences and interests. Because they were written by Euro-Americans, they provide more information about Native–Euro-American trade than Native-Native trade. When examined together, however, both sources of information can tell us much more about Chinookan trade than either can alone.

THE ARCHAEOLOGY OF LOWER COLUMBIA EXCHANGE

The archaeological record tells us most directly about the exchange of goods rather than ideas, since goods can be directly observed. Moreover, archaeology typically yields more information about long-distance than local exchange. Nonlocal products likely arrived through long-distance exchange, whereas items made of local raw materials do not necessarily signify exchange at all.

The clearest archaeological expression of exchange consists of artifacts made of raw material that does not naturally occur in the location where it was found. The only logical explanation for the Lower Columbia artifacts made from such materials as nonlocal stone, shell, animal bone, and native coppers is that humans brought the exotic material to the area. In many cases, no doubt, this process of importing goods occurred entirely through down-the-line trade that involved a series of intermediary exchanges that moved the product from source to destination. In other cases, Lower Columbia people must have ventured to a foreign source to obtain raw materials and products, negotiating passage and resource access with other groups. We can assume, then, that exotic artifacts generally reflect nonlocal exchange activity of some sort.

Exotic remains that can be sourced—that is, linked to a source area—are especially useful for reconstructing ancient trade routes. The most abundant sourceable material type recovered from the Lower Columbia is obsidian, a glassy volcanic stone that typically comprises less than 5 percent of flaked stone artifacts at Lower Columbia sites (Sobel 2006:165). Obsidian does not occur naturally in the area but is abundant to the south and southeast in the Willamette Valley, the Great Basin, the southern Plateau, and California. Each natural obsidian flow has a unique geochemistry, and it is possible to trace an obsidian artifact to a specific source. In essence, researchers identify the geochemical fingerprint of an artifact and then identify the natural source with the matching fingerprint. Analyses of hundreds of prehistoric artifacts from scores of Lower Columbia sites indicate that obsidian reached the Lower Columbia from geological sources in Oregon, Washington, California, and Nevada, from 50 to more than 500 kilometers from the Lower Columbia River. Other exotic artifacts recovered from Lower Columbia archaeological sites and linked to specific source areas include dentalia shells from the southern British Columbia coast, olivella shells from the Pacific Coast more broadly, and nephrite (a form of jade) from southern British Columbia (Ames and Maschner 1999; Carlson 1994; Galm 1994; Hayden and Schulting 1997).

The Archaeology of Precontact Exchange

Throughout the Archaic (10,500 BC–4,400 BC) and Pacific (4,400 BC–AD 1750) periods, archaeological materials along the Lower Columbia reveal three patterns of long-distance exchange. One is the northward flow of resources from central Oregon to The Dalles area, and then east and west along the river and northward onto the Plateau and along the coast. Much of the obsidian found in sites around The Dalles and at other points along this apparent route originated in central Oregon (Ames and Maschner 1999; Carlson 1994; Galm 1994; Sobel 2006, 2012), and it was undoubtedly one of many resources that was exchanged northward along the eastern flank of the Cascade Range to the Columbia River. We can only speculate about the specific resources traded southward in return (Hajda 1984:235; Stern 1998; Walker 1997).

A second pattern is the flow of products eastward from the Pacific Coast toward the interior along the Lower Columbia River. The earliest evidence of this pattern consists of multiple olivella shells, dated to 7000 BP, from Marmes Rockshelter along the mid-Columbia. Other artifacts made of marine shell, including olivella and dentalia, are from Archaic and Pacific deposits along the Lower Columbia, along the mid-Columbia, and on the southern Plateau (Ames and Maschner 1999; Carlson 1994; Galm 1994).

A third pattern is centered on The Dalles, a trade center where thousands of people congregated for a major fishery. Here, north-south and east-west travel routes intersected, and coastal and interior peoples and products came together. The Dalles area was a major center of regional and interregional exchange at the time of Euro-American contact, and the "complexity, age range, and sheer numbers of sites" at and around The Dalles suggest that the trade center has considerable antiquity (Galm 1994). Historically, the centrality of the place was fueled, in part, by the export of dried salmon. During late prehistoric times, exports also included ground soapstone beads, of which thousands in various stages of production have been recovered from archaeological deposits at The Dalles (Strong 1959:127).

Long-distance exchange activity by Lower Columbia inhabitants grew more frequent and extensive from the Early Archaic through the Middle Pacific periods. During the Late Pacific period (200/400–1750 AD), however, long-distance exchange activity may have stabilized or even declined (Ames and Maschner 1999:165–76; Carlson 1994; Schulting 1995:181–2).

The Archaeology of Protohistoric Exchange

The first documented interaction between Euro-Americans and Lower Columbia peoples took place in AD 1792, when the first ships entered the Columbia River. Long before that time, however, Euro-American activity indirectly affected Chinookan trade and culture. The protohistoric period in the Northwest corresponds to the last few centuries of the Late Pacific period, ca. AD 1600–1775 (Walker and Sprague 1998:138) or 1500–1774 (Boyd n.d.). Old World influences on Native Americans during this period are here called protocontacts.

Archaeological remains, oral narratives, and historical documents suggest that protocontact generally increased the intensity, geographic reach, and diversity of the Columbia River exchange network. The spread of horses into northwestern North America by the early 1700s was a crucial development (Haines 1938). Chinookans rarely owned or used horses, as they traveled mostly in canoes on waterways, but by the mid-1700s neighboring Plateau, Great Basin, and Plains peoples had adopted the horse as a major mode of transport and form of wealth. The improved ease of overland travel led them to participate more directly and intensively in Lower Columbia exchange, which increased both the geographic extent of the network and the diversity and volume of goods flowing through the hands of the Chinookans (Layton 1981; Stern 1998).

Protohistoric shifts in Lower Columbia trade activity also resulted from the arrival of Euro-American manufactures through down-the-line trade among Indians. Beginning with the Perez Expedition in AD 1774 and with increasing frequency thereafter, Spanish, British, and American maritime explorers and traders interacted with Native peoples both south and north of the Columbia River. Before that time, Euro-Americans circulated among Native Americans in midwestern parts of North America. Long before direct contact, Chinookans probably had heard about the newcomers and had obtained some of their manufactures.

Old World products also entered the Lower Columbia trade network through shipwrecks. By the 1600s, Japanese junks and Spanish vessels involved in cross-Pacific trade (Erlandson et al. 2001; Schurz 1939) drifted to the mouth of the Columbia River and nearby coastal areas. Chinese Kraak porcelain at both Meier (35CO50) and Cathlapotle (45CL1), for example, probably originated from the *Santo Cristo de Burgos*, a Spanish galleon that wrecked on the Oregon Coast in 1693 (Cromwell 2010). A Chinookan oral tradition, "The First Ship Seen by the Clatsop," recalls a wreck that carried not only a great deal of valued metal but also foreign men (Boas 1894:277; Gibbs 1877:237). The possibility that people as well as materials were among shipwrecks on Chinook shores is supported by the well-documented 1834 survival of three Japanese sailors on a boat that washed up at Cape Flattery, on the northwest tip of present-day Washington State (Hayes 1999; Ruby and

Brown 1976; Webber 1984). It is clear that Lower Columbia peoples relished the exotic materials, particularly metal, picked from amid ship wreckage (Boas 1894:277; Gibbs 1877:237). At first contact, in 1792, William Broughton observed that Lower Columbia peoples possessed "copper swords" and "a kind of battle axe made of iron" and that they valued these items too highly to consider trading them (Vancouver 1984:61).

The archaeological record has not told us much about protohistoric influences on Lower Columbia River exchange. At Cathlapotle in the Wapato Valley, an iron adze blade that has been securely dated to ca. AD 1450 must have reached the site by way of shipwrecks or other protocontact (Ames et al. 1999). The earliest Old World goods recovered from Cathlapotle consist mainly of small quantities of metal items (Sobel 2004:1070–100). The site also yielded hundreds of other Euro-American products, including glass beads, ceramic sherds, and metal projectile points. Arguably, the initial manifestation represents the protohistoric and very early contact periods, while the later manifestation represents the remainder of the contact period (Ames et al. 1999)

The strongest archaeological evidence for protohistoric intensification and expansion of exchange comes from the southwestern Plateau, which abuts the Lower Columbia. Compared to earlier burials, protohistoric burials in the region appear to contain higher quantities and a higher diversity of costly items (Schulting 1995:164), including Euro-American manufactures such as glass beads and copper and indigenous products such as dentalia shells (Schulting 1995:164; Stapp 1984:138–47). This shift may reflect a protohistoric intensification of exchange that incorporated trade items from the Lower Columbia River, the main travel route between the coast and the southern Plateau.

The Archaeology of Postcontact Exchange

Analyses of archaeological remains from Cathlapotle and Clahclellah (455A11) villages suggest that control over trade networks as a source of prestige was increasingly important during the postcontact period. At Clahclellah, the distributions of artifacts from precontact times suggest that large households with the most prestige did not necessarily control the flow of exotic trade goods. In postcontact times, however, high prestige households monopolized access to indigenous exotics, represented by obsidian artifacts, while both high and intermediate status households monopolized access to

Euro-American trade goods, represented by metal, glass, and ceramic artifacts (Sobel 2004:409–530; Sobel 2006:159–99). Likewise, at Cathlapotle before contact, access to exotics did not vary substantially among households. During the postcontact period, however, high prestige households dominated the obsidian trade while lower prestige households monopolized the flow of Euro-American manufactures (Sobel 2004:603–715; Sobel 2006:159–99).

The Clahclellah and Cathlapotle obsidian distributions suggest that high status households maintained and may have increased their control over long-distance trade in indigenous products. Euro-American artifact distributions imply that less prestigious households had an unprecedented opportunity to become important players in the exchange system through trade with Euro-Americans. Before contact, the ability of lower ranking households to gain prominence in long-distance exchange networks would have been constrained by the close linkage between social and economic systems. After contact, however, when it suited their aims, Euro-Americans sometimes developed exchange alliances favoring less prestigious Chinookan individuals and groups. Consequently, as the postcontact period progressed, interactions between Native Americans and Euro-Americans were less governed by those systems.

VARIATION AMONG COMMUNITIES IN FUR-TRADE ACTIVITY

Chinookan settlements played variable roles in exchange systems during the first decades of contact. This variability can be explored with data from three archaeological sites: Station Camp (45PC106), Clahclellah, and Cathlapotle.

Station Camp, also known as the McGowan site, is on Baker Bay on the Washington shore of the Columbia River estuary in Lower Chinook home territory. The site contains remains of at least one plankhouse dating to the early fur-trade era, between about 1790 and 1820 (Wilson et al. 2009:397). It has a low proportion of Chinookan domestic artifacts and indigenous trade goods such as obsidian and a high proportion of European and Euro-American trade goods, including "copper and glass trade beads, other copper artifacts, coins, brass tacks, nails, knives, musket balls and shot, fragments of creamware and porcelain ceramics, and glass bottles" as well as "copper bracelets, pendants, sheets, beads, awls, a hawk bell, thimble, and chain" (Wilson et al. 2009:ii). Station Camp was a warm-season Chinook settlement, focused on activities linked with the Euro-American fur trade. Baker

Bay was a major ship anchorage, and Fort Astoria (later called Fort George), just across the Columbia River from Station Camp, was the only Euro-American trading post in the region until 1825. Station Camp appears to have been a settlement that arose, in large part, from inhabitants' interest in managing and profiting from access to Euro-American products (Wilson et al. 2009).

Like Station Camp, Cathlapotle was inhabited by Chinookans intensively involved in postcontact trade, but it was a large, permanent town that had been established several hundred years before Euro-American contact. The settlement, which persisted until about 1831, was located in the Wapato Valley (Portland Basin) in Multnomah Chinookan territory. The hundreds of obsidian artifacts recovered from the site are traceable to geological sources in Oregon, California, and Washington. Active participation in the fur-trade economy is indicated not only by hundreds of Euro-American manufactures but also by the high proportion of stone scrapers recovered from postcontact remains (Sobel 2004). Flaked stone scrapers at Cathlapotle were typically used to process animal hides (Smith 2008), and the proportion of such scrapers from postcontact deposits is quite high at Cathlapotle compared to proportions from contemporary Chinookan townsites (Sobel 2004). Cathlapotle residents may have been intensively involved in the production of clamons (elk-hide armor) during the early fur-trade era (Sobel 2004). From the 1790s through about 1810, clamons were one of the main products the Chinookans traded to the British and the Americans, who then traded them to Natives on the north coast (Howay 1927, 1933; Ruby and Brown 1976:61, 116).

Cathlapotle stood near the intersection of four rivers within the Willamette-Puget lowland, a high traffic area accessible from all directions. Natives and eventually Euro-Americans from throughout the Northwest came to this part of the Lower Columbia to trade, attracted by the availability of wapato, the access to seasonal fish runs, and the chance to trade for Euro-American manufactures at Fort Vancouver (built in 1825). Cathlapotle residents aggressively sought exchange opportunities with passersby, and they monitored river traffic and launched canoes to intercept potential traders (Bell 1932:143–44; Lewis and Clark 1990:23).

Clahclellah was located along The Cascades in Cascades Chinookan territory. Like Cathlapotle, it was a sizable community involved in the exchange of Euro-American and indigenous products. Clahclellah's location farther east, however, suggests that its trade was oriented more to The Dalles, the largest Native exchange center in the Pacific Northwest. Trade by Clahclellah residents was also affected by its location along the main stem of the Colum-

TABLE 5.1. Exchanges of Euro-American goods for Native items

EXCHANGERS	GOODS EXCHANGED	SOURCE
Lewis and Clark	Blue beads—otter skins	Lewis and Clark 1990:83
Lewis and Clark—Kathlamets	Fishhooks—fish and wapato	Lewis and Clark 1990:89
Lewis and Clark—Clatsops	Fishhooks—Indian tobacco, wapato, another root	Lewis and Clark 1990:123
Lewis and Clark—Clatsops	A worn-out file, 6 fishhooks, spoiled pounded fish—3 mats, 2 bags, "panther" skin, roots	Lewis and Clark 1990:135
Nor'westers—Clatsops	1 fathom "smaller size Blue China Beads" —3 fathoms dried smelt	Henry 1992:697
Nor'westers—"old Clatsop" chief and followers	Canton blue beads—beaver "in meat," 3 trout, beaver skins, beeswax	Henry 1992:714

bia, beside a constricted, rapid-filled channel that was the only water route through the southern Cascade Mountains. Thousands of travelers boated through the area historically, and no doubt prehistorically. A high proportion of travelers portaged around the rapids on a trail that took them through Clahclellah and other Cascades settlements. Consequently, those who lived along The Cascades held a practical monopoly over Native and Euro-American travel and exchange. The Cascades residents profited by trading with the travelers and by assisting them with portages in exchange for goods or services (Boyd 1996:88; Sobel 2004:344–45). These factors, as well as the local seasonal abundance of salmon and other resources, made The Cascades one of several secondary trade centers in the Columbia River exchange network (Stern 1998:641–52).

Remains from Clahclellah imply that the local economy concentrated on long-distance exchange. This focus is suggested by archaeological evidence of a positive correlation between household prestige and trade activity and a lack of correlation between household prestige and production (Sobel 2004:816–26). Inhabitants profited tremendously from exchange activity, but not by producing and then exporting goods. Rather, they became important players in the Columbia River exchange system by exploiting the geographical factors that gave them some control over the physical movement of people and goods—for example, by serving as middle-persons in the flow of goods along the river, exchanging services (e.g., portage labor) to travelers, and exacting tolls.

SHIFTS IN THE GEOGRAPHICAL SCOPE
OF LONG-DISTANCE EXCHANGE ACTIVITY

Anthropologists have assumed that long-distance exchange activity by Lower Columbia peoples increased after contact, in both quantity and geographical reach. That increase is attributed to the economic effects of horses and the fur trade. Recent archaeological research, however, challenges this assumption. A comparison of precontact with postcontact obsidian artifacts from Cathlapotle, Clahclellah, and Meier (35Co5) indicates postcontact increases in the quantity of obsidian imported to Lower Columbia communities but not increases in the geographical distance of obsidian sources (Sobel 2012). The geographical scale of obsidian exchange apparently remained stable at Clahclellah and decreased at the other sites after contact. Thus, the obsidian data fit the traditional view of an increase in the intensity of exchange but contrast with the view of an increase in the geographical scope of exchange activity.

The obsidian evidence for a postcontact localization of trade activity may relate to the shifts in Native demography and intergroup relations that were the result of European epidemic diseases and horses (Sobel 2012). Epidemics would have robbed Native communities of many of the individuals who produced goods for export and who had specialized knowledge of travel routes and trade partners. While horses enabled the exchange of heavier objects over longer distances, they also sparked an increase in long-distance raiding (Hunn et al. 1998:378–79; Layton 1981; Shimkin 1986:519–23; Spier 1930:39–40; Stern 1998:456). Raiding affected intergroup relations and settlement patterns (Hunn et al. 1998:378–79; Layton 1981) and thereby weakened some trade relationships, even if it simultaneously strengthened others.

Several other archaeological obsidian analyses reveal temporal declines in the geographic scale of obsidian movement in the Lower Columbia and adjacent regions, including the Willamette Valley and portions of the Cascade Range, Plateau, and Great Basin (Baxter et al. 2011; Connolly et al. 2011; McClure 2011). These studies, however, do not indicate whether the declines began before or after European contact. Further analysis based on greater chronological resolution should show whether these declines, like those detected by Sobel (2012), can be attributed to postcontact developments.

Indian–Euro-American Exchange during the Fur-Trade Era

Foreign goods arrived at the Columbia along the same routes as Native goods did, although after 1792 they were brought to the mouth of the river as well. William Clark observed on April 16, 1806, that near The Dalles "the Skillutes precure the most of their Cloth knives axes & beeds from the Indians from the North of them who trade with white people who come into the inlets to the North" (Lewis and Clark 1991:129).

In 1795, just three years after the first Euro-Americans entered the Columbia, trader Charles Bishop (1967) reported that a Captain Moore had wintered over and that Indians "also informed us that Captain Adamson had been here in Mr Teasts Ship the Jenny" (57). Not only did local Indians already have muskets, powder, and foreign clothes, but they could communicate with English-speaking traders and foreign genes were being added to the local population. One of the officers on the *Jenny*, for example, fathered a child by a slave woman owned by a Chinook chief (56, 116, 118–19, 121–24). When Lewis and Clark (1990) arrived 20 years later, the Indians named 13 traders who had visited the mouth of the Columbia in the spring and fall and noted that the articles the foreigners brought found their way to the "most distant nations" on the river (155–56, 199). On January 14, 1806, Clark observed:

> This traffic on the part of the whites Consist in vending, guns, principally old British or American Musquets, powder, balls and Shote, (Copper and brass Kettles,) brass tea kettles, Blankets from two to three points, Scarlet and blue Cloth (Coarse), plates and Strips of Sheet Copper and brass, large brass wire Knives Beeds & Tobacco with fishing hooks, buttons and Some other Small articles; also a considerable quantity of Salors Clothes, as hats, Coats, Trouses and Shirts. . . . The nativs are extravigantly fond of the most Common Cheap Blue and white beeds . . . the blue is usially prefured to the white; those beeds Constitute the principal Circulating medium with all the Indian tribes on this river; for those beeds they will dispose of any article they possess. (205)

By this time, the Indians had become "great higlers in trade," as Lewis called them (Lewis and Clark 1990:164), a skill perfected with time so that in 1824 HBC's George Simpson (1968) called them "without exception the most

TABLE 5.2. Exchanges of subsistence goods for subsistence goods
(and beads)

EXCHANGERS	GOODS EXCHANGED	SOURCE
Clatsops—Tillamooks	Beads—blubber and oil	Lewis and Clark 1990:199
Kathlamets—Clatsops	Wapato—blubber and oil	Lewis and Clark 1990:199
"people below" and to the river mouth—Skillutes (at The Dalles)	Beads and trinkets—pounded salmon	Lewis and Clark 1990:204, 224
People in the Wapato Valley—Chillukkittequaws (White Salmon)	Wapato, dried eulachon, beads—pounded, dried salmon, shapallel, bear grass, acorns, dried berries	Lewis and Clark 1990: 98–100
Yamhill Kalapuyas—Clowewallas	Camas—dried salmon	Henry 1992:658, 664
Clatskanies—Skillutes (Oak Point)	Meat and roots—salmon	Henry 1992:641

intelligent Indians and the most acute and finished Bargain Makers I have ever fallen in with" (96).

Judging from the amount of food that the traders at Fort Astoria in 1812–13 were required to buy from the Indians, the beads and other foreign goods flowing from the fort must have been considerable. Although fort head Duncan McDougall (1999) did not mention which goods were exchanged for food, almost daily entries record the food that came in:

> October 27th [1812] . . . A small canoe arrived from up the River with 18 fresh Salmon which were purchased. . . . 28th. . . . Purchased from the natives near 40 fresh Salmon. . . . November 1st. . . . In the evening Comcomly with three Canoes arrived bring fresh Salmon etc. . . . 3rd. . . . Visited by several other Chinooks bringing Salmon and a few Geese. . . . 13th. . . . Comcomly & suite arrived in the afternoon, bringing upwards of five hundred smoked Salmon and a few furs. (132–35)

The Euro-Americans also traded for furs and occasionally distributed special gifts to Comcomly, Kiesno, and other chiefs.

Natives went to some lengths to obtain foreign goods, as indicated by the description Concomly gave to Bishop (1967) in 1795:

TABLE 5.3. Exchanges of subsistence goods for valuables

EXCHANGERS	GOODS EXCHANGED	SOURCE
People in the Wapato Valley— "people below"	Wapato—beads, cloth, "various articles," "most valuable articles"	Lewis and Clark 1991:36
"Indians"	Sea lion—slave and "an assortment of other articles depending on size"	Henry 1992:701
Indians on the coast who find a whale—other Indians	Chunks of whale meat— one blanket, string of dentalis, five shells longer than a fathom, or groundhog blanket	Boas 1894:262
Cascades man's wife—his elder sister (location not given)	Large seashell—dried pounded salmon and dried fish skin	Sapir 1909:227–29

> They go up the River Chinnook two or three hundred miles and come to Strange villages, where they land and offer trade with some trifling Pieces of Copper or Iron. The chief then gives the Signal and they all discharge their Pieces laden with Powder, into the Air. These people never having heard or seen such a Strange Phenomena throw off their Skins and Leather War Dresses and fly into the woods, while the others Pick them up, and leave on the Spott the articles first offered. They then Proceed to other Places in like manner . . . we soppose this mode cannot last long, as they will naturally be aware of a Second visit of the kind. (118–19)

Commenting on a "trading" expedition undertaken by Shelathwell and Concomly, who Bishop called ambitious "secondary chiefs," he wrote:

> we find they have not met with their Expected Success, each of the chiefs having got only five Dresses, and I am sorry to add that two of them where obtained at the Expence of the lives of the wearers. . . . This Discovery was made After we had bought their Leather War Dresses, upon Observing them Pierced with Muskett Balls. (21–22)

Women sometimes brought food and raw materials to the fort to trade. On April 27, 1813, McDougall (1999) said they were "Visited by Calpo's wife & sev-

TABLE 5.4. Exchanges of valuables for valuables

EXCHANGERS	GOODS EXCHANGED	SOURCE
"Indians"	Slave(s)—beaver skins, beads	Franchère 1969:102
"Indians"	Slave(s)—beads, beaver, otter, "etc."	Cox 1957:166
Women of a Cascades group—chief of another Cascades group*	Slave—beads	Henry 1992:654
Clatsop man—Lewis and Clark (trade not made)	Slave—gun and beads	Lewis and Clark 1990:360
Scanaway (Cowlitz chief)— a Thompson River Indian from the interior	Slave—gun, blanket, 2 yards of collar wire	Machlachlan 1998:57

* While Simpson (Merk 1931:98) said that wives were sent out to trade with their relatives on behalf of their husbands, this is the only example in the sources that might perhaps illustrate his observation.

eral of her people; traded some fish" (176). This bears out Astorian Alexander Ross's (2000) report: "In trade and barter the women are as actively employed as the men, and it is common to see the wife, followed by a train of slaves, trading at the factory, as her husband" (92). Women seem to have been trading their own products. On August 20, 1812, McDougall wrote: "Visited by great numbers of the natives, principally Women, bringing large quantities of waltap, Gum, etc." (118). In these cases, again, the return payment was not noted.

Indian-Indian Exchange

While most of the references to trade in the accounts focus on goods exchanged between Indians and Euro-Americans, some mention exchanges among Indians. William Clark, for example, described the "Great Mart of all this Country" near The Dalles:

> ten different tribes who reside on Taptate and Catteract River visit those people for the purpose of purchaseing their fish, and the Indians on the Columbia and Lewis's river quite to the Chopunnish [Nez Perce] Nation Visit them for the purpose of tradeing horses buffalow robes for beeds, and Such articles as they have not. (Lewis and Clark 1991:129)

While this suggests the existence of a true marketplace, where goods of all kinds were brought to trade, Alexander Ross (2000) saw the activities from a different perspective:

> The main camp of the Indians is situated at the head of the narrows, and may contain, during the salmon season, 3,000 souls, or more; but the constant inhabitants of the place do not exceed 100 persons, and are called Wy-am-pams; the rest are all foreigners from different tribes throughout the country, who resort hither, not for the purpose of catching salmon, but chiefly for gambling and speculation; for trade and traffic, not in fish, but in other articles; for the Indians of the plains seldom eat fish, and those of the sea-coast sell, but never buy fish. . . . The articles of traffic brought to this place by the Indians of the interior are generally horses, buffalo-robes, and native tobacco, which they exchange with the natives of the sea-coast and other tribes, for the higua [dentalia] beads and other trinkets. But the natives of the coast seldom come up thus far. Now all these articles generally change hands through gambling, which alone draws so many vagabonds together at this place. (117–18)

In short, goods were exchanged when people gathered at salmon-fishing and probably other resource-gathering sites, but the "buying and selling" familiar to Euro-Americans may not have been the primary means of accomplishing the exchange. With the exception of "beads and trinkets," the items exchanged were Native foods and, in one case, material used in basket making. People near the fort exchanged beads and trinkets for subsistence goods from groups from farther away. The Euro-American practice of using durable goods to buy food seems to have made headway among Indians as well by 1805. Another example is Alexander Henry's (1992) comment in 1813 that the Indians at the mouth of the river, who were usually short of provisions in March, could go upriver and purchase sturgeon and smelt from people above, "but few have the means to do this" (703) so they stayed home and ate roots.

There were exchanges of food and, except for wapato, Native durables. Two cases involved relatively rare sea mammals, and the distribution of whale meat in particular was surrounded by restrictions (Boas 1894:262). A Cascades man who gave a "large sea shell" for basic rations was forced to do so by famine and by a stingy elder sister's failure to observe the duties of a kinswoman (Sapir 1909b:227–29). In 1811, Gabriel Franchère (1969:95) reported that two Astorians who had been held by a chief on Sauvie Island

were ransomed for eight blankets, a copper kettle, an ax, a pistol, and a powder horn and shot. This might represent the equivalent of buying slaves, since
nonlocal captives were usually enslaved. Goods traded for slaves included
foreign items or the furs and skins exchanged for foreign goods. No other
mention of direct exchanges that might possibly be considered the trade of
valuables for other valuables were found, which implies that the foreign fur
trade had increased the trade of slaves among Indians.

Spheres of Exchange on the Lower Columbia

During the early 19th century, Indians were not freely trading all kinds of
goods for all others; rather, except in special circumstances, foods and raw
materials were exchanged for the same kinds of things and valuables were
exchanged for each other—allowing for the impact of foreign goods, to some
extent, on Native exchange.

EXCHANGE OF VALUABLES

In describing the "Great Mart" at The Dalles, Ross (2000) wrote that the
gamblers staked their "most valuable property" (90, 93). Other sources mentioned slaves, beads, dentalia, and blankets as the usual gambling stakes (Cox
1957:177; Simpson 1968:102), while Lewis and Clark said that beads and "other
parts of their most valuable effects" were gambled (1990:118–19).

Valuables changed hands in cases of marriage and dispute settlements.
Marriage required an exchange of valuables (gifting) between the families
involved. According to George Simpson (1968:98), families exchanged "presents" according to their means. One Astorian reported that a man and his
family presented to the woman's family slaves, dentalia, beads, copper bracelets, "etc.," while the wife's father returned "as many and sometimes more" to
the man (Franchère 1969:103). A second said the same, adding axes and
kettles to the list (Cox 1957:172), and a third said only that slaves and horses
were exchanged for canoes and "a certain return" (Stuart 1935:10). Charles
Cultee claimed that the return was on the order of four to five (Boas 1894:251),
and William Clark wrote in March 1806 that a canoe was given to the bride's
father "in exchange . . . for his daughter" (Lewis and Clark 1990:428), evidently unaware of the probable return gift.

A payment of valuables ("wergild," "blood money," and so forth) was
required to settle disputes of all kinds, whether arising from insults or murder (Franchère 1969:104; Simpson 1968:98–99). Simpson said that "in cases

of quarrels or misunderstandings with other Natives they either compromise matters by an exchange of presents or determine on fighting it out" (97). In 1814, the Cowlitz and Kiesno fought a battle over the Cathlacumups chief's failure to pay more than two blankets for a Cowlitz slave (Henry 1992:715–16). In the course of attempting to recover goods stolen by Indians at The Cascades in which two Indians were killed, the Astorians learned that they should pay for those killed with slaves or other goods and that the Indians believed they were entitled to keep some of the goods taken (Stuart 1935:11; Ross 2000:268; Cox 1957:149).

Fur traders were somewhat baffled by the Natives' readiness to assume an insult where none had been intended. In January 1796, Bishop (1967) wrote:

> this evening a Muskett Ball was fired by the Natives, which Passed close over our heads. Comcomolly wrestling or Playing with one of the officers, had received a blow in the Mouth, slight indeed to an Englishman, but to an Indian chief an Act sufficient to rouse him to revenge. He complained to me of it, but as I could not see any thing amiss I laughing told him, it was our manner of Play and where nothing ill was meant, with us, nothing ill as taken. He left the ship yesterday in apparent good humour. . . . Comcomally came on board Friday Morning. Said he fired the Ball at the Ducks and did not intend it near the ship as it was nearly dark: we gave this story (in our minds) the credit it deserved. (122–23)

The readiness to take offense with the implied or actual demand for recompense points to an important means for the distribution of valuable goods.

Shamans "live by their profession," Simpson (1968:100) wrote, and payments—unspecified, but probably valuables—were required for a shaman's services (Stuart 1935:9; Franchère 1969:103). Similarly, warriors were said to be paid for their services (Franchère 1969:104; Cox 1957:173), as were mourners at funerals (Ross 2000:97). The female relative who carried the bride over a "road" of dentalia was given dentalia (Boas 1894:251).

EXCHANGE OF FOOD

Food might be distributed or exchanged on the same occasions that valuables changed hands, but evidently not in exchange for the valuables themselves. Before Bishop (1967) left the Columbia, for instance, he received gifts of food: "he [Concomly] is going tomorrow in his canoe up the River to kill Wild Geese and Procure Some Fresh fish for us previous to our Sailing and Shelathwell is going away to get 'Wapatoes' (wild potatoes) as his Parting gift" (123). During a wedding ceremony, food was given to helpers and presumably to guests (Boas 1894:251).

A chief could serve as a center of food redistribution. In 1792, an old man who had guided William Broughton up the Columbia and "who appeared of some consequence" had "sufficient authority to demand part of the Sport every hunter or Fisherman had met with" (Manby 1992:199). In 1841, missionary Joseph Frost remarked that a hunter had brought an elk to the camp and, "according to custom, the most of it was taken to the lodge of the chief. Here a feast was prepared and the whole clan invited to partake" (Lee and Frost 1968:283). In short, the separation of goods seems to have held in situations other than direct exchange. It appears that subsistence goods were being exchanged or distributed in the context of ongoing relationships, with the intent of confirming and maintaining those relationships. Valuables were associated with situations where relationships, lives, and prestige were being changed or were at risk.

VALUABLES AND SOCIAL STRUCTURE

High rank depended largely on the possession of wealth, and any loss of valuables meant a loss of status. Gambling, for example, could mean a loss or gain in status, and disputes could lead to a break in relationships or to a serious loss of prestige. New relationships were established when a marriage took place. Shamans operated in situations of illness or other danger, as did warriors; mourners at funerals had lost a relative. If valuables had to be used to get food, a buyer's standing was reduced. The rarity of sea mammals was equated with valuables, and they might also be risky to get.

With the influx of foreign goods, new opportunities to obtain wealth were opened up, hence the "trading expeditions" of Shelathwell and Concomly. Simpson's (1968:97) remark that any Indian who owned a slave considered himself a chief reflects the rise in slave-trading with the increase in foreign goods. Euro-American artifact distributions suggest that lower-ranking households did indeed increase their standing by acquiring such items.

Spheres of Exchange Elsewhere

A similar system of restricted exchange was found in southwest Oregon and northwest California. Among the Tolowa-Tututni, the "prestige sphere" included shells, woodpecker scalps, rare pelts, obsidian blades, and certain regalia, with dentalia shells serving as a medium of exchange. These goods were exchanged in much the same contexts as on the Lower Columbia and could be used to buy food in cases of famine or for portions of a stranded whale. Ethnographer Cora DuBois (1936:51) pointed out that "scheming parsimony" and competitiveness characterized only those transactions in the prestige sphere; subsistence exchanges were marked by cooperation. Similarly, among the Yurok in northwestern California, valuables were termed "political goods," exchanged in low-frequency, high-ranking activities that were notable for competition among rivals. "Domestic goods and services," of low rank, were exchanged frequently by collaborating kin (Douglas and Isherwood 1996:131–37).

Social anthropologist Mary Douglas (1967) linked "restricted, ranked spheres of exchange" with "restricted, ranked spheres of status." By defining certain goods as valuables and linking them to status, elites in effect could limit access to status. When "restricted spheres of exchange are allowed to interpenetrate," she concluded, "the structure of privileges must collapse" (138). On the Columbia, when Euro-Americans freely exchanged all kinds of goods to obtain food, "just anyone" could acquire foreign valuables simply by providing the visitors with food. Though chiefs did their best to control the flow of imported goods, their efforts ultimately failed.

Exchange spheres also have been found in Oceania, Africa, and parts of South America (Pryor 1977:401–4), and they probably occurred in other parts of North America as well. The type of societies in which they might be expected to occur consists of relatively settled, autonomous, self-governing, local settlements linked by kin ties and cross-cutting social institutions but without higher-level organizations as found in, say, kingdoms (Fried 1967:109–10; Sahlins 1965:183).

CONCLUSIONS

Archaeology and ethnohistory give us different insights into the exchange systems of the Chinookan and other peoples of the Greater Lower Columbia. Archaeology, which concentrates on nonperishable trade items, can clarify the scope of long-distance exchange and shed light on the ways in which trade activity varied among households, communities, and social status groups. In addition, archaeology has begun to show how and why Native exchange networks developed in the context of Euro-American influences.

Ethnohistory and ethnography take us deeper into the role of exchange internally, in the social system. On the Lower Columbia, food and valuables circulated in different spheres. Food might be given to facilitate social relations and could be redistributed by high-ranking men, and valuables were exchanged whenever there was a shift in social relations, as in marriage, dispute resolution, and death. With the gain or loss of wealth, gambling could result in a change of status and hence a change in social relations. Possession of valuables was traditionally one way in which networks of high-ranking people could perpetuate their power, and it became a way for the *nouveau riche* to move up the socioeconomic ladder during the epidemic and fur-trade periods. The Native exchange system of the Lower Columbia was far more complicated and dynamic than first meets the eye, and archaeology, ethnohistory, and ethnography are only beginning to unravel its complexities.

SIX

HOUSES AND HOUSEHOLDS

Kenneth M. Ames and Elizabeth A. Sobel

> The household was the fundamental social, economic and cultural unit
> in western North America, including along the Lower Columbia River. On
> the Northwest Coast, houses were the physical manifestation of the house-
> hold and its social rank; they were theater and stage for social and spiritual
> rituals . . . they were also shelter in dank climate; they were food processing
> factories in which animal resources were butchered, roasted, smoked, ren-
> dered, dried, boiled, stored, and consumed: and they were the objects of
> tremendous effort and skill. Their interior arrangements were often a map
> of the relative status of the household's members . . . [and thought by some
> to be] maps of the . . . cosmos. (Ames and Maschner 1999:147–48)

Ancient and not so ancient houses, their contents, and associated dumps and
activity areas open windows into the lives of people in ways written records
or oral traditions cannot. Consequently, archaeologists have expended much
effort on excavating houses.

Households are central to understanding what anthropologists and others term complex societies—that is, societies that feature social stratification,
high population densities, monumental architecture, and an emphasis on
wealth. Most premodern complex societies practiced agriculture, which
enabled the high levels of food production that most researchers thought
were needed to support complexity. Northwest Coast peoples, however,
including those along the Lower Columbia and a few other known human
populations, had complex societies based on hunting-gathering economies
(Price and Brown 1985). For several decades, anthropologists have been trying to figure out how this happened. How did communities with only a
hunter-gatherer economy produce not only enough resources to meet basic

needs but also the surplus to support hereditary elites, high population densities, and the other resource-intensive aspects of complexity?

On the Northwest Coast, the answer lies at least in part with the household. The household was the fundamental unit of production, so household production must have been organized strategically, enabling the high output that fueled complexity. How were household members and property, including the house itself, mobilized to achieve such high production levels? We can find some answers to this question by examining the Chinookan household as an economic and social unit. Ethnohistoric and archaeological evidence can help us develop a picture of how houses sustained Chinookan culture and society immediately before the arrival of Europeans and to document some of the changes that occurred between the Vancouver expedition and the devastation of the epidemics (1792–1830).

CHINOOKAN HOUSEHOLDS

Chinookan households were part of larger communities of villages, towns, and regions, but the winter settlement or town was the primary community. Winter communities generally ranged in size from 40 to 500 individuals, although some in the Wapato Valley were larger. The mean number of individuals per community was highest in the Wapato Valley, intermediate at The Cascades, and lowest near the mouth of the Columbia River (Table 6.1).

The number of households per winter community in the Lower Columbia ranged from as few as one to at least 20, with each household having from about 10 to at least 100 individuals. Like community size, household size was largest in the Wapato Valley, intermediate at The Cascades, and lowest near the mouth of the Columbia. The core of each household was a kin-group of two or more nuclear and small extended families (Drucker 1934:32; Hajda 1984:169; Lewis and Clark 1990:221–22; Ray 1938:127); high status families and households were larger. A household also included any slaves owned by the resident families, and some households probably had skilled craftsmen temporarily living there (Drucker 1934:9–11, 32), as well as fictive kin, in-laws, orphans, and assorted hangers-on.

Chinookans had what anthropologists call corporate households. Each had an internal hierarchy with a leader, and many contained members of two or all three rank groups in Lower Columbia society—elites, commoners, and slaves. Members had certain obligations and privileges. They had to contribute to household production, for example, and could access the common household

TABLE 6.1. Estimated people per household in the Greater Lower Columbia River Region (from Hajda 1984)

REGION	LEWIS AND CLARK'S HIGH ESTIMATE*			LEWIS AND CLARK'S LOW ESTIMATE		
	HOUSES	PEOPLE	PEOPLE/ HOUSE	HOUSES	PEOPLE	PEOPLE/ HOUSE
Coast/River Mouth						
Total	286	5,160	18	31	500	16
Mean/Group	20	369	19	10	167	16
Median	16	225	16	11	200	18
Std. Dev	16	304	5	1	58	7
Wapato Valley						
Total	154	7,820	51	127	3,060	24
Mean/group	12	602	58	14	340	25
Median	6	400	50	6	200	25
Std.Dev	13	661	31	15	443	7
Columbia River Gorge						
Total	62	2,800	45	62	1,340	22

* Lewis and Clark produced two population estimates for the people they encountered: one developed in the fall of 1805, the second in the spring of 1806. The latter has been available in print as "Estimate of the Western Indians," while the former remained in manuscript until the 1980s (Boyd and Hajda 1987). Most GLCR population estimates (e.g., Mooney 1928, Kroeber 1939) are based on the "Estimate," which has higher population figures than the manuscript. Boyd and Hajda (1987) postulate that the differences between the two sets of figures reflect seasonal fluctuations in population along the river, with the lower figures representing a "core" GLCR population.

food supply (Lewis and Clark 1990:221–22; Swan 1972:161, 166). Finally, Lower Columbia households had multigenerational life spans, with houses inherited by children and household leadership passing from parent to child (Lewis and Clark 1990:221–22; Ray 1938:128; Spier and Sapir 1930:221; Townsend 1999:337).

CHINOOKAN HOUSES

There were three basic house types. The post-and-beam plankhouse, also called the winter or permanent house, was often maintained and reoccupied each year for decades and even centuries. The summer or temporary house, which could either be a mat lodge or a plank structure, was smaller and of lighter construction. The mat lodge had a pole frame covered by bark or mats. Some summer or temporary houses had light post frames covered with planks temporarily borrowed from a permanent house (Hajda 1984, 1994:180; Kane 1971b:34, 35; Ray 1938; Spier and Sapir 1930). The pit house or earth lodge was a common winter house on the Plateau east of the Cascade Mountains but historically existed in a minority of settlements in the eastern part of the Lower Columbia. Importantly, historical sources imply that all Lower Columbia settlements containing pit houses also contained plankhouses and that residents of these communities wintered in the pit houses and summered in the plankhouses (Lewis and Clark 1990:119; Wilkes 1845:382). This mix of surface plankhouses and semisubterranean pit houses in the same settlement also occurred along the Lower Fraser River in southwestern British Columbia during the last 2,200 years or so (e.g., Schaepe 2009). We know more about plankhouses than other Lower Columbia house types, and the plankhouse is much more closely linked, mechanically and symbolically, to the suite of indigenous household dynamics of interest here.

Plankhouse Construction

Throughout the Lower Columbia region, plankhouses shared some basic architectural features. The rectangular, gable-roofed houses, constructed primarily of western red cedar (*Thuja plicata*), ranged in size from 6 by 8 meters (about 20 by 25 feet) to 12 by 110 meters (about 40 by 360 feet), and even longer. The post-and-beam frame had upright posts or squared timbers set along the house's center axis, supporting the central ridge beam that formed the gable. Shorter posts or planks along the sides of the frame supported the eaves poles. Rafter poles linked these with the ridge beam. Ridge-beam supports were 4–5.5 meters (13–18 feet) or more high, while the eave posts were 1.5–2.2 meters (5–7 feet) high. Walls were split cedar planks set vertically into a trench beneath the eaves pole, with their tops lashed to it. Roofs were thin planks laid horizontally, vertically, or both and sometimes covered with cedar bark. Floors were earthen or planked; earthen floors were usually covered with mats.

People along the Lower Columbia, as elsewhere along the Northwest Coast, sometimes owned more than one house frame and shifted from frame to frame during an annual cycle, but they did not necessarily own more than one set of wall and roof planks. Consequently, they often took the wall and roof planks with them when leaving one house site and reattached the planking to the frame at the destination site (Hajda 1994:180; Ray 1938:126).

Small dwellings had a hearth set in the house's center, while larger structures had a hearth row down their long axis. As many as 10 hearths have been recorded for one house. Hearths were sometimes placed on the floor, sometimes in pits about 30 centimeters below the floor level, and inside framed boxes. These could be as large as 2.5–3 square meters (8–11 feet). Each served one or more family groups, which occupied the closest bench areas on both sides of the hearth (Hajda 1994). The presence of two or more hearths indicated that two or more families occupied a house.

Platforms for sleeping, storage, and other activities ran along at least the two sides of the house and perhaps at one or both ends. Material was stored on and under them, and sometimes the platforms were doubled, one above the other. The upper platform was reached by a ladder. Doorways—oval openings, roughly two by three feet, cut into a wide wall plank (Hajda 1994; Ray 1938:125)—were in one or both end walls and sometimes on sidewalls. Doors were usually pieces of plank, hide, or woven matting that could be pushed aside by those passing through (Hajda 1994:179; Ray 1938:125).

Many Lower Columbia plankhouses were semisubterranean, with floors and walls 0.3–2 meters (1–6 feet) below ground surface. In some instances, houses were erected over the excavation rather than in it, and the excavated areas were often floored over and used for storage. Archaeological investigations (Ames et al. 1992; Ames et al. 1999; Ames et al. 2008; Foreman and Foreman 1977; Smith 2006) show that extensive subfloor storage-pit complexes were common if not ubiquitous in Wapato Valley plankhouses. Pit complexes were located in two places: (1) below the sleeping benches and/or (2) below the floor planks that extended between the benches and the central hearth. In at least one instance, the excavation created a cellar (Ames et al. 1992; Ames et al. 2008). These pits were used for storage and for collecting refuse before throwing it out. The lack of documentary references to subfloor pits implies that they were not readily apparent to European and Euro-American visitors and that house occupants did not show them to these visitors.

Many documentary accounts describe painted and carved images on the interior surfaces of Lower Columbia plankhouses. Center posts, partitions, rear walls, the inner sides of the plank with the doorway, and the sides and ends of benches frequently bore carved and painted images, including geometric, anthropomorphic, and zoomorphic designs (Hajda 1994). The interior surface of the plank containing the doorway was often decorated so that the doorway composed the mouth or space between the legs of an anthropomorphic figure (Parker 1967:245; Vancouver 1984:77). Some observers noted freestanding painted wooden sculptures inside plankhouses (Hajda 1994), but historical accounts do not mention carvings or paintings on the exterior surfaces.

House construction differed among four areas within the Lower Columbia (Hajda 1994): the river mouth and outer coast, the middle Lower Columbia (Oak Point to Wapato Valley), The Cascades, and the upper Lower Columbia (Columbia Gorge Cascades to The Dalles area). Houses at the river mouth and outer coast were generally the smallest, with maximum lengths of roughly 30 meters (100 feet).

The largest houses were between Oak Point and the mouth of the Sandy River in the Wapato Valley. This region also had the only houses with internal partitions and the only large modular houses (those comprised of attached compartments). Meriwether Lewis and William Clark described a structure that was 69 meters (226 feet) long and divided into seven apartments, each roughly 10 square meters (30 square feet) in size. They and other sources apparently described large nonsegmented structures as well, ranging from 12 to 91 meters (40 to 300 feet) in length in this portion of the Lower Columbia (Hajda 1994). Archaeological excavations of Wapato Valley sites revealed both the segmented and large nonsegmented houses reported by Lewis and Clark. Of the six houses at the Cathlapotle site, at least four were subdivided into compartments (Ames et al. 2011). The Meier site, also located in the Wapato Valley, had a single large house featuring an open interior without compartments (Ames et al. 1992).

Houses along The Cascades portion of the river included structures longer than those near the coast but not as long as some of those in the Wapato Valley. Reported house sizes range from 11 by 10 to 49 by 14 meters (35 by 30 to 160 by 45 feet). Sources also describe a partition just inside the doorway of houses along The Cascades (Hajda 1994). Houses in the Columbia Gorge were distinct in at least two respects. First, they were relatively small compared to plankhouses in the Wapato Valley and at The Cascades, averaging perhaps 20 by 30 feet. Second, some settlements contained pit houses as well as plankhouses (Hajda 1994; Lewis and Clark 1990:119; Wilkes 1845:382).

Plankhouses have been used in the Lower Columbia for at least 2,800 years (Connolly 1992; Jermann et al. 1975), and archaeologists have investigated a large number of them (Table 6.2). Rectangular surface structures may have been built on the northern British Columbia coast as early as 6,000–7,000 years ago, with plankhouses constructed as early as 4,000–5,000 years ago. Rectangular surface houses were also present in southern British Columbia on the Lower Fraser River between 5,000 and 6,000 years ago (ca. 3000–4000 BC), much earlier than the Palmrose house (800 BC–AD 300) on the Oregon Coast. Plankhouse use seems to have been continuous on the northern coast after those dates, but there appears to be a gap of perhaps 1,000 or more years in their use (or in the archaeological record) on the Lower Fraser. The temporal pattern on the Lower Columbia before 2,800 years ago is unknown. After that, plankhouses were the dominant form of house in the region, although semisubterranean pit houses were also used in some locales (Bourdeau 2001; Minor et al. 1989:255; Pettigrew 1990:525; Warren 1958, 1960).

Archaeologists have identified over 20 sites with evidence of houses on the Lower Columbia. Only five of these sites have had excavations of sufficient scope to provide the information needed to reconstruct details of household organization and dynamics: Meier (35CO5), Cathlapotle (45CL1), Broken Tops (35CO57), Clahclehlah (45SA11), and McGowan/Station Camp (45PC106).

The Meier site, in the Wapato Valley near Scappoose, Oregon, contains the remains of one large plankhouse, about 14 by 30 meters (46 by 98 feet) in size, where an estimated 200 people lived (Ames et al. 2008). The site was occupied from ca. AD 1300 to 1800, into the fur-trade era. The house was used continuously between about AD 1400 to 1450 and site abandonment (Ames et al. 1992).

Cathlapotle, in the Wapato Valley near Ridgefield, Washington, is the site of a large town visited by Lewis and Clark on March 29, 1806. They estimated that it had a population of between 900 and 1,400 people. There is evidence for six very large plankhouses (ranging in size from 20 by 10 to 70 by 15 meters) in two rows paralleling the adjacent river. Four were modular houses. The town was established in its current location in around AD 1450 and abandoned by the mid-1830s. It is likely that the town was moved to its known location from another nearby place (Ames et al. 2011).

Broken Tops, in the Wapato Valley east of the Portland International Airport, contains remains of one or two rectangular plankhouse features

TABLE 6.2. Lower Columbia archaeological sites with house features

REGION	SITE	AGE APPROXIMATION	HOUSE SHAPE	ESTIMATED MIN. HOUSE SIZE (M)	MIN. NO. OF HOUSES	SOURCES
Dalles	Wakemap Mound	AD 900–1400 / AD 1400–1800s	Circular / Rectangular	? / ?	multiple	Butler 1960
Gorge	Caples (45SA5)	AD 1500–1700	Oval	6 × 4	41	Dunnell and Beck 1979
Gorge	Clahclehlah (45SA11)	AD 1700–1840 / AD 1500–1700	Rectangular / Oval	9 × 7 to 11 × 10; 4 × 3	7 / 11	Minor et al. 1989
Gorge	SKI*	Precontact (and postcontact?)	Circular and oval	6 × ? to 20 × ?	17	Warren 1959
Gorge	SK2*	Unknown	unknown	unknown	3	Strong 1959
Gorge	Wagon Wheel Park (CL8*)	Precontact	Circular	10 × 10	11	Warren 1959
Wapato Valley	CL14* CL3*	Precontact	Rectangular	12 × 7 to 36 × 7	4	Warren 1959; Strong 1959
Wapato Valley	Cathlapotle (45CL1)	AD 1400–1830	Rectangular	60 × 10 to 16 × 10	6	Ames et al. 1999
Wapato Valley	Meier (35CO5)	AD 1400– postcontact	Rectangular	30 × 12	1	Ames et al. 1992
Wapato Valley	45Cl.2*	Unknown	Rectangular	90 × 7.5	1	Strong 1959; Warren 1959
Wapato Valley	Broken Tops (35MU57)	AD 1375–AD 1500	Rectangular	unknown (9 × 3; 9.5 × 8.5)	2	Ellis and Fagan 1993; Ellis 2006
Wapato Valley	Herzog (45CL11)	Pre- and postcontact	Rectangular	21 × 10<	1	Foreman and Foreman 1977
Wapato Valley	Kersting (45CL21)	0 AD	Rectangular	8 × 5; 5 × 5>	3	Jermann et al. 1975
Wapato Valley	Lady Island (45CL48)	500 BC	Rectangular	unknown	1	Pettigrew 1981
Wapato Valley	Merrybell (35MU9)	900 BC	unknown	unknown	1, possible	Pettigrew 198

Region	Site	Date	Shape	Dimensions	Number	Reference
Wapato Valley	Pumphouse (35CO7)	AD 260+/-80 to postcontact	Rectangular	30 × 10; 17 × 7	2	Pettigrew 1981; Strong 1959; Warren 1959
Wapato Valley	Lyons (35MU6)	530+/-80 BP to postcontact	Rectangular	unknown	1	Pettigrew 1981
Wapato Valley	CL11* (Warren) CL4* (Strong)	Pre- and postcontact	Rectangular (and circular?)	37 × 7 to 12 × 7; 3.5 × 3.5 to 2.5 × 2.5	2–3; 2	Warren 1959; Strong 1959
Wapato Valley	Felida Moorage CL6*	Unknown	unknown	unknown	unknown	Strong 1959
Wapato Valley	Bachelor Is. (45CL43)	300 BC–AD 50	Rectangular	8 wide, 6 wide	2	Steele 1980; Ame et al. 2008
Wapato Valley	Ede (35CO34)	120 BC–AD 1000	Circular or oval	>7.5 × ?	1	Minor et al. 1985
Wapato Valley	Yale Reservoir (45CL420)	?	Circular or oval	unknown	1	Bryan 1992; cited in Wilson 1999
Wapato Valley	Long Jump (45CL460)	340+/-50 BP	Circular or oval	7 × 7	1	Wilson 1999
Wapato Valley	La Camas (45CL406)	AD 1670–AD 1810	Rectangular	20 × 7s	1	Chatters and Reid 1997
Wapato Valley	St. Johns (35Mr44–46)	AD 150–1805	Rectangular?	?	?	Pettigrew 2005
Estuary	McGowan/Station Camp (45PC106)	AD 1792–1829	Rectangular	8 × 10	1	Wilson et al. [year?]
Outer Coast	Palmrose (35CLT47)	300 BC–400 AD	Rectangular	>16 × 6	1	Connolly 1992; Phebus and Drucker 1979
Outer Coast	Par-Tee (35CLT20)	250 AD–900 AD	Circular	?	?	Connolly 1992
Outer Coast	Martin	~600 AD–?	?	?	?	Shaw 1977
Outer Coast	45(Cl01	1 AD–Contact?	Rectangular	?	2	DePuydt 1994

* Site number given by Strong and/or Warren; may not be current site number.

dating from ca. AD 1375 to 1500 (Ellis and Fagan 1993). The structures were smaller (8 by 9 meters) and less permanent than those at Meier or Cathlapotle, and they lacked the interior fittings described earlier. The site was probably inhabited seasonally, in spring and summer or both, by one or two small households engaged in subsistence tasks for immediate consumption and perhaps also to store resources for later consumption. It produced relatively few artifacts (Ellis 2006).

Clahclehlah, at the Middle Cascades on the northern or Washington shore, is probably the site of a town visited by Lewis and Clark in April 1806. The site was completely excavated in the late 1970s when a second powerhouse was constructed at Bonneville Dam. Seven plankhouses were aligned in two rows facing the Columbia River. While generally similar to the Meier and Cathlapotle houses, the Clahclehlah houses were much smaller, although they did have the standard interior fittings of Chinookan houses. The site appears to date from AD 1700 to perhaps as late as AD 1855 (Minor et al. 1985; Sobel 2004).

McGowan/Station Camp is located on Baker Bay on the Washington shore of the Columbia River estuary (Wilson et al. 2009). The bay was a major ship anchorage during the maritime fur trade, and the site was across the river from the fur-trading post of Fort Astoria/Fort George (1811–25). The McGowan/Station Camp site, which appears to have been occupied between about 1792 and 1820 (Wilson et al. 2009), contains evidence for one or more small (8 by 10 meters) plankhouses, although the remains may represent a single modular house. The structure was probably temporary and burned at least once, as archaeologists found burned planks that may be the remains of a wall or a shed-style roof. While the structure may have had sleeping platforms and interior pits, it did not have the large pit complexes found at upstream sites. The site also lacked domestic artifacts while having a rich assemblage of trade goods. It was probably a Chinookan trading depot (Wilson et al. 2009).

HOUSEHOLD PRODUCTION
Food Getting, Processing, Cooking, and Eating

Chinookan houses were the physical and organizational centers of an intensive food-getting economy. Lower Columbia peoples harvested a wide array of food resources, including mammals, fish, and plants; and large amounts of resources were transported to the house for processing. Many hunter-gatherers processed harvested resources in the field, but Chinookan people also used a great diversity and number of canoes, some capable of hauling several tons, so they hauled home everything from the largest elk to plant roots and berries. While some field processing did occur, most production activities took place in and around the house. Recent research in the vicinity of Cathlapotle, for example, suggests that food-processing activities were concentrated in and around winter residential sites (Daehnke and Funk 2005).

Initial food processing, including animal and fish butchering, occurred both inside and outside the houses. Salmon and sturgeon, for example, were processed inside the house (Sobel 2004). The archaeological recovery of articulated animal skeletal sections from subfloor storage pits also points to indoor food processing (Ames et al. 2011).

Cooking, including boiling and roasting, took place both inside and outside the house. Indoors, people cooked in and around the central hearth or hearths (Curtis 1970:92; Lockley 1928:59; Ray 1938:128–29; Swan 1972:111); outdoors, they used earth ovens and small hearths. Archaeological evidence for the large size and scale of indoor hearths and the high frequency of outdoor hearths and ovens shows the intense effort that people invested in food processing. Food was stone boiled by heating rocks in a fire and then dropping them into a container of water and food (Drucker 1934; Kane 1971b; Lewis and Clark 1990:215–17; Lockley 1928:59; Simpson 1968:103; Ray 1938:129; Spier and Sapir 1930:185); fish and meat were rendered into oil in this way (Lewis and Clark 1990:215–17). Meat and fish were roasted near or above the hearth fire (Lee and Frost 1968:300; Lewis and Clark 1990:215, 219; Ray 1938:130; Swan 1972:109), while roots, nuts, berries, moss, and meat were steamed and baked in outdoor earth ovens (Drucker 1934; Ray 1938:118–21; Lee and Frost 1968:181; Ray 1938:129; Spier and Sapir 1930:182–84).

Like indoor cooking, indoor eating generally occurred around hearths. In everyday situations and during feasts, individuals ate while seated on mats around hearths, with their food placed in containers or on mats. An entire family might eat food from a single container or mat (Boyd 1996:99–100; Curtis 1970:92; Drucker 1934:6; Lee and Frost 1968:299; Lewis and Clark 1990:118–20; Lockley 1928:59; Ray 1938:128).

Storage

Plankhouses were the major storage facilities along the Lower Columbia, as elsewhere along the Northwest Coast (Ames 1996). Great quantities of dried and smoked foods were stored, especially in late fall, when most winter provisions had been gathered. Euro-Americans described houses that were seemingly stuffed with provisions. In 1814, Alexander Henry (1992) observed that "the insides of these Indians Houses are crowded with smelt [eulachon] drying, suspended by the heads to poles, the roofs are lined every where excepting the fire place is full, all hanging tail downwards" (665). Nathaniel Wyeth (1973), in 1835, estimated that the house of one Lower Columbia "chief" contained four tons of dried fish, roots, and other food (175).

Many items were stored on or beneath benches, on the floor in other parts of the house, and in subfloor storage pits. Storage was not limited to foods, as an array of materials was kept in the subfloor pits, including raw materials, wealth goods, and trash. Butchered animal parts may have been stored for use as raw material (e.g., bone and tendons for making tools) as much as for food. The pits were probably lined with mats or baskets (Ames et al. 1992:283; Curtis 1970:95).

Objects were hung from rafters, ridgepoles, eaves posts, wall planks, and other structural members. A variety of foods, particularly those with high fat content and oil, were stored this way. Lamprey, salmon, eulachon, and sometimes berries and roots were suspended from the plankhouse ceiling (Swan 1972:111; Strong 1906:10). Perishable resources hung from the roof were dried and, to varying degrees, smoked by the hearth fires below (Henry 1992:665; Lewis and Clark 1990:378, 1991:27; Lockley 1928:59; Townsend 1999:347, 366; Swan 1972:111). Items stored on benches and floors were in boxes, baskets, and bags (Henry 1992:637; Lockley 1928:59), and those hung from ceilings and walls were probably in baskets and bags. A few sources indicate that stored items were sometimes concentrated in the rear parts of plankhouses (Curtis 1970:91; Drucker 1934; Lewis and Clark 1988:35).

Plankhouses could readily accommodate large volumes of stored goods. The Meier house had an estimated 1,000 meters or more of storage space under its eaves and in its cellar. Ames et al. (2008) estimate that the Meier cellar could have held over 20 tons of stores. While this probably was not typical, smaller houses still had substantial volumes of storage space.

Fabrication and Craft Production

Fabrication and craft production were key household functions and were often carried out indoors (Ray 1938:128). James Swan (1972:161–64) reported that in winter, when heavy rains limited outdoor activity, men and women often spent time making and repairing objects. For example, Swan wrote that women wove mats "on the lodge floor" by pounding two pegs into the ground, one at each end of the in-progress mat for the attachment of fibers, while men reportedly made and repaired spears, fishhooks, "daggers," wooden spoons, bowls, and dishes.

The archaeological visibility of fabrication activities is conditioned by preservation factors. The Lower Columbia archaeological record most directly reflects fabrication activities that involved nonperishable materials such as stone, bone, and metal. In contrast, fabrication activities involving perishables—basket making, for example—are often archaeologically invisible. Furthermore, most of the stone and bone artifacts commonly found by archaeologists were once parts of larger tools with nonperishable components. A stone net weight, for example, was once secured to a net woven of cordage, perhaps of nettle fiber, that did not preserve. Stone and bone artifacts are the visible tips of an invisible iceberg of technology. The iceberg's size is suggested by the Ozette site on the Washington Coast, which contains remains of several plankhouses dating to the early 1700s. The houses were buried beneath a vast mudslide that preserved the wooden objects in the houses. Archaeologists estimate that less than 5 percent of the tools at Ozette are of bone or stone (Croes 1996). The Sunken Village site, located on Sauvie Island in the Lower Columbia River (Croes et al. 2009), was likewise buried in wet mud. The many perishables recovered from Sunken Village hint at the range and diversity of wooden items that the Lower Columbia River houses probably contained. It is no surprise, then, that stone artifacts from Lower Columbia sites include many woodworking tools, indicating that carpentry was a major, ongoing effort.

Archaeological evidence for carpentry includes stone hammers or mauls, stone adze blades, antler splitting wedges, abraders for smoothing and sanding rough wood, saws, chisels, and wood shavings and chips. Among possible woodworking tools are beaver incisors, which may have been used as adzes for fine work and carving (Lyman and Zehr 2003). The diversity of tools indicates that the full range of woodworking and carpentry occurred at the houses. While it is possible that high status individuals at the Meier house engaged in more fine woodworking (e.g., carving) than other members of the household, they did not do so at Cathlapotle.

Fabrication also includes the acquisition of raw materials for tools and other items. Archaeology indicates that most of the stone for chipped stone tools was collected nearby and stored in the cellars against future need. Bone and antler were similarly locally available and were collected and stored. Other raw materials were imported through trade and travel. For example, obsidian and some high quality cherts were imported from other areas, and metals were obtained mainly from Europeans and Euro-Americans (Sobel 2012).

Fabricating activities occurred primarily inside, around the hearth, and the storage areas near the hearths are rich in fabrication debris, broken tools, and the like. They also contained evidence of racks and other small structures. The hearths themselves probably produced good light and sometimes quite high heat, required for working copper and treating some kinds of stone used for chipped stone tools. Less often, fabrication took place on the benches or outdoors.

The archaeological recovery of highly crafted items, such as those carrying decoration, is exceedingly rare. It is clear from museum collections, historical accounts, ethnographic data, and the occasional archaeological find, however, that such items were made. Small adzes, beaver teeth, stone gravers, perforators, and saws used for fine woodworking are ubiquitous but not abundant. At Meier, such tools are concentrated in the high status end of the house, suggesting that some high status individuals specialized in skilled woodworking. At both Meier and Cathlapotle, the distributions of faceted hammerstones, used to make groundstone objects, suggest focused work areas, which also implies specialization by groups within households (Ames and Smith 2010).

House Construction, Renovation, and Repair

The construction of a plankhouse was a significant investment in time and energy (Trieu 2006). The Meier house, for example, may have contained some 55,000 board feet of lumber, without a plank floor, to 75,000 board feet, with a plank floor. (Modern, single-family houses use 10,000–12,000 board feet). Building the house may represent the labor of from 1,400 to 2,600 people, if erected in a single day, as was the practice elsewhere on the Northwest Coast. Even the much smaller Clahclehlah houses each may have required the labor of as many as 400 people (Trieu 2006). The town of Cathlapotle likely contained over a million board feet of lumber at one time. These estimates do not include fittings—planking for storage boxes, hearth boxes, interior frames— nor the acquisition of wood for interior fires or the fabrication of tools.

Plankhouses were regularly repaired and rebuilt (Trieu 2006). Renovation included rebuilding houses almost from scratch, replacing and resetting eave support posts and ridge-beam support planks and filling, re-excavating, and refilling subfloor pits and post holes. Houses burned and were damaged by floods, and planks and beams rotted and were eaten by insects. Over its 400-year lifespan, the Meier house was repaired and rebuilt as many as 18 times (Ames et al. 1992); the house likely contained 500,000–1 million board feet over its lifetime (Ames et al. 1992).

Ceremonial Gatherings

The plankhouse was the primary setting for ceremonial gatherings in the Lower Columbia (see Sobel 2004). Ceremonial gatherings that took place partially or completely in houses included a series of life-cycle ceremonies, curing ceremonies, and winter spirit dances. The Lower Chinookans also held secular feasts or gifting ceremonies in the summer and fall to mark an individual's change in status from commoner to elite and ceremonies seeking spiritual aid in periods of food shortage (Ray 1938:48, 115). Ceremonial activity occurred primarily in the space that circumscribed, partially or completely, the hearth or hearths in a house. Feasts were sometimes, if not often, consumed in one house but prepared elsewhere. Wooden planks and posts were planted upright or laid horizontally on the house floor in various ceremonial contexts. The most sacred components of spirit dances took place in the rear of the house, while the front of the house was open to anyone who wished to attend.

Chinookan individuals with guardian spirits might possess one or more power boards or power sticks that individuals used while participating in spirit dances (Boyd 1996:122–26). At other times, they might display power boards and power sticks in their houses.

HOUSEHOLD SPATIAL ORGANIZATION AND SOCIAL STATUS

The interior arrangements of Chinookan houses, like those on the rest of the Northwest Coast, appear to have reflected the status of household members. The rear of the house had the highest status and was the most spiritually charged part of the dwelling (Sobel 2004), while the front carried the lowest status. This pattern applies to large houses with open interiors, such as Meier, but is more difficult to apply to segmented houses.

Archaeological data have been used to establish which compartments of the segmented houses were occupied by high status families. At Cathlapotle, in each of the four segmented structures, one or both of the end compartments were likely high status living areas, as they are much longer than the others and have more extensive subfloor pit complexes along both front and rear walls. In the excavated middle compartments, the subfloor pits are generally smaller and occur only along the back wall. House 1's largest compartment contains a cache of high status goods, including iron daggers. At Meier, prestige goods, such as copper bracelets, tend to be concentrated in the rear third of the structure, suggesting that the rear part of the house was a high status living area. Additionally, the only two anthropomorphic artifacts recovered at either site were in the high status areas, perhaps pointing to a high spiritual significance.

The documentary record is somewhat mixed about whether or not slaves were residentially separated from their owners. They may have lived and slept with their owners or near the front door. It is extremely difficult, however, to identify slaves in the archaeological record (Ames 2002, 2008).

The documentary record mentions several restrictions on women's use of space on the Lower Columbia. At various times, a woman was restricted to a partitioned area within the house in which she lived or to a small structure nearby. At the onset of her first menstrual period, a pubescent girl "ate, slept, and worked in a partitioned corner of the house" for a period of time—Ray reported five months (1938:68, 71–72), while Swan said one month (1972:171). Wacheno (Drucker 1934:25–27) noted that a reed hut within the house constituted the seclusion area, but he did not comment on the length of seclusion for Clackamas girls. Cultee (Boas 1894:246) suggested that the seclusion period lasted for about two months and that the girl used a "separate door" from other house residents. While in seclusion, her activities included eating, sleeping, basketry, and applying red pigment to her face, hands, and the part in her hair (Ray 1938:71). During all subsequent menstruations, the girl reportedly re-entered the seclusion area for five days (Ray 1938:71). Emma Luscier said that the seclusion was in a "partitioned corner of the house," though Cultee (Boas 1894:247) stated that a young woman left the plankhouse after her first two menstruations and resided elsewhere for five days.

Pregnant women were "secluded before delivery in a hut or partitioned corner of the house" (Ray 1938:68). During delivery, "the woman held to two upright posts"; afterward, "heated rocks were placed around her bed and water poured on to produce steam . . . to make sure that all the after birth would pass" (Ray 1938:68). The new mother stayed in the seclusion area for several days (Ray 1938:68). A woman also stayed behind a partition in the house for at least one month following her husband's death (Curtis 1970:99). The documentary record does not explicitly mention any restrictions on men's use of space.

HOUSEHOLD PRODUCTION, SOCIAL RANK, AND POSTCONTACT CHANGE
Specialized Production and Social Rank

Chinookan households did not apparently include full-time specialists. Archaeological evidence for all the production activities described earlier is found throughout each house, indicating that everybody, from the highest status families to the lowest, was involved in production necessary to support the family and the larger household. Some families within households, however, seem to have emphasized particular activities. At Meier, for example, although projectile points are found in all portions of the house, whole and broken projectile points are concentrated in the southern third of the house, suggesting an emphasis on terrestrial hunting by lower status members of this household. The high status end of the house contained only complete points, as though they were made there.

At Cathlapotle, projectile points were most common in the high status compartment of House 1, but most were broken. Similarly, worn adze blades at Meier were associated with only one hearth, hinting at the presence of woodworking specialists. Concentrations of stone tool-making equipment and waste also suggest the presence of specialists, although these occurred in most portions of the houses as if each segment or hearth group had stone toolmakers. The organization of labor appears to have been quite fluid.

Historical and archaeological information about hearths and associated thermally altered rock (TAR) also provide some evidence for differentiation of activities within households that may be linked to status or occupational specialization. Archaeologists working on the Northwest Coast generally recognize that hearths may represent social groupings, such as families, within the larger household. That assumption is also warranted for Lower Columbia houses.

Early accounts and historical paintings consistently portray large hearth boxes in the centers of Chinookan houses. Archaeologically uncovered hearths vary tremendously within houses. At Meier, the southernmost hearth box was at least 3 meters long and contained the remains of over 30 individual hearths. Evidence suggests temperatures sometimes in excess of 900° F, and the hearth contained bone, shell, and ash that were melted and welded together by the high heat. There were also indications of copper fabrication at this hearth. The surrounding storage pits were filled with great quantities of thermally altered stone from fires and boiling, indicating intense processing. By contrast, the northernmost hearth was relatively small, contained mainly wood ash, and lacked evidence of especially high heat. The middle hearth was similar to the northern hearth, and it contained the lowest quantity of TARs, although the number is still enormous. This all suggests that while food processing and fabricating activities requiring intense high heat occurred throughout the house, they were concentrated at the south end of the house, away from the high status area. So large-scale cooking for feasts and other ceremonials was probably concentrated at the south end and carried out by less elite or nonelite individuals within the household.

In Cathlapotle House 1, the hearths and TAR amounts differ from compartment to compartment. There are at least two very large hearths in the high status compartment (1d), and one was clearly in use during the lifespan of the house. Neither appears to have been in hearth boxes, or, if they were, the boxes were quite small. Both hearths lacked evidence for extremely high heat and intensive processing. One compartment (1c) contained a classic hearth box, which was used during the lifespan of the house. Like the southernmost Meier hearth, it was a processing hearth, although temperatures were never as consistently high in it nor the processing as intense. Surprisingly, the TAR data suggest less-intensive heat-related activity in this compartment. The hearth in the compartment was built directly on the earthen floor. While it did not at all resemble the high temperature hearth in the Meier house, the TAR evidence suggests intensive heat-related processing. This compartment also contained a large cache of copper tools, so the high heat may be related to fabrication. All the hearths in House 4 were built directly on the sandy floor and none had hearth boxes, although there appears to have been relatively intensive heat-related processing through this house. The intensity of processing activities varied within houses, from hearth to hearth. Some hearths were associated with very high heats and intensive processing activities, while temperatures elsewhere were kept cooler. It is also perhaps telling that the highest heats were not in the high status areas.

In summary, then, everybody did everything; but within each household, some families, hearth groups, compartment groups, or status groups emphasized specific activities such as hunting land mammals or working copper. They do not appear to have done this, however, at the exclusion of other activities. Additionally, different households had different productive emphases. At Meier, there seems to have been a focus on fine woodworking, while at Cathlapotle there was a focus on hide working. What we do not yet know is how these skills were integrated into the larger economy. For example, did the person working the copper exchange his or her products for other goods, perhaps ground stone mauls, or was making such items among their obligations to the house chief or the household (see Ames 1996)?

We also have not yet generated or recognized archaeological evidence for gender roles in household production. On the coast, women's labor was particularly important in processing resources (e.g., Walter 2006), but it is difficult to tease out gender roles archaeologically.

Beyond individual households, there may have been production differences between communities. Some production differences between Meier and Cathlapotle may be ecological. The sites differ, for example, in the diversity of mammals represented. While this could reflect differences in local habitats, it could also reflect different trade patterns. Archaeological data indicate that Cathlapotle people were much more engaged in hide working. Cleaned and boiled elk hides, known as clamons, were a major export from the Lower Columbia and Willamette Valley during the fur-trade period. European and Euro-American fur traders took bales of clamons, widely used as armor, north along the coast to trade for sea otter pelts. Cathlapotle residents were probably heavily involved in this trade, as the distribution of scrapers indicates a postcontact increase in hide processing at the site. The comparative lack of involvement by Meier residents in hide working may relate to the fact that Cathlapotle was located near the Columbia River and therefore regularly was visited by European and Euro-American traders, while Meier was several miles from the river (e.g., Cromwell 2010). Woodworking increased at Meier after contact (Fuld 2011), which points to some degree of community specialization in production

Production differences between Meier and Cathlapotle may also relate to different abandonment dates. Meier may have been abandoned 10 to 20 years earlier than Cathlapotle, which was deserted sometime between 1830 and 1836 (Boyd 2011). Therefore, direct involvement in the fur trade lasted perhaps twice as long for Cathlapotle residents as for Meier residents. Cathlapotle households had much more opportunity to alter production in relation to Euro-American contact and colonization.

We do not know whether Chinookan households shifted their production activities as a direct consequence of the fur trade. Did they, for example, increase production of foodstuffs or craft items so they would have materials to trade? The introduction of firearms probably had no impact on production levels, as they were apparently not important trade goods during the pre-reservation era. Archaeologically, gun parts are extremely rare, and while both Cathlapotle and Meier produced hundreds of thousands of pieces of chipped waste, they produced no gunflints (and one percussion cap). The only musket barrel in either site had been cut off the gun and rammed into the ground to support an eave post.

The progressive depopulation of the Lower Columbia during the fur-trade years must have had more impact than the fur trade itself on household production. At some point in the 18th century, Meier residents allowed the cellar to fill with dirt and covered the floor with clay. Perhaps the household population had shrunk to the point that the plank floor (15,000 board feet) became too costly to maintain. Such a decrease in membership would have constrained household production. Changes in the sizes, numbers, and locations of hearths in Chinookan houses also may point to depopulation (Gardner-O'Kearny 2010). Over time at Cathlapotle, hearths increased in number while decreasing in size. The pre-existing interior hearth arrangement broke down as hearths were built directly on the house floors rather than in boxes and were not aligned with the central hearth rows. One possible explanation for this pattern is that as villages like Meier were abandoned, the survivors moved to towns like Cathlapotle, where they were accommodated in the pre-existing houses. This may be why Cathlapotle had a relatively large population and an apparently productive labor force until it was abandoned.

SUMMARY AND CONCLUSIONS

Winter plankhouses were the largest human constructions on the Northwest Coast, including along the Lower Columbia River. Given the resources and labor required for their construction and maintenance, they are certainly examples of monumental architecture (e.g., MacDonald 1983). For more than two millennia, they were the centers of the cultural, social, economic, and political lives of their occupants. Archaeologists and other scholars have learned a great deal about how these institutions operated, but there is much more to learn. It is clear, for example, that prodigious volumes of resources were harvested and processed into stores. What remains less clear is how that work was organized and coordinated and what role, if any, specialists played. We do not fully understand the sources of variation in house form along the river. Some of it is seasonal, but other factors must have been at play. Finally, we have barely touched here on the spiritual and cultural roles of these structures. It is not hard, however, to look at the excavated hearth boxes along the central line in the Meier house and visualize elders in the winter firelight, instructing children through songs and stories.

Excavated cellar and storage pits of a plankhouse at the Meier site, near Scappoose, Oregon. The Meier house, excavated by Portland State University in the 1980s, dates between A D 1400 and ca. 1820. A large cellar is a distinctive feature of the large winter houses in the Wapato Valley. The Meier cellar could hold 166 cubic yards of stored material. (Courtesy of the Wapato Valley Archaeological Project, Portland State University)

Mountain Landscape with Indians, by John Mix Stanley (1814–72), oil on canvas, 1870–75. Stanley's painting is the only known depiction of a traditional Chinookan settlement. Although the scene is near present-day Hood River in the Columbia River Gorge, the structures depicted are probably typical of village sites throughout the Chinookan area. The painting is apparently based on a drawing from one of Stanley's 1846–53 visits to the Pacific Northwest. (Courtesy of the Detroit Institute of Arts, USA, gift of Wayne County Medical Society, The Bridgeman Art Library)

Tsinistum with a clam basket. Tsinistum, or Jennie Michelle (several spellings), was a well-known Clatsop basket weaver. Women were traditional gatherers of plants and shellfish, and in this photo Michelle carries an open-work clam-gathering basket on her back. Lewis and Clark described other gathering tools, such as digging sticks for roots and women's wapato canoes. (Courtesy of the Oregon Historical Society, ORHI49251)

SALMON FISHING AT CHINOOK.

Salmon Fishing on Chinook Beach, by James Swan, early 1850s. This drawing, published in Swan's *The Northwest Coast* (1857) and based on his original sketch (in the Beinecke Library, Yale University), shows seine fishing, the usual method of catching salmon during major runs in the main stream of the Columbia River. (Courtesy of the Oregon Historical Society, bb010070)

MRS. WILSON, A KATHLAMET WOMAN

Ch'isht (Catherine George), a Willapa woman wearing dentalia shell frontlets. Dentalia, traded from the West Coast of Vancouver Island, were a Chinookan wealth item and medium of exchange. The photograph is from the frontispiece to *Kathlamet Texts*, by Franz Boas (1901), where she was misidentified as "Mrs. Wilson, Kathlamet." (Courtesy of the Oregon Historical Society, bb010081)

Indian (Chinook) Lodge, opposite Fort George, Henry Warre, watercolor, 1845. Despite the title, this watercolor was probably the Clatsop lodge shown adjacent to Fort George in the Warre/Richardson painting. It is the best extant depiction of a typical Lower Chinook plankhouse. (Courtesy of the American Antiquarian Society, Philadelphia, Sir Henry James Warre Collection, No. 51)

Cathlapotle Plankhouse. This plankhouse was constructed in 2005–2006 near the Cathlapotle town site, on the US Fish and Wildlife Service's Ridgefield Refuge outside Ridgefield, Washington. It was built by members of the Chinook Tribe, volunteers from the Ridgefield community, and the US Fish and Wildlife Service. The plankhouse project won one of the first Advisory Council for Historic Preservation Director's Award for Federal Achievement in Historic Preservation and the Secretary of the Interior's Cooperative Conservation award in 2006. (Courtesy of the US Fish & Wildlife Service, District 1 OR, Friends of Ridgefield Refuge, Kenneth M. Ames, photographer)

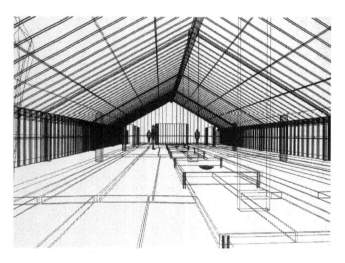

Meier Plankhouse interior, computer model. The single plankhouse at the site was quite large, 80-by-12 meters. (Courtesy of the Wapato Valley Archaeological Project, Portland State University, reconstruction by Darin Molnar)

Casanov, Noted Warrior, Chief from Fort Vancouver, Paul Kane (1810–1871), oil on paper (9.75 x 8.125 inches), ca. 1846–47. Kiesno was chief at Cathlacumups village near St. Helens (to 1830) and Wakanasisi near Fort Vancouver (to 1848). Besides Concomly of Chinook village, he was the most influential Lower Chinookan of the early 1800s, with kin ties at The Cascades, Willamette Falls, and Chinook, and he had a special relation-ship with the Hudson's Bay Company. (Courtesy of the Stark Museum of Art, Orange, Texas, 31.78.201)

Charles Cultee. Cultee was Franz Boas's main informant for *Chinook Texts* and *Kathlamet Texts*. This photo is from the frontispiece to *Chinook Texts*, 1894. (Courtesy of the Oregon Historical Society, bb010085)

Victoria Wishikin Howard, 1919. Mrs. Howard, Melville Jacobs's main informant for *Clackamas Chinook Texts*, is shown here sorting basket materials. Most of her work with Jacobs dates from 1930. (Courtesy of the Barbara Danforth Private Collection)

Cradle model, 1841. This model of a Lower Columbia canoe cradle was collected by the US Exploring Expedition. Portland Basin cradles had a different shape; both were used for head-flattening. (The model does not include the woven pad of grass that was used to flatten the infant's head.) The doll has features and body designs typical of the Chinookan Art Style. (Doll and Cradle courtesy of the Peabody Museum of Archaeology and Ethnology, Harvard, Peabody ID number 18-12-10/87342, individual image digital file number 54040019)

Interior of a Lodge, Columbia River, Paul Kane, oil, 1847. In this painting, probably executed near Fort Vancouver, Kane shows a spirit board, to the left, and in the chief's quarters at the back of the lodge, a monumental figure that served as a model for the Cathlapotle Plankhouse upright. The painting is a model for house interiors at the Meier and Cathlapotle sites. (Courtesy of the Stark Museum, Orange, Texas, 31.78/120)

Indian Grave Near the Entrance of the Columbia River, N.W. Coast of America, Henry James Warre (1819–1898), watercolor heightened with gum glaze over graphite on paper, 1845. Interment in raised canoes was a preferred mode of burial among Lower Chinookans. There are several early 1800s depictions, notably by Paul Kane, but Warre's painting is one of the better examples. (Courtesy of the Amon Carter Museum of American Art, Fort Worth, Texas, 1996.4.12)

Fort George, Thomas Richardson, oil, based on a sketch by Henry Warre, 1845.
Fort Astoria, established in 1811 and later called Fort George, was the major Lower
Columbia trade center throughout the early 1800s. It was situated adjacent to the Clatsop villages and across the Columbia River from the Chinook villages. Richardson's oil
reproduces better than the original Warre sketch, but it substitutes an East Coast style
birch-bark canoe for the dugout in Warre's original. (Courtesy of the Oregon Historical
Society, neg. no. 35111, dig no. ba020149)

CAMP ON THE TREATY GROUND.

Treaty in the Chehalis between Gov. Stevens and 5 tribes Chinooks, Chehalis, Cowlitz, Queniult, & Satsops, James Swan, February 1855. The treaty failed, though the Quinault treated later and were rewarded with a reservation. The Chinook never successfully treated with the US government. The painting is from Swan's *The Northwest Coast* (1857); his original sketch is in the Beinecke Library at Yale University. (Courtesy of the Oregon Historical Society, bb010071)

Indians Dipnetting for Salmon at Willamette Falls, Joseph Drayton, 1841. Portland Basin Chinookans took salmon by dipnet at The Cascades Rapids and at Willamette Falls. This is Drayton's original sketch; the version published in Charles Wilkes's *Narrative* has several modifications. (Courtesy of the Oregon Historical Society, bb010070)

WM. CAMERON McKAY, M.D.
PENDLETON, OR.

Dr. William McKay, a medical doctor, was the son of Concomly's daughter Timmee and trader Tom McKay. The author of several papers on Native culture, he delivered an address in Chinuk Wawa to the Columbia River Centennial celebration in 1892. The photograph is from *History of the Pacific Northwest* (vol. 1, 1889). (Courtesy of the Oregon Historical Society, bb010082)

SILAS B. SMITH,
SKIPANON, OR.

Silas Smith, a lawyer, was the son of settler Solomon Smith and Celiast, whose father was Clatsop Chief Coboway. He was the author of several articles on Native culture dating from the turn of the 20th century. This image is from *History of the Pacific Northwest* (vol. 2, 1889). (Courtesy of the Oregon Historical Society, bb010094)

Emma Millet Luscier, 1953. Mrs. Luscier was Verne Ray's principal informant for *Lower Chinook Ethnographic Notes* (1938). This photo is from the original owned by Ella Frank of Bay Center, Washington, as published in *Rolls of Certain Indian Tribes* (reprint, 1969). (Courtesy of the Oregon Historical Society, bb010086)

SEVEN

SOCIAL AND POLITICAL ORGANIZATION

Yvonne Hajda

A T the beginning of Euro-American contact, the Lower Columbia River had a relatively rich and diverse resource base and a larger and greater density of population than almost anywhere else in Native North America north of Mexico. Exchanges among people permitted the development of a relatively complex sociopolitical organization. To classify the Lower Columbia as a complex hunting-gathering (or fishing-gathering) society is to assume that other social features depend on that base. The subsistence mode is assumed to limit or allow population numbers and densities required for social organization to develop. Exchanges beyond the local group, however, expand the subsistence base by allowing access to resources available elsewhere.

Sociopolitical organization throughout western Oregon and Washington consisted of relatively settled, autonomous, self-governing local groups linked by kin ties and crosscutting social institutions but without any higher-level organization. Groups such as these have been classified as "tribes," intermediate between "bands" or "simple egalitarian" societies and "advanced chiefdoms" (Sahlins 1968, 1972), or as "rank" societies (Fried 1967:109). As a region, the Lower Columbia, with many small, independent but interdependent groups, consisted of overlapping networks formed by exchanges of people, information, and goods. Within groups, unequal exchanges between higher- and lower-ranked people created bonds of dependency, linking people of differing status.

Social organization can be seen as a response to the needs of a group of people to perpetuate and maintain itself. Socially recognized forms of behavior emerge to accomplish these ends: marriage, living arrangements, and kinship, for instance, become regularized, and beliefs about the rightness of these arrangements develop. Once developed, social organization is not simply a reflex of the environment or a mode of subsistence; rather, it mediates between people and between people and the environment. It channels action in certain directions, but it can be changed because it depends on individual choices.

During the late 18th and early 19th centuries—with the arrival of foreigners and their diseases, trade goods, and cultural practices—the social organization of Native groups of the Lower Columbia went through enormous changes. From first direct contact in 1792 to the beginning of the malaria epidemics in 1830, Indians were a majority of the population and foreigners had to reckon with functioning societies.

TRIBE AND NATION

While tribes were not Native realities, the records so often use the word that it has to be reckoned with. Today, when "tribe" is used for Northwest Coast groups, it refers to a group that shares a language or dialect and a common culture and lives in a particular area, often a watershed (e.g., Suttles 1987). From the remarks of early white observers, it seems certain that, as on the Northwest Coast generally, no political unity existed beyond that of a single village or small group of related villages and that cultural and social bonds cut across language differences and whatever political entities existed. Euro-Americans, however, were not familiar with such situations and attempted to create larger conceptual units. When the ship *Columbia* entered its namesake river in 1792, it anchored in Baker Bay off the village "Chinoak," the village name evidently being the source of the later "tribal" name (Howay 1990:398). Some 150 years later, Emma Luscier, of Chinook descent, said that "Chinook" used to be just one place until the whites came and "spread it all over" (Harrington 1942–43: reel 17, fr. 683). In 1795, Charles Bishop (e.g., 1967:116, 118–19) used "Chinook" to identify a number of villages and for the Columbia River. Lewis and Clark (e.g., 1990:154) referred to a collection of villages as Chinook, as did Nor'wester Alexander Henry in 1814 (1992:700). Most such "tribal" names appear to have originated as village names.

The term "tribe" was loosely applied to nearly any group. In 1796, Bishop (1967) spoke of "Taucum the chief of the Chinnook Tribe," but he also wrote that "Taucum . . . is gone with his tribe a good way to the Northward up Woolquet [Wallacut] River," omitting other Chinook groups (114, 116, 127). His comment about "the Chinnook tribes united" included more than Taucum's group.

In 1805–6, Meriwether Lewis and William Clark attempted to come to grips with what constituted a "tribe" or "nation" on the Lower Columbia. Speaking of people on and near Sauvie Island, they wrote:

> All the tribes in the neighbourhood of Wappatoo [Sauvie] Island, we have considered as Multnomahs; not because they are in any degree subordinate to that nation. . . . they are . . . linked by a similarity of dress and manners, and houses and language, which much more than the feeble restraints of Indian government contribute to make one people. (Allen 1814: 227)

Language differences, however, did not prevent them from grouping Salish-speaking Tillamooks and Chehalis, Lower Chinook-speaking Clatsops and Chinooks, and Upper Chinook Cathlamets and Wahkiakums who "resemble each other as well in persons and dress as in habits and manners" (Lewis and Clark 1990:89, 168, 183–84, 432–33, 437).

After 1811, land-based fur traders also grouped people together who lived around the Lower Columbia. Astorian Alexander Ross (2000) went further than Lewis and Clark, combining not only the groups they listed but also Kalamas, "Cattleputtles," Clatskanies, and Multnomahs as "descended from the same stock" (Ross 2000:87–88). In 1828, HBC Governor George Simpson (1968) concluded that all Indians below The Cascades "may be considered one and the same Nation although speaking different languages" (96).

While Lewis and Clark (1990) sometimes used "tribe" to mean a subdivision of a "nation," as with the Sauvie Island groups, at other times they used either word to refer to the same group or a single village, as with the 14-house "Quath-lah-poh-tle nation" or village and the one-house Nechacolee village or nation (457, 477, 478). Clearly, the village was the salient unit.

HOUSEHOLD AND VILLAGE

The largest sociopolitical unit was the village or local group, consisting of one or more households linked with other households and villages through kinship ties created by marriages outside the units. The permanent or winter house could hold several families. Meriwether Lewis provided the most complete early description of household composition:

> Several families of these people usually reside together in the same room; they appear to be the father & mother and their sons with their son's wives

and children; their provision seems to be in common and the greatest har-mony appears to exist among them. The old man is not always rispected as the head of the family, that duty most commonly devolves on one of the young men. They have seldom more than one wife, yet the plurality of wives is not denied them by their customs. (Lewis and Clark 1990:221–22)

From this it appears that the household was a corporate unit, there was no strict seniority in leadership, the core of the household was a group of males, a wife joined her husband in his family's extended household, and polygyny was practiced.

A "family," as Euro-Americans used the term, seems to have referred to a man and his wife or wives and children. The number of people comprising a family, at least for Lewis and Clark, can be approximated by comparing their estimates of population, houses, and families per house. Four hundred Chinooks in 28 houses and 200 Clatsops in 14 houses averaged 14 per house; upriver at Nechacolee, 100 people in a single house with 7 "apartments" again averaged 14 people per "apartment." Lewis and Clark (1990:218) reported that a house might hold one or two families but that sometimes three or four or more lived in "one room," so a family might have consisted of as few as 4 or 5 or as many as 14 people.

Ross (2000) estimated larger "families." He never saw more than four fires in any house, which meant 80 people, including slaves (98); that is, each family had its own fire, and by his estimate a family consisted of some 20 people. Slaves counted as part of a household, as Lewis and Clark (1990:167) indicated; and, to judge by estimates of population, relatives and other visitors sometimes were present. Each family grouping had its own space on a bed platform, marked off by ridgepole supports and, often, partitions. Fireplaces along the centerline of the floor were used by the nearest family group, as Ross indicated.

The responsibilities of the household head are nowhere spelled out; but because "their provision seems to be in common," he probably directed the acquisition and allocation of resources for the household. He may well have given advice and had a hand in settling disputes as well, but families were otherwise able to do much as they pleased.

The primary division of labor was between men and women, but the distinction was blurred by the existence of slavery. Slaves, whether men or women, did the hardest work. Rich people with many slaves may have done little work of any kind, while the work of the poor was similar to that of slaves. Lewis and Clark (1990) apparently did not distinguish between the work of slaves and that of free people:

> The men of these nations partake of much more of the domestic drudgery than I had at first supposed. they collect and prepare all the fuel, make the fires, assist in cleansing and preparing the fish, and always cook for the strangers who visit them. they also build their houses, construct their canoes, and make all their wooden utensils. the peculiar provence of the woman seems to be to collect roots and manufacture various articles which are prepared of rushes, flags, cedar bark, bear grass or waytape [cedar roots]. the management of the canoe for various purposes seems to be a duty common to both sexes, as also many other [domestic] occupations which with most Indian nations devolves exclusively on the woman. their feasts which they are very fond are always prepared and served by the men. (436)

While women's work seems fairly clear, men's work was said to overlap with it to some extent. In 1811, Astorian Gabriel Franchère (1969) observed that men were seen "more frequently than the women with a needle in their hands" (100). The men may have been slaves. As Simpson (1968) reported: "In Spring Summer & Autumn they are chiefly occupied in Fishing and feasting, their Slaves collect Roots. . . . [and] are made to Fish, hunt, draw Wood & Water in short all the drudgery falls on them" (101, 103). William Clark mentioned that a slave boy offered for sale to the explorers by a Clatsop man was the man's cook, confirming that male slaves were doing "women's work" at least some of the time (Lewis and Clark 1990:360).

While a woman after marriage typically moved out of her home village to join her husband's, a man usually stayed in his father's village. An excellent statement of other possibilities was related in an 1855 letter to Joel Palmer, superintendent of Indian affairs in Oregon:

> The Clackamas Chief enquired of me, where Thos. was, that he the chief had included Thos. and family in the no. of his band. . . . Thos.—the Clackamas Indians, and John the Linn City chief, are all related on their mothers side, and were of the North of the Columbia river about eight miles below the Dalles, on a small stream Thlat-en cat [Klikatat]—Thos.'s father was of the Dalls tribe, and Thos.'s wife of the Kaskade tribe, so you find the relationship, much "mixed up." As Thos. has lived (as suited him) at those places these recognized his right of possession. John, the Linn City Chief says

Thos. right is as good as his (John's). . . . Thos. claims his possessory right with the Linn City Indians although he had lived with me for 3 years and has been permanently in the Willamette since the Kayuse difficulty [1848], and before that time occassionly here and there as suited him. (Jennings 1855)

Thomas's "right of possession," then, was linked to places where he had relatives and where he had lived for a time.

SEASONALITY

The permanent village, where people spent the colder months, was often near a fishing site or other important resources. The site was corporately owned by the village, which might consist of a single house. In 1835, settler John Ball (1835) described some lower Willamette Valley houses as "two hundred feet in length . . . and a whole village live in one house." More often, several houses were grouped together. In 1824–25, Governor Simpson (1968:95) noted that from The Cascades to the coast Indians lived in villages of from 10 to 15 houses, though some might have been larger (Lewis and Clark 1990:478).

Resources—especially the culturally and nutritionally important salmon and other fish—were available only in restricted locations at certain times of the year, but only some of the population resided in those places. To better balance resources and people, two strategies were employed: exchanges and distributions moved resources to people (see ch. 5 in this volume); and families dispersed in warmer weather, leaving the permanent villages to move to one site after another where and when resources were available and returning to the permanent villages as winter approached (Boyd and Hajda 1987). As Ross (2000) put it, "In winter they live in villages, but in Summer rove about from place to place" (98). The widespread network of kin—wider for the rich than for the poor—brought with it rights to use the resources of many places and the ability to be safe while traveling.

Some people near the mouth of the Columbia moved away from the river during the winter, into "the woods" or up smaller streams (McDougall 1999:46; Franchère 1969:92; Bishop 1967:114). Such movement probably accounts for the "large village of 36 houses deserted by the Inds." that William Clark saw at Point Ellice in November 1805 (Lewis and Clark 1990:48). Rather than leaving a permanent village, particularly if it was near a crucial resource site, some stayed home and were joined by others. This was apparently the case on Baker Bay, perhaps to maintain control of important fishing sites or in response to the presence of the fur traders or both. In early January 1814, Nor'wester Alexander Henry (1992) observed:

> The great smoke which now rises from the three Chinook villages denotes the return of these people to their winter quarters, which is usually at this period. They will contrive to augment in numbers daily, as the smelt [eulachon] fishing is approaching fast and then the sturgeon fishing follows, and, as the Spring draws near, the salmon fishing approaches, the natives from the Northward will also bend their course here. (637)

The Fort Astoria journal noted in early February 1812 that Indians who had been on the bay below the fort for the previous three months had just gone upriver to catch eulachon, which had begun to enter the river a few days before (McDougall 1999:70).

Fish runs attracted people to the rivers. In the 1820s, Simpson (1968) reported that "the whole of the Interior population flock to its [Columbia's] banks at the Fishing Season" (94). The Fort Astoria journal (McDougall 1999) noted in late July 1811 that the Chehalis "are all assembled in Baker's Bay for the purpose of catching Sturgeon," and the Chinook chief Concomly said that great numbers of the Indians from the north lived with his people in summer and fall (37, 148).

Fish runs were important, but people moved about for other resources as well. In August and September 1813, for example, a great many people from the area of Oak Point and Sauvie Island were in the vicinity of Fort Astoria drying berries and perhaps for other reasons (McDougall 1999:213, 215). On descending the Columbia in the fall of 1805, Lewis saw one wooden house and 24 temporary structures at Ne-er-cho-k-oo; returning upriver in spring, they saw only the house. The inhabitants explained:

> their relations who were with them last fall usuly visit them at that season for the purpose of hunting deer and Elk and collecting wappetoe and that they had lately returned to the rapids [The Cascades, their permanent home] I presume to prepare for the fishing season. (Lewis and Clark 1991:38)

People from The Cascades often visited "at every season of the year for the purpose of collecting wappetoe" (38). The abandoned house at Nemalquinner near Sauvie Island, Clark wrote, belonged to the "Cush-hooks Nation who reside at the falls of this river [the Willamette] which . . . they make use of when they Come down to the Vally to gather Wappato" (59). The inhabitants had recently returned to Willamette Falls to fish.

NETWORKS: MARRIAGE AND KIN

Villages and households were linked through marriage and kinship. Bilateral kinship prevailed on the Greater Lower Columbia, as it did throughout the central part of the Northwest Coast culture area. Descent traced bilaterally, through both parents, creates a series of overlapping kindreds: each person's set of parents, siblings, cousins, and so on differs to some extent from everyone else's. Unilineal societies, while recognizing relationships through the other parent, trace "legal" kin through mother or father only and so tend to develop mutually exclusive lineages and clans. The networks of kin created in bilateral societies thus tend to be more extensive than those found in unilineal societies.

On the Lower Columbia, a marriage was an alliance between two families not known to be related. The alliance was ratified by an exchange of valuables such as slaves, canoes, furs and hides, shells, and imported beads and metal objects. The woman's family generally returned about as many valuables to the groom's family as they had received (Franchère 1969:103; Cox 1957:172; Boas 1894:251). For the poor, such exchanges were likely to be minimal. A wife typically moved in with her husband and his family (that is, residence was typically virilocal and patrilocal), but a man without resources might join his wife's family.

A man could take more than one wife, but the goods required to cement several alliances probably limited the practice to the wealthy. Charles Bishop (1967), captain of the English trader *Ruby*, which wintered on the Columbia in 1795–96, commented: "These people have as many Wives as they can Purchase or Provide for, thus Taucum has ten" (127). Plural marriages probably increased for some as the influx of foreign goods enriched certain men. When they did occur, all the wives lived in the husband's house.

Since people in a village tended to be relatives, spouses usually came from different local group; that is, village exogamy (outmarriage) was the rule. Differences of language or "tribe" were irrelevant. The poor probably married close to home; but for those of high rank, marriages might link distant places, creating a regional system of class or rank. The Chinook chief Concomly had at least five wives: two from upriver Chinookan groups, one from a Lower Chinook group, one from the Chehalis, and one from the Willapa (Lewis and Murakami 1923:75–78). In 1795, a young chief, probably Quinault, was on the Columbia to arrange a marriage with the daughter of the Chinook chief Shelathwell (Bishop 1967:119–20). After a marriage, exchanges of gifts and visits between the families, which might include seasonal shifts of residence, helped maintain ties.

In addition to links created by his own marriages, Concomly had contacts that included Grays Harbor, where a brother was chief (Douglas 1904:253, 333). One daughter was married to Coalpo, a Chinook chief at the village by Fort Astoria; another was married first to Duncan McDougall, head of the fort, and then to Kiesno, chief of the Cathlacumups village near Fort Vancouver. Several others were married to other Euro-American fur traders. Few of Kiesno's ties are documented, but in addition to his link to Concomly and relatives at The Cascades, two of his brothers-in-law were Tualatin Kalapuya and Clackamas (Jacobs 1945:160–3; Landerholm 1956:86, 92).

Documented marriage ties reveal that the Greater Lower Columbia regional network comprised, at a minimum, the Quinault to the Alsea on the coast, upriver to The Cascades, along the lower Willamette and Clackamas Rivers, and groups bordering those along the rivers (Hajda 1984:123–32, 151–52, 327–33; see also Suttles 1987, 1990:12–14). Certainly by 1812, if not long before, Salish-speaking Chehalis were intermarried with the Chinooks, as the Clatsops were with the Tillamooks (Seton 1993:92; Boas 1894:273).

The network probably extended farther. The distribution of Chinook-style head flattening, for example, characterized free people of both sexes as far upriver as The Dalles. Beyond that and in neighboring interior groups, some women with flattened heads might be seen (Lewis and Clark 1988:345). Parents might have flattened a female infant's head to reduce the chances of her being seized as a slave, to increase her chances of marrying a richer Chinookan-speaking man, or both. To encounter another flat-headed person, then, was to meet a possible relative or a relative of a relative.

STATUSES

Freedom, wealth, and ancestry marked off statuses within a hierarchy of chief, commoner, and slave, while the status of shaman (or "Indian doctor") was marked by a special kind of knowledge.

Chiefs

Euro-Americans in the Pacific Northwest and elsewhere referred to certain Indian men as "chiefs," but they were not talking about tribal chiefs. Lewis and Clark, for example, named six chiefs for the Chinook proper, one for every 67 people and four to five houses. The numbers for the Clatsops were similar (Lewis and Clark 1990:154–55, 416). These men were, at most, heads of villages or at least heads of households or extended families. Meriwether Lewis described the chief's position this way:

> These families when associated form nations or bands of nations each acknoledging the authority of it's own chieftain who dose not appear to be heriditary, nor his power to extend further than a mear reprimand for any improper act of an individual; the creation of a chief depends upon the upright deportment of the individual & his ability and disposition to render service to the community; and his authority or the deference paid him is in exact equilibrio with the popularity or voluntary esteem he has acquired among the individuals of his band or nation. (222)

One Astorian commented that each village had a chief who "does not seem to exercise much authority over the others" (Franchère 1969:102), while another claimed that the principal chief "possesses an arbitrary power without any positive check, so that if he conceive a liking to anything belonging to his subjects, be it a wife or daughter, he can take it without infringing the law; but he must, nevertheless, pay for what he takes" (Ross 2000:88). A third claimed that "most generally the power of deciding controversies and of punishing offenses is entrusted to the chief" (Stuart 1935:11). It is possible that as the wealth of chiefs increased through control of trade, contact with fur traders also increased their power. Certainly, Lewis and Clark "made chiefs" by giving medals to men they saw as outstanding. Those who would control trade with Euro-Americans gained wealth and influence and were regarded as chiefs by the traders. The policy of the Hudson's Bay Company was to seek out indigenous men whose interests seemed to dovetail with the company's, dealing with local groups through these men as representative of their communities (Harmon 1998:28).

As Lewis and Clark indicated, chieftainship did not pass automatically from father to son; several potential candidates might be on hand (see also Stuart 1935:10). Such leaders were generally members of a high-ranking family—sons, brothers, cousins, or nephews of a chief. Controversies might arise among the claimants or their supporters. Missionary John Frost wrote of hearing gunfire from the north side of the Columbia in the summer of 1842, when after the death of Concomly's successor, Chenamus, the claim to the Chinook chieftainship by Chenamus's son was contested by a "royal" rival (Lee and Frost 1968:97–98). Ranald MacDonald, Concomly's grandson, recalled that some of the old people considered him the heir after Concomly died in 1830, as did two Hudson's Bay Company men (Lewis and Murakami 1923:23, 78).

The choice of one candidate or another, as Meriwether Lewis observed, would depend on his "upright deportment" and "his ability and disposition to render service to the community" (Lewis and Clark 1990:222). One way this was done was to act as a center for the redistribution of food (and perhaps other goods as well). In 1792, Thomas Manby (1992) wrote about the old man who had guided William Broughton's vessel up the Columbia and "who appeared of some consequence," supplied them with fish and other food; he had "sufficient authority to demand part of the Sport every Hunter of Fisherman had met with" (199). Much later, in the fall of 1840, before the autumn salmon season began, Reverend Frost recorded that a Clatsop hunter had managed to kill an elk and "according to custom, the most of it was taken to the lodge of the chief. Here a feast was prepared and the whole clan invited to partake." No doubt such redistributions contributed to the "popularity or voluntary esteem he has acquired among the individuals of his band or nation" (Lee and Frost 1968:283).

Fur traders emphasized wealth, followers, and contacts as chiefly prerequisites. Simpson (1968), for instance, said that Concomly was a "principal man" of the Chinooks because he was "the most wealthy having a number of Slaves and a large stock of Hyaques [dentalia shells] Beads and other property" (97). Wealth enabled a man to trade for slaves and acquire more wives, with their contacts to outside resource areas. In 1812, Astorian Robert Stuart (1935) noted that "he who exceeds in the number of his wives, male children and Slaves is elected" (10).

So-called chiefs appear to have differed in rank. Bishop named five chiefs (Lewis and Clark also named four of them 10 years later), of whom he said that Taucum was "chief of the Cinnook Tribe," Shelathwell and Concomly were "the two chiefs next to Taucum," and Telemmeks and Chinini were evidently among "several inferior chiefs." A visitor from Quinault "was but a small chief" (Bishop 1967:116). Lewis and Clark (1990:154) still ranked Taucum ("Stockhome") first, Concomly and Shelathwell ("Sil-lar-le-wit") second and third, "Nor-car-te" fourth, and Chinini fifth. They did not mention Telemmeks, but later referred to Delashelwilt.

As a chief acquired or lost wealth and prestige, his rank would change, and the fur trade seems to have accelerated such changes. Concomly, for example, rose from secondary chief to "principal man of the Chinook tribe," one of the "three Chiefs or principal Indians" on the Lower Columbia, according to George Simpson (1968:86, 97), evidently due to his ability to capitalize on his location at the mouth of the Columbia and his access to foreign fur traders. Early on, he and Shelathwell had "traded" (raided is more accurate) with upriver people for furs and hides, once bringing in some "war dresses" with musketball holes in them (Bishop 1967:118–19, 121–22). He married one daughter to Coalpo, the chief located near Fort Astoria, and several to the Euro-American traders, including Duncan McDougall. After McDougall left the country, that daughter was married to Kiesno, the chief near Fort Vancouver who Simpson referred to as "next man to Concomly in the River." After Fort Vancouver was established, Concomly and Kiesno nearly went to war over control of the flow of furs (Simpson 1968:253). Access to the goods supplied by the forts was facilitated by those marriages. Concomly attempted to control the flow of furs from interior and upriver groups to the foreign traders by telling each side of the hostile intentions of the other (Ross 2000:77–78).

Commoners

Nothing is really known of free people who were not considered nobles or royalty. Bishop (1967) referred to the "inferiour people," and distinguished "Chiefs and the free people" from slaves (116, 127). Lewis and Clark (1990) presumably included free commoners when they referred, for instance, to "Comowooll the Clatsop Chief and 12 men women & children of his nation" (342). Some of those commoners probably included poor relations of the chief or the nobility, dependent on their higher-ranking kin for support and protection in return for labor and services. Some may have had slave ancestry. The descriptions do not generally distinguish between commoners and slaves.

Slaves

Here the sources have more to say. Slaves might have been acquired through raids on distant groups, among which relatives would not be found (Bishop

1967:127, Stuart 1935:11), but they were more often acquired through trade with neighboring groups for valuables such as beads or furs or through the exchange of valuables at a marriage, payment of a debt, gambling, and so on. Most slaves were said to originate in areas south or east of the Lower Columbia (Franchère 1969:102; Lewis and Clark 1990:365, 476; Bishop 1967:127; Stuart 1935:11), areas in which flattening the heads of freeborn infants was not practiced. By prohibiting slaves from practicing head deformation, free persons could be distinguished from slaves by their appearance. Some slaves, however, came from the north, probably increasingly so as traffic between forts accelerated (Gibbs 1877:189; Ross 2000:92; Smith 1901:255–56). Those people may have been commoners, who were less likely to have flattened heads than was true on the Columbia, or they had heads deformed in styles other than the Chinook (see Hajda 2005).

Slaves were originally foreigners and always outsiders. If they had been captured as adults, they spoke languages other than Chinookan. Even if they had been captured as children or born to local slaves and so spoke the local language, they were social outsiders. Though slaves lived with a family, Lewis and Clark's rosy view that they were treated very much like "their own children" (1990:365) has to be viewed skeptically. They did all the hard work, as Simpson (1968) said, adding that they

> form the principal article of taffick on the whole of this Coast and constitute the greater part of their Riches . . . they feed in common with the Family of their proprietors and intermarry with their own class, but lead a life of misery, indeed I conceive a Columbia Slave to be the most unfortunate Wretch in existence; the proprietors exercise the most absolute authority over them even to Life and Death and on the most triffling fault wound and maim them shockingly. (101)

When slaves became ill, they were neglected; when they died, the corpses were tossed in the water or the woods (Franchère 1969:102; Simpson 1968:101; Bishop 1967:127; Ross 2000:97). A few slaves were apparently adopted or freed. One Astorian said that an occasional favorite slave might even be allowed to flatten an infant's head (Ross 2000:99–100). If that happened, another claimed that the former slave could marry a free person and his children "by undergoing the flattening process, melt down into the great mass of the community" (Cox 1957:166).

Shamans

Many individuals had special abilities for one or another task, credited to the acquisition of guardian spirits who bestowed the power to do these things. Shamans were always referred to as men, but Ross (2000) said that both men and women might be an "Indian doctor" who relied on "roots and herbs" for curing (96–97). Shamans had guardian spirits that permitted them to use their power to cure disease or, on occasion, to harm others. Some might be chiefs (Scouler 1905:165, 275). It is possible, though undocumented, that slaves might have acquired (or had before capture) spirit power that enabled them to become shamans, either turning over their earnings to their owners or perhaps gaining freedom in this way (Ray 1938:53). One Astorian said that shamans were paid only if the sick persons recovered (Stuart 1935:9), but another said they were paid no matter what the outcome (Franchère 1969:103). Simpson (1968) claimed that they "live by their profession" (100).

Power could be used for curing or for sorcery. Simpson said that the shamans were "much respected by all classes who never venture to question their skill and conceive that they have the power of conjuring or praying them to Death at pleasure and even from a distance" (100). In 1825 and 1826, Dr. John Scouler (1905) mentioned two instances in which it was suspected that deaths were caused by a shaman's sorcery. In one case, two of Concomly's sons were treated by a neighboring chief who "pretended to great skill in medicine, & cured diseases by singing over his patients." They both died, and the "medicine chief" was accused of using "enchantment" to cause their deaths (165–66). In the other instance, a chief who died had eaten camas six months before at the house of a Cowlitz chief "who was famed for his skill in medicine." The shaman was killed in retaliation. Scouler said that such suspicions frequently led to wars (278–80).

CONFLICTS AND CONFLICT RESOLUTION

Franchère (1969) observed that "each village having its particular chief, it sometimes happens that quarrels occur among them which usually end in an exchange of presents befitting the nature of the offense" (104–5). In general, insult or injury, from accidental breaking of a dentalium shell to murder, had to be settled by a payment of valuables. If the payment was considered inadequate, then the conflict escalated. In a society where wealth was an important measure of status, it could be expected that insults and injuries might be perceived where none was intended, as Euro-Americans often found out (e.g., Bishop 1967:122–23). Between villages, linked by kinship and marriage but with no overall political structure, a dispute not settled by the proper payment might lead to what Euro-Americans called war.

Several intraregional "wars" were recorded. In 1813, there was a battle between Kiesno's Cathlacumups and the Tillamooks and Clatsops over a murder, with Concomly as mediator, since he was related to the chiefs on both sides (McDougall 1999:206–9). In this case, by the time Concomly arrived, the Cathlacumups had not produced enough goods to satisfy their opponents and the battle had already begun. In 1814, there was an interlocking series of disputes between the Chinooks and Clatsops, the Chinooks and Chehalis, and the Chehalis with unnamed people to their north. In an 1814 conflict between the Cowlitz and Kiesno (Henry 1992:700–1), the Cathlacumups again offered an inadequate payment to his antagonists (Henry 1992:715). Suspected ensorcellment was the cause of war in two cases in 1825 (Scouler 1905:165–66, 276–77).

Franchère (1969) described what a "war" entailed (see also Simpson 1968:97–98):

> if the transgression is very serious, a murder for instance (which is rare) or the kidnapping of a woman (which is frequent), a battle ensues, each side having paid a number of young men to come to its aid. They let it be known what day they will go to attack the other enemy's village (differing in this respect from the barbarous custom of other North American tribes who fall upon their enemies by night, massacring men, women, and children). These on the contrary arrive in their war canoes, paddled by the women, who follow their husbands in these encounters. Having arrived near the enemy's village they begin to parley; both sides do their best to effect a reconciliation and they often succeed. If they are unable to agree they start the action, which never lasts long, for as soon as one or two fall, those who have lost them admit defeat and retreat. If it is the villagers who are defeated, the conquerors do not leave until they have been given presents. (104–5)

Stuart (1935) wrote: "they seldom make prisoners, but when this is the case, they are always well treated and never reduced to slavery" (11). Only if a settlement could not be reached, even after a battle, would a night attack be planned (Henry 1992:716).

The carefully circumscribed nature of the hostilities resulted from the need to preserve the network of relationships among local groups. One observer reported: "The spring of the year seems to be the season wherein all their national disputes are adjusted, so as to allow them full scope during the salmon fishery to provide for the ensuing winter, without any molestation from their neighbours" (Henry 1992:716).

CHANGE

During the years after Euro-Americans first entered the Columbia River, new people with unfamiliar customs and foreign goods became established in the area. First Fort Astoria and then Fort Vancouver became centers of settlement as well as trade, attracting Indians from a greater distance. Many traders formed alliances with Native women and had families with them. Still, Native people were in the majority, and their society retained most of its familiar form.

Beginning in 1830, devastating epidemics of malaria killed some 90 percent of those in areas around Fort Vancouver, and somewhat fewer at the mouth of the river. Chief Concomly died, as did most of Kiesno's people. Earlier disease outbreaks had had an impact, but none had been so destructive. Some villages, such as those on Sauvie Island, were entirely depopulated; remnants of others joined together in new groups, as was the case at Wakanasisi near Fort Vancouver. Indians from other areas began to move in to take over the places where their relatives had lived.

Before 1830, no Euro-American women lived in the area, and fur traders took Indian wives and raised mixed-blood children. In the mid-1830s, missionaries and their families arrived, and waves of American settlers with their families appeared in the early 1840s. Previously, Indian customs and social arrangements had prevailed, but they were being replaced by different values and traditions. As the decade progressed, local people were increasingly being forced off their land. Treaty negotiations to legitimize land claims and establish reservations took place in the 1850s.

Some Native people, such as those in southwest Washington and northwest Oregon, were never included in the treaties. Some joined relatives on reservations, but others remained in their old territories, though they were overrun by white settlers. Now under the control of the American legal system, Indians were often powerless as their social organization gradually disintegrated. Slavery persisted for a long time—and its stigma even longer—

but it eventually died out. The first American farmers in the region some-times bought slaves from the Chinooks (Clark 1927:1:57; Davenport 1885:3; Hussey 1967:117), as slavery was still an unsettled question in the United States. In spite of these changes, many people remembered their ancestral connections and maintained ties with their relatives. They remembered the old ways and, to the extent possible, continued to carry out old practices.

EIGHT

CHINOOKAN ORAL LITERATURE

Dell Hymes and William R. Seaburg

Most of our knowledge of Lower Chinookan oral literature comes from three talented Native consultants interviewed by anthropologists between 1890 and 1936. In the summers of 1890 and 1891, Franz Boas worked with Charles Cultee (Kathlamet, Clatsop, Kwalhioqua; d. ca. 1897), who dictated Chinook stories as well as Kathlamet myths and tales. In the introduction to *Chinook Texts,* Boas (1894) noted that his work was facilitated by "Cultee's remarkable intelligence. After he had once grasped what I wanted, he explained to me the grammatical structure of the sentences by means of examples, and elucidated the sense of difficult periods" (6)—all through the medium of Chinuk Wawa, the regional trade language (see Boas 1901; Boxberger and Taylor 1986; Cole 1999). For two months in July-September 1929 and for two additional months in January-March 1930, Melville Jacobs (1958–59) worked with his remarkable Clackamas consultant Victoria Howard (Clackamas, Molale; d. 1930). Mrs. Howard "exhibited fine humor, sharp intelligence, and excellent diction in both Clackamas and English" (1; see also Senier 2001). Both the Cultee and Howard collections were recorded by hand, first in the Native language and then translated into English. Between 1931 and 1936, Emma Millet Luscier (Kathlamet, Lower Cowlitz; d. 1954) dictated a handful of Chinook texts to Verne F. Ray (1938) as part of his fieldwork for *Lower Chinook Ethnographic Notes* (see McChesney 1969). Tragically, the three collections undoubtedly represent only a fragment of Lower Chinookan stories that once constituted a vigorous oral tradition.

Like Native stories throughout the Northwest, Chinookan stories were told to instruct, to caution or warn, to explain, to validate, and, above all, to entertain. Each myth or tale was told for multiple purposes, depending on the storyteller, the audience, and the occasion of its telling. The proper time to relate myths—maybe tales, too—was at night and only during winter. Telling stories at the wrong time had real-world consequences for Northwest peoples. Myths told out of season, for example, could delay the onset of spring, and the Upper Chehalis reportedly stopped telling stories as soon as spring arrived "in order to make the spring last a long time" (Adamson 1934:xii).

Many oral traditions in the Northwest linguistically differentiated myths from other kinds of stories (Miller 1989:125). The Clackamas word for myth is *k'ani*, and the Chinook and Kathlamet employ closely related forms. Mrs. Howard described a Clackamas chronological sequence that began with a long Myth Age, followed by probably much shorter Transitional Times—including the time when the people were coming soon—followed by "a brief modern period whose actors and events were of kinds which modern people experienced" (Jacobs 1958–59:195). The Nehalem Tillamook peoples to the south of the Clatsop Chinookans acknowledged a similar succession of time: the Myth Age, the era of transformation, and the era of "relatively recent history"—that is, a time usually described as "before the nineteenth century" (Jacobs 1990:ix).

SOCIOCULTURAL CONTENT AND THEMES

Jacobs was one of the first folklorists in the Northwest to seriously study the cultural meanings of Chinookan myths and tales. In what could be called a "projection" theory of folklore, he hypothesized that a story's content highlighted "points of stress in the society." In other words, "events and social relationships portrayed in an oral literature connected with relationships which were unsatisfactorily resolved by social structure and custom" (Jacobs 1959b:130). This theory blends the image of a movie projector onto a film screen with the psychodynamic concept of projection (1959b; see also Jacobs 1958–59:127–30).

Jacobs argued that not every aspect of a people's culture received expression in its oral literature. Some topics or themes were stressed more than others, and some were relatively ignored or omitted altogether. In the Clackamas collection (1958–59), social relationship themes receive repeated attention, including relations between siblings, husband and wife or wives, in-laws, high-class and lower-class peoples, and the like (132). Actor personality traits, primarily inferred from characters' behavior, are another facet of the literature. Jacobs (1959a:211–19) listed more than 150 male actors in the 64 Clackamas myths and tales, although relatively few appeared in more than one story. Major male actor personalities include Coyote, Blue Jay, Skunk, Grizzly, Coon, Crane, and Thunder, among others. Over 100 female characters were projected onto the myth and tale screen, including Grizzly, Seal, Bear, Meadowlark, Crow, Greyback Louse, and Sun. Scores of other named and unnamed minor actors appear briefly and function as little more than plot expediters.

Other sociocultural themes emphasized in the Clackamas collection include humor, value ideals, worldview, and songs. Some topics were relatively ignored or omitted from the Clackamas folktale screen, including shamanism and religious rites—for example, First Fish ceremonies and spirit power acquisition; ceremonial rites, such as a girl's puberty ceremony or marriage negotiations; and economic activities.

A complementary approach to Jacobs's analysis is in Dell Hymes's retranscription of the English translations of Chinookan texts into ethnopoetically structured lines, verses, stanzas, scenes, and acts. Hymes argues that the traditional narrative style content is often at least partly expressed through rhetorical form and organization.

Stylistic Features

Chinookan oral literature shares many if not all nonlinguistic features of style with other Native oral traditions in the Northwest. By processes of diffusion, including intermarriage with other groups, extensive trade networks, and the sharing of common resource sites, stylistic features of Northwest oral literatures spread throughout the southern Northwest Coast and Plateau. Jacobs (1972) lists 21 classes of areal stylistic features.

STYLIZED STORY OPENINGS AND CLOSINGS

Chinookan myths use a relatively small selection of stylized introductory phrases, such as "Coyote and Skunk lived there" (Clackamas), "There were Blue-Jay and Robin" (Chinook), and "One day the Crab and her elder sister, the Seal, were hungry" (Kathlamet). In some Coyote myths, a proper opening might describe Coyote moving about—that is, "Coyote was coming. He came to Gōt'át (*gut'át*)" (Chinook). Introductory phrases like these frame the narrative by introducing the leading actors of the drama. Other Native language versions of myths in the Northwest use opening phrases analogous to the Chinook ones. Typical openings include: "There were Crane and his son Eagle" (Takelma, Rogue Valley); "A house was there; Coyote, indeed, was traveling about all by himself" (Takelma); and "They were living in one house" (Alsea, Oregon Coast).

Many Chinookan stories also use, although not consistently, stylized closings or ending words or phrases, such as "Myth myth; tomorrow we shall have good weather" (Chinook and Kathlamet) or "Myth myth" (Kathlamet and Clackamas). Another form has a myth actor announcing the way things will be in the future, when the people (i.e., Indians) come into the land. The Chinook narrative, "The Panther Myth," ends this way:

> Now [the panther] took the woman at her arm. He carried her out of the house and shook her so that all her flesh fell down. He threw her down and said: "Your name shall be Chicken-hawk. Henceforth you shall not make chiefs unhappy. When you see a snake you shall eat it. My name will be Panther."

Clackamas Transitional Times stories might end this way: "Now the people are very close by." For comparison, Takelma texts provide a nice example of a stylized, patterned ending phrase: " 'Tis finished. Go gather and eat your baap-seeds" (Sapir 1909a). Jacobs (1972) noted that stylized introductions "displayed much greater similarity over the region" (13) and were more common than stylized endings, although he was not sure why.

PATTERN NUMBERS

The dominant overt pattern number for the Chinookans was five and its multiples, although two-patterns were also present. Thus, a story might describe five siblings or fellow villagers acting out five-pattern scene repetitions, in sequence from oldest to youngest, with the youngest and smartest actor succeeding where his companions had failed. In other literatures of the region, such as that of the Sahaptins of the Middle Columbia, the successful youngest actor would have revived his dead companions by stepping over their bones five times.

Chinookan oral literatures contain scores or more of recurring motifs shared with all oral literatures in the region (Jacobs preferred "plot expeditor" or "plot device" to "motif"). Motifs straddle the boundary between content and style, and Jacobs (1972) described them as slices of "expressive content that functioned primarily in a stylistic way" (14). He (1959a) called the Clackamas motifs "explanatory elements" (232–50):

- bride comes: an unmarried young woman travels forth on her own initiative to a marriageable man's house and becomes his wife.

- excrement as advisor: Coyote's "excrements" serve as his spirit-power advisors, who are often verbally and sometimes physically mistreated by Coyote.

- monster killed from within: various myth-era monsters are physically invaded by less powerful actors, who usually manage to kill their adversaries by cutting out their hearts.

- nongenital conception: the Clackamas motifs of oral impregnation join an imaginative host of regional-wide motifs of conception by other-than-genital means (Midge Dodge [2005] identified approximately 50 different nongenital conception motifs from the Northwest Coast and Plateau areas).

- arrow-chain ladder to Sky Country: people ascend to the Sky Country by means of arrows shot into the sky, one notched into the back of another, forming a scalable ladder.

- child picks out unknown father: only the biological child is able to identify its biological father.

- the explanation for Robin's red breast and food habits.

DESCRIPTIONS OF NATURE

Descriptions of natural surroundings are sparse to almost nonexistent, unless important for the plot action. As myth actors travel from one village to another in a story, we do not find gratuitous mention of weather conditions, cloud formations, or descriptions of flora and fauna, the condition of the trail, and the like. Such detail is often found in Native stories dictated in English rather than the Native language.

Unless required by the plot, reference to movement and travel often involve little more than "she left," "she went along," "she arrived there." Virtually nothing is learned about the journey. Such extraneous details would have been considered stylistically unaesthetic.

REFERENCES TO MOODS, FEELINGS, AND PERSONALITY

An actor's moods and feelings often are deduced from plot action rather than expressed in words or phrases. In the same way, knowledge of an actor's personality traits must be deduced from plot action and social relationships. Typically, a headman is not said to be knowledgeable or generous and a shaman is not described as powerful or bad. Such conclusions are gleaned from the behavior of the actors. As Jacobs (1972) summarized: "All the evidence points to an extreme of laconicism in depiction of action, movement, travel, feelings, relationships, and personalities, with great speed in plot action" (16).

DIALOGUE

A stylistic feature not listed in Jacobs's 1972 inventory but studied by Hymes, Seaburg, and others is dialogue or constructed speech. One difference between a story that is told and one that is performed is the presence of dialogue—both within a character (interior monologue) and between characters. Dialogue is an important involvement strategy for drawing the audience into the story, helping them experience the artistic performance of the narrative.

SONGS

Like some other features of style, songs straddle the murky divide between expressive content and style. Reasons for songs varied, according to Jacobs (ca. 1971), "from expression of affection to declamation of aggression; from confirmation of relationship to a supernatural to mockery of another myth actor." Songs probably were stylistically more integral to precontact myths and tales than they were to stories performed by 20th-century acculturated storytellers. Only a few visiting anthropologists in the Northwest carefully noted song texts or musical structure; Jacobs (1958–59) recorded some from Mrs. Howard.

Tale-Types

By tale-type we mean a basic plot (structure or sequence) that recurs as a recognizable narrative unit (variations) from culture to culture. Chinookan oral traditions shared a number of tale-types with regional oral literatures, such as the five abstracted below:

- Panther and Lynx (myth): Older Panther hunts while younger Lynx tends the fire. While playing, Lynx lets the fire go out and steals a firebrand from the five Grizzly Bears living across the river. One by one, the Grizzlies retaliate by attacking Panther because of the stolen fire. Each time Panther is almost killed, Lynx breaks a Grizzly's legs with an ax. Finally, all of the Grizzlies are killed and their house is burned. Panther abandons Lynx because of the trouble his negligence has caused.

- Black Bear and Grizzly Bear (myth): Black Bear warns her children of her impending murder by Grizzly Bear. Black Bear's oldest child kills Grizzly's children to avenge her death, and Grizzly is killed in her attempts to pursue and kill Black Bear's children.

- They Deserted the Mean Boy (tale): A mean boy who mistreats other children is abandoned by his parents and fellow villagers. While fishing, he encounters a water supernatural, who becomes his wife. She magically creates a large house filled with quantities of food and gives birth to two sons. Hearing of the boy's good fortune, the villagers attempt to return to the village but drown in a storm created by the boy's wife. Feeling guilty for the storm her husband has forced her to create, she leaves him and returns to the water. The father and sons metamorphose into mountain creatures.

- Raccoon and his Father's Mother (myth): A hungry Raccoon rejects the food his grandmother offers him and instead consumes all of her stored acorns. His grandmother punishes him with a partly burned stick that produces Raccoon's black stripes. Raccoon flees to berry bushes, followed by his repentant grandmother. He chokes her with a ball of mashed berries and thorns, and she transforms into a pheasant. Raccoon encounters and kills through trickery a succession of four Grizzly Bears. The fifth Grizzly outwits Raccoon and announces his future status as a mere raccoon who will no longer murder people.

- Coyote and Skunk (myth): "Coyote ties his reluctant younger brother Skunk's musk sac and successively calls out to Doe, Buck, Horned Buck, and Elk to help him carry Skunk outside, on the pretext that Skunk is dying from spirit-power illness. Each time Skunk discharges musk, an animal faints; Coyote kills and devours each one before Skunk revives.

The fifth and last animal, perhaps Grizzly, kills Coyote and decrees that Skunks will be harmless in the future" (Jacobs 1959a:576).

PERFORMANCE

No one has conveniently assembled the many verbal features of Chinookan narrative performance. Those mentioned here include, in no particular order, archaic myth-era words and phrases; puns; onomatopoeia; falsetto, high monotone, and other vocal mannerisms; stylized singing; stylized laughter; a past tense verbal prefix reflecting the story's placement in the distant past; diminutive and augmentative consonant symbolism; rhetorical lengthening; stylized phrases such as "I do not know how long a time"; and stylized repetition.

A Clackamas Coyote myth, "Coyote Went around the Land," illustrates several verbal features of an onomatopoetic morpheme, stylized repetition, rhetorical lengthening, and dialogue and internal monologue, used widely in oral literatures throughout the Northwest. In this excerpt, Coyote meets a man who farts with every step he takes. Coyote talks the man into trading anuses so Coyote can walk in a similarly distinctive fashion.

> Then he [Coyote] went along, he broke wind *p'u* (it sounded) as he went,
> he broke wind *p'u p'u p'u p'u*. "Oh dear me!" he thought, "this is quite nice."
> And so he went along. Soon afterwards as he was on his way he saw a deer.
> He thought, "I shall kill it." He approached it stealthily (but) he broke wind
> *p'u p'u*. He said to it (to his noisy anus) in vain, "Be still! I am trying to kill
> a deer." He moved just a little, (a loud) *p'u*. . . . it sounded. And that deer ran
> away. "Hm," he thought. "Had I had my own anus, I would have killed the
> deer." (Jacobs 1958–59:94–95)

In his transcriptions of Howard's texts, Jacobs (1958–59) paid especially close attention to characters' meaningful modulations of voice, including rising and falling tones, as suggested in these examples:

> "Hm!" (growl of anger) she replied to him.

> "Oh no!" (in a pained tone).

> "Oh! (falling tone implying[,] Isn't that nice, I'm glad) younger sister!"

None of these features of Clackamas verbal art has yet to be carefully noted or systematically studied.

Nonverbal features of performance included a storyteller's gestures and dance movements and facial expressions and required postural and other responses by both the storyteller and the audience. Such nonverbal aspects of performance are either poorly documented or undocumented for the Chinookans, as they are for most Northwest Native groups. The ethnographic literature does offer information on storytelling etiquette, especially for children. Sleeping during a myth recital, for example, was proscribed for Upper Chehalis children (Adamson 1934:xii–xiii), the Skokomish peoples of the Hood Canal area (Elmendorf 1960:430), and the Wishram Chinookans (Sapir 1909b:189). During Nehalem Tillamook (Jacobs 1990:vii) and Upper Chehalis (Adamson 1934:xii–xiii) storytelling sessions, children were cautioned to lie down or recline. Among the Santiam Kalapuyans (Jacobs 1945:81), they could sit but not stand during myth narrations. In all three groups, failure to observe proper storytelling posture resulted in becoming humpbacked. In many areas of the Northwest, audience members were required to utter frequent signals of continued attention throughout the narrative recital, words often loosely translated as meaning "we are listening."

THE SHAPE OF ORAL NARRATIVE

All oral traditions, it seems, organize narratives, not in terms of paragraphs but in terms of lines and sets of lines (Hymes 2004; 2003). This is true in narratives in Kathlamet, Clackamas, and Shoalwater Chinook. Probably the best known of Charles Cultee's Shoalwater narratives is "The First Ship Seen by the Clatsop" (Boas 1894:275–78). Here is an English translation in lines and verses.

THE FIRST SHIP SEEN BY THE CLATSOP

He was dead, that one old woman's son.   [i] (A)
    She wailed all the time.
One year she wailed all the time.
    and she became silent.
Now a long time,   5
    and she went.
        There to the slough at Seaside she went.
        There she stayed all the time at Neacoxie,
        and she returned.

She came,   (B)
    she came,
        she came,
            she returned [there] to the beach.
            She nearly reached Clatsop.

Now she saw something.   (C) 15
She thought, "A whale."
Nearly she reached it.
Now two spruce trees stood upright near her.
She thought,
    "Oh! Behold it is not a whale."   20
    "Behold it is a whale."
    "Behold a monster."

She reached that thing lying there.   (D)
Now all outside it was copper. [thus]
Now ropes were all tied to it at those spruce trees.   25
    and (it was) full of iron.

Then a bear came out.   (E)
He was on that thing,
    that thing lying there.
        Just like a bear it looked.   30
Behold! His face was that of a person.

Then she went home.   [ii] (A)
Then she remembered her son.
Now she cried.
She said, "Oh! That son of mine.   35
    He is dead, that son of mine,
        And what is told about in tales has landed."
She nearly reached the town.
She cried.

[—]"Ah! A crying person comes.   (B) 40
Perhaps she has been struck."
The people made themselves ready.

They took their arrows.
They took all their arrows.

"Well, listen," an old man said   45
Then the people listened.

Now she kept saying,   (C)
   "That son of mine is dead
     and what is told about in tales has landed."
Then the people said,   50
   "What may it be?"
Then they went to meet her,
   those people ran.
She was spoken to,
   "What is it?"   55
"Ah, something lies around the point.
   There are two bears maybe,
     or people maybe."

Then the people ran.   [iii] (A)
Then that something lying there was reached.
Now those people held them—   60
   something or other,
     it was two buckets of copper.

Now that one arrived at them first.   (B)
Then again one arrived.
Now thus the person did to his mouth.
Now they were given those buckets.   65
Those buckets had lids.

Thus it was done to them,   (C)
   they pointed inland,
     they were sent for water.

Then those two persons ran inland.   [iv] (A)   70
At a log
   and they hid themselves.

Again they returned,
    they ran toward the sea.

One climbed up,   (B) 75
    he entered it.
        He went down into that ship.
He looked about the interior of the ship,
    it was full of boxes, that ship.
He found brass buttons,   80
    strings that long [half a fathom].

He went outside.   (C)
He intended to call his relatives,
    Already something that lay there was set afire.
He jumped down there.   85

Now there were two persons below.   (D)
That something burned.
Now it all burned,
    that something burned just as fat.

There they gathered that iron.   (E) 90
They gathered that copper,
The Clatsop gathered that brass.

Then all the people learned about it.   [v] (A)
Those two persons were taken to the Clatsop chief.
Then their chief said at one of their towns,
    "I shall keep that one with me."   95

The people almost fought.   (B)
Now he was taken to one town, one.
Now good became the heart of that one chief.

Then the Quinault learned about it,   (C)
    then the Chehalis learned about it,   100
        then the Cascade learned about it,

> then the Cowlitz learned about it,
> > then the Klikitat learned about it.

All those up the river went down the river.
They came to Clatsop.   105

Two fingers wide of copper   (D)
> one slave,
> > and it goes around at the arm.
Thus (half the length of the radius) long of iron (=) one slave.
Nails were bought.   110
If a good cured deer skin,
> then they exchanged some for them.
> > It was bartered.
If long dentalia,
> then several were exchanged for those nails.   115
> > those people bought them.

The Clatsop became chiefs (rich).   (E)
There and for the first time iron was seen.
Brass was seen for the first time.

Now those people were kept,   (F)   120
> one at one chief,
> > at a point of Clatsop land one was kept.

The overall configuration can be indicated in a profile:

[i]   ABCDE
[ii]   ABC
[iii] ABC
[iv]   ABC
[v]   ABC
[vi]   AB CD EF

Such internal relationships are found in other narratives told by Cultee (e.g., the Kathlamet "Sun's Myth"), Victoria Howard (Clackamas), and Louis

Simpson (Wishram). They reflect the two major pattern numbers among the Chinookans, three and five, which go with pairing, and the use of certain line initial words as markers.

Cultee's "First Ship Seen by the Clatsop" is reproduced here because little attention has been given to the internal form of narratives in Shoalwater Chinook. The case is different with Kathlamet and Clackamas myths. Cultee's "Sun's Myth" has become widely known. Hymes first narrated it at the 1975 annual meeting of the American Folklore Society in Portland, Oregon. Victoria Howard's "Seal and Her Younger Brother Live There" has appeared in Japanese, as well as in a collection of women's narratives.

What is striking about "The Sun's Myth" is that it depicts the destruction of a people by one of its own members, its chief. The three scenes of the first part have a happy ending: abundance of wealth of the kinds available to Indian people. The three scenes of the second part show a choice made by the chief, an act of hubris that leads him to destroy the five villages of his people, one by one. The hubris is in wanting to possess power beyond the human, the power of the Sun herself. We cannot but think that power beyond the control of Indian people has to do with power involving whites.

Here is the scene that ends the first half, a moment in which times seems to have stopped.

THE SUN'S MYTH
A long time he stayed there;
    now he took that young girl.
They stayed there.
In the early light,
    already that old woman [Sun] was gone.
In the evening,
    she would come home;
she would bring things,
    she would bring arrows;
sometimes mountain goat blankets she would bring,
    sometimes elkskin armors she would bring.
Everyday like this. (Boas 1901:29; Boas 1901:26–33)

In the second half, or fourth act, the chief becomes homesick, which happens often in such narratives. The Sun offers the chief every kind of wealth, but he has become fixed on the shining thing she hangs up at night on her return (= the power of the sun). He wants only that. Finally, she gives it to him (one cannot forever refuse a guest, and a relative), but she also gives him an ax.

He starts back. As he approaches one of the villages of his people, the ax begins to sing: "We two shall strike your town, we two shall strike your town." The chief tries to hold back, but he cannot and loses consciousness. When he recovers, he sees the village of his people destroyed. This happens five times. Each time he approaches a village of his own people he tries harder and harder to be rid of the ax, but he fails. Then comes the end of the second part, and the myth, a sixth act corresponding to the third shown above.

> He looked back. (A)
> Now she is standing near him, that old woman.
> "You,"
>> she told him,
>>> "You.
>> "In vain I try to love you,
>>> in vain I try to love your relatives.
>> "Why do you weep?
>> "It is you who choose.
>> "Now you carried that blanket of mine."
> Now she took it, (B)
>> she lifted off what he had taken.
> Now she left him,
>> she went home.
> He stayed there; (C)
>> he went a little distance.
> There he built a house,
>> a small house.

These last two stanzas are not in terms of three or five, but of two pairs for the Sun and two pairs for the chief. We cannot but think that they indicate that male power (3, 5) has been replaced by female control (2, 4).

Victoria Howard's telling of "Seal and Her Younger Brother Lived There" is again a further thinking through of a widespread myth. There are various versions of a plot in which a man (or two men) travels to the Sky Country to take revenge on a headman or chief. To gain access, the avenger disguises himself as a woman of the house. He may be almost discovered several times.

Late at night, he climbs up to the man's bed (or is already in it), still disguised as a wife. At that point, a child calls out that there is a penis (or a knife) but is shushed. The "wife" goes uncaught, kills the man, and escapes. The audience presumably is satisfied, the story having been told from the standpoint of the person seeking revenge.

Howard told Jacobs a version in which the story is from the standpoint of the child, who notices that the "wife" sounds like a man when they all go outside to urinate (distance from the ground) but is shushed (scene 1). She feels something come onto her face when they are in bed at night (she is below, the "wife" and husband above) but is shushed. Then she rises, raises a light, sees her uncle dead, and screams (scene 2). In the final scene, she laments her uncle and her failed attempt to rouse her mother, while her mother simply keeps making a formal lament (scene 3) in which she invokes the house posts, which is indicative of status (see Jacobs 1958–59:340–41; 1960:238–42; Hymes 2004, ch. 8).

SEAL AND HER YOUNGER BROTHER LIVED THERE

[i. The 'wife' comes]

They lived there, Seal, her daughter, her younger brother.	(A)
After some time, now a woman got to Seal's younger brother.	
They lived there.	(B)
They would 'go out' outside in the evening.	
The girl would say,	5
she would tell her mother:	
"Mother! Something is different about my uncle's wife.	
It sounds just like a man when she 'goes out'."	
"Shush! Your uncle's wife!"	
A long long time they lived there like that.	(C) 10
In the evening they would each 'go out'.	
Now she would tell her:	
"Mother! Something is different about my uncle's wife.	
When she 'goes out' it sounds like a man."	
"Shush!"	15

[ii] [The uncle dies]

Her uncle, his wife, would 'lie down' up above on the bed.	(A)
Pretty soon the other two would lie down close to the fire,	
they would lie down close to each other.	
Some time during the night, something comes on to her face.	(B)

She shook her mother, 20
    she told her:
    "Mother! Something comes on to my face."
"Mmmmm. Shush. Your uncle, they are 'going'.
Pretty soon now again, she heard something escaping. (C)
She told her, 25
    "Mother! Something is going t'uq t'uq
    I hear something."
"Shush. Your uncle, they are 'going'.
The girl got up, (D)
    she fixed the fire, 30
        she lit pitch,
            she looked where the two were:
                Ah! Ah! Blood!
She raised her light to it, thus: (E)
    her uncle is on his bed, 35
  his neck cut,
      he is dead.
        She screamed.

                      [iii. The women lament]
She told her mother: (A)
    "I told you,
        'Something is dripping.'"
    You told me,
        'Shush, they are 'going'.'"
    I had told you,
        'Something is different about my uncle's wife. 45
        'She would 'go out',
      with a sound just like a man she would urinate.
        'You would tell me,
            'Shush!'"
She wept. 50
Seal said: (B)
    "Younger brother! My younger brother!
    "They are valuable standing there.
    "My younger brother!"
She kept saying that. 55
As for that girl, she wept. (C)

She said:

    "In vain I tried to tell you,

    "Not like a woman,

    With a sound just like a man she would urinate,

        my uncle's wife."   60

    You told me,

      'Shush!'

    "Oh oh my uncle!

    "Oh oh my uncle!"

She wept, that girl.   65

Now I remember only that far.

These examples demonstrate that when Native Americans on the Columbia were encountered by others, they were not without verbal art. What we know of their verbal art can move us even today. We are fortunate to have evidence of that, although unfortunate, as are their descendants, to have only a portion of what must have been a rich ability and heritage. Yet we can honor what they have left us and go further to make clear the forms and imagination at work.

The situation is similar to that of Old English literature and its one surviving great work, *Beowulf*. As Seamus Heaney has stressed with his translation of *Beowulf*, it took a scholar who was also a creative writer, J. R. R. Tolkien, to establish that *Beowulf* was not simply a survival but also a work of imagination, a work of art with its own integrity and distinction (Heaney 2000:xi). There is much to be done to bring out the ways in which many Native American narratives are works of art, having integrity and distinction of their own (Hymes 2003).

NINE

LOWER COLUMBIA CHINOOKAN CEREMONIALISM

Robert T. Boyd

T RADITIONAL Chinookan ceremonies or religious rituals were particularly vulnerable to the rapid changes that came with Euro-American contact. Change and loss occurred after the epidemics of the 1830s removed many specialists and broke apart the critical mass of people needed for group performances; and in the early 1840s, when missionaries at the surviving settlements at Willamette Falls, The Cascades, and the mouth of the Columbia discouraged traditional life rites. After such experiences, the details on what was practiced and the belief system behind it remained mostly in the minds of a few traditionalist survivors.

This reconstruction of what went before is based on two sets of data: eyewitness accounts of practices from the early contact period and ethnographic information collected from Chinookan informants between 1890 and 1936. Extant accounts were compared, identifying both recurring elements and passages that are judged to be particularly reliable, and recombined into configurations or geographically limited clusters. Complete firsthand or remembered accounts of single ceremonies have been especially valuable sources.

Anthropologists like to discuss religious systems under two broad categories: belief systems and the rituals that often act out the beliefs. Lower Columbia belief systems—a species of animism, or belief in nature spirits—are explored by Dell Hymes and Bill Seaburg in this volume (ch. 8). In cultures where traditions are passed on orally, ceremonials tend to vary a great deal from performance to performance, from place to place, and from one time to another. Anthropologists of religion have noted that ceremonial segments, or elements, may easily be dropped or added and moved around and that this accounts for much of the variation in ceremonial practices in the

Pacific Northwest (e.g., Gunther 1928; French 1955). At the same time, however, a common purpose, or theme, tends to hold them together. Ceremonials have been interpreted as a cultural means of giving meaning to otherwise inexplicable biological events or ecological realities (Malinowski 1948), such as changes in the life cycle or recurring yet variable fish runs, and of bringing together and anchoring groups of people to their own shared intuitive non-material cultural or belief systems, as in winter spirit dances.

Ceremonials can be discussed under two broad headings: calendrical rites and rites of passage. Calendrical rites mark recurring (usually annual) natural or social events—for Lower Columbia Chinookans, the First Salmon ceremony and winter spirit dances. Rites of passage mark changes in the life cycle, such as birth, puberty, mating (marriage), and death (funerals) and the social statuses that go along with them: child, adult, spouse, ancestor. All ceremonials are saturated with specific ritual behaviors that may be hard to comprehend when viewed in isolation; but when they are matched with what is known from the underlying belief system, such behaviors may be eminently logical. I will discuss two calendrical rites—the First Salmon ceremony and winter spirit dancing—and two rites of passage in the life cycle—head flattening and the practices and beliefs surrounding death.

FIRST SALMON CEREMONY

The First Salmon ceremony is a defining trait of the Northwest Coast culture area, occurring among almost all of the Native cultures from the Alaska Panhandle south to the Klamath River. It is the most prominent of a series of First Food rites that celebrate the arrival of seasonally important wild foods, found throughout the region but more diverse in the interior Northwest (or Plateau culture area). The common thread in these rituals was the belief that each species had a spiritual manifestation that had to be ritually honored if it was to return in abundance year after year. Given the fluctuation in most of these species' natural cycles and without the control over supply that domestication brings, it is not surprising that ritual behaviors tended to cluster around economically important animals and plants. This is particularly the case with that resource most important to Native Northwest Coast peoples' survival, salmon (see ch. 4 in this volume). Lower Columbia Chinookans also may have celebrated First Food rites for sturgeon (Ray 1938:110; Jacobs 1958–59:222) and elk (Lee and Frost 1968:283; Boas 1894:265).

The data on the Lower Columbia Chinookan First Salmon ceremony come from over a score of accounts, full and partial, ethnographic and historical. The most important is a cluster of descriptions from the journals of the Astorians, a detailed record from the missionary Joseph Frost in 1841, George Gibbs's summary from the 1850s, and later accounts from three river-mouth Chinook and one Clackamas informants—Silas Smith (1901), Charles Cultee (Boas 1894), Emma Luscier (Ray 1938, 1942), and John Wacheno (Drucker 1934).

The June 6, 1811, entry in the headquarters log of the Pacific Fur Company at Fort Astoria records the first encounter of the fur traders with this unusual ritual:

> They [Chinooks] have salmon in great plenty, but from a superstitious idea they entertain that boiling & cutting it across will prevent them from coming into the River until the next new Moon, they have brought us Very few & those they insisted on dressing & roasting themselves. We at first suspected it was from some plan they had formed to starve us. (McDougall 1999:20)

Eight days later, "Comcomly & Kamaquiah paid us a visit, the former brought 15 small Salmon for a feast, but the whole to be eaten before sun set, & had it prepared by his own people" (24).

Alexander Ross (2000) explained and elaborated on what the Astorians recorded:

> When the salmon make their first appearance in the river, they are never allowed to be cut crosswise nor boiled, but roasted, nor are they allowed to be sold without the heart being first taken out, nor to be kept over night; but must be all consumed or eaten the day they are taken out of the water; all these rules are observed for about ten days. These superstitious customs perplexed us at first not a little, because they absolutely refused to sell us any unless we complied with their notions, which we of course consented to do. (97)

Astorian Gabriele Franchère (1969) added that the Chinook believed that if these rules were not followed then "the river would be obstructed and the fishing poor that season" (96).

Taken together, the earliest accounts present the basic elements of the Lower Chinook First Salmon ceremony, which recur in the later records:

failure to observe the ritual will negatively affect the run; the heart must be removed (and treated ritually); dogs must not eat the heart; the fish must never be cut crosswise (lengthwise was prescribed); fish caught in the morning must be eaten that afternoon, always before sunset (less often stated: all in one day); the usual mode of cooking is roasting; ritual restrictions and/or sale to outsiders continued for about a month (Ross's "ten days" probably refers to some restrictions, not all).

By far the most detailed description of the Lower Chinook First Salmon ceremony comes from Methodist missionary Joseph Frost (1934) at Clatsop in 1841. On April 24, Frost (and his wife, assumedly) "were invited to partake of three very fine" salmon "by the people of Wasalsal's lodge; the first taken by them this season." Frost described the butchering of the salmon in great detail: flanks were removed and roasted on spits, and the rest of the fish was cooked on a scaffold. The host did all the preparation but did not eat; the missionaries were served first, then guests, then lodge inhabitants. The proper preparation of the fish, always indoors, and consumption, always in the afternoon, seemed to constitute "a kind of sacred right [sic]" that was "strictly observed by all the natives in this region" "until the strawberries [salmonberries is intended] ripen." After that, restrictions were lifted, trading started, and everyone could "cook and eat their salmon as they see fit." If the ritual was not followed, Frost was told, then "the weather would become stormy & they would not be able to catch any more salmon" (162–63).

Frost did not stop with a simple description of the practices. As Christian communion is explained by the story of the Last Supper, the missionary searched for the story behind the behavior. He found it in a "Talapus" (Coyote) myth. As Frost retold it, Coyote came "from the south" and, "finding the people" with no food but land animals and birds, "made" salmon. He then "made a seine," with Coyote in a canoe and Snake ashore with the land line, which he threw, and caught "a great draught of salmon" that he took to the people to eat. Coyote then

learned their fathers how to cut the fish and roast them, and told them that for some time they must eat only in the afternoon of each day, and that if any of them should touch a dead body, or . . . if their women, under certain circumstances ["circumstances" being a circumlocution for menstruating] should look upon a salmon net . . . until the berries began to ripen . . . which is about the first of June . . . the salmon would all leave the river. . . . But as soon as the specified time arrived they were at liberty to cook the salmon as they might see proper, and sell them to whom they pleased . . . they fully believe that this is a law imposed upon them by their deity, and that distressing results would follow, namely, the removal of all the salmon, if this law should be transgressed. (300–1)

Frost's description is the most comprehensive one available, but it does not mention everything. An important omission is the ritualized treatment of the heart, first noted by Ross and mentioned in half of the accounts. A more complete description of this comes from 1835: "Before the fish is split and prepared for eating, a small hole is made in the breast, the heart taken out, roasted, and eaten in silence, and with great gravity" (Townsend 1999:162). Details vary, but disposition of the heart appears to have been important. Many accounts say that if a "stranger" or a "dog" ate the heart, then the salmon runs would fail (e.g., Wilkes 1845: 324, 119). The fear of a dog eating the heart is clearly akin to the proscriptions on those who touched a corpse or on menstruating women: all were ritually unclean. It is a common theme in Northwest Coast religion that spirits are offended by ritual impurity or uncleanliness and that they will stay away or be driven away if such people or actions are present.

There is also more to say about Frost's statement that the first salmon were those taken "by the people of Wasalsal's lodge" and that the fish were prepared "by one man, and only one" who did not eat the fish himself. Who was this person? On the Lower Columbia, Emma Luscier said, "The fisherman obtaining the first salmon. . . . acted as ritualist" (Ray 1938:110), and it was he who invited the guests to his lodge for the ceremonies. When the Astorians were finally invited to eat salmon, it was "Concomly and Kamaquiah," local chiefs, who supervised the goings-on. On Puget Sound, the family that owned the local weir or, more specifically, the family head who had access to net-making materials was in charge (Meeker n.d.). So it may be that the high-ranking man who owned the seine that caught the first fish was ritual leader on the Lower Columbia.

Lower Columbia Chinookans did not take spring-run chinook, probably because lower river levels restricted the fish to the deep waters of the middle of the river, where seines could not be used. Instead, "first fish" were caught in June when higher river levels brought the runs closer to shore. Also of interest is the month-long period between the arrival of the first salmon and the appearance of salmonberries, when ritual restrictions applied, fishing of salmon was off-limits to outsiders, and salmon was not traded. This period of restricted access may have been a cultural response to the unpredictability of the summer runs and may have prevented overharvest.

So, the First Salmon ceremony on the Lower Columbia was unique. It did not have many of the better-known elements of the ceremony farther north, including a "salmon priest," an altar with fish treated as high-ranking guests, a fish's head pointed upstream, and the return of the bones to the river. There is no mention of salmon spirits living across the sea, in human form, donning salmon clothing for the run, and returning as spirits to the ocean to repeat the cycle again (Drucker 1965:95). The Lower Columbia ceremony emphasized proper preparation in a single lodge and observance of taboos for a month before everyone was allowed to fish without restrictions. The mythological "charter" that has survived from the Chinook does not identify the first fish as "chief of salmon" who leads his flock upstream and who must be honored ritually if he is to return and lead the runs in following years. Instead, the background myth highlights Coyote's Myth Age introduction of salmon and fishing methods, plus a lengthy list of taboos that must be observed if the runs are to be maintained.

Frost's salmon story appears to be a shorter version of a myth that Franz Boas collected twice from Charles Cultee in the 1890s. Cultee's "Coyote Myth" dates from the Myth Age and is concerned with the institution of seine fishing and taboos related to salmon fishing and processing, though neither version emphasizes the introduction of salmon per se. Cultee's versions have Coyote fishing for salmon, on the first day successfully and on the second day unsuccessfully. Then, in frustration, he asks his "sisters," resident in his gut, what he did wrong. (The "sisters" recur in many Coyote myths, always at hand, always advising Coyote on proper behavior.) This happens many times in succession, and each time the sisters relate a new set of taboos that must be observed if the fish are to return to be caught (Boas 1901:45–49). The *Chinook Texts* version, which is longer, begins at Neacoxie Creek in Clatsop territory, and the "sisters" advise on proper butchering (lengthwise, not crosswise), cooking (on spits), roasting, and keeping the fish away from menstruating women or those who have touched corpses (Boas 1894:101–6).

Then, interestingly, Coyote moves upstream from Neacoxie, fishing at new places and encountering new and unfamiliar taboos at each location. The myth clearly expresses his increasing frustration with the many rules and probably is a projection of how many Chinooks actually felt. But it also indicates—and this is an important point—that first salmon taboos, and probably ceremonial elements as well, differed for each village and drainage system on the Lower Columbia. For the neighboring Tillamook, Boas (1923) wrote, "There was a separate method of treating the fish for every river. . . . The methods of cutting the fish were different" (9–10).

There are only a few records of First Salmon rituals for Chinookan peoples between Kathlamet and The Cascades. In 1934, John Wacheno recalled some distinct elements: five "crane heads" of wood were set up on the river's banks; the first five salmon taken had their heads burned off; there was no gambling at this time; and when "cooked"—roasted not specified—"everyone took a bite." Then—and this is the only clear documentation of this element for the Lower Columbia—"Salmon bones thrown back in river, became salmon again" (see Boyd 1996:128, 174; Boas 1923:9–10; Jacobs 2003:204).

From The Cascades, there is only the following:

B.B. Bishop, one of the earliest builders of steamboats on the Columbia . . . told the writer that the Indians at The Cascades had a spring festival with the first run of salmon. They would boil whole the first large salmon caught, and have a ceremony in which the whole tribe would pass in procession around the fish, each taking a bit. They exercised the utmost care to leave the skeleton intact, so that at the end it had been picked clean but with not a bone broken. (Lyman 1915:382)

WINTER SPIRIT DANCING

Compared to the First Salmon ceremony, documentation for what was undoubtedly the major ceremonial activity of the Lower Columbia Chinookans, the cycle of winter spirit dances, is sparse. Early white observers were rarely privy to these rituals, so the more complete documentations come from Charles Cultee, Emma Luscier, and Clackamas-speaking Victoria Howard. Verne Ray (1942), the compiler of *Lower Chinook Ethnographic Notes*, was very interested in the winter ceremonies, though much had already been lost by the time he collected his information from Emma Luscier in the early 1930s. By comparing the Chinook notes to data from upriver Plateau peoples, however, he was able to generate a general outline for the winter spirit dances.

Spirit dancing took place during the coldest two months of winter and consisted of five-day dances held sequentially in different houses. Hosts might be shamans, wealthy men, or fathers seeking public recognition of the new guardian spirit of their offspring. The dances were open to all, and consisted primarily of individual singing and dancing representing, symbolically, one's guardian spirit. Recognition of new spirit powers and power performances by people with unusual and strong powers might occur. Gifts were distributed, usually to guests, at the end of each five day session, but sometimes at other points in the ceremonies.

Accounts are rare, so we must turn to a myth text for the flavor of the river-mouth spirit dance. Cultee's "*úpənpən* [skunk] her story" describes a spirit dance held by Myth Age people. Skunk is "a chieftainess" who "made a large house and invited the people." Blue-jay is her assistant and gift distributor. Several spirit people come and dance, and the songs they sing hint at their identity. The "Maggots" dance first, singing "We make move the rotten meat." Blue-jay gifts them with a mountain goat blanket. They are followed by geese, who sing "We pull out the sea grass, the sea grass" and are gifted with a goose-skin blanket. Then elks: "We hiss on bluffs" and are gifted with an elkskin gift; and wolves: "We carry deer-fawns in our mouths; we have our faces blackened" and are gifted with a wolf blanket. Grizzlies follow, along with *ínc'x* birds, gray cranes, and rabbits, each with characteristic songs and gifts. The myth ends with a miraculous performance by skunk, the hostess, who "made wind [farted] and the whale fell down dead." The assembled guests then feast on whale meat (Boas 1894:147–48).

Melville Jacobs (1929–30) recorded several spirit power songs from Mrs. Howard. The animal power songs—rabbit, owl, grizzly, mouse, bear, chipmunk—are cryptic and descriptive like Cultee's songs. Mrs. Howard sang others, however, that were not animals—sunset, fire, lightning—and many that she could not identify. "In some songs," she told Jacobs, "they kind of name their power in the song so people know what the power is, but in other songs the people can not tell what the power is." The songs could be a kind of charade, or they might simply mystify (adding to the power). Mrs. Howard never knew what her own mother's power was, but her maternal grandmother's was fog. When her grandmother performed, she wore her hair long and loose and sprinkled with goose down, painted her face red, and danced with "arms outstretched . . . hands and palms facing out," apparently alternating with thumping on the floor with her cane. She sang: "Towards dawn the early morning mist e . . . ai" and "the others in the crowd followed her song and danced as she danced" (see Jacobs 1959a:ch. 15).

Both Emma Luscier and Mrs. Howard described how the guardian spirit power of "novices" (post-spirit quest youths) was recognized and initially expressed at the spirit dances. According to Luscier, the novice—who had been experiencing the type of malaise called "spirit illness," indicating that he had acquired a guardian spirit—neither slept nor ate during the five-day run of the dance, "until he heard a song which satisfied him, relieved his illness" (Ray 1938:81–83). Mrs. Howard told of a young man who fainted during the ceremonies and did not respond to a burning ember on his hand, both signs of spirit possession. Following this public display, his father had to throw a five-day dance and give-away recognizing his new power (Jacobs 1958–59:544, 658–59).

Winter dances were compulsory for people with unusual and strong spirit powers to express them publicly. The records record a few "power performances" cryptically and three in more detail. As on the British Columbia Coast, some of these involved a degree of legerdemain, while others were more or less straightforward. It is not possible to say how much was fact and how much was illusion. Emma Luscier mentioned "holding hot stones" and said that "Sam Millet's spirit was an owl, and like the owl he was able to swallow snakes" (Ray 1938:84). John Wacheno said: "Person with power from fire—could light pipe without fire (holding in sun), handle hot stones drink boiling water."

"Dog-eating," well known as a ceremonial element from the British Columbia Coast and fully documented from The Dalles (Boyd 1996:130, 138–39), is also reported from Willamette Falls:

> May 23, 1845 . . . A year ago last winter at the Falls of Wallamette an Indian thus ate a dog after which his long hair was cut off, singed & cut off by him. If he lived through this operation he was to be denominated a great doctor among his people, also a chief or ruler. He was sick sometime & came very near dying but finally recovered & lives to enjoy the acknowledged honors. (Alvan Waller, cited in Boyd 1996:138)

In everyday life, dogs were considered to be the animals closest to humans and never were eaten.

Similar to dog-eating was what Mrs. Howard called "Bird blood spirit-power," but here the performer drank bird blood. Blood was food for the dancer's guardian spirit, and sometimes the performer cut his arms and drank the blood (Jacobs 1958–59:505–6). This last behavior—gashing—may be a different power performance from blood-eating. At The Dalles, people who gashed themselves during spirit dances were demonstrating strength and invulnerability to pain, and the scars remained as evidence of their bravery. Outside of a ceremonial context, gashing was observed near Fort George in the early 1830s:

> In times of pretended inspiration, and communion with the Great Spirit, they seize a fleshy part of the body, about the stomach and ribs, in one hand, and plunge a dagger right through the fold, without drawing blood. This act is taken as a proof of their invulnerability—a favour granted by the Great Spirit [more properly by a particular guardian spirit]. I have seen some of them thus gashed all over the front of the body. While I was in charge of Fort George, one of these crafty old priests prepared to perform this operation in my presence. He grasped a handful of his flabby flesh, and drew his dagger. But I instantly checked him. (Dunn 1844:91–92)

Cultee said that each gash represented a person killed (Boas 1893a:41). All of the other activities were outlandish or risky, if not outright dangerous, and all indicated strong powers.

The performances that are more frequently reported from Lower Columbia Chinookan lands involve magical movements of inanimate objects: effigies, power sticks, and power boards. A Kathlamet tale related by Cultee describes a dancing figure: "one man at Nisal sang his conjurer's song. A small figure of a supernatural being was made of cedar wood. When this man, who had a supernatural helper, sang, then the cedar figure moved and danced. . . . it went to and fro five times in the house. . . . All the people went to see it. They were surprised" (1901: 201–3). Wacheno described a half-Kalapuya Clackamas whose spirit power controlled "wooden dolls which he could make dance by his singing" (Drucker 1934).

"Dancing stick" performances were recorded from Kathlamet (Gibbs 1955–56:137–38) and The Cascades (Kuykendall 1889). In her description of a performance, Emma Luscier said the sticks were the same as the batons used as drumsticks on the roof rafters and were several feet long, with feathers and other objects attached two-thirds of the way up (Boyd 1996:123–24). Gibbs (1955–56) said that the sticks were "carved and painted." In the spirit performances, the sticks moved magically by their own power: at Kathlamet, "a rapid and tremulous motion was communicated to them, the operator holding them near one end." Other people tried to stop their movement, but could not, and "their hands become clenched so that they cannot be disengaged" until the operator blew on them. The action stopped when the spirit power owner suddenly threw his hands in the air (137–38).

At The Cascades, the power owner passed the sticks to someone in the audience, who was unable to let go and was "jumped up and down around the lodge" until "the stick raised up violently, uplifting the man's arms," and he fell down in "a state of cataleptic rigidity." Not until the power owner made movements over him was the man able to let go and "awake." The power sticks were also reported to "stand or dance about alone and even remain suspended in the air." Informants described a "sensation" like "electric current" while holding the sticks: "Their muscles were thrown into a state of tonic spasm, so that they found it impossible to let go." This statement might sound suspicious if it were not duplicated by another account collected from a Twana elder in southern Puget Sound in the 1930s (see Elmendorf 1992:185; Adamson 1934:193; Olson 1936:155).

Beyond individual spirit songs, dances, and power performances, there is little evidence that Chinookan peoples possessed anything like the "dancing societies" of the northern Northwest Coast. The complex North Coast form of the potlatch was absent, though gifting was pervasive. Mrs. Bertrand said that Concomly gained knowledge of the form of a dancing society through purchase of a northern slave (Ray 1938:91) and Cultee described a potlatch performance (Boas 1894:268–69), but Ray (93) believed both to be late overlays from the north. My survey of the historical and ethnographic literature turned up no other examples.

HEAD FLATTENING

Pregnancy and birth constituted a particularly dangerous transition period for both mothers and their babies, and a cluster of taboos surrounded those events. Immediately after birth or shortly following, children were placed in a special cradle for head flattening, one of the hallmark customs of the Lower Chinookans (see ch. 7 in this volume). A practice that was more closely related to social ranking than to rituals of transition, head flattening was described by almost all who wrote about Chinookan peoples from 1792 into the early 1900s, and we have over 30 separate accounts on the custom.

We know about two varieties of head-flattening cradles that were characteristic, more or less, of the lower river and the Portland Basin. In 1834, John Townsend (1999) reported:

The Wallammet Indians [observed at Clackamas village at Gladstone] place the infant soon after birth, upon a board, to the edges of which are attached little loops of hempen cord or leather, and other similar cords are passed across and back, in a zig-zag manner, through these loops, enclosing the child and binding it firmly down. To the upper end of this board, in which is a depression to receive the back part of the head, another smaller one is attached by hinges of leather, and made to lie obliquely upon the forehead, the force of pressure being regulated by several strings attached to its edge, which are passed through holes in the board upon which the infant is lying, and secured there. The mode of the Chinooks, and others near the sea, differs widely. . . . A sort of cradle is formed by excavating a pine [cedar] log to the depth of eight or ten inches. The child is placed in it, on a bed of little grass mats, and bound down in the manner above described. A little boss of tightly plaited and woven grass is then applied to the forehead, and secured by a cord to the loops at the side. (127–28)

The downriver version is often compared to a canoe, which James Swan says was called "canim" or "canoe." Charles Wilkes collected one of these cradles in 1841, and it is now at the Peabody Harvard Museum (for the upriver version, see Kane 1971b:246).

Two-thirds of the accounts mention the time span for head flattening—an average of one year, though Silas Smith (1901:258) said "some mothers continu[ed] it longer than others," a practice related to rank. Infants were released from their bonds only for cleansing; for feeding, the cords were loosened and the cradle pressed to the breast (Corney 1965:150). The effects on the skull are clear in several illustrations, including those of Charles Cultee. The face is broadened, and the front-to-back radius of the skull has been flattened. In 1796, Charles Bishop (1967) described it as "resembling an human face carved out of a Flatt Piece of Plank, the thickness of the head from the Back Part to the Eye Brows often seen to be not more than half the Breadth of the face. In a front view it gives them a fine open countenance" (126). Several descriptions compare the shape of the head to that of a "wedge." In profile, there was "a straight line from the crown of the head to the top of the nose[,] considered by them [to be] the acme of beauty" (Hale 1846:216).

The process was controlled by loosening or tightening the cords that held the flattening board (Duflot de Mofras 1937:182). In the first year, before the sutures closed, the skull was soft and could be shaped (Smith 1901:258), "partly by actual compression, and partly by preventing the growth of the skull" (Hale 1846:216). Narcissa Whitman was shown a child at The Cascades whose head, at the back, "was of a purple colour as if it had been sadly bruised" (Drury 1963:99), and almost a third of the observers commented on the "goggle" eyes of the children. Despite this, there was near unanimity that the process caused no pain and did not affect intelligence. HBC Governor George Simpson (1968) reported that "this operation does not seem to give pain as the children rarely cry and it certainly does not affect the brain or understanding, as they are without exception the most intelligent Indians and most acute and finished Bargain makers I have ever fallen in with" (96). In fact, very few observers applied negative value judgments to the custom. Edward Belcher (1843:206) compared it to the binding of Chinese women's feet, and missionary Joseph Frost said that when he asked a Chinookan why they flattened heads, he answered: "Why do your ladies make themselves so small about the waist" (Lee and Frost 1968:103).

Ideas of beauty aside, the main reason for Chinookan head flattening was social: free people flattened their heads, while slaves were not allowed to. It was a visual marker of social separation (see ch. 7 in this volume). Head flattening also indicated kinship, and flat-headed people did not take slaves among neighbors who also had flat heads. They went further afield and took them from communities of round heads (Hajda 2005). Head flattening was apparently difficult to do right, and the technique may have been privileged information.

DEATH AND BURIAL CUSTOMS

Death was a rite of passage not only for the deceased but for the survivors as well. The only description of a funeral in the literature is Sal-tsi-mar's in 1853 at Willapa Bay (Swan 1972:185–89); otherwise, there are thumbnail accounts that mention a few elements. The body lay in state in the house for five days, and the corpse was washed and clothed by paid specialists. For Clackamas, morticians received special powers from "blue flies" and may have been the same as the "corpse handlers" at The Dalles (Boyd 1996:108–9). After the body was removed, the house was abandoned or burned.

Mourners cut their hair—to the earlobes, according to Emma Luscier—and fasted for a period, usually stated as a month; morning and evening, they sang dirges. For the Clackamas, close relatives avoided fresh food (Drucker 1934; Jacobs 1958–59:501). Swan (1972) described the mourning songs at Willapa Bay:

The burden of the song . . . is simply an address to the dead, stating their love for her, the many years she had lived with and taught them, that she was not poor, and had no occasion to go to a better country, and they saw no reason why she should go to the land of the dead. . . . Every day, at sunrise and sunset this chant is repeated by the relatives for thirty days. (187)

Close relatives might mourn longer. The name of the deceased was tabooed and dropped out of circulation, and close relatives might change their names. That was the case with Concomly on the death of his two sons in the "mortality" of 1824–25. On that occasion, Concomly wore "the worst clothing he c[ould] possibly procure & abstain[ed] from washing . . . for eighteen or twenty months" and changed his name to "Madsu" (Scouler 1905:168). James Swan (1972:189) stated that the name taboo remained in force until reburial—or perhaps when the soul had departed to the second afterlife— and named five people who changed their names following the deaths of close relatives. Wilkes (1845:118) mentioned a dance of several women at Astoria that marked the end of mourning for a widow and her eligibility for remarriage.

In addition to flattened heads, the most conspicuous, unusual, and commented-on custom of Lower Columbia Chinookan peoples concerned their modes of burial and cemeteries. Graves were noted and described by almost every visitor to the Lower Columbia, particularly after the epidemics of the 1830s. The most comprehensive and concise account comes from John Dunn (1844) at Fort George in the early 1830s:

On the death of one of these people, the body was formerly wrapped, in skins or mats (. . . now they use blankets), and disposed in a small canoe; the deceased's arms, and other articles of general use, being laid beside him. The canoe is then placed on a platform by the river side, or on rocks out of reach of the tide, and other mats tied over it. Sometimes these sepulchral canoes are suspended from boughs of trees, six or eight feet from the ground. The canoe in which the body is placed is perforated at the bottom, for the twofold purpose of letting out the water that the rains may have deposited in it, and of preventing it from ever being used again by the living. When his friends can afford the expense, a large canoe, reversed, is placed over the lower, to protect it from the rain; and both are firmly tied together. . . . Formerly on the death of a chief, or other person of wealth and importance, one or more of his slaves was put to death. (86–87)

William Clark described the supporting platform:

> 4 pieces of Split timber are Set erect on end, and sunk, a fiew feet in the
> ground, each brace having their flat Sides opposit to each other and Suffi-
> ciently far asunder to admit the width of the Canoe in which the dead are
> to be deposited; through each of those perpindicular posts, at the hight
> of 6 feet a mortice is Cut, through which two bars of wood are incerted;
> on those Cross bars a small canoe is placed. (Lewis and Clark 1990:97)

There was some consistency to the grave goods and where they were
placed, inside or outside the canoe. Grave goods were always gender-specific
and included only personal, movable property. A man's bow and arrow, guns,
fishing harpoon, and paddle were placed inside the canoe, as was jewelry.
Outside the canoe, usually on poles, were hung a woman's kitchen utensils:
wooden bowls, tin kettles, pans, baskets, and blankets, which might be shredded before being affixed to the poles. Later accounts noted that grave goods,
like the canoes themselves, may have had holes punched in them. One early
source reported that "boards painted with rude resemblances of the human
figure" (Scouler 1905:280), probably spirit boards, were placed next to burial
canoes. Cultee said that a man's guardian spirit "baton" and a shaman's rattle
were "placed next to" or "hung" on the canoe (Boas 1894:257). The rationale
for grave goods was not, apparently, what Euro-Americans thought—that the
dead would use them in the next world—but, as Swan (1972) stated, to appease
the ghosts: "The Chinooks say that the dead revisit the earth at night and
would be very angry if they found their property in use by others, for which
reason it is put by their graves. They [the ghosts] value these things much, and
come to look after them" (317).

Particularly splendid grave goods, of course, accompanied the wealthy. In
1847, one canoe-coffin on Mount Coffin, assumed to be that of a chief's wife,
contained "sixty-six finger rings" and "forty ankle and wrist ornaments"
(Thornton 1849:281–82). In the Cowlitz cemetery (but not noted in any Chinookan burial site), dentalia might be placed in the mouth and over the eyes;
at Clackamas, dentalia beads were strung on the hair of the deceased (Drucker
1934; Jacobs 1958–59:630).

Well-to-do, high-ranking Chinookans, in addition to having better
canoes and more grave goods, might be reburied after several years, the second time in a box. This is what happened to Concomly, as related by Dunn
(1844): "The noted chief, Concomly, was buried with great ceremony, in a

canoe near Fort George in 1831. His body was afterwards taken out of the canoe, for greater security, by his relations, and placed in a long box, in a lonely part of the woods" (94). Reburial may be why we have two surviving illustrations of "Concomly's grave," one a canoe (Kane 1971b:fig. 170), the other a raised box (Wilkes 1845:320–21), which were constructed and used at different times.

Canoe-burial was the preferred mode of interment for Lower Columbia Chinookans and their non-Chinookan neighbors as far upriver as the downstream half of Sauvie Island. Above that point, known historic cemeteries in the Portland Basin practiced variant forms. At Clannaquah village on the east bank of Sauvie Island in 1844, the cemetery was "laid out in streets," and burials consisted of cedar uprights supporting horizontal boards of up to "three tiers," on which wrapped corpses were laid. On the west shore of the island, on a ridge behind the village of Cathlanaquiah (*gaɬánaqʷaíx*), an early settler recalled that bodies were placed in branches of oak trees and that "stone images sometimes occur[red] on the ground beneath." The people at Gladstone village on the lower Clackamas in 1841 interred their dead under "a broad head-board . . . frequently painted or carved with grotesque figures." At The Cascades cemetery—on the north side, just below the rapids—wrapped bodies, perhaps of extended families, were placed in eight-foot-square wooden "vaults," on the model of houses, with doors sometimes "curiously engraved." Grave goods were on the roof or upright poles, and William Clark saw "Several wooden Images, cut in the figure of men" beside the tombs (Lewis and Clark 1988:361). The usual type for Chinookans of the Columbia Gorge and The Dalles were burial houses on midriver (Memaloose) islands (Boyd 1996:106–8, 246–63; ch. 2 in this volume).

Many Chinookan customs concerning funerals, treatment of the dead, and cemeteries can be interpreted as reflecting a fear of ghosts. Houses of the deceased were burned and possessions destroyed, and only people with protective powers handled corpses. Mourners were "disguised" by cutting their hair and wearing old clothes, and the names of recently deceased people were no longer spoken. Cemeteries were in isolated places avoided by the living.

In 1834, at Mount Coffin, an observer explained why Indians were rarely encountered at burial grounds:

The vicinity of this, and all other cemeteries, is held so sacred by the Indians, that they never approach it, except to make similar deposites; they will often even travel a considerable distance out of their course in order to avoid intruding upon the sanctuary of their dead.... After we embarked, we observed an old withered crone with a long stick or wand in her hand, who approached, and ... wav[ed] her enchanted rod over the mouldering bones. (Townsend 1999:131)

Swan (1972:68) explained that it was fear of ghosts that kept them away.

To understand this fear, we need to look at Chinookan beliefs about ghosts and the afterlife (see Cultee's story of his grandfather's visit to the Land of the Dead and Mrs. Howard's myth, "Dead Persons Come to Purchase the Unmarried Girl," in addition to Swan 1972:174, 212–13, 316; Jacobs 1959a:13). There were two Lands of the Dead: the first for those recently deceased, who could still visit the living, and the second for those gone longer than about 10 years. Ghosts—the souls of the deceased (spirit powers of dead people were another category)—were lonely; they hung around cemeteries where their worldly things were and, if they had the opportunity, enticed their closest relatives and friends to join them. Ghosts were awake at night and asleep during the day and tended to do many things opposite of the living. In the otherworld, where they resided, things were not always what they appeared to be. Mrs. Howard's "unmarried girl," for instance, was purchased by a dead man at night; in her new home, her husband and his people "danced all night" but reverted to bones at daylight (Jacobs 1958–59:380–88). When Cultee's grandfather visited the Land of the Dead, he thought he saw "two people carrying a stick." They were house posts. He thought he saw a man "dragging his intestines," but on closer look it was a woven mat (Boas 1894:247–48). In "Blue-jay and Io'i's Myth," Bluejay caught what he thought were leaves, branches, and a log. They were trout, salmon, and a whale, food for the dead (Boas 1894:169). The otherworld was located at the end of a trail or across a river, somewhere to the west. It was not a bad place. Clatsop Silas Smith (1901) apparently did not exaggerate much when he said:

Their conception of the spirit land is quite beautiful and pleasing. There it is always spring or summer; the fields are perpetually green, flowers blooming, fruit ripening, and running waters diversify the scenery of the beautiful landscapes, with always an abundant supply of game, and of course the inhabitants are in a continuous state of felicity. (260)

Swan (1972) wrote: "departed spirits enjoy themselves so much in their new state of existence that they wish all their friends to join them" (181).

So it is not surprising that souls of the living, once they were in the Land of the Dead, might be tempted to stay there. The traditional Chinookan belief system included no concept of heaven or hell or of sin or good works that determined where one went after death. The otherworld was especially attractive to infants, who if not treated well on earth might opt to return to the "Land of the Babies" (Jacobs 1958–59:286). The beliefs also help explain one form of curing ceremony, which assumed that sickness was caused by the initial departure of the soul to the Land of the Dead, where shamans (or their spirit powers) visited in an attempt to rescue the soul before it was too late. The concept of two afterworlds also appears to be related to the two-stage burial sequence: in a burial canoe while the flesh remained on the body and, when only bones were left, in a burial box. Sometimes, it appears, high water levels picked up burial canoes before they reached the second stage (e.g., Scouler 1905:278). As the otherworld was supposed to be to the west and the body was oriented in that direction, it seems that the survivors had prepared their dead well for such a happenstance. The second Land of the Dead was more vague, a place where the deceased became "lost" (Swan 1972:316) or "vanished entirely" (Jacobs 1959a:13).

There is much more to Chinookan ceremonialism, including complexes relating to birth, ear piercing, the first menstruation, and the all-important spirit quest. Always, Chinookan belief systems and ritual practices backed up each other, made perfect sense, and fitted seamlessly into their world.

TEN

LOWER COLUMBIA RIVER ART

Tony A. Johnson and Adam McIsaac
with Kenneth M. Ames and Robert T. Boyd

T HE Lower Columbia River Valley is the focal point of the distinctive and little-known Chinookan Art Style. Chinookan art is steeped in social and religious meaning, with a focus on individual spirit powers. The Chinookan Art Style, which appears in the utilitarian objects of material culture, uses geometric shapes as elaboration and in representational figures, while employing a unique perspective on human and animal forms, here termed Chinookan Anatomical Art.

Although the focal area of the Chinookan Art Style was the string of Chinookan villages from the mouth of the Columbia River to just above The Dalles in present-day Oregon, the style was found over a much wider region that roughly corresponds to the Greater Lower Columbia River region (Hajda 1984) and was created by peoples other than Chinookans. Here, we will concentrate on artwork that was created between Astoria, Oregon, and The Cascades, about 130 miles upriver. Upriver Chinookan pieces from the Columbia River Gorge and The Dalles, however, are essential for comparison and for defining the parameters of the larger style.

Within the Chinookan Art Style there is a continuum of variations along the river and important relationships with other regions. Chinookan Style clearly influenced the art of people who lived in the larger region, and comparisons can be made among them. The wood, bone, and stone art of the Lower Columbia is markedly similar in both form and function to that of the Salishan people of western Oregon and Washington, and to a lesser extent southern British Columbia. Chinookan Art Style objects have been collected from locations in the Pacific Northwest that are well outside the area of influence of its people's art. Without provenance, it is often impossible to deter-

FIGURE 10.1. Chinookan spoon, spruce, H: 4 inches × L: 7¼ inches × W: 5 inches, 1820–60. A Chinookan spoon that is typical in both form and associated imagery (a man and presumed coyote), by an unidentified maker on the Lower Columbia River, The Dalles, Oregon. (Thaw Collection, Fenimore Art Museum, Cooperstown, New York, T0149, John Bigelow Taylor, New York City, photographer)

mine the area of manufacture for these pieces except to say that they originate from the Greater Lower Columbia River.

ATTRIBUTES OF THE CHINOOKAN ART STYLE

The distribution of Chinookan Art Style pieces at contact demonstrates an indigenous interest in collecting and owning these objects. Early fur traders continued this interest, and Chinookan art objects exist in private collections and museums worldwide. Today, individuals and institutions are again recognizing the value in this compelling style, and a growing number of artists are working to perpetuate it.

The style takes advantage of an incredible range of materials. It is clear that Columbia River Chinookans (and their neighbors) were compelled to produce it. Carving, both two-dimensional and three-dimensional, was primary, and painting was secondary, although some items received elaborate applications of paint. The distribution of artifacts made from wood, stone, bone, horn, and antler implies that availability was a significant factor in determining what material was used.

Lacking abundant sources of suitable wood, the people of The Dalles emphasized stone, bone, and horn, while those nearer the mouth of the Columbia found wood more readily available. Whalebone clubs and adzes came from the coast, while mountain sheep horn bowls and ladles came from the interior; both were traded widely from their source areas. Heavily used woods included the easily worked western red cedar for larger pieces and the harder alder, maple, ash, and yew for smaller items and containers (Ray 1938:131). Bone and elk antlers, which lend themselves to fine work, were used for figurines, effigies, adzes, wedges, pins, and awls. Around Lake River, effigies were often modeled in clay—sometimes fired, sometimes not. Worked stone pieces included materials from pumice to Columbia River basalt (Petersen 1978). Woodcarving tools were made of local stone and beaver incisors, while jadeite was acquired from sources in the Fraser River valley.

Basketry materials included sweetgrass sedge, cattail, hazel shoots, spruce root, red cedar bark and root, Indian hemp, and rushes. Beargrass, slough sedge, cedar bark, and eelgrass were typical items used for designs. A variety of dyes was applied to the sedges, beargrass, and cedar bark, while white to golden beargrass and black eelgrass were also used. Red and yellow were the most typical dyes seen on basketry; supplemented with the natural blacks, browns, and whites of the base material, the baskets were very colorful. Paint colors were typically red and black, with yellow, blue, green, and white also used.

Chinookan Style Art does not often stand alone. Typically, it can be seen as decoration or adornment of material objects, including adzes, bark shredders, baskets, bows, bowls, bunk rails, burial canoe uprights, canoes, clubs, combs, cradles, cups, digging stick handles, house posts, ladles, mat creasers, mortars and pestles, pins, pipes, "slave killers," and spoons. The most notable examples of stand-alone pieces are made of stone, clay, and antler. Scale was determined by the object being decorated, and forms within the art were often derived from the materials themselves. The art can be extremely small in scale, at times nearly microscopic (Figure 10.2). Most decorated surfaces are rounded, not flat. Architectural carvings—where flat, split cedar planks are the typical material—are exceptions and are also exceptional in terms of scale.

Basic geometric shapes, appearing as either raised or incised elements, are

FIGURE 10.2. Zoomorphic image, ⅝ inches × ⅜ inches. This is a near microscopic example of a Chinookan Style zoomorphic image that contains all of the classic elements of the style. (Courtesy of the Judy and Victor Reeder Collection)

the backbone of the style. Concentric geometric shapes and bands of interlocking positive zigzags are typical and often help define larger positive background spaces. They also appear integrally in anthropomorphic and zoomorphic imagery. The primary shapes are circles, triangles, rectangles, constricted rectangles (hourglass), squares, diamonds, crescents, almond shapes, pie shapes, and parallel and perpendicular lines. The word "geometry" is misleading, and it may be most appropriate to refer to this attribute of the art as "organic geometry." The artists were wholly aware of both positive and negative space and used both to develop forms. This concern over positive and negative is expressed by carving, incising the form of the objects themselves, and piercing.

Lower Columbia Art involves both zoomorphic and anthropomorphic figures and is strongly influenced by an aboriginal perspective of anatomy. Bodies are geometricized, and faces are composed of planes applied to geometric shapes such as diamonds, circles, and octagons. Observers often have noted the "skeletal" or "x-ray" attributes of the art. Figures often have overlapping body parts and extremities, while some lack key parts of anatomy altogether. Our use of the term Chinookan Anatomical Art is new.

Chinookan Art is dynamic. Its ability to combine flowing and diminishing lines, combined with the tension of geometric shapes interacting with each other and bold anthropomorphic and zoomorphic images in a single composition, adds to the inherent strength and unusual qualities of the artworks. The forms have genuine concern for each other and build tension by flowing into or rebounding off each other. The negative spaces created within the compositions are essential.

Chinookan Art is spiritually loaded. Images often represent spirits in human or animal form or both. Some are recognizable, while others are ambiguous and unfamiliar from a non-Native perspective. Many images, like Coyote, have their origins in regional mythology, while many are clearly veiled representations of their owner's spirit power(s). Numerical sequences, a significant concern in Chinookan lifeways and mythology, are evident in the style as well. The number five has great significance, and element sequences of three and, more typically, five are evident. Double imagery is also present, with forms being seen as different based on the viewer's perspective. Often these appear to be transformational type images that likely also represent personal spiritual experiences or the transformation of myth characters.

GEOMETRIC SHAPES

Mountain sheep horn bowls (Figure 10.3) often exemplify how geometric forms are used in complex compositions. Triangles are most often seen in interlocking patterns, where they create positive zigzag lines. Circles, rectangles, squares, diamonds, and their concentric versions are found both independently and representing "body parts." Crescents and repeating crescents function similarly. Geometricized body parts usually include "organs," leg and arm joints, ribs as well as heads, and their associated features. Almond shapes most often appear in the context of heads and eyes, as well as animal forms, although they can stand alone. Pie shapes are usually seen as negative space defining positive imagery, and constricted rectangles are found as independent negative images. Robin Wright (1991) notes the similarity of the constricted rectangle shape to net gauges of the region.

These elements can appear with as little as a row of interlocking triangles, forming a positive zigzag on the belly of a bow, or in an intricate use of space decorating the entirety of a horn bowl's complex surface. Typically, a combi-

FIGURE 10.3. Sheep horn bowl, 4.5 inches × 7.25 inches × 5.5 inches. This sheep horn bowl both exemplifies Chinookan Anatomical Art in its anthropomorphic images and beautifully illustrates the use of varied geometric shapes to complete a composition. (Courtesy of the Lee and Lois Miner Collection)

nation of shapes creates a complete composition, and designs can exist with or without zoomorphic or anthropomorphic imagery. A great deal of tension is generated in the art by the flowing and diminishing lines generated through these shapes and their interaction.

Chinookan basketry uses similar shapes and proportions. Triangles that form positive zigzags (Figure 10.4) are extremely common in the basketry west of the Portland Basin (see Crawford 1983:57–63). Anthropomorphic imagery, especially east of the Portland Basin, shows the same concern for anatomy typical in carving. Negative shapes may be formed by piercing, whether defining the attributes of an animal or human or simply piercing an object. Again relevant is the number of piercings seen on each individual piece. The numbers three and five are prevalent, with five being dominant.

LOWER COLUMBIA ANATOMICAL ART NO. 1: HUMAN FACES

Three main face types occur in the Chinookan Art Style: three-plane, two-plane, and the so-called tsagiglalal style. The human face is typically broken

FIGURE 10.4. Clatsop basket, mid-19th century, sweetgrass sedge, beargrass, and eel grass, 6 inches × 11.5 inches × 3 inches. This uniquely shaped Clatsop basket features geometric and zoomorphic imagery typical of the westernmost Chinookans and their neighbors. (Courtesy of the Hallie Ford Museum of Art, Willamette University, Salem, Oregon, gift of Richard D. Slater)

into planes, with a strong nose and brow ridge. The nose is almost always long, thin, and straight, terminating at the brow ridge. Faces are usually circular, though they also can assume other shapes, such as elongated ovals, triangles, diamonds, and octagons. Many recall the head-flattening tradition of the Greater Lower Columbia, either showing a strongly pushed-back forehead plane or, in the tsagiglalal type, elongating or squeezing the entire head. Details of hair and headdresses are usually present. The style's approach to the human face is relatively flat. Deeper, more three-dimensional carving is typical in stone and also possible in wood.

Tsagiglalal

The tsagiglalal type is named for the most famous image of this type, a pictograph near Old Wishram village, upriver from The Dalles on the north shore of the Columbia. Tsagiglalal, commonly known as "she-who-watches," is most associated with the easternmost Chinookan villages.

Tsagiglalal-type images should not be mistaken as representing the character tsagiglalal. Instead, they should be understood as a convention for representing the "human" face, primarily by easternmost Chinookans. When archaeologist B. Robert Butler (1965) showed an image of this type to an Upper Chinook (Wishram) woman, he got this response:

> I showed . . . a Wishram woman who was considered to be knowledge-able about "the old ways" . . . [a small tsagiglalal style] piece. She threw her hands over her eyes in great alarm and asked me to put it away. . . . She said that the carving was Tsi'La, 'watersnake,' a very powerful guardian spirit. She implied that Tsi'La was a very dangerous guardian spirit. I specifically questioned her about the grinning face motif. In reply she said, "people grin like that when they're sick" and "when people look at you like that, you get sick." (9)

The Wishram woman's reference to sickness, which likely recalls the spirit sickness that was a result of an encounter with a guardian spirit, speaks to the spiritual nature of the art.

Tsagiglalal-type figures vary immensely in size and material. A classic image of this type from Sauvie Island is a lava upright almost two feet tall (Wingert 1952:pl. 6). While the carving on a very small and remarkable pipe tamper (Figure 10.5) is typical, the tamper was carved in the round, which makes it unique among such objects. It can also be considered a fine example of double imagery. The strong flowing and diminishing lines share many superficial similarities with the Form Line Style to the north, but it is wholly representational of this type of face in the Chinookan Art Style.

The tsagiglalal face type is characterized by almond-shaped eyes and a strong brow line that arches down to define the eyes. The eyes are concentric, positive shapes defined by incising. Positive lines developed in this way typically grow and diminish. The negative incised lines and planes form "hollow" eyes, forehead, lower cheeks, and the mouth's interior. The mouth grows from the corner of the eyes, producing a "grinning" appearance, and it most often includes a tongue or tooth. The nose flows into eyes, eyebrow, and cheek. The overall shape of the face may be perfectly round or may appear to be stretched or elongated toward the forehead; it is typically an elongated flat oval. Beyond this, there is much variation. The face may have "ears" atop its head, giving it a zoomorphic appearance; it may have a flattened head with hair parted down the middle; or it may have a headdress.

FIGURE 10.5. Pipe tamper, precontact, horn, 2½ inches × ⅜ inches. This pipe tamper is a remarkable object, in size and design. It is of the tsagiglalal type typical of the easternmost Chinookans. (Courtesy of the Portland Art Museum, Portland, Oregon)

Three-Plane Type

This face type is characterized by clearly divided forehead, cheek, and chin planes. Each plane is recessed or pushed back into the plane above it, with a distinct step up to the next plane. Eyes and mouths are unusual, with the exceptions of power boards, house posts, and other large-scale carvings. When present, the chin plane holds the mouth, and the cheek plane holds eyes. Both mouth and eyes are often represented by incised crescent-shaped lines, although they can take numerous shapes typical to the art. Other elaborations on individual planes are possible. Occasionally, face paint or tattoo lines appear on chin or cheek planes. Most often, elaboration occurs on the forehead plane and may include explicit or hinted-at hair, headgear, hats, and so forth. The nose always terminates at the brow ridge, which can be the forehead or the brow line, and the forehead is almost always pushed back to represent head flattening. The nose may simply run into the forehead, but it usually pushes back below the forehead plane, resulting in a step up to the forehead plane. This approach to carving a human face appears to have had currency throughout the Greater Lower Columbia.

FIGURE 10.6. Burl mortar, early 19th century, maple burl, $5\frac{5}{8}$ inches × $6\frac{1}{4}$ inches diameter. Bold anthropomorphic images on this burl mortar highlight the strong shapes associated with the art style. The obvious clavicle and hip that connect these individuals are wholly typical yet unique in their presentation as joining elements. (Courtesy of the Portland Art Museum, Portland, Oregon, gift of Miss Winifred Myrick, through Mrs. David L. Davies)

Classic three-plane face examples include the faces on the house post in Paul Kane's *Interior of a Lodge, Columbia River,* on the coyote and man spoon (Figure 10.1), on the mountain sheep horn bowl (Figure 10.3), and on the contemporary Cathlapotle plankhouse image (Figure 10.15).

Two-Plane Type

Another representation of the human face is the two-plane style, in which the cheek, chin, and mouth form one unbroken plane with the forehead and nose forming the other. As with the three-plane style, the cheek planes are recessed or pushed back into the brow ridge or forehead, and the nose terminates at the brow ridge or forehead, which can be the forehead or the brow line. The forehead is almost always pushed back to simulate head flattening. Cheeks and other aspects of facial contours are typical in this type, but no cut line or plane identifies these additional features (Figure 10.6). Unlike the three-plane style, the two-plane often has eyes and mouth represented by incised lines, although relief eyes raised above the cheek plane are also known (Figure 10.12).

LOWER COLUMBIA ANATOMICAL ART NO. 2:
THE HUMAN BODY

The human torso is most often represented from a frontal perspective, although some profile imagery, especially in stone carving, is known. The relationship of positive and negative forms—defining sternum, clavicle, and arms—is based on human anatomy and generates a dynamic spatial intensity. Limbs are often represented as perpendicular or as growing and diminishing lines defined by incised negative space, carved geometric shapes, or piercing; they are often essential for containing the torso. Other body parts may be represented with a special emphasis on joints, ribs, and "organs." The term "organs" is used loosely here, because objects represented inside the body can also be of an expressly spiritual nature. Two body types are typical: the true anatomical and the underdecorated.

The most common representation of the human form by Lower Columbia artists includes anatomical detail such as clavicle, sternum, ribs, pelvis (hip or belt or skirt), limbs, joints, and "organs" (Figures 10.1, 10.3, 10.5, 10.7, 10.9). A strong and often naturalistic clavicle is expected on the upper body, as is a pelvis (belt or skirt) line often parallel to it. Arms characteristically run perpendicular to these, with an often undefined termination to both. A sternum

FIGURE 10.7. Shoto clay images. These images are rife with elements of the style. (Courtesy of the Burke Museum of Natural History and Culture, Seattle, Washington)

is usual between the arms and, while terminating at the clavicle, may or may not extend to the hip line. This sets up the typical format for expressing the human torso: three more or less parallel lines (arm-sternum-arm) terminating into perpendicular lines at top (clavicle) and bottom (pelvis, belt, skirt). Within this contained space are ribs and, sometimes, "organs." Ribs are often determined by parallel lines, chevrons, and crescents that can either be carved as planes or incised. Concentric circles, elongated ovals, almond shapes, and others typical of the art represent "organs" within this space as well. Limbs often show joints at shoulder, elbow, and knee; they may be represented as simple protrusions but often are formed by concentric circles, squares, or elongated rectangles. Hands and feet are not usual, although positive shapes may hint at their presence. Most often, limbs simply terminate into another positive line, such as the belt line.

The underdecorated type of representation is defined by strong positive shapes that lack recognizable anatomy beyond the basics: typically clavicle, arms, and pelvis. These are defined by pierced negative lines or geometric shapes that often are recessed. Contour may hint to anatomy other than the torso itself, but recognizable parts defined by incised or otherwise carved negative space are rare. Like the true anatomical type, limbs usually start at the shoulder and end at the "belt" line (Figure 10.6).

A unique medium for Columbia River Art is fired clay, represented by the well-known "Shoto clay" figures (Figure 10.7). These are most often anthropomorphic figures that, as a subgroup, are mostly simplified and sometimes even crude. The body, when represented, often is simply defined by incised lines and, at times, as a primary shape. Features are sometimes only roughly indicated and eyes are slits, although more typical representations of faces and body parts also are possible.

Shoto images also often hint at head flattening, hairstyle, and head gear or headdresses. The use of patterns in the clay can define negative and positive space. Wilbert (2010) examined a collection at the Burke Museum in Seattle and concluded that the designs and motifs on the clay were local and present on other media. These are the only fired clay figurines on the Northwest Coast or in the broader region, and they do not appear to have been made after contact.

LOWER COLUMBIA ANATOMICAL ART NO. 3: ANIMAL FIGURES

Animals may or may not be recognizable in the art. These representations are typically naturalistic but rely on geometry and strong positive and negative shapes to define them. Certain favored species tend to cluster in different media—for example, coyote, bears, and birds in wood; "dogs" and cervids in basketry; and salamanders, owls, beavers, and seals in stone. Many of the figures are depictions of spirit helpers.

Anatomical features are the focus. Multiple images, zoomorphic-zoomorphic or zoomorphic-anthropomorphic (Figure 10.5), may be combined, and it is often unclear where one individual ends and another begins. Numerous images may appear together, and details are often reduced to the point of lacking eyes, mouths, and other small details. Applied images are typically found standing atop handles or on a platform seemingly built for their use (Figure 10.8). Piercing is typical, and negative spaces are almost always concerned with the primary shapes of the art. The zoomorphs are compact, which allowed the artist to take advantage of the limitations of the material in which they are carved (Brown 1998).

Anthropomorphic images tend to have strong positive forms that define legs joined with hips or shoulders (Figure 10.1). This is clearly related, as a design sensibility, to the most common representation of human bodies, focused on the strong positive clavicle and hip elements that are joined by strong perpendicular elements of arms, sternum, and legs. In zoomorphs, we call these strong positive elements "hip-leg forms" and "shoulder-leg forms." In Figure 10.1, for example, the coyote's head is mounted on the front of the

FIGURE 10.8. Sheep horn ladle, mid-19th century, mountain sheep horn, 8¼ inches × 4⅜ inches × 5½ inches. This finely carved Chinookan ladle is a master work of the Chinookan Art Style. (Courtesy of the National Museum of Natural History, Smithsonian Institution, #E701–0, collected by George Gibbs, received 1862)

shoulder-leg form from a protruding neck that is a continuation of the body; the tail is likewise mounted on the rear of the hip-leg form. Birds will typically include a single hip-leg form. This form, when viewed from the front, creates a planklike platform, or plane, on which the head is mounted. This mounting of the head onto a flat surface can be seen in anthropomorphic and zoomorphic images on items such as power boards, house posts, image canoes, and spoons.

Bone and Antler Objects

A primary medium of the Chinookan Art Style is bone and antler, which allow for a tremendous amount of detail. Some of the best-known pieces have been produced in these materials, and it is clear that they have been a favorite material of artists for a very long time. Stand-alone objects include the well-known Sauvie Island woman and child at the Burke Museum. The straight adze, the primary woodworking tool of the style, had handles usually manufactured from elk antler or whale bone and was often highly decorated. Other decorated items carved from bone and antler were pins, awls, amulets, and gaming pieces.

Sheep Horn Bowls and Ladles

The carving and manipulation of the horn of bighorn sheep (mountain sheep) border on the miraculous. The transformation from raw horn to bowl (Figure 10.3) or ladle (Figure 10.8) is an extremely complex and time-consuming process, involving long periods of soaking, boiling, and/or steaming along with carving, shaping, and thinning. Once complete, these vessels are extremely durable, and examples can be assumed to have survived generations. Based on the wear and patina on many of the objects, it is clear that such objects were not always destroyed or sent with their owners into the afterlife. Some have been found in graves and show obvious signs of having been "killed," but there are numerous examples that exhibit a level of wear far beyond a human life span.

Sheep horn is a material that allows for a great deal of detail and, once shaped, is easily carved. Its resistance to splitting and breaking allows for zoomorphs that are often carved more finely than most wood species allow (Figure 10.8). The material is particularly well suited for chip carving, and there are numerous examples of fine detailed geometric decoration over the majority of a bowl's surface area. While ladles are often highly decorated, they usually do not have the quantity of decoration seen on bowls. Ladles are also most typically decorated with zoomorphs that are carved to perch or stand on the end of the handle. They can be carved integrally to the handle or stand on what often seems to be a surface expressly for that purpose. Bowls almost always have "ears"—raised projections on two sides that rise above the rim of the bowl. These are a product of the bowls' manufacture and are most often pierced and sometimes highly decorated. Anthropomorphs, especially faces, are most often represented on bowls.

Wooden Spoons

Chinookan-style spoons are typically carved with a bowl and an integral handle that is attached either at the rim on the back of the bowl or partway down the bowl's back. At times, handles can consist entirely of an anthropomorphic or zoomorphic image or both (Figure 10.1); at others, they include a "perch" upon which the image stands or is mounted. The bowls of spoons are usually

FIGURE 10.9. Elk hide armor, early 19th century, leather and paint, 38 inches × 40½ inches × 1⅝ inches. This is an exceptional example of Chinookan painted elk hide armor, known to the early fur trade as a clamon. Many of the obligatory elements of Chinookan anthropomorphic art are seen here and show a clear relationship to their carved counterparts. (Courtesy of The Field Museum, Chicago, Illinois, © The Field Museum, A114359_02d, John Weinstein, photographer)

carved to a canoelike form, which suggests that it was steamed and bent to expand the size of the spoon's bowl (like a canoe or sheephorn bowl or ladle).

Painted Objects

With the exception of pictographs, which are most common in eastern Chinookan territory and highlight the flat design associated with the Chinookan Art Style, stand-alone painted objects are rare. One example of a two-dimensional painted object is a spectacular clamon, or elk-hide armor (Figure 10.9), in the collections of the Field Museum in Chicago; it is the only known surviving example in Columbia River Style. Clamons, which were commonly mentioned in the historical literature, were made of elk hide and traded north—in the early contact era, by Euro-American traders—where they were used in intertribal warfare. Alexander Ross (2000) described them this way: "of elk-skin, dressed and worked to the thickness of nearly half an inch, and arrow-proof. The clemal nearly covers the whole body, with an opening left on the right side to allow the arm free action in combat" (89). So few examples of painted images exist that it is impossible to say how typical the image on the clamon is. It is clear, though, because of its provenance and the form of the imagery associated with it, that it is from the Lower Columbia. The focus on anatomy, the "planed" faces, and the concentrics place it firmly in the Chinookan Art Style.

STONE SCULPTURE

The level of detail in Chinookan stone sculpture varies by the material used and the intent of the artists. Some materials, such as basalt, do not lend themselves to a high degree of detail; others, like pumice and soapstone, are readily carved and can exhibit a great deal of detail. While pumice objects carved in the style can be highly detailed, they are more commonly quite simple. Some of the most intricately carved items are in soapstone and take the form of tubular pipes. These pipes, some long and thin, some stout and short, are sometimes very detailed. Often, zoomorphs stand asymmetrically on the side of these pipes, while others are embellished with geometric shapes.

Lower Columbia stone sculpture emphasizes both zoomorphs (Figures 10.11, 10.12) and anthropomorphs (Figure 10.7). Two varieties of anthropomorphic stone sculpture are common: stone bowls with human faces and upright figures. Numerous stone bowls were made on the Columbia River for utilitarian purposes. These can be finely shaped, deep vessels, but Columbia River bowls that appear to be integral to zoomorphic or anthropomorphic imagery are generally shallow. The function of these bowls is not always known. "Human" face-type bowls typically range from 5 to 12 inches high and seem to have been more prevalent in eastern Chinookan territory near The Dalles. While humanlike, they may represent any number of creatures—human, supernatural, and otherwise.

The exceptional 22.5-inch-high zoomorphic upright from Sauvie Island (Figure 10.11) exhibits aspects of double imagery and is a fine example of classic Chinookan stone art (Wingert 1952:pl. 5). Viewed from above, the object is clearly an animal. The spine with three shallow bowls is obvious, with ribs extending from both sides and shoulders reminiscent of the clavicle ground

FIGURE 10.10. Salamander bowl, precontact, basalt. Objects of the type of this fully carved and quite lifelike stone salamander "bowl" have often been misidentified as "beaver." While zoomorphic carvings are primarily ambiguous, the prominence of salamander and newt in the Greater Columbia River's mythology likely explains the frequency of these images within the art. (Courtesy of the Portland Art Museum, Portland, Oregon)

FIGURE 10.11. Zoomorphic object, 22½ inches, w. 13¾ inches. A unique perspective of typical Chinookan Art Style forms is seen on this large zoomorphic object. (Courtesy of the Oregon Historical Society, Portland, #bb010115)

FIGURE 10.12. Anthropomorphic figure, precontact, basalt, 55.5 inches × 17 inches × 6.5 inches. A typical two-plane face, headdress, and obligatory anatomy are obvious on this very large anthropomorphic figure. (Courtesy of the Portland Art Museum, Portland, Oregon)

the outstretched arms to the body. The "claws" are somewhat unusual, and a nose ridge is present, but no brow. The round eyes are characteristic of the style, and the mouth and presumed teeth are clear, setting the direction of the face (looking up). The cheek line, however, can double as a brow ridge and creates a distinctly human face when considered from another perspective. It is likely that this piece was mounted upright in the ground.

Upright Figures

Overlapping with the last class are large upright figures, often with shallow bowls in the top. Significant examples come from both Sauvie Island and The Dalles, with a size range of from several inches to over four feet tall. In 1841, Hudson's Bay Company Governor George Simpson (1968) described the Sauvie stone: "a block of black basalt, rudely chiseled by the Indians of ancient days into a column of four feet in height and three feet in diameter" (175). Touching the stone was supposed to cause rain. This is likely the upright sculpture now owned by the Portland Art Museum (Figure 10.12) (Mercer 2005: 20).

In 1856, George Gibbs (1955–56) described the Multnomah stone as one of a type of "weather stone":

> Yahotowit, an intelligent Klikitat, stated that the Multnomah stone was not the only one that produced rain. There are a great many in different places. They were a race of Skookums (Chinuk Wawa: monster or powerful spirits) who have been changed to stone, and if anyone sits down upon them, as a squaw when gathering berries, it speedily rained. (311)

Gibbs also listed several other weather stones in the area.

Other Stone Pieces

There are numerous examples of large zoomorphs carved in the Chinookan Art Style. Some are fully carved and include the shallow bowls typically seen in the area. One carving, reminiscent of the Pacific giant salamander (Figure 10.10), is unusual for being fully carved and for its lifelike appearance, while others are embellishments on naturally shaped stone, some of which are carved in place while others are portable. These large stone carvings were often ambiguous, although some clearly represented spirit powers. Guardian spirits were never to be identified outright, although a knowledgeable observer might recognize hints regarding the nature of the power. Others personified local stories and were meant to educate or warn viewers.

Large-Scale Carving: What the Explorers Saw

Most of the wood art pieces from the Lower Columbia have not survived due to time, conditions that are not conducive to the preservation of wood, and the cultural practice of "killing" or burning items owned by individuals at death. In the 1890s, for example, when Willapa Bay resident Mary Armstrong Riddell (Satsop) died,

> she had a huge canoe, about forty feet long, housed in a split cedar shake shed located above high tide. Some of her possessions were put in the canoe all was burned in ceremonial fashion. She was buried in the Bay Center cemetery, and as the grave was filled with Earth, Captain Jim Huckquist (Lower Chinook), who was married to her sister, Susan, threw in her beads and other trinkets. (Wiegardt Perrow 1971)

Canoes often were used as burial canoes, and power boards were used to support them. Killed items, which typically was done by punching holes into them, were placed with the body. Canoes used as burial canoes also were pierced to ceremonially "kill" them and for the practical purpose of allowing drainage.

Museum collections hold some of these "killed" objects, as they were favorites of early grave robbers. Many Chinookan Art Style pieces also exist in tribal communities. More undoubtedly will see the light of day, but much of what once existed on the Columbia River was recorded only in the minds of elders and the descriptions of early explorers.

House Posts

Like their neighbors to the north, Lower Columbia peoples often carved posts and planks inside their lodges with anthropomorphic and zoomorphic figures. Many early explorers mentioned this practice. In 1814, at Chinook village, Alexander Henry (1992:613) passed between the legs of a "large rudely carved figure of a man" just inside the door of a Native lodge. At The Cascades, he reported that bed planks and interior partitions were "carved and painted [with] uncouth figures of eagles, tortoises, and other animals" (Henry 1992:630). In late March 1806, at Kathlamet village, Meriwether Lewis reported:

> these people are very fond of sculpture in wood of which they exhibit
> a variety of specimines about their houses. the broad peices supporting
> the center of the roof and those through which the doors are cut, seem
> to be the peices on which they most display their taist. I saw some of these
> which represented human figures setting and supporting the burthen on
> their shoulders. (Lewis and Clark, 1991:9–10)

Power Boards and Power Figures

Power boards and power sticks represented items infused with the power of a person's personal guardian spirit, and both were used in guardian spirit and shamanistic ceremonies. For Portland Basin Chinookans, we have Paul Kane's depiction of a spirit board; for the river-mouth Chinooks, there are two near-contemporaneous descriptions from the lodge of Chenamus (Concomly's son) at a Chinook village. In 1836, John Townsend (1999) wrote: "In almost every house there is a large figure, or idol, rudely carved and painted upon a board, and occupying a conspicuous place" (253). The best description comes from an unpublished journal from the 1839 Belcher expedition:

> we found the chief seated "a la torque" [legs crossed] on a mat placed on an elevated platform at the extremity of the building. . . . Behind the seat of the chief was a black board painted red with a slight relief of coloured rings; and again behind this, forming the extremity of the house was a gigantic figure of red and black with long arms and five projecting ribs. A triangular red face, and horizontal figure-of-eight eyes; they pointed upwards to explain its medium. Two others of smaller size were stationed opposite to each other at the sides. (Hinds 1836–42)

George Gibbs (1955–56) recorded in the 1850s that, following the adolescent spirit quest at Willapa Bay, "an early task was to represent his tamahnous [guardian spirit] in some suitable form, as by painting or carving upon a board. This device was placed in some conspicuous situation in the lodge during the life of the owner, after his death near his grave" (127). An exceptional example of this type of power board was collected and photographed at Bay Center in 1898. It is currently housed at the American Museum of Natural History in New York City.

Power figures are mentioned in the historical record in three contexts: in the rear of the lodge near the chief's bed (like power boards), in shamanistic ceremonies, and at gravesites. Hinds (1836–40) saw what were certainly power figures on three sides of the chief's platform at the back of the house; and at The Cascades, Henry (1992:649) recorded four two-feet-high crowned figures and "two large painted stones" around the chief's bed.

Artists Alfred Agate (1841) and Paul Kane (1847) drew the interior of Chinookan lodges, showing house posts carved in anthropomorphic fashion. A modern example exists in the reconstructed Cathlapotle longhouse in the Ridgefield National Wildlife Refuge north of Vancouver, Washington. Both Kane's and Agate's paintings illustrate the significant aspects of Chinookan monumental sculpture. Geometric (Agate) and geometric and zoomorphic (Kane) bunk rails can be clearly seen lining the walls. Anthropomorphic images are seen in both images on the rear house posts. A power board rests at the end of the sleeping bunk on the left of the Kane image. While not presented in detail, it clearly includes an anthropomorphic spirit figure.

"Image Canoe" Carvings

There were several types of Lower Columbia canoes, separable by form and function (see Boyd 1996:61). As with northern canoes, painting, carving, and inlay were forms of adornment. A special class of Chinookan canoes, which became known as "image canoes," had carvings that were of a scale unrivaled on the Northwest Coast. There were two primary types: cutwater, with a near perpendicular bow that had an image mounted on a platform carved on it, and double image, with a near perpendicular bow and stern and images on both ends.

For cutwater images, Alexander Ross (2000:98) noted a man or a "white-headed eagle" on the bow, and Alexander Henry (1992) described a Clatsop chief's war canoe as having a "carved figure of a carnivorous animal with large ears erect, and arms & legs clinging to the upper extremities . . . grinning most horribly. . . . The large ears are painted green, other parts red and black" (679).

On November 4, 1805, on the Columbia near what is now Portland International Airport, Lewis and Clark (1990) met "a large Canoe . . . orniminted with *Images* carved in wood the figures of <man &> a Bear in front & a man in Stern, Painted & fixed verry netely on the <bow & Stern> of the Canoe, rising to near the hight of a man" (18). The explorers called the place Image Canoe Island (now Hayden Island). On February 1, 1806, below The Cascades, Lewis described others:

> some of them particularly on the sea coast are waxed painted and orni-
> mented with curious images at bough and Stern; those images sometimes
> rise to the hight of five feet; the pedestals on which these immages are fixed
> are sometimes cut out of the solid stick with the canoe, and the imagary is
> formed of separate small peices of timber firmly united with tenants and
> motices without the assistance of a single spike of any kind. . . .their immages
> are representations of a great variety of grotesque figures. (Lewis and Clark
> 1990:263, 265)

Two sketches in the Lewis and Clark journals depict a man on the bow and either a bird or bear on the stern. An exceptional double-image canoe model (Figure 10.13) at the American Museum of Natural History has a bird on its bow and an apparent bear on its stern.

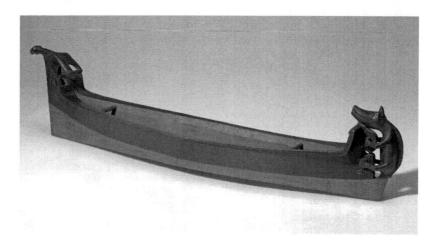

FIGURE 10.13. Double-ended image canoe. This rare example of a double-ended image canoe is one of the true master works of the Chinookan Art Style. (Courtesy of the Division of Anthropology, American Museum of Natural History, Lower Columbia River canoe catalog number 16.1/1786 A)

ARCHAEOLOGY

The small sample of artifacts from controlled archaeological excavations includes stone sculpture, carved bone and antler objects, and clay objects. Rock art, both petroglyphs and pictographs, is plentiful in and above the Columbia River Gorge (e.g., Keyser 1992), but some have been found on the Lower Columbia. The most famous is Tsagiglalal (She Who Watches), which overlooks the upstream end of the Columbia River Narrows, a major fishing and trading locality.

Also rare in the archaeological sample is basketry and carved and worked wood. Conditions in most sites on the lower river are such that these items do not preserve. Recent work at a waterlogged site on Sauvie Island in the Wapato Valley (Croes et al. 2009), however, demonstrates that there are sites with the right conditions in the Lower Columbia, so we may anticipate the recovery of such items.

On the Northwest Coast, objects carrying design elements date to as early as 3000 BC (Ames and Maschner 1999). The earliest in the Lower Columbia region, recovered from the Palmrose site in Seaside, Oregon, date to between 800 BC and AD 300. Only a few of the large number of carved antler and bone objects at Palmrose have been studied or described (Connolly 1992), but it is clear that the Chinookan Art Style was well established by this time. Ames

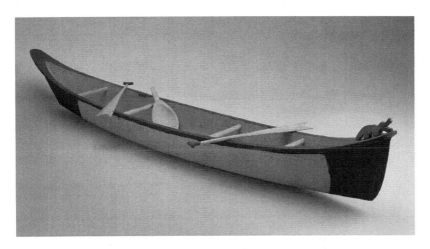

FIGURE 10.14. Cut-water image canoe, alder and paint. The classic cut-water type image canoe is represented here with associated paddles and bailer. (Courtesy of The Field Museum, Chicago, Illinois, © The Field Museum, A114959d_018, John Weinstein, photographer)

and Maschner (1999) found resemblances between the Palmrose objects and contemporary art in southern British Columbia and also with much later art objects on the lower river. One zoomorph, for example, is an owl form, historically one of the common animal figures of the Chinookan Art Style.

Excavations at the Meier and Cathlapotle sites in the Wapato Valley produced small samples of design-bearing objects dating between about AD 1400 and 1840. Most of these are of bone and antler, while a few are of stone or pumice. Most of the bone and antler appear to be pendent fragments. One, from Meier, carries a series of triangular forms that might represent houses but that are similar to basketry motifs. A charred fragment from a hearth at Cathlapotle exhibits deeply carved form lines in an abstract design. Stone sculpture at both sites was limited to a few bowls, zoomorphic mauls and pestles, and two anthropomorphic faces carved in pumice. The Meier artifact is elaborate, with faces carved on both sides. The two Meier faces, of the three-plane type, differ somewhat in that they have large eyes and open mouths; the two sides, however, are not identical. The Cathlapotle example is much simpler and smaller and does not fit into either the three- or two-plane category. It is also of pumice but is almost sketchlike in its simplicity. The Meier and Cathlapotle artifacts were recovered in similar contexts, at the rear of houses. Those sites also yielded fragments of pumice bowls with incised geometric designs.

FIGURE 10.15. Wealth post, Cathlapotle plankhouse. The final "wealth" post at the Cathlapotle plankhouse in Ridgefield, Washington, is seen here during construction. The post was designed by Tony A. Johnson and primarily carved by Adam McIsaac. (Courtesy of Adam McIsaac, photographer)

Neither site produced the large anthropomorphic or zoomorphic sculpture for which the Lower Columbia is known (e.g., Wingert 1952). The only such sculpture that may be in its original exterior location is the large "beaver bowl" on Fisher's Landing (Keyser et al. 2006). Peterson (1978) inventoried Lower Columbia River art, describing and illustrating a large number of smaller sculptures, including bowls. Most originated in the Columbia River Gorge, but a few were collected in the Wapato Valley. Many may have been taken from graves.

The tradition of art on the Lower Columbia experienced a precipitous decline with the introduction of alien diseases in the late 1700s. Many artists and craftsmen and women with specialized knowledge died, taking their skills with them. The Indian Shaker Church and Christianity led to the decline of spirit beliefs and the substitution of white for Native technology, which also contributed to a decline in traditional art. Looting and the Native American artifact trade resulted in many surviving pieces being dispersed and lost to the public (Butler 2007).

Despite this long decline, Chinookan Style Art is finally taking its rightful place in the communities of its origin. Today, large installations and individual pieces can be seen in art galleries, public parks, and buildings and homes.

PART II

After Euro-American Contact

ELEVEN

LOWER CHINOOKAN DISEASE AND DEMOGRAPHY

Robert T. Boyd

I N the first century of contact, the Lower Columbia Chinookans suffered more from the effects of introduced diseases and depopulation than almost any other Native peoples in the Northwest. Yet they survived, and their numbers are increasing. This chapter is a history of Lower Chinookan disease and population, from the aboriginal state, through the disruptive early contact years, up to the rebound and revitalization of the last century.

ABORIGINAL HEALTH AND DISEASE

Like other Northwest Coast peoples contacted by whites in the late 1700s and in common with early contact hunting-gathering peoples around the world, Lower Columbia Chinookans were relatively healthy. The explorers and traders who first met them said as much. On November 1, 1805, after spending nearly a year in lower-river Chinookan territory, William Clark wrote: "The nativs of the waters of the Columbia appear helthy" (Lewis and Clark 1988:373). In 1811, Astorian Alexander Ross (2000) recorded: "If we may judge from appearances, these people are subject to but few diseases" (98). And as late as 1824, Hudson's Bay Company Governor George Simpson (1968) proclaimed: "they are however wonderfully healthy being rarely afflicted by any other than Imported Diseases" (99).

This relative health, however, did not mean that Lower Columbia Chinookan peoples were disease-free. They had their own inventory of diseases, which were related to a fishing and foraging lifestyle, residence in relatively small villages, and seasonal movement to resource areas. Most of the diseases were chronic, arising from dietary imbalances, bone wear, and parasites, all maintained in individuals and rarely very contagious. We know about these diseases from the early historical literature, anthropologists' interviews with Chinookans, studies of disease traces in bones, and epidemiological comparisons with neighboring peoples (Table S11.1 online).

For hunting-gathering peoples, living in high-latitude temperate regions had advantages and disadvantages. The most important advantage was that colder climates support fewer parasites and disease-causing micro-organisms than do warmer ones. The biggest disadvantage was seasonal food shortages in late winter and early spring, which led to nutritional problems and occasional starvation. On the Lower Columbia, eyewitness accounts describe such shortages, and several myths and tales tell of starvation. A key resource was salmon, which is known for its inconsistent runs. In early April 1806, Lewis and Clark (1991) met several canoes of Cascades peoples on their way to the Wapato Valley. On April 1, Lewis wrote "that their relations at that place were much straightened . . . for the want of food; that they had consumed their winter store of dried fish and that those of the present season had not yet arrived" (49). Two days later, he wrote: "these poor people appeared to be almost starved, they picked up the bones and little pieces of refuse meat which had been thrown away by the party" (62). John Ordway, a member of the expedition, reported on April 5: "they inform us that the natives above the great falls [The Cascades] have no provisions and many are dieing with hunger. this information has been so repeatedly given by different parties of Indians that it does not admit of any doubt" (Lewis and Clark 1995:286).

Myths and tales with starvation themes include "A Famine at The Cascades" (Sapir 1909b:227–29), "They Died of Hunger" (Clackamas; Jacobs 1958–59:458–66), "The Spirit of Hunger" and "Winter All the Year Round" (Kathlamet; Boas 1901:207–15, 217–20), and "The GiLä'unaLX" (Chinook; Boas 1894:229–33). Several other texts note starvation in passing. Causes for starvation included a cold and late winter with snow and ice, the exhaustion of stored food supplies, and the failure of major food resources. Some people suffered more than others. In "The Spirit of Hunger," for example, "Many old people were dying . . . poor children died of hunger" (Boas 1901:207). That myth also personified hunger as a spirit who hoarded and withheld the wild foods: "She was very lean; she was only bones, but she was braided" (212).

The personal hygiene of Lower Chinookans was good. Meriwether Lewis wrote of people in the Wapato Valley: "they are fond of cold, hot, & vapor baths of which they make frequent uce both in sickness and in health and at all seasons of the year. they have also a very singular custom among them of baithing themselves allover with urine every morning" (Lewis and Clark

1991:33). The ammonia in urine would be an effective cleanser, and both frequent bathing and the urine wash are noted elsewhere (e.g., Simpson 1968:103; Jacobs 1958–59:400; Jacobs 2003:92–93).

Refuse disposal was a problem, as it is with semisedentary people everywhere. Solid waste accumulated over time, and salmon-processing attracted flies (e.g., Henry 1992:624, 702). Regular seasonal movements—from winter villages to warm-season camps—were a major way of dealing with this problem. Several sources describe abandoned winter villages infested with "fleas" (e.g., Lewis and Clark 1990:142; Cox 1957:76; Ross 2000:99; Simpson 1968:62). From the standpoint of disease transmission, however, lice were a bigger problem and the real parasitic villains among precontact Northwesterners. Myths from the Kathlamet and Clackamas give complete inventories of lice varieties and their characteristics, and "greyback" (body) louse was a myth character (Boas 1901:12–13; Jacobs 1958–59:394–95). Lice were removed manually (e.g., Ray 1938:153–54; Jacobs 1958–59:340) or in the heat of the sweat lodge (Boyd 1999b:285–86).

TRADITIONAL CURING

Clackamas Chinook recognized three broad classes of curing: minor ailments, treated by natural medicines; aches and pains and minor fevers, treated by sweating in sweat lodges; and more serious problems, handled by specialized curers in ritualized treatment sessions. The first class included "cuts, infections, burns, and broken bones," dealt with by "poultices, herbs, and splints" (Jacobs 1959a:14). Willapa Bay people had several more specific medicines, including teas and grease ointments (Swan 1972:178). Herbalists were said to be mostly women (Ross 2000:97).

Sweat bathing was seldom mentioned below Kathlamet, but all upriver Chinookans practiced it. Although Emma Luscier described two types—a plank structure and a willow-branch "beehive" oven—the second is the only one clearly defined in the historical records. David Douglas's 1825 description of sweat baths downriver from Vancouver is the best we have (1959:114–15). The sweat lodge was made by digging a hole, one to three feet deep and five feet in diameter, on a river or stream bank and covering it with a round frame of willow sticks and "turf" or mud. Hot stones were added to the hole (apparently not heated in place), and the occupant (rarely more than one) entered with a bowl of water, which he poured over the stones to make steam. After remaining in the enclosure for from 15 minutes to an hour, or until he was "parboiled," he ran out of the lodge and jumped into the cold water. Sweating, which removed body odor and "purified," was done before hunting and as an adjunct to several ceremonies. Although sweating and the cold plunge worked well with prewhite aches and minor fevers, the treatment could be deadly with introduced febrile diseases.

Curing ceremonies conducted by shamans—"curers," "medicine-men," "Indian doctors"—were, like head flattening and canoe burial, unusual and fascinating to Euro-Americans. Including ethnographic recollections, there are over 20 accounts from the Lower Columbia Chinookan area. The best— from Gabriele Franchère, Joseph Frost, and James Swan—are based on or describe a single curing session. Franchère's (1969) 1811 account is the earliest and most concise and can be used as a template to describe the elements of the curing procedure.

> As soon as an Indian feels indisposed . . . the medicine man is called and, having received a present, begins his operations as follows: The patient lies on his back with his family and friends gathered about him, each holding a long stick in one hand and a shorter one in the other, the medicine man intones a lugubrious chant and the others take up the same tune beating time on their sticks. . . . the medicine man goes about curing the patient, kneeling beside him and pressing with both fists against his stomach. . . . At the end of each verse or couplet of the song, the medicine man joins his hands, brings them up to his mouth and blows, repeating often until, having spat out of his mouth a small white pebble that he has hidden in it in advance, he shows it triumphantly to all. . . . [and] blow[s] the sickness into the fire. (102–3)

Shamans had obtained a spirit power (or several) that gave them the power to cure. They normally endured long and difficult quests to obtain these powers and did not begin curing until later in life. Two sources indicated that there were special initiation dances for shamans during the winter ceremonies (Emma Luscier merely noted the initiation dance; John Wacheno actually described one). Chinookan people also believed that with the power to cure diseases came the power to cause them. So, an evil shaman was commonly assumed to have sent the object/spirit intrusion, and fully half the sources noted that this belief frequently resulted in the killing of an alleged disease-causing shaman.

Curing ceremonies always took place indoors and were attended by family and friends of the ill person. The patient reclined on his back, on mats, sometimes elevated. Shamans were invited to cure, usually by messengers, and could decline treatment after giving a preliminary diagnosis. They normally began by singing, accompanied by the audience, who beat wooden poles on the ceiling and sang. Lower Columbia Chinookan sources do not address the timing of sessions, but they probably were more flexible than elsewhere in the Northwest, where they took place at night and for several nights in succession. Some sources described the building tension of the audience and the frenzy of the shaman, which suggest lengthy sessions.

How a shaman cured depended on his diagnosis. Chinookans believed that the more serious, potentially deadly ailments had supernatural causes. The most frequent was what anthropologists call "object intrusion"—that is, the entry of a foreign object-cum-spirit—usually sent by a malevolent outsider such as an evil shaman. In the Lower Columbia Chinookan area, the object was removed most often by pressing on the torso, as Franchère describes (sources also indicate that contact ranged from passing one's hands over the body to kneeling on it). Less frequent, but still common, was the "sucking cure," in which the shaman placed his mouth on the affected area. Both of these procedures resulted in the production of some small object, either in the mouth or the hands, which was quickly displayed to the audience and then disposed of. The sources list white pebbles, shells, pieces of bone, feathers, skin, or a "bug" (according to Wacheno, as the object was perceived to be animate), which rarely were accompanied by pus or blood if produced from the mouth (see also Jacobs 2003:159). The object might be thrown into the air with a quick movement of the hands, tossed into a fire, or dunked in a container of water.

Less commonly reported but apparently present throughout the Chinookan area was the belief that some diseases were caused by the loss of the soul, which had to be retrieved from the Land of the Dead by shamans or their spirit helpers. In the elaborate Spirit Canoe ceremony, soul loss and retrieval are well documented and often thought to be characteristic of neighboring western Washington Salishan peoples. A simpler form is reported in both river-mouth and Clackamas Chinookan sources, so it was probably typical of the Lower Columbia as well. Silas Smith (1901), who was half Clatsop, described the ceremony this way:

> They believe that when a person becomes very sick the spirit leaves the
> body and seeks the shores of the spirit land, and unless it is recaptured and

returned to its original tenement, the person will of course surely die. In such cases the services of a skillful tamanawas doctor are engaged, and an assistant is furnished to accompany him . . . to the land of the dead. The assistant is given a baton, ornamented in the upper part with plumes of birds and claws of beasts. The doctor manipulates his assistant until he has him mesmerized; also the baton, which is in a constant state of agitation; he then places himself in a trance state, meanwhile keeping up a vigorous chant, and they start on their excursion to the shadowy shores. . . . If they should be fortunate enough to find the absconding spirit, the doctor secures it and brings it back . . . restoring it to the patient. (260–61)

In the Puget Salish Spirit Canoe ceremony, an actual canoe was employed, and a bevy of shamans acted out the trip and soul recovery. Although Cultee spoke of "three or four seers . . . who go and visit the guests" (Boas 1893:39) and an 1840s source reported "priests" who "retire into a canoe to hold a consultation" (Dunn 1844:91), no Lower Columbia source describes a real Spirit Canoe ceremony. References to "mesmerism" (hypnotism), however, occur often in Chinookan spirit-dancing accounts. The Nehalem Tillamook description of soul retrieval, for example, has the shaman "lie dead" for a day (Jacobs 2003:169). A myth told by Charles Cultee (Boas 1894:158–60) and notes from Mrs. Howard (Jacobs 1958–59:516, 1959a:14) simply mention soul retrieval. Unlike object/spirit intrusion, soul loss was attributable to ghosts or errant souls, so shamans were blameless and shaman killings were not associated with it (Gibbs 1955–56:136).

POSTCONTACT DISEASE HISTORY

Before contact with whites, Lower Chinookan peoples had a "disease pool" of several chronic, not very contagious ailments that persisted in individuals and a curing system consisting of herbal treatments, sweat bathing, and shamanistic curing sessions. Although based on a theory of supernatural causation, the curing system nevertheless helped ameliorate minor ailments and, for those it could not cure, provided some psychological closure. There is no evidence that curing practices made any disease situation worse.

As soon as Euro-Americans arrived or their influence was felt on the Lower Columbia, however, the system was thrown out of balance. New diseases appeared, and the indigenous curing system was unable to deal with them. There were several epidemics, people died, populations dropped. What happened to the Lower Chinookan people in the first century of contact was a local example of what is now called the Columbian Exchange (Crosby 1972), the interchange between the Eastern and Western hemispheres of plants, animals, peoples, technologies, and disease-causing microorganisms that followed Christopher Columbus's 1492 landing in the Americas. Of the 10 most prominent and virulent diseases generally accepted by historical epidemiologists as making the voyage from Eurasia and Africa to the Americas (Boyd 1999b:table 2), four of the deadliest—smallpox, malaria, viral influenza, and measles—were documented on the Lower Columbia. Whites also brought tuberculosis and venereal syphilis, found elsewhere in Native America, to the Lower Columbia (Table S11.2 online). Though the Chinookan peoples survived, the cumulative impact of this onslaught on their numbers and cultural traditions was devastating (see Boyd 1999b). Here, I will summarize what we know from the Lower Columbia, emphasizing the two most important diseases, smallpox and malaria.

Smallpox

The first imported disease to arrive among the Chinookan peoples was almost certainly smallpox, one of the most deadly and contagious diseases that affect humans. Three epidemics are documented among Lower Columbia Indians, but there may have been more. Smallpox is caused by a virus and spreads by face-to-face contact, usually through a sneeze ("droplet infection") or by touch, rarely through objects. The disease follows a predictable pattern of about 10 days latency, followed by a rash on the extremities that spreads and develops into lesions, during which time the carrier is infectious. An average 30 percent of those infected die after about a month, while the remainder, often with pockmarks, survive and become immune to reinfections. Smallpox vaccine was rare and largely unavailable in the Northwest during the presettlement period.

In February 1806, Meriwether Lewis recorded the first evidence for Chinookan smallpox: "The small pox . . . prevailed about 4 years since among the Clatsops and distroy several hundred of them. . . . I think the later ravages of the small pox may well account for the number of remains of villages which we find deserted on the river and Sea coast" (Lewis and Clark 1990:285). Two months later, in April, near *ničáqʷli* (the Blue Lake village), William Clark wrote: "an old man . . . brought foward a woman who was badly marked with the Small Pox and made Signs that they all died with the disorder . . . which

She was verry near dieing with when a Girl. from the age of this woman this Distructive disorder I judge must have been about 28 or 30 years past" (65). Two epidemics are noted here, the first (using Clark's calculations) in 1776–78, the second in winter 1802. These dates are supported by records from other parts of the Northwest, suggesting regional epidemics, not just local outbreaks (see Boyd 1999b:ch. 2).

There is considerable controversy over the exact date of the first recorded epidemic and the possibility that smallpox penetrated the Northwest earlier. One hypothesis holds that the first great American smallpox epidemic, brought with Cortez to Mexico in 1520, spread throughout North and South America (Dobyns 1966; Campbell 1989). Also, vessels from smallpox-source areas may have gone astray or been wrecked on the Oregon or Washington Coasts before the Spanish explorations of 1774–75. These include Sir Francis Drake's 1579 voyage on the *Manila Galleon,* which debarked annually from Acapulco starting in 1565 (Schurz 1939) and Japanese junks that wrecked several times on the coast in the 1900s and assumedly in earlier centuries as well (Brooks 1876). In 1900, Silas Smith, a grandson of Clatsop chief Coboway, recorded three traditions of pre–Robert Gray wrecks, including the "beeswax ship" and the wreck that left the metalworker Soto behind. Despite the intriguing possibilities, however, there is no hard evidence for disease introduction from any of these sources.

There is also controversy over the precise date of the earliest epidemic noted by Lewis and Clark, how far it spread, and how it got to the Northwest (Boyd 1999b:32–38). Since 1973, researchers have fallen into two camps: one favoring introduction by a Spanish coastal voyage of the 1770s (Cook 1973; Fortuine 1989) and another claiming that smallpox spread in the early 1780s from the Plains through mounted Indian intermediaries (Harris 1994; Fenn 2001). A recently discovered oral tradition from just south of Chinookan lands gives added support to the coastal theory and the introduction of the disease in the early 1780s. It is not a definitive answer, however, and it may well be that smallpox entered the Northwest at approximately the same time from both directions.

In 1845, settler John Minto (1915) interviewed Cullaby, a Clatsop man, aged about 50. Cullaby related a tradition that dated to the time of his grandparents' marriage, which would have been sometime between about 1765 and 1775. In Nehalem Tillamook lands, just south of Clatsop, people heard booms and saw fire at sea; on the beach, they found three corpses and a survivor with red hair. The red-haired man stayed with the Nehalem and married a local woman. Then, in about 1782—recalled as a decade after the wreck and 10 years before the first ships entered the Columbia—another boat came close to shore:

> Some of its people made a landing in small boats. When they went away, they left two sick men who soon afterwards died. Soon many of the Tilla-mook became sick in the same way. The disease caused their skins to turn very red and their faces to swell, making them almost blind. Many, many of them died, and the faces of those who survived were left spotted ever afterwards. This deadly sickness soon reached the Clatsops from the Tilla-mook people. (71)

The red-haired man died, too, but not before he warned the Nehalem to flee in small groups to the hills.

There is not much question about the origin of Lewis and Clark's second reported epidemic in the winter of 1801–2; it most certainly arrived via the northern Rockies route. Mortality was less, probably concentrated among nonimmunes under the age of 20 (Boyd 1999b:39).

Other than Lewis and Clark, evidence for the early smallpox epidemics comes from archaeology and from records of the Astorians. It is difficult to isolate, archaeologically, evidence of the smallpox epidemics from others that followed, but the likeliest example appears to be at the Sauvie Island village Clannarminamon excavated by the Oregon Archaeological Society in 1968, where "over 90 . . . skeletal remains were encountered throughout the entire excavation area at the same depth and all in complete disarray" (Jones 1972:182). This was the site where an 1812 observer reported that a formerly "very powerfull tribe" had been "reduced by the small Pox to 60 Men" (Stuart 1935:32).

Several years after the smallpox epidemics, the Astorians recorded how Chinookan peoples responded to what I call "a heritage of fear" in *The Coming of the Spirit of Pestilence*. There are two well-known examples. The first is the saga of the Cree-speaking female berdache Kauxumanupika, who accompanied explorer David Thompson down the Columbia in the summer of 1811. On the return trip, the explorers had to protect her because she had threatened Indians along the way with smallpox in order to extort furs from them. At Fort Astoria, fort head Duncan McDougall (1999) said: "if we had not taken him [*sic*] under our protection from the moment he arrived, he would have fallen sacrifice to the dread they entertain of his power to introduce the SmallPox, which he very imprudently boasted of on his way down" (30). At The Cascades, Thompson (1962) had to reassure the people that the whites were not bringing "the Small Pox to destroy us" (367) and "2 Men of enormous Size to overturn the Ground &c" (earthquakes?). Upriver, the threats of Kauxumanupika may have spawned a religious reaction, which fed into the nativistic religions that arose in the mid-1800s (Spier 1935:25–29; DuBois 1938:8–9; Boyd 1996b:175–76).

The second event, supposedly carried out by McDougall himself, may have been inspired by Kauxumanupika, but its immediate impetus was the massacre of the crew of the *Tonquin* off Vancouver Island, which frightened the isolated Euro-American colony at Fort Astoria. McDougall brought together the headmen from both sides of the river and produced a small flask. He warned: "See here . . . in this bottle I hold the small-pox safely corked up; I have but to draw the cork and let loose the pestilence, to sweep man, woman, and child from the face of the earth" (Irving 1976:80). Concomly and the other leaders were cowed and did not attack the fort. Twenty-nine years later, another American, John Dominis, threatened Native Americans, both on the Lower Columbia and off Cape Flattery, with "disease in a bottle."

Native American myths from the Lower Columbia and adjacent regions (Alsea and Lower Chehalis) contain a motif of a person who travels from village to village, with each visit followed by the death of all inhabitants. Myths are not history, but this certainly sounds like the effects of a highly infectious epidemic disease. One Chinook myth, "The Transformers" (Curtis 1970:116–23), has people dying after a woman laughs in their faces (droplet infection?); another, "The Sun's Myth" (Hymes 1975; excerpt in ch. 8 in this volume), contains elliptical passages that may refer to pockmarked skin. Both appear to be attempts to control and capture, through symbolic expression, the horrifying experience of the early epidemics.

Smallpox may have appeared on the Lower Columbia a third time, in 1824–25, though the sources are not clear. Concomly lost two sons and "8 individuals of his family" (Scouler 1905:277) during this time, and scattered references from other parts of the coast refer to a "mortality." If it was smallpox, it was reappearing every generation, claiming mostly nonimmune people born since the prior epidemic. In 1853, a final smallpox epidemic attacked surviving Chinookan communities, killing nearly 50 percent of the people at the river mouth and at The Dalles (Boyd 1999b:161–64).

"Fever and Ague"

Smallpox, reappearing in waves among Lower Chinookans, was devastating, but worse—from the standpoint of suffering, number of casualties, and effect on cultural continuity—was a disease that first appeared in summer 1830 and that we now know was malaria. The disease was then known as either "fever and ague" (or shaking) or "intermittent fever," after its most prominent symptoms, alternating fits of fever and chills (the term "malaria," after its supposed cause, "bad air," was not generally used before the mid-1800s). Cases of the fever had popped up on the Lower Columbia before 1830 (e.g., two members of the Astor Expedition), always imported from elsewhere. The Lower Columbia Chinookans believed that the disease was introduced by an American captain, John Dominis, and his ship the *Owyhee*, which sat at anchor off the lower tip of Sauvie Island for most of a year in an abortive attempt to capture the Indian trade from the Hudson's Bay Company.

The *Owyhee* pulled anchor in mid-July 1830, and it was during that month that the first cases of "intermittent fever" appeared at Fort Vancouver. By month's end, almost everyone at the fort had experienced fits, and the supply of medicine was exhausted, to be replenished in mid-August by the annual supply ship. We do not know whether Indian settlements were hit simultaneously or later, but August and September were apparently the deadly months. On October 11, in separate letters, fort head Dr. John McLoughlin (1941) wrote: "The Intermitting Fever . . . has carried off three-fourths of the Indn. Population in our vicinity" (88). At Fort George, botanist David Douglas (1905) wrote: "A dreadfully fatal intermittent fever broke out in the lower parts of this river about 11 weeks ago, which has depopulated the country. Villages, which afforded from 1 to 200 effective warriors, are totally gone" (202). McLoughlin's "vicinity" probably referred to the Portland Basin, while Douglas's "lower" river stretched from The Cascades to the river mouth. The two Multnomah villages and Cathlanaquiah, on the southeast and southwest shores of Sauvie Island, filled with corpses, were burned on order of McLoughlin to prevent further infection. Several members of Kiesno's family expired, although he received medicine and survived. At the river mouth, Concomly died. Archaeological records of the devastation may be preserved at sites on Lake River and near Kalama, where clusters of human remains escaped the ravages of early artifact hunters (Kenneth Ames, personal communication, 2012).

There were two reasons for the great differential in mortality. First, the whites had medicine—barely enough, it seems, for themselves—and with almost all personnel sick at the same time, they could not attend to Natives. Second, the Indians, without medicines, treated the alternating hot and cold spells with their own sweat lodge/cold plunge treatment, or "Maddened by fever" they "rush[ed] headlong into the cooling stream" (Ogden 1933:97). Both actions caused sudden death. The last new case of "intermittent fever" was recorded at the fort on November 12.

A century later, Victoria Howard recalled what her Clackamas mother had told her about the arrival of "fever and ague":

> they said, "The ague (fever and shivering) is on its way here. Dear oh dear!"
> . . . Soon but I do not know just how long after, then some one person got
> the ague. He lay with his back to the fire, he got only colder. . . . His whole
> body shook. So long a time and then it stopped. Now he got feverish, he
> got thirsty for water. They gave it to him, he drank it. So many days, and
> then he died. Then some other person too, and also I do not know how
> many others got the ague. Soon then a great many of them, I do not know
> how many. Their village was a large one, but they all got the ague. In each
> and every house so many of the people were ill now. They said that when
> they had fever, . . . they would run to the river, they would go and swim in
> it, they would go ashore, they would drop right there, they would die. . . .
> The (Clackamas) people died, I do not know how many. Only a few did
> not die. It (the epidemic of ague) quit even before they gathered them
> (the corpses that were lying around), they buried them. They were at last
> through with (burying) them all, and then they (the survivors) lived there.
> (Jacobs 1958–59:546–47)

Malaria recurred with remarkable regularity every summer and autumn after 1830, though with decreasing intensity. In 1831 and 1832, the disease took hold in July, peaked in early fall, and then tapered off with cold weather. In 1830, the disease was limited to the Lower Columbia, but in 1831 it appeared in the remainder of the Chinookan zone in the Columbia River Gorge to The Dalles and to the (non-Chinookan) Kalapuyan peoples of the Willamette Valley. In 1832 and 1833, it spread to southwest Oregon and the California Central Valley.

The Chinookan people of the focal area suffered most, experiencing not one but several annual back-to-back epidemics. People who managed to escape one year's outbreak would be infected the next. Another geographic characteristic was that fewer people were infected close to the ocean or in the dry interior. The HBC people saw these patterns and recognized that it was not a contagious disease spread by human contact—it was environmental in nature—but they thought it was caused by miasma, foul air associated with stagnant water and rotting vegetation (Ogden 1933:97).

Malaria, we now know, is transmitted by mosquitos that carry a parasite that invades blood cells, reproducing and causing them to burst all at once, producing fits of heat and cold and anemia. Once the parasite is in the blood, it can be picked up by a second mosquito and spread to other hosts. The malarial parasite appears to have originated in Africa and spread to the Americas after contact. Only one genus of mosquito, the *Anophelines*, carries malaria; *A. freeborni* is the Northwest representative, which breeds in stagnant water during warm weather. On the Lower Columbia, spring melts caused a June freshet, which backed water and debris into sloughs and lakes that began to decay with summer evaporation—an ideal mosquito-breeding environment. The treatment for malaria, quinine (distilled from cinchona, also called Peruvian bark), kills the malarial parasite; "powdered dogwood bark" was used as a backup in the Northwest to alleviate fever, but it did not cure the disease.

Until the late 1800s, the miasmatic theory held sway in Western thought, while Lower Columbia Indians uniformly attributed the origin of the disease to Captain Dominis of the *Owyhee*. Dominis, suffering in competition with the HBC for the Indian trade, reportedly had borrowed a leaf from the Astorians and had threatened the Chinookan villagers with a vial before opening it and releasing the fever (see, e.g., Lee and Frost 1968:108). There were variations on this theme at different places. In addition to or in place of the vial, for example, Dominis "hung up some bad sail in a tree" (a flag?) or threw "a parcel containing poison" into the river (Lee and Frost 1968:108). The disease was said to emanate from a shell attached to river survey sticks (Tappan 1854), glass trade beads (McWhorter, n.d.), or even smoke from the ships' cannons (Clarke 1905:132). In the Chinookan mind, Dominis was acting like an evil shaman, and many of these items were functional equivalents to the bones, shells, or claws that they believed entered bodies and caused disease.

POPULATION HISTORY TO 1854

There are several issues in Lower Chinookan population history: the size of the population at and before contact with Euro-Americans; the reasons for and magnitude of subsequent decline; the rate and size of population rebound in the 20th century; and the amount and significance of intermarriage with Euro-Americans. Demographers like to point out that no census is perfect, even today. This was even more the case 150 to 200 years ago, and the problems multiply when trying to determine the population of seasonally mobile, preliterate peoples. Nevertheless, the population history of the early contact Chinookan peoples is one of the best known for a Native American group. President Thomas Jefferson asked Lewis and Clark to estimate Indian populations on their route, and they did so with what appears to be commendable accuracy. The Hudson's Bay Company took a census of the Northwest tribal peoples they traded with after 1824, and there was a great interest among Euro-Americans in the depopulation caused by the "fever and ague" epidemics. Finally, when government control was established and treaties became imminent, knowing Indian numbers became important.

Lewis and Clark's "Estimate of the Western Indians" (Table 11.1) is our benchmark for Columbia River indigenous populations. The explorers used several methods, especially house counts, and estimated lower-river numbers twice, probably in autumn 1805 and spring 1806. By comparison with spotty estimates preceding and following Lewis and Clark—the Vancouver Expedition's canoe-capacity estimates in 1792 and Robert Stuart's 1812 villages estimates of adult males—and with fever-and-ague loss figures, they appear to be quite reliable. The "Estimate" has two major characteristics: the numbers are large for preagricultural peoples, and there is great seasonal variation in village size.

In 1825, HBC Governor Simpson (1968) reported: "The population on the banks of the Columbia River is much greater than in any other part of North America that I have visited as from the upper Lake to the Coast it may be said that the shores are actually lined with Indian lodges. . . . the whole of the Interior population flock to its banks at the Fishing Season" (94). Lewis and Clark's first estimate probably approximates a core resident Chinookan population; their second estimate appears to include many visitors to seasonal fisheries (Boyd and Hajda 1987). For Chinookans from The Cascades to the ocean, the base total is 7,560; with fishery visitors, the estimate is 14,640. The actual Chinookan population was probably greater than the first estimate's minimum and perhaps two-thirds of the fishing season total, or up to 10,000 people.

But what was the precontact number? Here there is very little to go on. By 1805, Chinookans had already experienced two smallpox epidemics, one a

TABLE 11.1. Lower Chinookan peoples in Lewis and Clark's estimates[1]

NAME	ETHNICITY	ESTIMATE 1	ESTIMATE 2	DIFFERENCE
Sha-ha-la Nation y-e-huh Clah-clel-lah Ne-er-cho-ki-oo	Cascades Chinookan (fishery visitors: Northwest Sahaptins)	1,500	2,800	1,300 (46%)
Wap-pa-to Nation	Multnomah Chinookan	2,210	5,290	3,080 (58%)
Ne-cha-co-kee		100	100	
Mult-no-mah	(visitors: diverse)	200	800	600 (75%)
Clan-nah-quah		130	130	
Shotos	(visitors: Northwest Sahaptin)	180	460	280 (61%)
Quath-lah-poh-tle		300	900	600 (67%)
Cal-la-maks		200	200	
Cath-lah-cum-ups	(visitors: Athapascans?)	150	450	300 (66%)
Clack Star		350	1,200	850 (71%)
Clan-nar-min-a-mow		280	280	
Clan-in-na-tas	(visitors: Kalapuyans?)	100	200	100 (50%)
Cath-lah-nah-quiah		150	400	250 (63%)
Cath-lah-com-mah-tup		70	170	100 (59%)
[Clackamas] villages	Clackamas Chinookan	1,350	2,850	1,500 (53%)
Ne-mal-quin-ner		100	200	100 (50%)

(continued)

TABLE 11.1 *(continued)*

NAME	ETHNICITY	ESTIMATE 1	ESTIMATE 2	DIFFERENCE
Clark-a-mus	(visitors: Molala?)	800	1,800	1,000 (56%)
Cush-hooks	(visitors: Kalapuyan?)	250	650	400 (62%)
Char-co-wah[2]		200	200	
[Cathalamet] villages	Cathlamet Chinookan	1,800	3,000	1,200 (40%)
Skil-lutes	(visitors: Cowlitz)	1,500	2,500	1,000 (40%)
Wack-ki-a-cums	(visitors: Athapascan)	100	200	100 (50%)
Cath-lah-mahs		200	300	100 (33%)
[Lower Chinook]		700		
Chin-nooks		400		
Clat-sops		200		
Kil-laxt-ho-kles[3]		100		
Total		7,500	14,640	7,080 (48%)

1 Based on Boyd 1999b:table 15. Lewis and Clark's original two estimates are in Lewis and Clark 1990:473-89.

2 In 1999, I excluded Char-co-wah on the basis of the "Ch," which is usual at the beginning of Kalapuyan (Willamette Valley) place-names. By location (above Willamette Falls, west bank), however, Chinookan is more likely; and since ethnographers at the turn of the 20th century considered the village "probably Chinookan" (Hodge 1971(1):235), it is here reinstated.

3 Listed in the "Estimates" as somewhere on the coast north of the Columbia, probably on the Long Beach Peninsula of Willapa Bay. In 1901, Franz Boas (1901:196) recorded Naqctxō'kᴌ *naqɬtxúkɬ* for North River, which is clearly related, and in 1905 he gave the Lower Chinook spelling of Kil-laxt-ho-kles as Gaᴌā'qstxoqᴌ *gatʰáqstxuqɬ*, which is the same as Naqctxō'kᴌ *naqɬtxúkɬ* but with the prefix "people of" (Hodge 1971(1):688). So Kil-laxt-ho-kles appears to be a Lower Chinook name for "people of the North River" or, more broadly, Willapa Bay (Henry Zenk, personal communication, 2009).

few years before and the other a generation back. In 1999, I estimated an aboriginal number by starting with Lewis and Clark's base and assuming average smallpox mortality (30 percent in a "virgin soil" outbreak; less in the second) and no rebound (unlikely in a short time span), for a total of 13,968 in about 1770. There are many caveats, and the total was probably larger, perhaps significantly so. Starting with an 1805 base of 10,000 would raise the number, as would assuming a greater-than-average mortality in the first smallpox epidemic. Both are likely, so it is safe to assume a minimum population of 15,000 Lower Columbia Chinookans before white contact. To date, we have no other good methods of approximating aboriginal populations. Perhaps in the future, archaeological site counts, carrying capacity estimates, density comparisons, or some other method will help firm up this number.

Population decline from the first smallpox epidemics has to be estimated, but depopulation from the fever-and-ague years is very clear—and dramatic. We have both loss estimates and postepidemic numbers, and (allowing for some unreliable figures) they are consistent and match. In 1835, a visiting missionary said that "probably seven-eighths, if not, as doct. McLaughlin believe nine-tenths have been swept away" since the start of the fever-and-ague epidemics (Parker 1967:178). In 1841, Horatio Hale (1846), a member of the Wilkes Expedition, wrote: "the region below the Cascades . . . suffered most from the scourge. The population, which before was estimated at upwards of ten thousand, does not now exceed five hundred" (245). Portland Basin peoples were hit the hardest: "From the river Cowlitz to the falls of the Columbia 'Kassenow' claims authority. His tribe . . . has lost more than 2,000 souls by fever" (Slacum 1972:15). In 1837, there were 37 people at Kiesno's village, the only village near Vancouver that was still inhabited. Counts from 1841 showed 574 at the mouth of the river (Hudson 1841), 150–200 at The Cascades, and about 300 each on the Clackamas and the Columbia from Cathlamet to Vancouver (Wilkes 1925:296). Using Lewis and Clark's figures, there was an estimated Lower Columbia Chinookan decline of 82 percent from 1806 to 1841.

On the ground, these statistics translated into several things. First, abandoned villages were everywhere, particularly in the Portland Basin. In 1833, for example, Kalama "a few years ago contained two or three hundred inhabitants, but at present only its superior verdure distinguished the spot from the surrounding country" (Tolmie 1963:183). Second, Indian cemeteries were filled to overflowing. From the perspective of whites, an impediment to settlement had been removed (e.g., Wyeth 1973:149). From the standpoint of the Lower

Columbia Chinookans (particularly in the focal area), several local polities and families were gone; much accumulated cultural tradition, both in practice and in memory, was lost; and the few survivors suffered a palpable depression and fatalism. At Willamette Falls, for example, "after the fever had ravaged, people expect to die any day; and that is why, these poor natives say, they no longer take the trouble to build" (Landerholm 1956:81; see also Ball 1925:99).

In 1838 and 1851, two sets of censuses of local Chinookan groups—the first taken by the HBC, the second in association with the 1851 treaty negotiations— show internal trends in Chinookan populations. The first is a low percentage of children, indicating populations that were experiencing difficulties replacing themselves. In 1838, children made up 30 percent of 288 Chinooks and Clatsops (Frost 1934:58); in 1845, the local Methodist minister said there were fewer than 14 in a Chinook/Clatsop population of about 400 (Gary 1923:275). From 1851, two Chinook/Clatsop counts show another trend: intermarriage with whites. Of 279 Indians in one count, 17 were women married to whites, with 53 children among them (Gibbs 1851). The second count of 251 showed 54 "half bloods," or 22 percent (Shortess 1851). Outmarriage, of course, was a Chinookan cultural preference; but with a diminished core population and a rapidly increasing white majority, there was a danger that the numerous mixed-blood children, especially those resident in white communities, would self-identify as white and be lost, culturally and biologically, to a continuing Chinookan entity.

After the 1847–48 measles and the 1853 smallpox epidemics, another census was taken of Lower Columbia Chinookan populations, which came in with a total of 525 (Boyd 1999b:table 17). This was the last period of major decline, and it was concentrated among Clackamas (78; measles the likely culprit) and peoples at the river's mouth (279; smallpox). In 1902, Silas Smith recalled:

> along in the 50's, of my best judgment, there were about 500 full blooded Indians inhabiting the Columbia river from Point Ellis to what is known as Ilwaco now. . . . the smallpox epidemic was in the winter of '52 and '53 and a good many Indians were killed by that disease. I could not say how many. I will say that even after the smallpox, there were a great many Indians. I would not say there were less than 300. (US Court of Claims 1902:226, 242)

The "epidemic era" among the Lower Columbia Chinookan peoples ended in 1853, and, despite horrendous mortality, they had survived. In less than a century, however, their population had plummeted from in excess of 15,000 to just over 500 survivors living on the margins of a culturally different and rapidly increasing non-Native immigrant population of 12,000 (Bowen 1975:181). Disease was the major engine of change among the Chinookan peoples in their first century of contact with Euro-Americans. In the second century and beyond, they had to deal with a new set of threats.

REBOUND AND RECONSTITUTION, 1855–2011

With the passing of the 1853 smallpox epidemic, Lower Chinookan populations transitioned into a new period characterized by gradual rebound, extensive intermarriage with whites, and reconfiguration of tribal units. Because the Chinook Tribe was without government recognition, data on population numbers and trends are nowhere near as complete as they are for recognized tribes who fell under direct government supervision. This is true even for those Chinookans who were enrolled at multitribal reservations such as Grand Ronde and Quinault, because separate records on tribal affiliation were rarely kept.

The best summary of population history after the 1850s is Stephen Dow Beckham's 1987 *Chinook Indian Tribe: Petition for Federal Acknowledgement*. Beckham reproduced family statistics from the 1880 and 1890 federal censuses in Pacific and Wahkiakum Counties, the special counts by Charles McChesney in 1906 and Charles Roblin in 1919, and tribal rolls from 1953 and 1987. Neither the federal censuses nor the special counts are complete, and the populations counted are not comparable.

Total counts for Chinook descendants number 187 in 1880, 289 in 1890, 124 in 1906, and 257 in 1919. In 1880, the five largest population centers in the two-county area were Chinookville, Wallicut, Brookfield, Cathlamet, and Bay Center; in 1890, they were Bay Center, Ilwaco, Brookfield, Cathlamet, and Nemah. Three names appear on both lists, a discrepancy that represents either an undercount or internal migration—probably both. The most notable characteristic of the 19th-century census sample is the large number of Indians married to white settlers and the large number of half-blood children. In 1880, 21 Chinook women were married to white men (no Chinook men were married to white women). They had a total of 61 children; and out of the total population of 187, at least 121 (65 percent) appear to have been half or quarter blood. The Wahkiakum County population was more heavily mixed, with several half-blood women married to whites, with quarter-blood children. The trend of Native women espousing white settlers, in place since 1811, continued and intensified as the white settler population increased in numbers and proportion to the diminished Indian communities. A second trend, which began early but does not show in the two county censuses, is that many Chinook women who married white men moved away from their aboriginal homeland. A third trend, which intensified nationally in the century after 1854, was for offspring of less than half-blood to no longer identify as Indians and no longer to report themselves to census takers as being of Native American descent.

Nationally, Native American numbers reached a nadir just after the turn of the 20th century. Then, first with improved health care on reservations and by mid-century with an increased willingness to recognize Indian ancestry and identify as such, Native American populations began a dramatic rebound. After World War II, Indians began to migrate to urban areas, a trend that shows clearly in the 1953 Chinook tribal roll.

Membership in the Chinook Tribe today is determined by annuity payments or by demonstration of descent from an ancestor named on the McChesney or Roblin lists. In 1953, of 978 enrolled Chinook, the largest communities were Bay Center (93 members), Astoria (91), and Taholah on the Quinault Reservation (64). In the 1987 roll, membership had doubled, to 1,980, and members were concentrated in the Portland metropolitan area (143), South Bend/Raymond (108), and Longview/Kelso (108). Bay Center remained the most heavily Chinook community, with 62 enrolled members.

In 2011, the population of those with Lower Chinookan ancestry and who self-identify as Chinookan is large and on the way to recouping the dramatic losses of the first century of Euro-American contact. The Chinook Tribe—incorporating descendants of the river-mouth Chinook, Clatsop, Wahkiacum, Kathlamet, and Willapa peoples—has 2,910 enrolled members (Chinook Tribal Office, July 2011). The membership of the Shoalwater Bay Tribe, largely Chinook but with Lower Chehalis blood as well, numbers 360 (Tony Johnson, personal communication, 2011). Some Clatsops are enrolled in the Clatsop/Nehalem Tribe (total 200), nearly all of whom have some Clatsop ancestry (Douglas Deur, personal communication, 2011).

Determining Chinookan proportions at the two large multitribal reservations where they have a significant presence—Quinault and Grand Ronde—is difficult because of intermarriage and because separate figures are not kept. Judging from allotment records, however, about 40 percent at Quinault (Beckham 1987:157) and 15 percent (Willamette Falls and Cascades) at Grand

Ronde (Henry Zenk, personal communication, 2011)—1,157 of a total of 2,893 at Quinault and 780 of a total of 5,200 at Grand Ronde—are ballpark figures (enrollment figures courtesy of tribal enrollment offices, July 2011). Some people of predominantly Chinookan heritage are enrolled elsewhere. The classic case is the Cascades people, with descendants at Grand Ronde, Warm Springs, Yakama, and Cowlitz (see Williams, ch. 15 in this volume). All told, there may be 4,627 descendants of Lower Chinook and Kathlamet speakers and another 780–plus descendants of the Portland Basin Cascades, Willamette Falls, and Wapato peoples. As of the first decade of the 21st century, the Lower Chinook have recouped their contact-era losses, and descendants of the Portland Basin Chinookans, tragically diminished by the 1830s epidemics, are clearly still with us.

TWELVE

THE CHINOOKAN ENCOUNTER WITH EURO-AMERICANS IN THE LOWER COLUMBIA RIVER VALLEY

William L. Lang

C HINOOKAN-SPEAKING peoples likely first came into contact with Euro-Americans during the late 18th century. The first recorded encounters are notations in ships' logs that describe trading between maritime merchants and Chinookans on the Pacific Coast and the Lower Columbia. Early documented contacts underscore the primary cause of new people coming to the Chinookan homelands—trade and economic exchange.

Contact with Japanese or other cross-Pacific mariners likely took place earlier, during the 17th and early 18th centuries, but there are no written records; the evidence comes from Native oral tradition and archaeology (Brooks 1876; Erlandson et al. 2001). For example, a Chinook informant told anthropologist Franz Boas that a Clatsop woman—probably in the mid-18th century—had seen what she thought was a whale, but with two spruce trees seemingly attached:

> Oh! Behold it is not a whale.
> Behold it is a whale.
> Behold a monster. (Boas 1894:277–78)

The "monster" was a ship that subsequently wrecked and was stripped of its metal trappings and cargo; two survivors were enslaved by Chinookan headmen.

While there may have been an older maritime contact, the earliest documented Euro-American contacts with Native groups in the region were coincident with the maritime fur trade that boomed in the 1780s after Englishman James Cook's last voyage to the Pacific. News and material goods from those early encounters surely affected Chinookan groups on the Lower Columbia and the Oregon and Washington Coasts. The maritime trade in the North Pacific brought attention and investment in a risky business, where enormous profits hinged on Euro-American traders acquiring valuable furs from Native people in exchange for inexpensive manufactured goods. Each party in the trade had their eyes on a scarce commodity, and each pursued strategies they had long used. The trade brought the world to the North Pacific and latched Native people to an economic exchange that wrapped around the globe. The encounter between Chinookans and Euro-Americans also marked the beginning of a long history of commercial exploitation of natural resources in the Pacific Northwest, an exploitation that brought more and more nonindigenous people to the region (Gibson 1992; Clayton 2000).

The first documented contact between Euro-Americans and the Chinooks was in May 1792, when American merchant sea captain Robert Gray floated his ship across the dangerous bar at the mouth of the Columbia. He had found the great coastal river that European cartographers had long speculatively inscribed on their maps as the "River of the West," a major artery that drained the Pacific Northwest interior. Gray's charting of the Columbia's estuary was important to the history of exploration in the North Pacific, but his contact with Chinook people was in many ways even more consequential (Pethick 1979; Gibson 1992:22–35; Ruby and Brown 1976:61–84).

Gray and other maritime traders had contact with Chinookans in a relatively narrow cultural context. Their encounters were episodic and single-minded: acquiring furs in trade that would bring wealth to their investors. The Indians also connected to the traders in culturally limited ways, for they perceived the traders primarily as sources of new material wealth. Just as the traders likely understood little about Chinookan culture, the Chinookans probably had little interest in the personal histories of traders (Lang 1992). Gray's contact was true to type. In spring 1792, he coasted south from the Strait of Juan de Fuca, stopping to trade at Grays Harbor, where he put his crew on alert because of fear-provoking sounds from Chehalis who canoed near his ship. He already had dealt forcefully and aggressively with Indians on Vancouver Island and was ever-ready to enforce his terms of trade with weaponry (Nokes 1991:13–15).

On May 11, 1792, Fifth Mate John Boit described the scene on entering the Columbia:

> We directed our course up this noble *river* in search of a Village. The beach was lin'd with Natives, who ran along shore following the Ship. Soon after above 20 Canoes came off, and brought a good lot of Furs and Salmon, which last they sold two for a board Nail. . . . they appear'd to view the Ship with the greatest astonishment and no doubt we was the first civilized people that they had ever saw. (Nokes 1991:397)

Boit's description suggests that Natives anticipated trading for metal. Oral traditions and reports of stranded Euro-American mariners from ships that visited the coastal areas before Gray suggest that the Chinook were prepared for trading in 1792, and Gray himself had traded with Tillamooks who lived farther south on the coast in 1788 (Boas 1894:277-78; Henry 1992:620-21; Franchère 1969:124). For several days, the ship anchored at locations as far as 10 miles upriver, trading daily with Chinooks. Boit wrote in his log that the Chinooks were honest traders, that a chief named Polack directed their trade, and that all "appear'd very civill (not even offering to steal)" (Howay 1990:398-99).

Chinookan traders on the Lower Columbia had significant advantages. Positioned at the meeting point of maritime trade and goods coming downriver from interior tribes, villages near the river's mouth acted like a venturi by facilitating trade from as far north as Vancouver Island and to the east in the Columbia River Basin and beyond. Early Euro-American traders commented on the exchange of dentalia shells found on the west coast of Vancouver Island as currency in trade for natural and manufactured products from the interior, including elk hides that were used as protective armor. The shells were strung together in prescribed lengths that equated agreed-upon values (Silverstein 1990:536-37; Scouler 1848:228-52; Ray 1938:37; see Boyd and Hajda 1987:309-26). The trade had flourished for hundreds of years, but Euro-American traders added considerable wealth and a broad range of manufactured goods that enriched trading chiefs on the Lower Columbia. As their wealth increased, so did their importance to other Chinooks and their power in conducting trade with Euro-Americans. Chinuk Wawa, a trade language that developed with continued contact, eventually eased cross-language communication problems and offered an abbreviated vocabulary that made trading more efficient (Harris 1994:28-36; ch. 13 in this volume).

Gray's was not the only sailing ship to anchor in the Columbia estuary in 1792. He had passed along his chart of the river to George Vancouver, commander of a British exploring expedition that reached the Columbia in October. Vancouver's ship, the *Discovery*, could not safely cross the bar because of the low river flow—Gray had crossed the bar in May, with the Columbia running full (see Meany 1907:83–84; Nokes 1991:218–19)—so he sent the tender, the *Chatham*, commanded by William Broughton, to anchor in the ten-mile-wide estuary. When the *Chatham* anchored, it encountered the *Jenny*, a British merchant ship captained by James Baker that was trading with Chinooks. Following Vancouver's orders, Broughton ascended the Columbia in two cutter boats, which his sailors oared more than a hundred miles to just above present-day Washougal, Washington (Ruby and Brown 1976:54; Howay and Elliott 1929:197–206).

Broughton surveyed the Columbia as an explorer, not a trader. For Chinookans, the distinction likely made little difference, but the upriver survey surely concerned them. What might these armed men in the cutters intend? Were they an invasive force that sought slaves, as other intruders had? Did they mean to challenge the Chinookans' control of river trade and passage? Could friendship with this group provide them some advantage? As the British sailors made their way upriver, village chiefs tried to engage them, but Broughton avoided much contact as he sounded the river and assayed tributaries. On October 26, he was invited to stay in a sizable village about 50 river miles from the mouth (Cathlapotle), but he remained cautious and stayed on the opposite side of the river (Barry 1932a:31–42). The next day, more Chinookans joined a flotilla that followed Broughton's boats, until nearly 200 men in canoes came near. Edward Bell (1932) noted in his log: "A large Stout Man who sat in the Canoe nearest to us seem'd to be the leading Chief amongst them. In case of a sudden attack from this powerful fleet, we had regulated everything in the best manner for our defence, the Swivel was primed, and a Match kept burning . . . Mr. Broughton . . . fired a Musket with a Ball in it into the Water" (143).

Broughton completed his survey of the river in early November, creating the first detailed chart of the lower reaches of the Columbia. Publication of his chart in Vancouver's *A Voyage of Discovery* in 1798 announced the river's location, its dimensions, and its inhabitants. The book also included notation of more than 20 trading vessels that had spent time on the Lower Columbia between 1794 and 1796 and that had provided Chinookans with a steady opportunity to acquire a broad range of European goods. Shelathwell and

Concomly, two village chiefs who dominated trade with Euro-Americans on the lower river, created conditions that fostered mutually beneficial exchanges. They became more and more discerning in their trade with Euro-Americans, a talent that sometimes annoyed traders, whose complaints document the controlling positions Chinook headmen held in exchanges along the Columbia (Bishop 1967:57n1; Lewis and Clark 1990:427). Traders on the *Ruby*, a British merchant ship that worked the lower river in the spring of 1795, recorded that the Indians had set their own prices after seeing the cargo goods the day before: "we were plagued the whole day to break trade on their own terms, but knowing our stay here would be at least ten days, we suffered them once more to depart with their skins." A day later, the traders gave in to the Chinooks' price structure: "we broke trade with the Natives and tho' not bought so cheap as they have been at this place, was more reasonable than we had expected to have procured them" (Bishop 1967:57). The *Ruby* left the river to trade up the coast, only to return in October, when they resumed their relationship with Shelathwell and Concomly. The *Ruby*'s captain, Charles Bishop, described his relationship with the Chinook as amicable and trusting, even to the extent that he allowed Concomly to bed down in his cabin. Bishop took his connection with Concomly as a sign of a good trade connection, but it was likely Concomly who held the upper hand. The chief understood the importance of familiarity and discretion in trade, and he told Bishop (1967:117) that he and other chiefs had a short list of white traders "they are at war with, if ever they come here again," because of their use of violence and aggressive behavior.

The sight of a trading ship had become common to Chinookans by the late 18th century, but a flotilla of canoes carrying more than 30 armed people downriver was news. There is no way of knowing whether Chinookan headmen had been forewarned of the arrival of Meriwether Lewis, William Clark, and their entourage in the fall of 1805, but their presence on the lower river substantially altered Chinook history. Thomas Jefferson, United States president and an advocate for the scientific and commercial exploration of western North America, had taken notice of British explorations, especially Alexander Mackenzie's overland trek to the Pacific in 1793 and Vancouver's survey of the Northwest Coast. In early 1803, he manipulated Congress to finance a major military expedition up the Missouri River and westward to the Pacific, including descent of the Columbia into Chinookan homelands. Led by Captains Lewis and Clark, the expedition—known as the Lewis and Clark Expedition, or the Corps of Discovery—had important scientific ambitions, but the main rationale was geopolitical: Jefferson hoped the explorers would find a navigable river route across the continent and establish beneficial political and economic relationships with Native nations. By the fall of 1805, the group had traveled more than 3,400 miles from their starting point near St. Louis and had met with dozens of Native groups (Lewis and Clark 1990:447–61). Once in the Columbia River Basin, the explorers were in territory that was unclaimed by Euro-American nations (see Kukla 2003; Ambrose 1996).

During the descent of the Snake and Columbia Rivers, the explorers expressed increasingly negative opinions about the Natives they encountered. In their journals, they complained that Indians they allowed in or near their campus were stealing goods, especially metal objects. When the expedition reached the Columbia, Lewis and Clark were prepared to trade with Natives, as they had throughout their journey, but they were running low on time. Besides, they were not traders; their mission was exploratory, and their goals were to create maps, describe natural features, and establish friendly relations. There was something about the Columbia, its rough currents, and its people, however, that put the exploration party on edge, even before they reached the lower river in November 1805 (Lang 1996:141–48).

During the first week of November 1805, the expedition drifted down the Columbia below The Cascades and past the Sandy River, which joins the Columbia from the south, and then past islands near the mouth of the Willamette River, a tributary they did not notice. On the south shore of the Columbia, Clark noted one large house, more than 20 straw houses (*ne-er-cho-ki-oo*), and more than 50 canoes. The explorers stopped, visited, tasted, and bought four bushels of cooked wapato roots before continuing on (Lewis and Clark 1990:1–18; see Moulton 1983:maps 80, 81). Lewis and Clark had entered an intense trading zone, a stretch of river highway that facilitated exchanges between the upriver Cascades and The Dalles areas and the mouth. Interior goods came downriver while coastal goods went upriver, and all Chinook villages acquired wealth through the trade. The explorers had visited central trading places during their journey—along the Missouri and at Celilo Falls on the Columbia—but those centers drew horse Indians from all points of the compass. On the Lower Columbia, trade was conveyed on a linear causeway, largely by canoe. The captains determined early on that the Chinookans were unlike upriver groups, especially given their decorated, large-prowed canoes, which Clark reported rose "to near the hight of a man" (Lewis and Clark 1990:1–18; see Ronda 1984:169–71).

On November 5, the Corps of Discovery continued downriver in a steady rain, through a valley landscape that William Clark described as "fertill and handsom . . . at this time Crouded with Indians." They passed and described a village of 14 houses (Cathlapotle), an active trade center that specialized in making elk-hide armor. Although the men had brief contact with villagers, Clark noted that it was "the first night which we have been entirely clear of Indians Since our arrival on the waters of the Columbia River" (Lewis and Clark 1990:24). They had seen muskets in Indian hands, "one wearing a Salors dress" (32) and other evidence of regular trade with Euro-Americans, including an encounter with two canoes of Indians who mentioned trading with a ship captain and who had retained a few words of English. Expecting more intense trading locations as they proceeded downstream, Lewis and Clark eagerly anticipated arriving at the ocean, where they thought they might encounter trading ships and a prime location for American enterprise. Clark even mistakenly shouted in his journal on November 7, "Great joy in camp we are in View of the Ocian," when they were actually looking at the Columbia's broad estuary (33). What they found, once they finally made it to the Pacific Ocean, was not the world they had imagined (Ronda 1984:176–77).

After several miserable days hunkered down in the face of lashing winds and pouring rain in what Clark called "this dismal nitch," the Corps moved to within sight of the ocean, where they first met people they identified as "Chin nooks" (Lewis and Clark 1990:50). After a few Chinook had been in their camp, Clark wrote in his journal on November 15:

> I told those people that they had attempted to Steal 2 guns &c. that if
> any one of their nation stole any thing that the Sentinl. whome they Saw
> near our baggage with his gun would most certainly Shute them, they all
> promised not to tuch a thing, and if any of their women or bad boys took
> any thing to return it immediately and Chastise them for it. I treated those
> people with great distance. (Lewis and Clark 1990:50)

Trading with the Chinooks aggravated the captains, who increasingly characterized the Indians as unreasonable bargainers. "It is bad practice," Clark noted on November 17, "to receive a present from those Indians as they are never Satisfied for they receive in return if ten time the value of the articles they gave" (Lewis and Clark 1990:61). Nevertheless, when Lewis and Clark desired exchange for an item they fancied, they willingly acceded to the bargain driven by Chinook chiefs Concomly and Shelatwell. Clark wrote on November 20:

> found maney of the Chinooks with Capt. Lewis of whome there was 2 *Cheifs Com com mo ly* [Concomly] & *Chil-lar-la-wil* [Shelathwell] to whome we gave Medals and to one a flag. One of the Indians had on a roab made of 2 Sea Otter Skins the fur of them were more butifull than any fur I had ever Seen both Capt. Lewis & my Self endeavored to purchase the roab with different articles at length we precured it for a belt of blue beeds which the Squar [Sacagawea] . . . wore around her waste. (72–73)

Clark had misjudged his hosts, not realizing that they were a very practiced trading people who had more than a decade of experience with Euro-Americans and hundreds of years of making exchanges with other keen trading parties on the river and the coast.

The captains realized that the winter would be hellish without durable shelter. Querying Chinook villagers on the north bank, they learned that the lands south of the river offered the best hunting, and a quick poll of the exploration party decided the question. After finding a suitable site near the Netul River a few miles from present-day Astoria, Oregon, the Corps finished a substantial fort by the end of December. Fort Clatsop was named by the captains for the people who lived in villages on the south shore of the Lower Columbia, on Young's Bay, and on the coast near the Tillamooks, a Salish tribe. By building their winter quarters in Clatsop territory, the Corps of Discovery took a chance that they might be less demanding traders than their neighbors to the north, but they found Clatsop headman Coboway to be just as skillful in trade as Concomly and Shelathwell. The fort itself, however, represented an important change in Chinook experience with Euro-Americans. The Corps of Discovery had appropriated the Clatsop lands with little or no ceremony or approval, and it was the first of many structures that would signal a new engagement with Native people in the Columbia River Basin. It was also the beginning of a three-month relationship between the explorers and the Clatsops that would test the patience of each (see Ronda 1999:3–22).

Clatsops saw the fort and its inhabitants as an opportunity to enhance their wealth, not unlike making deals with visiting maritime traders or collecting goods from wrecked ships. The Corps, however, saw the fort as sanctuary and drew a clear line between their compound and the surrounding landscape. The captains laid down rules for Indian visits, because they feared losing control of their men, running low on provisions, and diminishing their trade items. The orders included announcing the entry of each Indian into the fort and removing anyone who acted in a manner deemed unacceptable, especially theft. The promise of good hunting came only with daily effort, and the Americans often found it necessary to rely on trade with Clatsops to sustain their needs. The Clatsops tried to maintain primacy over the Chinooks in having access to the fort (Lewis and Clark 1990:156–57). For Lewis and Clark, all Indian visitors posed the same question: How much engagement was appropriate?

The captains generally characterized the Clatsops as "great higlers in trade" (Lewis and Clark 1990:165), but they perceived Indian traders from such a narrow viewpoint that they seemingly missed the obvious: Lower Chinook traders on both sides of the river bargained for items they considered desirable and wealth-enhancing. Lewis thought Clatsops foolish in trade. "I therefore believe," Lewis wrote on January 4, 1806, "this trait in their character proceeds from an avaricious all grasping disposition. . . . for their disposition invariably lead them to give whatever they are possessed off not matter how usefull or valuable, for a bauble which pleases their fancy, without consulting it's usefullness or value" (165). Perhaps more important, the captains misunderstood the way trade worked on the Lower Columbia. Clatsop and Chinook chiefs conducted trade and had some means to affect its content and direction, but individuals were also free to make their own exchanges, and they expected, given the rules of reciprocity, the freedom to take items from the Corps, especially unusual or ubiquitous goods. The captains interpreted and evaluated all trade relations against business behavior in Virginia, which led them to miss the desirability and usefulness of goods they considered "a bauble" (165) and to label as theft any taking of found items around the explorers' camp.

The captains worried that trading sexual favors for goods, which was frequent during the winter at Fort Clatsop, would diminish their store of trade items. Some trade in sex seemed organized, at least in the case of the "old baud," a Chinook woman who brought several slave women to the fort on more than one occasion, but most visits were by individuals (Ronda 1984:208–10). At the same time, high-ranking women were offered as marriage partners. Clark told of a Clatsop man who "brought me out of gratitude his sister. . . . She staid two or three days in next room with Chabono's wife. She was quite mortified at being refused by C[lark]. She declined solicitations of the men" (Jackson 1978:503).

Among the most revealing trade sequences during the 1805–6 winter was the Corps' pursuit of a canoe for their planned ascent of the Columbia. The captains had marveled at the canoes, which represented hundreds of hours of careful labor, great design skill, and artistic investment. They described the canoes in detail in their journals (e.g., Lewis and Clark 1990:267–72), and on March 21, 1806, Patrick Gass recorded seeing "as many as an hundred canoes at one burying-place of the Chin-ooks, on the north side of the Columbia" (Lewis and Clark 1996:199). Surely they recognized the central importance of these great river transports to Chinookan culture. Nonetheless, when Lewis and Clark failed to acquire a canoe, they broke one of their cardinal rules— to treat Native people with honesty and fairness—by stealing one. Noting on March 17 that a canoe "is an article of the greatest value except a wife," Lewis complained: "Clatsops will not sell us one at a price which we can afford to give we will take one from them in lue of the six Elk which they stole from us in the winter" (Lewis and Clark 1990:426). The "stolen elk" referred to carcasses that had been cached in early February, which Clatsops had taken from Corps hunters. Coboway had provided compensation to Lewis and Clark to retain good relations, but evidently it had not been enough (see Lewis and Clark 1990:27, 299, 336). So, while Coboway visited the fort on March 18, four men stealthily made off with the canoe, an event that Lewis left unrecorded in his journal. Ironically, on the day the Corps left Fort Clatsop, the Chinook chief Delashelwilt offered to sell a canoe to Lewis, but with the stolen canoe in hand they no longer needed one (Lewis and Clark 1991:7; Ronda 1999:10–11).

During the winter stay at Fort Clatsop, the captains collated information they had accumulated on their outward trek, including copious materials on Native nations. In their "Fort Clatsop Miscellany," they included descriptions of Columbia River conditions, the locations of Indian villages, estimates of their populations, plus descriptions of houses, burial vaults, and material goods such as canoes and weapons. When they departed their winter quarters in late March, the captains left the fort structure to Coboway, along with an official list of the expedition members, a document that Coboway retained for several years. The farewell and the gift to Coboway put a fine point on the larger truth of the expedition's four-month stay. They had never been part of the larger community on the Lower Columbia, even as they interacted with Chinook, Clatsop, and Kathlamet men and women. Unlike the close connections the captains made on the upper Missouri with Native nations, their relationships with the Chinookans were distant, overtly nonpolitical, and occasioned by their needs. Trading with Chinookans arose from necessity and offered no promise of a long-term relationship, and the Corps made no mention of anyone building a trading fort at the mouth of the Columbia. In his post-expedition communication to President Jefferson, Lewis portrayed the Columbia as a poor commercial link for cross-continental trade; it would only serve maritime commerce, he advised. Relationships with local Indian traders had been amicable, but as Lewis declared in his journal on March 20, the Corps "had accomplished every object which induced our remaining at this place except that of meeting with the traders who visit the entrance of this river" (Lewis and Clark 1990:441). Clearly, the major attribute of the area was the river's mouth and estuary. To that end, Clark drew detailed sketch maps of the headlands, the main channel, and potential harbor areas at the river's mouth (Jackson 1978(1):319–21; see Lewis and Clark 1983:maps 82, 83, 91, 92).

Lewis and Clark (1990) left the Columbia estuary with a thorough dislike of the region and an unflattering image of its residents (see, e.g., 330–31). On the way upriver, the explorers passed villages that offered them meals and conducted some minor trading, but the Corps had little to trade. When it became apparent that the Indians were interested in establishing a trading relationship, the captains (1991:16) gave a Kathlamet headman a Jefferson medal, but it was merely a gesture, not a commitment to future relations. The villages were more populated than during the expedition's descent of the Columbia in the fall, and the captains learned from their occupants that habitation and trade extended up the major tributaries—the Cowlitz, Lewis, and Willamette. They learned about regional trading patterns and seasonal movements, which led them increasingly to recognize that a relatively large population lived in the Columbia River Valley downstream from The Cascades. They also noted an extensive trade between coastal groups and inland villages, as when lower-river Chinooks traded European goods for wapato, a key plant food that grew no closer than 15 miles upriver and in abundance some 100 miles from mouth of the Columbia (Lewis and Clark 1991:27–28, 34–36; see Cutright 1969:259–65).

On April 2, 1806, Clark recorded his trip up the lower reaches of the Willamette, a tributary they had missed in their descent of the Columbia. Clark and seven men paddled upriver for about seven miles, guided by a Willamette Falls villager, to a village (Nemalquinner) dominated by a sizable house. Clark was told about a major fishing area at falls some distance upriver and the existence of more than a dozen Clackamas villages along a river of that name (Lewis and Clark 1997:438–39). On Clark's way to the mouth of the Willamette, his experience at Ne-er-cho-ki-oo is revealing. The village, on the south bank of the Columbia a few miles east of the mouth of the Willamette, was populated by Chinookan-speaking people who had come downriver from The Cascades. The "Columbian (or Wappato) Valley," bounded on the east by the Sandy River and on the west by the Cowlitz, included significant wapato harvesting sites and seasonal village locations. When Clark entered a "large double house" to trade for wapato, he was rebuffed. On April 2, he recorded his engagement with women in the house and seemingly reveled in his own intimidating behavior, an imperiousness that may well stand as an expression of his attitude toward Chinookan people in general.

> I had a Small pece of port fire match in my pocket, off of which I cut a pece one inch in length & put it into the fire and took out my pocket Compas and Set myself doun on a mat on one Side of the fire, and a magnet which was in the top of my ink Stand the port fire cought and burned vehemently, which changed the Colour of the fire; with the Magnit I turned the Needle of the Compas about very briskly; which astonished and alarmed these nativs and they laid Several parsles of Wappato at my feet, & begged of me to take out the bad fire . . . this measure alarmed them So much that the womin and children took Shelter in their beads and behind the men. (Lewis and Clark 1991:57–58).

The Corps proceeded upriver beyond the Chinookan villages, with a generally positive perception of the people living in the Wapato Valley, some 150 miles upriver from the mouth. Clark commented on the hospitality of the people of Ne-er-cho-ki-oo, the care they took with their aged population, and the geographical information one chief provided on the Willamette's course (Lewis and Clark 1991:66, 1983:map 79). As they ascended the Columbia, the captains seemed to have evaluated Chinookans on a sliding scale, with their most critical comments directed at the trading intransigence of villagers nearest the Pacific and fewer criticisms as they got closer to The Cascades. The captains had trouble at the falls, where they ordered sentinels. Lewis recorded on April 11, 1806, that if "they made any further attempts to steal our property or insulted our men we should put them to instant death" (Lewis and Clark 1991:105). By the time they made the mouth of the Snake River, they felt relieved to finally leave the Columbia.

The consequences of the Lewis and Clark Expedition on Chinookans were significant but remained largely beyond the purview of chiefs and villagers along the Lower Columbia. They could not have foreseen the people who would invade their country during the following two decades. When the Corps paddled out of sight, the Chinookans remained in control of trade on the river and looked forward to more profitable exchanges with their familiar maritime traders. They were eager to interact with new people—whatever their purposes or intentions—but they would do it on their own terms.

Evidence of this attitude came in May 1810, when two Massachusetts brothers, veteran maritime traders Nathan and Jonathan Winship, brought their ship, the *Albatross,* across the Columbia River bar. At anchor in Baker Bay, they hired a Chinookan guide to help them find a suitable location for a trading settlement on the lower river, complete with a log fort, cultivated land, and an anchorage to accommodate shipping. The Winships selected a bench about 40 miles upriver, but the location was too low and a spring freshet destroyed their half-built structure. When the brothers and their crew relocated, armed Chinookans demanded that the Winships return to their territory so that they could benefit from the trade. A few musket shots from the Indians, plus superior numbers, convinced the brothers to abandon their plans and leave the river. As one of the Winship men remarked: "The country was theirs" (Ruby and Brown 1976:119–24; Jerzyk 1940:175–81; Victor 1886:129–35; Busch and Gough 1997).

By 1810, Chinookan chiefs and villagers had engaged with Euro-American traders for most of two decades. The consequences had been significant. Certain chiefs, such as Concomly, had enriched themselves and gained more influence, but trade with the cloth and iron traders had affected everyone on the lower river. The arrival of another ambitious group of Euro-Americans, however, introduced changes that would lead to a steep three-decade decline in Chinookan control of their homelands. When John Jacob Astor's Pacific Fur Company traders arrived on the Columbia to establish a fur post, the Chinooks and Clatsops saw them as another potential source of wealth, but this new invasion brought more than increased commerce. The new fort represented a bold investment, with Astoria planned as headquarters for an international trade with China (see Ronda 1990). Astor sent the *Tonquin* by sea, an overland party from Missouri, and in 1812 a second ship, the *Beaver,* to supply and staff the new post. The *Tonquin* arrived in early 1811 with livestock, trading goods, and an international crew that included Hawaiians. Chinook and Clatsop chiefs aided the party in selecting a location for the post, a few miles up the Columbia on the south bank, just east of Youngs Bay.

More than 70 by 80 feet in size, Fort Astoria included a large warehouse and store, land for gardens, areas for boat construction, a fenced ground with several cannon for protection, and bastions. Indians came to watch construction and to trade, with upwards of 50 or 60 at times eager to trade skins (McDougall 1999:17; Ruby and Brown 1976:135).

Relations between the Astorians and Chinookans pivoted on the viability of the fur enterprise. On the one hand, as Pacific Fur Company clerk Alexander Ross (2000) put it, there was nervousness prompted by "rumours from all quarters and suspicious appearances . . . that the distant tribes were forming some dark design to cut us off, and reports . . . were daily brought us by Comecomly and his people." Regular trade with Concomly had convinced Astorians that he had their interests at heart, but they soon changed their opinion, calling him "crafty" and deciding to "set about counteracting" his intrigues (94–95). The Astorians were careful, as clerk Alfred Seton (1993) put it, to "always keep a strict guard night & Day & allow only a certain number to enter within the pickets" (91). On the other hand, the fur men had to rely on Chinookan goodwill, which began with Indian canoeists saving fur company men who had foundered at sea trying to navigate the Columbia bar. Dhaitshowan, headman at the Clatsop village at Point Adams, a few miles west of Fort Astoria, had greeted them "very amicably and hospitably," welcoming them to the territory (Franchère 1969:99). That kind of relationship augured well for fur traders who knew that their economic success depended on mutually beneficial economic exchanges with Indian groups, especially men like Concomly who controlled trade. But maintaining good relations while ultimately desiring to control trade made for an uneasy partnership with Chinookans.

The history of relations with Concomly offers a window on the larger significance of the Astorians' brief existence to the destiny of Chinookans on the Lower Columbia. From late summer through winter 1811–12, Concomly regularly traded furs at the fort and provided salmon and other foods when provisions were low at Astoria. Nonetheless, the Astorians were wary, remarking that they had "good reasons to believe, particularly from his late conduct and several suspicious circumstances that have taken place, his pretended friendship all along has been a mere train of deceit" (Seton 1993:41–42). Kathlamets from upriver and Clatsops from Point Adams also traded regularly with the Astorians, but Concomly managed most of the trade, sometimes serving as intermediary when potential intertribal warfare might disrupt the peace on the river and also by acting as a broker, especially with the Quinault, who lived north of the Columbia (Seton 1993:171, 206; Ronda 1990:222). Concomly ran an account at Fort Astoria, bringing salmon, eulachon, and even cedar boards for canoe building in exchange for blankets, iron, and manufactured items (Henry 1992:732). Duncan McDougall (1999), the leading business partner at the fort, took Concomly's daughter in marriage to guarantee good relationships and a steady trade. The sizable bride price included "5 new guns, and 5 blankets, $2\frac{1}{2}$ feet wide, which makes 15 guns and 15 blankets" (Whaley 2007:677–78). In addition to enriching Concomly and establishing a kinship tie with the Astorians, the marriage gave Concomly's daughter some position in trade. Concomly may have gained more by this relationship than the Astorians, because marriage ties often meant more stable business exchanges and more control over dispersal of manufactured goods, but he also entangled himself in a larger, international set of economic and geopolitical connections that no marriage arrangement could control (Seton 1993:116; McDougall 1999:203).

The Pacific Fur Company's operation at Astoria fell victim to two powerful developments, the War of 1812 and the struggle among rival fur-trading companies over the resources of the Columbia River Basin. In an ironic turn, the American victory in the war left Britain in possession of Fort Astoria, renamed Fort George, with an agreement that allowed both nations to settle in the region. The North West Company, based in Montreal, pushed over the Continental Divide in 1810, led by David Thompson, perhaps the greatest land geographer in continental history. In July 1811, Thompson descended the Columbia from hundreds of miles upriver in a cedar canoe with eight aboard. He introduced himself to McDougall and Pacific Fur Company men, took nearly a week surveying the estuary for one of his highly detailed maps, and headed upriver (McDougall 1999:33n72; Ross 2000:101–2). On his descent of the river, at the mouth of the Snake, he had literally staked out the region for his nation and fur partners. "Here I erected a small Pole," Thompson (1994) recorded in his journal, "with a half sheet of Paper well tied about it, with these words on it: Know hereby that this Country is claimed by Great Britain as part of its Territories and that the NW Company of Merchants from Canada . . . do hereby intend to erect a Factory in this Place for the Commerce of the Country around" (152; see also Ross 2000:138–39; Ronda 1990:232–34; Nisbet 1994:202–5).

In 1813, when the spoils of war had been sorted out, the North West Company received the Pacific Fur Company's properties, including several interior posts. When the Pacific Fur posts were combined with North West posts established by Thompson in present-day British Columbia and Montana, the new traders managed a weblike network of posts in the Columbia country. Fort George remained the key post, in the same geopolitical and economic position as Fort Astoria, an embarcadero for shipment of furs to the world market. A new order had come to the Columbia, one that responded to the dictates of international relations and included land and sea operations and significant capital investment (see Mackie 1997:17–28; Harris 1997:38). Concomly discovered the new shape of trade relations on the river when he adhered to his alliance with the Americans and offered to defend Astoria against the British, only to have McDougall wave him off. He would continue to prosper only if he adjusted to the new reality. For Coboway, the Clatsop chief, the stark knowledge of the new arrangements came in May 1814, when he came to trade at the fort and showed Alexander Henry the younger, a North West Company official, his coveted Lewis and Clark document, which listed the members of the exploration party. Henry took the list, crumpled it up, and tossed it in the fire, while presenting the chief a paper declaring that the North West Company owned the fort grounds (Ronda 1999:11; see Henry 1992:622; Franchère 1969:150–53; Ronda 1990:294–301; Keith 2008:27–40).

Chinookans continued to trade with the fur men, mostly Scots, French Canadians, and Iroquois who had stayed to work for the new managers. The North West men fanned out to villages throughout the region, but they often failed to make good connections with headmen who saw little advantage in tying themselves to the men at Fort George. There were also open conflicts—for instance, between Iroquois employees of the company and villagers on the Columbia and its tributaries—and inevitably bands of Chinookans used alliances with the company men to pursue their own ends (Barry 1932:366–67). Concomly, for example, had complex relations with Kiesno, a Chinookan headman at the mouth of the Willamette who wielded control over trade on the middle river. In at least one recorded instance, Concomly vied with Kiesno for trade supremacy, which made clear that relationships among Chinookan traders on the river were well beyond the control of Nor'westers. Nonetheless, Concomly and Kiesno had offered service to Nor'westers, and both had been granted preferential status by the company men (Ruby and Brown 1976:154–55, 164–66; Henry 1992:2:670–71, 715–16; McDougall 1999:206–8; see Spencer 1933:19–30). Yet, the North West Company did not prosper on the Columbia. It traded at a disadvantage to maritime traders, while their competition with Hudson's Bay Company over control of the

Saskatchewan and Winnipeg trade further diminished their ability to develop the Columbia River region.

Parliament put an end to the mutually destructive competition between the two fur enterprises in 1821 by forcing a merger, which effectively handed over the North West Company posts in the Pacific Northwest to an enlarged Hudson's Bay Company. By 1825, HBC had surveyed the conditions and decided to establish its regional post upriver from Fort George near the confluence of the Willamette and Columbia Rivers on Jolie Prairie, a site Chinookans called *skičútx*ʷ*a*, where the company built Fort Vancouver, a 250-by-150-foot structure. The fort was headquarters and fur depot for a vast region that extended east to the Continental Divide, north to Alaska, and south to California (Simpson 1968:64; see Gibson 1997:142–43; www.nps.gov/history/history/online_books/fova/clr/clr1–3a.htm; Mackie 1997:100–2; Koppel 1995:19–126, 56–60). The workforce eventually reached more than four hundred in various positions, including French Canadians, Iroquois, Hawaiians, and Chinookans. Chinookans called the fort King George, and for more than 25 years it represented a profound reordering of trade relations in their homeland, including a shift in the center of Columbia River trade from the mouth to the upriver wetland areas (see Harris 1997:32–33).

Chinookans interacted with HBC in several ways. As fur-gathering traders, they did not impress company men. James Douglas, for example, commented on "the natural indolence and improvidence of the Columbia Indn. He must be urged [to] exertion by the most pressing wants" (Mackie 1997:101). HBC employed Chinookans as laborers, fish providers, farmworkers, and guides. Near Fort George and Fort Vancouver, close relationships included trade and social connections. One of Concomly's daughters married chief trader Archibald McDonald, for example, and gave birth to Ranald McDonald, who later became famous for his travel and residency in Japan. McDonald and other children of Chinookan–fur trader unions received education at the Red River colony in Manitoba, making them influential in English-speaking and Native worlds (Ruby and Brown 1976:169–70). Yet, despite the importance of Concomly, Kiesno, and other headmen, HBC officials remained cautious about ongoing relationships with Indians. George Simpson, HBC head of the Northern Department, noted in his tour of the Columbia in 1824 that Chinookans battled each other for primacy in trade, which left HBC to contend with a constantly shifting set of relationships. John McLoughlin, HBC's chief factor at Fort Vancouver and nearly a law unto himself in the vast region, complained that Chinookans traded with anyone, including American ship captains, rather than engaging consistently with HBC men. More trying to McLoughlin, Chinookans took advantage of any opportunity to enrich their villages. When the barkentine HBC ship the *William and Ann* ran aground on Clatsop Spit in 1829, with a loss of everyone aboard, Clatsops grabbed up as much as they could from the wreck, only to discover that McLoughlin had no intention of allowing them their found merchandise. Sending a representative downriver, McLoughlin made it plain that he would "not be duped by Indians" and that they would deliver up the goods or else. When the Clatsops resisted, McLoughlin had their village leveled (McLoughlin 1941:71–73, 80–81; Simpson 1968:98–99).

HBC did not employ heavy-handed relations as a rule on the Columbia, but it is clear that company clerks and factors meant to create a predictable trading regime, which included a reformation of Chinookan culture. For McLoughlin and others, Indian social practices and behavior threatened moral order. They tried to quell disputes among Chinookan groups, arguing that peace was the best social environment for trade. HBC officials particularly disliked the practice of slavery and often remarked on the practice of head flattening, although they did little or nothing to halt those practices; trade was their objective. McLoughlin also recognized that the social scourges introduced by Euro-Americans, such as liquor, threatened Chinookans and often perverted trade. Continued traffic in alcohol, McLoughlin (1941) warned in 1827, would lead to wrecked relations "and ultimately it will cause Blood to be Shed" (48).

A much different calamity intervened to change everything for everyone on the Lower Columbia, especially the thousands of people who lived in villages along the waterways. Fever and ague or "intermittent fever," 19th-century terminology for malaria, struck in 1829–30 and roared up and down the Lower Columbia River (see Boyd 1999b:84–115; ch. 11 in this volume). "The Intermittent fever has appeared at this place," McLoughlin (1948) wrote HBC governors in October 1830, "and carried off three fourths of the Indian population in our vicinity." By December, McLoughlin told his superiors in London "to attempt to describe our situation during this dreadful visitation [of malaria] is impossible" (140, 175). When naturalist John Kirk Townsend (1999) visited villages devastated by malaria on the Lower Columbia in 1834, he stood in shock:

A gentleman told me, that only four years ago, as he wandered near what had formerly been a thickly peopled village, he counted no less than sixteen dead, men and women, lying unburied and festering in the sun in front of their habitations. Within the houses all were sick; not one had escaped the contagion. . . .Some were in the dying struggle, and clenching with the convulsive grasp of death their disease-worn companions, shrieked and howled in the last sharp agony. (170–71)

The four-year epidemic was the most important episode in the Chinookan encounter with Euro-Americans. "It is no unusual thing," fur trader Francis Ermatinger (1980) wrote in February 1831, "to see two or three dead bodies, in a short excursion along the river. Some of the villages were entirely depopulated" (140). Population numbers among Lower Chinooks and mid-river Chinookans dropped dramatically (see ch. 11 in this volume). Concomly, the master of lower-river trading, succumbed in 1830, although Kiesno survived and became a major trading chief. Nothing in Chinookan life escaped its consequences, not in local economy, not in social relations, not in spiritual life. Their world had shattered in 48 months of unforeseen devastation—a cultural earthquake (Boyd 1999b:264; Lewis and Murakami 1923:78n48; Ruby and Brown 1976:198–200).

During the 1830s, the Chinookan encounter with Euro-Americans reached a major transition point. The population crashes in the wake of the malaria epidemic introduced dependency to the Chinookans' world. Where they had been masters of the lower river and often resistant to the methods and schemes of Euro-American traders, they found themselves with many fewer cultural resources and in far more need of what the invaders to their homeland might provide. Although most families continued to pursue traditional sources of sustenance, more and more Chinook people became enmeshed in economic exchanges with Euro-Americans, dominated by HBC, and in cultural relations with Protestant and Catholic missionaries. Chinookan survival depended on how well they could get some of the wealth the whites' trade had created on the Columbia.

Fort George at Astoria and Fort Vancouver were centers of an increasingly important economic geography that drew in many Chinook households. The trade, usually meted out in exchange equivalents of beaver pelts and manufactured blankets, connected Chinook people to an imperialistic world of international capital investment and economic competition. To casual observers, such as Lt. Charles Wilkes (1845) of the US Exploring Expedition, the "numbers of Indians . . . always to be seen lounging about" (322–23) Fort George seemed to indicate indolence rather than labor or trade. But that typically American evaluation hid an important economic relationship. It was important enough that HBC protected its trading relationships with Chinookan villagers along the Columbia. William Slacum (1972), an American government official who spent two months on the Columbia in 1836–37, described HBC attempts to prevent Chinooks from trading with any other companies or free traders. In the noncurrency economy on the Columbia, trade for the Chinooks meant exchanging gathered natural resources or their labor for manufactured goods at HBC stores. In 1840, for example, Middle Chinooks could purchase four handkerchiefs at Fort Vancouver by paddling a canoe for four miles, while 10 to 15 salmon could purchase one shirt at Fort George in 1846 (Mackie 1997; Frost 1934).

Chinooks participated in the new economy through direct labor relationships, primarily in transportation, repair and maintenance of canoes, excavation and construction work, and the cultivation and tending of gardens. HBC posts in the Columbia Department had long employed Indians as laborers, but many had shunned such work, considering it fit only for slaves. Increasingly, though, as conditions offered few alternatives, they acceded, hiring on with the company generally on a seasonal basis or as part-time workers. Native full-time laborers at Fort Vancouver in 1840, for example, accounted for fewer than 5 percent of the workforce (Mackie 1997:295–300). The occasional laborers at the headquarters post worked as plowmen, river pilots, and canoe ferrymen and in one instance as salmon seiners to supply HBC's cured salmon trade. At Fort George, HBC Factor James Birnie hired Chinooks as paid laborers in the gardens, weeding and cultivating potatoes (Lattie 1963:222). Birnie also expected Chinook fishers to trade considerable salmon during the annual runs. Hired labor aside, Chinooks also maintained their traditional ways, especially in salmon harvest. As Neil Howison (1913), an American naval officer, reported in 1846, Indians on the Lower Columbia were "wonderfully superstitious respecting this fish; of such vital importance is his annual visitation to this river and its tributaries that it is prayed for, and votive offerings made in gratitude when he makes his first appearance" (47; see Roberts 1962:183; Morison 1927:111–32).

By the early 1840s, the Chinook pursuit of traditional ways emphasized the cultural distance that continued to separate them from the traders and missionaries who had first come to the Lower Columbia in the mid-1830s. In 1834, Methodist missionaries established a mission near present-day Salem along the Willamette River among the Kalapuya people and later added missions among Chinookans at Willamette Falls and on Clatsop Plains on the

Lower Columbia. Jason Lee, the founder of the Willamette Mission, ambitiously believed in Christianity's power to revolutionize Indian lives, but he quickly found that the ravages of disease among the Chinooks and the Kalapuyas left him with few potential converts. Nonetheless, when Lee returned east in 1838 to secure reinforcements for his enterprise, he took two mixed-blood Chinookan boys to represent what he saw as both the challenge and the reality of Chinook youth in need of Christianity, a visceral prompt for potential recruits to a reinforcement of the Methodist enterprise in Oregon. As perhaps a sign of the ultimate futility of the missionary work, however, the boys took education in New York and Massachusetts and settled out in white society (Ruby and Brown 1976:202; Lee and Frost 1968:262; see Loewenberg 1976; Schaeffer 1963:41–54).

At Willamette Falls in 1840, the Methodists established a mission under the ministrations of Alvan Waller, one of Lee's recruits in the so-called Great Reinforcement, which brought more than 50 new missionaries to the Oregon country on the ship *Lausanne* in 1840 (Frost 1934). Chinookans near Willamette Falls occupied two villages, one nearly adjacent to the falls on the west side of the Willamette and another on the east side a few miles up the Clackamas River. Some of the new missionaries did not share Waller's ambitions at the falls, describing the Chinooks as "degraded" and perhaps beyond reach. "Surely, thought we," Gustavus Hines (1850) wrote, "it will require the labor of many years to elevate these Indians from the depths of their pollution into a civilized and Christian people" (91–92). Charles Wilkes (1845:346), however, took note of the Chinooks' fishing prowess, describing their dipnet techniques and the engagement of men and women in the harvest. By 1846, British agents surveying the Oregon country reported that the mission at the falls was no longer, but a Methodist chapel in its place served some of the nearly 300 residents of Oregon City (Schafer 1909:51). The Methodists at the falls, like those at Willamette Mission, had shifted their denominational efforts to the incoming Americans (Boyd 1996:28).

At Clatsop Plains, Methodist Joseph H. Frost established a mission to the Clatsops. Solomon Smith, an HBC employee who had married Celiast, a Clatsop woman, lived at Clatsop and aided Frost in establishing the mission. During less than two years of labor, however, Frost tired of the struggle, which was compromised by conflicts among Chinook and Clatsop families and his unrealistic hopes for mass conversions. In his diary, Frost confessed: "I am quite confident, from all the observations which I have been enabled to make relative to their moral and physical condition, that there never will be anything like a permanent Christian church raised up for them" (Lee and Frost 1968:295). For Frost, the failure was wholly the Clatsops'. He had committed himself to the task, but the potential parishioners had remained tied to their traditional ways. It was the result, Frost argued, of their "defective" language, which prevented them from grasping the power of the word. They were a people, he concluded, who "are a law unto themselves," a people who could not abandon their culture for a new way (313; see Ruby and Brown 1976:203–6).

The Methodist failure among the Chinookan people stands as a marker of two dynamics at work during the mid-19th century in Oregon country. For the Chinooks, the way forward did not include an abandonment of their spiritual lives or their traditional culture, but it was clear to them that their economic future would necessarily be tied to the capitalistic world the traders had brought to the Columbia. The other dynamic centered on the invasion of the Chinook homeland by wealth-seeking Americans, land-hungry migrants who dreamed of creating an agricultural empire in Oregon. The tide of Americans who rushed into the region during the 1840s radically altered conditions by claiming land, surveying it, and parceling it out to landowners. Howison (1913) saw it clearly in 1841: "In speaking of the Indians, I would respectfully suggest that this moment is, of all others, the most favorable for extinguishing titles to the land. Miserable as they are, they show some spirit and jealousy on this subject" (47).

Howison's admonition to grab Chinook land became policy by the early 1850s, when the machinery of imperial acquisition brought the power of the American government to the Chinooks in myriad ways, including treaty-making. It was the end of an era and the beginning of a sharply different world for the Chinooks. The arc of their history, from the first meeting of the maritime traders to the advent of the American settlers, was a punctuated decline in power and the ability to pursue their desires and, ultimately, to defend their interests. The era of trade subtly gave way to a time of colonization, and what had begun as an enriching relationship for Chinookans devolved into a loss of power and land, a condition that challenged them to be resilient or perish.

THIRTEEN

CHINUK WAWA AND ITS ROOTS IN CHINOOKAN

Henry B. Zenk and Tony A. Johnson

T HE name "Chinook" appears in two ship's logs documenting the first recorded visit by non-Natives to the Lower Columbia River. In May 1792, the American trading ship *Columbia Rediviva* under Captain Robert Gray crossed the hazardous river bar and anchored near a village they called "*Chinoak*" or "*Chinouk*" on the river's north bank (Howay 1990:398, 437). Almost a hundred years later, a descendant of the Native people encountered by Gray and his crew noted that the name, properly *c'inúk*, comes from the language of the Lower Chehalis people, who lived just north of the early seafarers' "Chinook" (Boas 1911:563). In the forms "chǐ'nook," "chǐ'nŭk," the name has entered the region's indigenous languages as well as the regional English of the Pacific Northwest, where it is today often heard as "shǐ'nŭk."

Throughout the Greater Lower Columbia, English and indigenous-language speakers alike have applied the name "Chinook" to Native groups along the lower river, as well as ambiguously to two categorically different species of language historically associated with the majority of those groups: their own original tribal languages and a regionally much more widely known pidgin hybrid, based largely on local tribal languages but, in contrast to them, featuring a small basic lexicon and few, simple grammatical rules. In this volume, Chinookan designates a language family consisting of two languages, Lower Chinook (spoken at the mouth of the Columbia River) and Upper Chinook (spoken from Grays Bay to The Dalles); or, following Mithun's (1999:382) revision, three languages, adding Kathlamet (spoken from Gray's Bay to Rainier, Oregon; elsewhere classified as the westernmost dialect of Upper Chinook). We reserve Chinook both for the dialect of Lower Chinook spoken on the north side of the Columbia estuary and for the original speakers of that dialect; while preferring the local Native term Chinuk Wawa for the pidgin hybrid, which in local English is also known as Chinook Jargon, or simply Jargon.

Chinuk Wawa arose among Chinookan speakers under circumstances and at a time that remain subjects of debate. During the early contact period, Chinuk Wawa served as a "trade language," facilitating at least minimal communication between local Indians speaking a variety of indigenous tribal languages and non-Natives speaking English and French. As rapid social change from the mid-19th century on brought Indians from disparate tribes together on reservations and work crews, at hopyard encampments, and in Indian quarters of towns and cities, Chinuk Wawa assumed considerable importance as a medium of intertribal communication. During this period, it developed an embryonic written literature, consisting mostly of religious texts composed by missionaries who adopted it as an alternative to the perplexing variety and forbidding complexity of Northwest tribal languages. Chinookan, the principal indigenous source of Chinuk Wawa, had a reputation for being exceptionally difficult to learn even among speakers of other Northwest languages. While the Chinookan roots of Chinuk Wawa are beyond dispute, scholars still argue about the language's origin, social functions, and linguistic description (Grant 1996). In this sketch, we attempt to convey some sense of what Chinookan and Chinuk Wawa look like as languages, while contributing our own point of view on the origin and nature of Chinuk Wawa.

A LANGUAGE "FOREIGNERS SELDOM ATTEMPT TO ACQUIRE" (HALE 1846:562)

Chinookan languages, at this writing, are represented by but a few elderly speakers of Kiksht, the easternmost dialect complex of Upper Chinook. The surviving dialects are Wishram, indigenous to the north bank of the Columbia River, and Wasco, indigenous to the south bank, at an ancient dipnet fishery since inundated by The Dalles Dam. Wasco-Wishram speakers are a minority among speakers of Sahaptin, the majority indigenous language of the Yakama and Warm Springs Reservation communities. While English is now predominant, Kiksht, Sahaptin, and Chinuk Wawa were languages of daily life among these people as recently as the first quarter of the 20th century. While individuals bilingual in Sahaptin and Chinookan sustained much of the region's intertribal communication, this was a distinctly asymmetrical bilingualism: hardly any Sahaptin speakers spoke Chinookan, while many Kiksht speakers spoke Sahaptin; Chinuk Wawa served the purpose when individuals' tribal-language repertoires happened not to overlap. In 1843, the missionary Henry Perkins noted this asymmetry: "While the Walla-walla and Klikatak [both terms referring to Sahaptin] are spoken by numbers of the [Kiksht-speaking] Chinook, not one of the former tribes, to my knowledge, can speak the [Kiksht] Chinook readily" (in Boyd 1996:34). Several decades later, Edward Sapir (1909b) noted the same asymmetry and offered a linguistic explanation: "most of the Wishrams speak, or at least have a smattering of, Klickitat [Sahaptin], as well as their own language and the Chinook jargon; very few, however, if any, of the Sahaptin-speaking Indians, can also speak Wishram, the language having a reputation for great difficulty, chiefly, it is probable, because of its harsh phonetics" (x). This explanation is surprising, considering that the basic sounds or phonemes of Chinookan are comparable to those of Sahaptin. Both languages share arrays of uvular, glottalized, and fricative consonants that may sound harsh to speakers of English and French but that seem perfectly natural to speakers of Northwest indigenous languages. The only phonetic trait clearly distinguishing Chinookan from Sahaptin is the greater degree to which consonants may adhere, or cluster, in Chinookan. The Chinookan verb, in particular, is remarkably compact, often consisting of a string of individually short meaning-bearing units or morphemes, as illustrated by the following examples simplified from Boas (1911), in which the verb proper is highlighted in bold type:

1. *amłaxšgámx̣* (respelled from Boas 1911:576):

a-	*m-*	*ł-*	*a-*	*x̣-*	*-šg*	*-am*	*-x̣*
[tense]-thou-	it-	her-	from-	**take**	—finish	—habitually

Thou wert in the habit of taking it from her (Boas's translation).

2. *iqtílux̣* (respelled from Boas 1911:672):

i-	*q-*	*t-*	*i-*	*l-*	*u-*	**-x̣**
[tense]-	somebody-	them-	him-	to-	[direction]-	**do**

He had them (shots) done to him (=he was shot).

Especially relevant to the Chinookan roots of Chinuk Wawa is the frequent use in all dialects of the auxiliary verb *-x̣* 'make, do, become' (invariably inflected, as in example 2), which can be paired with an uninflected verbal particle or linked to one or more nouns inflected to agree with it.

3. *λq'up gačíuẋ; λq'up galíẋuẋ* (respelled from Sapir in Boas 1911:676):

λq'up	*ga-*	*č-₁*	*i-*	*u-*	*-ẋ*
cut	[tense]-	he₁–	him-	[direction]-	**do**

He cut it (*λq'up*=verbal particle; subscript-1=transitive subject form).

λq'up	*gal-*	*í-₂*	*ẋ-*	*u-*	*-ẋ*
cut	[tense]-	he₂–	self-	[direction]-	**do**

He got cut (subscript-2=intransitive subject/transitive object form).

4. *úlu aktáẋ tílxam* (respelled from Boas 1894:260.11–12):

u-₁	*-lu*	*a-₁*	*k-*	*t-₂*	*a-*	*-ẋ*	*t-₂*	*-lxam*
the₁-	hunger	she₁–	on-	them₂–	[direction]-	**do**	the₂-	people

The people are hungry (subscripts-1, 2 =cross-agreeing nominal-verbal prefixes).

Morphological complexity is not unique to Chinookan. Tribal languages spoken by the Chinookans' neighbors did not lack for structural complexities of their own. Even so, the morphologies of neighboring languages—those of the Athapaskan, Sahaptian (including Sahaptin), Salishan, and Kalapuyan families, plus Molala, a language isolate—show nothing quite like the Chinookan inflected verb, which may combine a dozen or more individually short grammatical and lexical elements into one seamless "sentence-word." It is not surprising, therefore, that the perception of Chinookan as difficult appears to have been widely shared by speakers of other local languages.

The picture for downriver Chinookan and its neighboring Salishan languages (Tillamook, Lower Chehalis, Cowlitz) appears to parallel that sketched here for Kiksht Chinookan and Sahaptin. By the time Franz Boas reached the Lower Columbia in 1890, only a few Lower Chinook and Kathlamet speakers could be found, and all of them were using principally Salishan languages—Lower Chehalis on the north bank of the river, Tillamook on the south—in their own families and communities (Boas 1894:5–6; Rohner 1969:119–20). According to Clara Pearson, a Tillamook speaker visited during the 1930s and 1940s by several linguists and anthropologists (Seaburg in Jacobs 2003:47–52), Clatsop (the dialect of Lower Chinook neighboring Tillamook) was an "awful hard" language (Jacobs 1933–34(107):87). In 1942, linguist John P. Harrington was unable to find any lower-river Chinookan descendants who were still fluent in Chinookan, although a number still did speak local Salishan languages (Snow 1969:4). Chinuk Wawa survived on the lower river about as long as local Salishan (Harrington 1942–43:reel 18.0209–0499; Tony A. Johnson, personal information); and next to Lower Chinook, Lower Chehalis is the most important local source of Chinuk Wawa words (Kinkade and Powell 2005). During the period of fur-company hegemony on the Lower Columbia, from 1811 to about 1843, Chinuk Wawa was the principal medium of communication between Chinookans and European and Canadian newcomers. Writing from Fort Vancouver in 1838, Fr. Modeste Demers observed: "The real language of the Chinooks is almost unlearnable; it differs entirely from that of all the neighboring tribes; but they speak the jargon also, which is used as the medium between the Canadians and the whites in general and the Indians who are settled near the fort" (Blanchet 1983:65–66).

The shift from Chinook to Lower Chehalis and Chinuk Wawa was in progress among the Chinooks by the 1850s, to judge from this observation by James Swan (1972). He attributes this shift explicitly to the perceived difficulty of Chinookan:

> The [Lower] Chehalis language is that most usually spoken at present, for
> the ancient Chenook [Chinookan] is such a guttural, difficult tongue, that
> many of the young Chenook Indians can not speak it, but have been taught
> by their parents the [Lower] Chehalis language and the Jargon. The Jargon
> is the medium with which the Indians hold [intertribal] intercourse with
> each other and with the whites. (306–7)

Swan's observation that Chinuk Wawa sustained Indian-with-Indian as well as Indian-with-white communication suggests that asymmetrical bilingualism coexisted with Chinuk Wawa on the lower river, just as it did upriver. No doubt bilingual Chinookan speakers carried much of the burden of cross-language communication in both places; but just as there were Kiksht speakers with only "a smattering" of Sahaptin, not all lower-river Chinookans were equally adept in local Salishan. Moreover, Indians from outside the local area had always come into the Lower Columbia as visitors or new residents, a trend surely accelerated by contact but that had precontact antecedents in aboriginal trade and slavery as well.

These observations suggest that social conditions on the Lower Columbia favored the development of a contact medium, or secondary language adapted for relative ease of learning. While such conditions are most apparent for the early postcontact era, it is entirely possible that asymmetrical bilingualism, like intertribal visiting and in-migration, had an aboriginal background. This raises the possibility that some sort of Lower Columbia intertribal contact medium predated the first visits of white explorers and traders.

CHINUK WAWA'S HYBRID CHARACTER

Determining what a (putative) aboriginal Chinuk Wawa would have looked like is not easy. Chinuk Wawa is at its grammatical and lexical core a hybrid, in which Chinookan-derived basic elements are fused with equally basic elements imported from Nootka (now often termed Nuuchahnulth), a language indigenous to the West Coast of Vancouver Island some 200 miles to the north of the Lower Columbia. An additional nearly 20 percent of the 500–700 simple (as opposed to compounded) Chinuk Wawa words in most frequent use on the Lower Columbia come from French and English. It has long been suspected that the Nootka portion of the lexicon was introduced by Europeans and Euro-Americans, since many of the first British and American seafarers to visit the lower river had been at the Vancouver Island trading hub of Nootka Sound (Howay 1943). In the course of these earlier trading forays, the seafarers had used a drastically simplified and phonetically reduced form of Nootka, the so-called Nootka Jargon (Samarin 1988; Lang 2008:15–42; Clark 2005). While the Nootka contribution to Chinuk Wawa is not large (about 5 percent of the Lower Columbia lexicon), it provides the usual Chinuk Wawa words for some of the most basic meanings known to human language: go; come; make, do; see, look; woman; give; many, much; little; know, understand; good; no, not. The Nootka contribution is also central to the grammar of Chinuk Wawa, with the Nootka-derived auxiliary verbs *mamuk-* ('make, do, cause to be') and *čagu-* ('become, get to be') assuming the grammatical work reserved in Chinookan for the inflected verb *-x* 'make, do, become' (examples 2, 3, 4 above).

TABLE 13.1. Sources of earliest-recorded words attributed to
Lower Columbia Indians

CLARK 1805	THOMPSON 1811	CHINUK WAWA	ASSUMED SOURCE
Clouch	"Thloos: good;	łuš 'good'	N łuł 'good, pretty'
com ma-tax	"Kummen tacks [Kummertacks]: I understand, or know it;	kəmdəks 'know'	N kamat-aḥ 'known+[irrealis]' N kamat-ak-s 'known+ [durative 1 sing.]
	"Knick me	naika 'I, me, my'	Chinookan naika 'I, me, my'
wake	"Week no	wik 'no, not'	N wik 'no!'
	"se ye: far off;	saya 'far'	N sayaa 'far off'
	"Perhuk [Pesheek]: bad."	pišak 'bad'	N p'išaq 'bad, ugly'

Note: Nootka(N) words as spelled in Powell 1991, except kamat-aḥ, spelled following Silverstein 1996:128; and kamat-ak-s, spelled following Clark 2005.

The first recorded example of connected speech attributed to Lower Columbia Indians is indistinguishable from Nootka Jargon: "every [Clatsop] man . . . looked at the gun the Size of the ball which was 100 to the pound and Said in their own language *Clouch Musket*, [English word Musket] *wake, com ma-tax Musket* which is, a good Musket do not under stand this kind of Musket &c" (Lewis and Clark 1990:121). The three non-English words are from Nootka. Moreover, they appear to show distortions of Nootka word-forms and morphology identical to ones met with in the Chinuk Wawa of later record (Table 13.1). These same three words, in their same distorted "Chinuk Wawa" forms, reappear several years later in a journal entry by David Thompson (1994) on July 13, 1811, at The Cascades (present-day Cascade Locks, in the homeland of the *wałáła* and *wáyaxix* Chinookans) during his descent of the river to Fort Astoria: "A fine day. The people on the right Side or North Side are called Waw thloo las [*Wan-thlus-lar*]—on the [South] side We yark eek [*Woe-yark-Eek*]. Thloos: good; Kummen tacks [*Kummertacks*]: I understand, or know it; Knick me week no se ye: far off; Perhuk [*Pesheek*]: bad. After much delay we were obliged to set off" (155; alternate readings from Elliot 1914:61–62). Thompson's somewhat garbled entry documents five Nootka Jargon words alongside the first known recorded instance of a Chinookan pronoun (Table 13.1).

Gabriel Franchère (1967:203–4) and Alexander Ross (2000:342–49), two clerks who were already at Fort Astoria when Thompson arrived in 1811, left longer word lists that reveal a mishmash of Chinookan, "broken" Chinookan, and Nootka Jargon/putative Chinuk Wawa. Franchère's and Ross's spellings of words of what was later known as Chinuk Wawa are in general more suggestive of indigenous-sounding pronunciations than they are of English-sounding pronunciations. For example, Franchère, a French-speaking Canadian, writes "Thlounasse" for Chinuk Wawa/Chinookan λ'únas/ƛúnaš 'perhaps', while Ross, a Highlands Scot and in all likelihood a Gaelic speaker, writes "Thlun-ass" for the same word; for Chinuk Wawa/Chinookan tq'íx 'want, need', Franchère writes "Ste kech," Ross "Tekeigh"; for Chinuk Wawa/ Chinookan ixt 'one', Franchère writes "Icht," Ross "Ight." Similar considerations apply to Thompson's spelling of the word for 'good', which suggests the sound ł (a voiceless lateral fricative), characteristic of later-recorded Indian pronunciations of this word (compare "Tlòsh," Ross's spelling of the same word)—as opposed to the cluster written cl or kl, an English speaker's typical approximation of voiceless "l"-sounds in local indigenous languages.

THE CHINOOKAN CONTRIBUTION TO CHINUK WAWA

The accurate records of Chinookan and local Indian Chinuk Wawa secured from the late-19th century on, when linguists trained in modern methods began appearing on the scene, permit us to expand on the foregoing suggestive historical passages. One striking feature of Chinuk Wawa is that the part of its basic lexicon derived from Lower Columbia languages, comprising at least half of the 500–700 simple (that is, noncompounded) words in most frequent use on the lower river, includes many words derived from Chinookan pronouns, nouns, and particles; but comparatively speaking, hardly any derived from Chinookan inflected verbs (like those described in the discussion of Chinookan examples 1–4 above). The examples appearing in Table 13.2 include three of the no more than ten Chinuk Wawa words derived from Chinookan inflected verbs. By contrast, all six Chinuk Wawa personal pronouns are based on Chinookan pronouns, while about 30 percent of its Chinookan-derived words are from Chinookan nouns and about 50 percent are from Chinookan particles (Zenk and Johnson 2005).

Chinuk Wawa, as recorded from Lower Columbia Indians, faithfully preserves the basics of Chinookan pronunciation and morphological form (see Table 13.2). Most Chinookan-contributed Chinuk Wawa words are derived from whole Chinookan words. Even when they are not, they respect Chinookan morpheme boundaries. In the case of noun-derived words, the

TABLE 13.2. Chinookan sources of selected Chinuk Wawa words

CHINOOKAN WORD-CLASSES (AFTER HYMES 1955)	CHINOOKAN	CHINUK WAWA/CHINOOK JARGON: INDIAN PRONOUNCED (SIMPLIFIED FROM JACOBS 1936, HARRINGTON 1942); (WHITE PRONOUNCED AFTER GIBBS 1863)
Pronouns	náika '1 sg.'	náika [Ní-ka] 'I, me, my'
	máika '2 sg.'	máika [Mí-ka] 'thou, thine, thee'
	yáxka '3 sg. (masc.)'	yá(x)ka [Yáh-ka, Yok'-ka] 's/he, hers/his, her/him'
Nouns	i-k'áinuɫ 'tobacco'	k'áinuɫ [Kí-nootl, Kí-noos] '...'
	i-ʔíčxut 'black bear'	ícxut [Its'-woot, Its'-hoot] '...'
	ɫ-čúq 'water'	cuq, cəqʷ [Chuck] '...'
	š-iá-xušt 'his (two) eyes'	siyáxus(t) [Se-áh-host] '...'
	tí-lxam 'people'	tílixam [Til'-i-kum] 'person, people'
	ú-lu 'hunger'	úlu [O'-lo] 'hungry'
Verbs	í-šgam 'take it!'	iskam [Is'-kum] 'to take, get'
	mə́-ɫait 'thou sit!'	míɫait [Mit'-lite] 'to sit, stay'
	-x(ə́)-laqɫ 'open' [stem]	xálaqɫ [Háh-lakl] 'open'
Particles	c'əm 'marked'	c'əm [Tzum] '...'
	k'au 'tied'	k'au [Kow] '...'
	ɫq'up, λq'up 'cut'	ɫq'up [Tl'kope] '...'
	λxʷap 'hole'	ɫxʷap [Kla-wháp] '...'
	λ'mən 'mashed'	λ'mən, λ'ímin [Klim'-min] '...'
	λ'ap 'find'	λ'ap [Klap] '...'

exceptions are rule-governed: stressed Chinookan number-gender and possessive prefixes being retained as Chinuk Wawa (siyáxus(t), tílixam, úlu), unstressed such prefixes usually being dropped (k'áinuɫ, ícxut, cúq). Nor are there any obvious phonetic characteristics that would enable foreign hearers to readily separate inflected verbs as a class from other kinds of Chinookan words.

Any hypothesis concerning Chinuk Wawa's origin and early development must account for these facts of linguistic form, which taken together point to a systematic avoidance of Chinookan morphological complexity. Note that while the Chinookan morphology of Chinuk Wawa's large Chinookan contribution is unmistakably simplified, it is by no means mangled—as we might expect had it originated with foreigners' reproductions of Chinookan words whose internal constituencies they did not comprehend. This generalization applies as much to the Chinook Jargon of English-speaking visitors and set-tlers as it does to the Chinuk Wawa of local Natives. The two varieties show basically identical word forms (see Table 13.2); only certain indigenous pro-nunciation features that, by and large, are preserved faithfully by local Indi-ans are badly mangled by English speakers. These distortions are readily explained: ɫ, q, x̣ and the glottalized consonants are simply very difficult for English speakers to pronounce correctly. Evidently, both of these Chinuk Wawa varieties go back to one ancestral Chinuk Wawa.

THE GENESIS OF CHINUK WAWA

Chinuk Wawa's hybrid character and European-mediated Nootka influences have provided fodder for scholarly dispute. Samarin (1986, 1996) revives Howay's (1943) proposal that Chinuk Wawa was a creation of the same British and American seafarers who introduced Nootka words to the Lower Colum-bia. Lang (2008:55–121) thinks that the seafarers and land-based traders who followed them at Fort Astoria and Fort Vancouver were capable of sustaining, at most, an unstable mishmash that combined Nootka Jargon with elements of broken Chinookan, the real genesis of Chinuk Wawa coming later when the local Indian wives of fur-company employees began adapting this mish-mash to the task of raising the first generations of ethnically mixed or Métis children born on the Lower Columbia. Thomason (1983) argues that Chinuk Wawa's markedly indigenous phonology and word orders, which she (1981) documents with reference to a wide range of sources, are best explained as structural lowest common denominators shared by indigenous languages brought into contact on the Lower Columbia, presumably as a result of that region's exceptional development of indigenous trade and slavery. In her model, the seafarers' Nootka Jargon is a later graft on what is at core an indig-enous (and, most likely, aboriginal) Lower Columbia pidgin.

We have tried to make the case that, to be convincing, any hypothesis of Chinuk Wawa's genesis must explain the medium's roots in Chinookan, as revealed by the linguistic features we have touched on here. For the rest, we must admit that we ourselves are unable to agree on a likeliest scenario for explaining the genesis of this singular linguistic phenomenon. Johnson finds Thomason's arguments most convincing. Zenk wonders whether the reputed exceptional difficulty of Chinookan led to an exceptional development of "foreigner Chinookan," driven by Chinookan speakers' motivated avoidance of the most productive aspect of Chinookan morphology—its system of verbal and nominal prefixation. He is inclined to emphasize the agency of the Chinookans themselves, who must have been primarily responsible for dropping inflected verbs (save for a few simple imperative and stem forms) and for disconnecting (dropping entirely, or retaining for sound-value only) the number/gender and possessive prefixes that in Chinookan mark nouns for agreement with verbs.

In either case, Lower Columbia Chinuk Wawa in its fully crystallized historical form (Hale 1846:635–50; Gibbs 1863a; Demers et al. 1871) also owes much to the early American and British seafarers. It was they who contributed the Nootkan-derived auxiliaries *mamuk-* ('make, do, cause to be') and *čagu-* ('become, get to be'), which Chinookans learned to use in place of the Chinookan inflected auxiliary verb -*x̣* ('make, do, become', as in examples 2, 3, 4 above). Substituting Nootka Jargon *mamuk-* and *čagu-* for Chinookan -*x̣* would have removed much of the necessity for using Chinookan verbs and nominal agreement prefixes, setting the stage for a Chinookan-derived lexicon in which verbs and nominal agreement prefixes were simply avoided. Chinookans could have drawn on a pre-existing Lower Columbia pidgin, Chinookan foreigner-talk, or both to constitute such a lexicon.

For all their reputed difficulty, Chinookan languages also feature a lexicon distinguished by an exceptionally large number of words of simple morphological form—in particular, its plethora of uninflected (or minimally inflected: sometimes suffixed, never prefixed) particles, many of which convey onomatopoeic or semi-onomatopoeic sound-associations (see Boas 1911:627–36). While Chinookan clearly deserves its historical reputation for difficulty, it also comes with a considerable repertoire of built-in means for its own simplification. It is not impossible that both of these aspects of Chinookan are rooted in the historical position of Chinookans as regional trade middlemen. Further linguistic, sociohistorical, and even archeological investigation may yet clarify the disputed genesis and early development of Chinuk Wawa.

CHINUK WAWA IN FULL BLOOM

Chinuk Wawa has also been the subject of vigorous debate surrounding its status as a rule-governed linguistic system—or language, in the usual sense of that term. Among world languages are some that, like Chinuk Wawa, lack an inflectional morphology; all such languages rely instead on word order to encode grammatical information. But some linguists have claimed that Chinuk Wawa word order follows no regular pattern, instead being perpetually open to negotiation. Silverstein (1972, 1996) and Thomason (1983) have disagreed vehemently on this point. Silverstein argues that every speaker fashions his or her own Chinuk Wawa grammar, based necessarily on the patterns of his or her primary language(s). Thomason points to records from disparate times and places evincing the same basic Chinuk Wawa word orders again and again.

Our own view is that the regional Chinuk Wawa word orders cited by Thomason are default patterns, as intrinsic to full mastery of the language as Chinuk Wawa's regional lexicon (see Kaufman 1971:277; Grant 1996:1186). They do not preclude a speaker being influenced by his or her other languages. If the Chinuk Wawa word order of a newly arrived settler struggling to communicate, "Chinook" dictionary in hand, appears indistinguishable from that of his mother tongue, then this is only natural for an adult learning a new language. This seems to have been the view of Methodist missionary Myron Eells (1893), although the published version of this quote (Eells 1894:31) reads as if it endorses Silverstein's position (see Silverstein 1996:239)—the result, we suspect, of an editor's too-heavy hand.

> There is no settled authority in regard to the order of the words in this language. They are generally placed in much the same order as they are in the language which the speaker has been accustomed to use, if he be not well acquainted with the language. An English speaking person will place them in much the same order that he would in English, but there are many phrases where this is not true, the order of which must be acquired by practice: for instance *halo nika kumtuks* not I understand, is far more common than *nika halo kumtuks*.

Equally, the Chinuk Wawa of a skilled Native interpreter, able to switch instantly between Chinuk Wawa and other languages in contact, may be no less impressively fluid and effective for also bearing telltale indications of the speaker's background and place of origin, including his or her first language or languages (Zenk and Johnson 2003).

The intimate connection between default word order and word meaning in Chinuk Wawa is illustrated by two sentences from Mr. Wilson Bobb (1891–1985), an elder of the Grand Ronde Indian Community, Oregon.

kə́ldəs ya hayu-wáwa
merely he ongoing-talk
He's just talking.

wík hayu-kə́ldəs-wáwa!
not ongoing-worthless-talk
Don't be talking nonsense!

The word *kəldəs* has two meanings based originally in the multiple positions it can occupy in a sentence: (1) as an adverb positioned clause-first in front of pronoun (if present) and verb, it means 'just, merely'; (2) appearing anywhere else in the sentence, it usually has the sense 'worthless, of little value'. While not all Chinuk Wawa words can occupy different sentence positions, many can. Once fixed by common usage, a word's alternate meanings are then available for extended usages, as in the case of the widely known regional idiom *kəldəs-pałač* 'a gift', in which an originally adverbial *kəldəs* 'just, merely' becomes attached to *pałač* 'to give; a gift', yielding 'merely given' or 'mere gift' (and not necessarily, something of little or no worth), as in something given with no expectation of return.

As far as we know, there were no monolingual adult speakers of Chinuk Wawa, and even fluent speakers may betray telltale indications of being influenced by their other languages. The last generations of fluent speakers in Mr. Bobb's home community of Grand Ronde shared at least local English as another language. Chinuk Wawa remained in late use in this community primarily with conservative older household members who preferred not to use English—or at least not all the time. The language had also acquired symbolic associations with group identity. Under these circumstances, speakers could mix features of their different languages quite freely, mixing and resorting both words and word orders. At the same time, Chinuk Wawa word orders that monolingual speakers of English would not be expected to introduce, lacking an autonomous Chinuk Wawa "target grammar" (Thomason 1983:830–33), were frequently used by all these speakers (Chinuk Wawa Dictionary Project 2012:30–51).

Autonomy as a linguistic system is but one issue. Another is posed by Chinuk Wawa's claimed lack of expressiveness due to its limited lexicon and grammar. Were such limited resources "not fully expressive either of the indigenous cultures or of the transplanted [European] ones and their complex religious doctrines," as Roth (1994:172) maintains, or do we underestimate "the irrepressible creativity of language" (George Lang, personal communication, 2005) at our peril? A promising avenue for exploring this issue is provided by the considerable Catholic missionary literature preserved in Chinuk Wawa (Pilling 1893:entries for Blanchet, Bulmer, Demers, Durieu, Eells, LeJeune, St. Onge; Robertson 2003, 2005, 2011; Vrzić 1999). One of the first Catholic missionaries on the Lower Columbia, Rev. Modeste Demers (who arrived there in 1838), was not reluctant to translate abstruse theology into Chinuk Wawa, for example, in a text published in Latin with an accompanying Chinuk Wawa translation, under the title: "Definitio Dogmatis Immaculatæ Conceptionis Beatissimmæ Virginiæ Mariæ | a SS. D. N. Pio PP. IX. Eadom in eam Linguam translata quæ vulgo Jargon Tchinook | dicitur, quæque obtinet in tota Oregonensi Provincia; | auctore Episcopo Vancouveriensis Insulæ" (Pilling 1893:20). While Pilling mentions seeing this at Georgetown University, we have been unable to locate a surviving copy there or elsewhere, nor are we aware of any other Chinuk Wawa text addressing the "Immaculate Conception" of Mary. But consider the treatment of the Virginal Conception of Jesus in Mary's womb, in the catechism attributed to Fr. Demers and published by Frs. Blanchet and St. Onge (Demers et al. 1871:54–55; we are indebted to Fr. Martinus Cawley of Our Lady of Guadalupe Trappist Abbey, Lafayette, Oregon, for clarifying the differences between these two church doctrines). The Chinuk Wawa syntax of the latter is clear, straightforward, and entirely in keeping with regional Chinuk Wawa word-order patterns (Figure 13.1).

Some sense of the role and significance of Chinuk Wawa in the lives of generations of Lower Columbia Indian and Métis speakers can be gathered from the life story of another Grand Ronde elder, Mrs. Clara (Menard) Riggs (1892–1983) (see Hymes and Zenk 1987). Although Mrs. Riggs claimed Chinuk Wawa as her native—her *first*, but equally, her *Native*—language, she spent her later childhood and early adulthood away from Grand Ronde speaking only English. Much of her fluency as an elder speaker stemmed from a more recent 18-year period of household residence with her mother-in-law, Jennie Riggs, a conservative, English-shunning older woman. While we have no record of any monolingual adult Chinuk Wawa speaker, predominantly Chinuk Wawa–speaking children are documented at the Lower Columbia contact communities of Fort Vancouver (Hale 1846:644) and French Prairie (Shepard 1935:194–95); and most of the elderly Grand Ronde speakers interviewed by Hajda (1977–80), Zenk (1978–83), and Johnson (1998) had acquired the language in the course of varying degrees of childhood exposure.

Ikta okuk chako man?
what? that-one become-man
(1) *What is it to become man?*

Spos iskom iltuil pi tomtom kakwa nsaïka, okuk chako man.
if   get   flesh and spirit   like   us   that-one become-man
(2) *To get flesh and spirit like us, that is to become man.*

Pus ikta, iaka chako man ok Saḥali Taï iaka Tanas?
for-what?   he   become-man that High-Chief   his   child
(3) *Why did the Son of God become man?*

Saḥali Taï iaka Tanas iaka chako man pus mamuk tlak nsaïka kopa lempel.
High-Chief   his   child   he   become-man for   do-off   us   from hell
(4) *The Son of God became man to deliver us from hell.*

Kopa tlaksta tluchmen iaka chako tanas?
in   who?   woman   he   become-child
(5) *Of which woman was he born?*

Kopa Mali kwanesom tlush iaka chako tanas.
in   Mary   always   good   he   become-child
(6) *Of blessed Mary he was born.*

Tlaksta mitlaït pus iaka Papa?
who?   be-there for   his   father
(7) *Who was there as his father?*

Wek tlaksta man pus iaka Papa, kopet iḥt okuk Saḥali Taï iaka Papa. . . .
   no-who   man for   his   father   only-one that-one High-Chief   his   father
(8) *There wasn't any man as his Father, his father was God alone. . . .*

Saḥali Taï Saït Espli iaka potlach iaka kopa Mali.
High-Chief   Holy-Spirit he   give   him   into Mary
(9) *God the Holy Spirit gave him into Mary.*

FIGURE 13.1. Excerpt from *Lesson VIII:* The Incarnation (Demers et al. 1871:54–55). Word orders are basic regional Chinuk Wawa. Regionally familiar compounds are *saxali-tayi* 'God' (literally, 'high-chief'), *pus-ikta* 'why?' ('for-what?'), *mamuk-ɬaq* 'remove' ('do-off'), *wik-ɬaksta* 'no-one', *kupit-ixt* 'alone' ('only-one').

By 1891, close to the year Clara Riggs was born at Grand Ronde, the super-intendent of the reservation laconically reported that "nearly all" of his wards "understand the English language more or less, but seldom try to speak it" (Lamson 1891:369). Apart from English, only Chinuk Wawa was shared by the entire turn-of-the-century Grand Ronde community (Zenk 1988), and there were adult community members who felt more at home in "Jargon" than in any other language known to them. Such persons included both Clara Riggs's mother, who died when her daughter was a small child, and her mother-in-law to be, Jennie Riggs. Visiting the Grand Ronde home of Sam, Clara, and Jennie Riggs in 1934, the anthropologist Joel Berreman (1934) had this to say about Jennie Riggs: "She talks English with some difficulty. Claims to speak jargon fluently, and to be able to understand Clackamas and Klicki-tat" (pt. 1:54). Other elders who knew Jennie Riggs confirm that she spoke fluent Chinuk Wawa, not to the exclusion of English but in definite prefer-ence to it.

Jennie Riggs was still a child when she and her Clackamas Chinookan mother were brought to Grand Ronde, part of the mid-19th-century forced relocation of western Oregon Native people to reservations. Her mother died not long after their arrival, and at the age of 17 she was married to Solomon Riggs, the 60–something chief of the Umpqua (Athapaskan-speaking) tribe, in what according to Clara Riggs was the last full-scale traditional wedding at Grand Ronde. Apart from likely early-life exposure to Clackamas Chinookan and Klikatat Sahaptin, Jennie Riggs spoke principally Chinuk Wawa all of her long life. The significance of Chinuk Wawa to her life story does not end there, assuming that the man she identified as her biological father, "Billy *məkái*," was the well-known frontier Oregon physician Dr. William C. "Billy" McKay.

Born at Astoria in 1824 to a Chinook mother and a Scottish-Ojibwa fur-company employee, Dr. McKay belonged to one of the first cohorts of native-born Lower Columbia Métis, the very individuals Lang identifies as the "founders" of Chinuk Wawa. Be that as it may, Chinuk Wawa certainly played a crucial role in this man's adult career, which straddled the two worlds whose historic meeting had given him existence. As a member of government treaty commissions, a commander of US Army Indian scouts, and (for the greater part of his career) an agency physician on Oregon Indian reservations, Dr. McKay had many occasions to use the Chinuk Wawa he doubtless acquired in early life. May 11, 1892, the centennial anniversary of Robert Gray's landing at the village *c'inúk* or *činúk*, found him back at Asto-ria, appropriately commemorating the occasion with a "Chinook" (Chinuk Wawa) "address," in which he reminded the audience of Captain Gray's hos-pitable reception by the lower-river Chinookans (Zenk 1999), the people whose signal contribution to the subsequent transformation of the Pacific Northwest was the very medium in which he spoke.

FOURTEEN

NOW YOU SEE THEM, NOW YOU DON'T: CHINOOK TRIBAL AFFAIRS AND THE STRUGGLE FOR FEDERAL RECOGNITION

Andrew Fisher and Melinda Marie Jetté

O N July 3, 2002, Chinook Tribal Chairman Gary Johnson attended a White House luncheon to honor Native Americans who had provided aid to the Lewis and Clark Expedition in 1805–6. The invitation to meet with President George W. Bush seemed a fitting culmination to the tribe's long struggle for federal acknowledgment, which the outgoing Clinton Administration had granted in January 2001. As Johnson dined with the president and other tribal representatives, he could savor not only the expensive food but also the knowledge that the federal government finally regarded him as an Indian and as a Chinook. Two days later, before Johnson had left the nation's capital, the memory of the meal soured when he received word that the Bureau of Indian Affairs (BIA) had overturned the decision to grant recognition to the Chinook Tribe. According to a letter from Assistant Secretary of Indian Affairs Neal McCaleb, the Chinooks had failed to meet three of the seven criteria required by the Federal Acknowledgment Process (FAP). Johnson, who had been called to the nation's capital as the official leader of a recognized tribe, returned home an ordinary American citizen, as the Chinooks once again ceased to exist in the eyes of the United States. But he came home unbowed. "If the government thinks we're going away because they have made this decision," he declared, "they're absolutely wrong" (Shaw 2002).

The Chinook Tribe's fight for recognition illustrates the capricious nature of the federal acknowledgment process. Established in 1978 to review the petitions of hopeful groups, the BIA's Branch of Acknowledgment and Research (BAR) aimed to provide a consistent, fair, and expeditious route to federal status. To receive recognition, unacknowledged tribes had to satisfy seven mandatory criteria outlined in FAP regulations. The petitioning group must (1) demonstrate that it has been identified as an American Indian entity on a substantially continuous basis since 1900; (2) show that a predominant portion of the petitioning group comprises a distinct community and that it has existed as a community from historical times until the present; (3) demonstrate that it has maintained political influence or authority over its members as an autonomous entity from historical times until the present; (4) provide a copy of the group's governing document, including its membership criteria; (5) demonstrate that its membership consists of individuals who descend from the historical Indian tribe or from historical tribes that combined and functioned as a single, autonomous, political entity and provide a current membership list; (6) show that the membership of the petitioning group is comprised principally of persons who are not members of another acknowledged North American Indian tribe; and (7) demonstrate that neither the petitioning group nor its members are the subject of congressional legislation that has expressly terminated or forbidden the federal trust relationship. If these criteria seem clear enough, they are anything but easy to meet, given a history of colonization that tended to invent, shatter, and reassemble the very groups from which the FAP demands an unbroken record of cohesion.

As historian Mark Miller (2004) has noted,

the majority of acknowledgment determinations are cloaked in shades of gray. In any government forum, determining whether a group really is an Indian "tribe" is a patently ambiguous pursuit because it involves concepts as slippery as ethnicity, community, culture, political allegiance, and psychological motive all rolled into one seemingly all-encompassing "package" of tribe—itself a contested term that arguably obscures more than it illuminates. In this light, it is not surprising that the recognition process is a recipe for controversy. (5–6)

The passage of the Indian Gaming Regulatory Act (IGRA) in 1988 further complicated the issue by forging a link in the public mind between recognition and tribal casinos. Many politicians and non-Indians now assume that every petitioning group is simply trying to parlay its indigenous heritage into piles of cash. Such cynicism seems especially unfair to those unacknowledged tribes, such as the Chinook, that initiated their bids for recognition well before IGRA became law. Exploiting popular prejudices is easier than explaining complicated histories, however, and the Chinook Tribe was forced to fight an uphill battle against public skepticism as well as the legacy of past government policies.

The origins of the controversy over Chinook recognition can be traced to the 1850s. Although Congress recognized aboriginal title in the enabling legislation for the Oregon Territory in 1848, and later established an early treaty process, the federal government did not negotiate any treaties for the Oregon Territory before approving the Oregon Donation Land Act in 1850. By formally encouraging Americans to settle on Indian land before treaties were ratified and aboriginal title extinguished, the United States set a precedent for Indian policy in the Pacific Northwest. Beginning in the 1850s, regional Native groups and Indian Office representatives grappled with federal policies that were fundamentally flawed due to a miscomprehension of indigenous land and resource use systems, administrative and legal inconsistencies, and an unwillingness to protect Indian treaty rights.

In June 1850, just four months before approving the Donation Land Act, Congress reorganized Indian Affairs in the Oregon Territory, establishing a new treaty process and creating the post of Oregon superintendent of Indian affairs. When the first superintendent, Anson Dart, arrived in Oregon in 1851, one of his priorities was to negotiate treaties with the Native groups of the western valleys and to organize their removal, preferably east of the Cascade Mountains, in order to allow the resettlement of their lands by incoming American citizens. Dart's work to negotiate treaty agreements and extinguish Indian land title was intended to resolve conflicts over land and resources that had developed between regional Indian groups and American settlers since the early 1840s and which intensified following the passage of the Donation Land Act (Coan 1921:53–57).

Seeking to resolve the Indian land question in the Lower Columbia River region, Superintendent Dart convened a treaty council at Tansey Point, on the south shore of the Columbia River estuary, in early August 1851. Assisted by Indian agents Henry Spalding and Josiah Parrish, Dart negotiated a series of treaties with seven Lower Chinookan bands, the Athapaskan-speaking Clatskanie (misidentified as Chinook), and two Tillamook groups, identified as the Lower Band and the Nehalem Band of Tillamook. These treaties reflected the efforts of tribal leaders to reserve a communal land-base and the right to harvest and gather food and fuel resources within their indigenous territories. Through the treaties, tribal leaders also sought to secure 10-year annuity payments for their relinquished lands and access to goods and services through the Indian Office. The seven Lower Columbia Chinookan groups that concluded treaties at Tansey Point included the Clatsop Tribe of Indians (August 5, 1851), Nue-que-clah-we-muck Tribe of Indians (August 7, 1851), Waukikum Band of Chinook Tribe (August 8, 1851), Konnaack Band of Chinook (August 8, 1851), Kathlamet Band of Chinook (August 9, 1851), Wheelappa Band of Chinook (August 9, 1851), and Lower Band of Chinook (August 9, 1851) (Coan 1921:58–61; Beckham 1987:7–9; Deloria and DeMallie 1999:205–28).

Anson Dart carried the Tansey Point treaties to Congress in November 1851. By the fall of 1852, however, Oregon territorial delegates Joseph Lane and Samuel Thurston and their congressional supporters had successfully blocked the ratification of the treaties. The delegates opposed the treaties largely because the agreements recognized the Indians' right to remain on reserved lands within their larger aboriginal territory rather than compel their removal east of the Cascades. Senate opponents also objected to the tribal leaders' insistence that the annuities for their relinquished lands be made in cash and goods over a ten-year period. In the context of increasing American settlement in the Pacific Northwest during the 1850s, the failure of Anson Dart's treaty program left the Chinook people without ratified treaties, thereby severely constraining their ability to protest the expropriation of their land and resources and to seek redress from the US government (Coan 1921:63–68). The absence of formally ratified treaties later became a major obstacle in the Chinook Tribe's quest for both federal recognition and for a satisfactory resolution of their land claims petition against the government (Porter 1990).

A second treaty initiative a few years later raised the hopes of local Native groups, but it also failed to produce a ratified agreement. In 1853, Congress created the Washington Territory out of the northern portion of the Oregon Territory and appointed Isaac I. Stevens territorial governor and ex officio Washington superintendent of Indian affairs. In late February 1855, on the Chehalis River near Grays Harbor, Stevens finally met with the Native peoples of southwestern Washington Territory, including the Queet, the Quinault, the Satsop, the Lower Chehalis, the Upper Chehalis, the Cowlitz, and the Chinook (the Quileute and several smaller bands were absent). After several days of tense negotiations, representatives from the groups in attendance refused to sign the Chehalis River Treaty. They opposed the terms of the proposed land cessions and the provisions that required them to leave their indigenous lands and become consolidated on one large reservation, and they were dissatisfied with the federal government's unwillingness to honor the Tansey Point treaties of 1851. Angered by the Natives' rejection of his terms, Stevens refused to compromise and stormed out of the treaty council. At the time, he believed that a treaty suitable to the government could be concluded at a later date (Coan 1922:17–18; Marino 1990:171). Although the nonratification of the Tansey Point treaties and the failure of the Chehalis River council again left the Chinook peoples without a legally binding treaty, several developments over the ensuing decades did bring them a measure of "administrative recognition" from federal authorities. This limbo status has persisted to the present as the tribe has faded in and out of the view of federal officials.

Puget Sound Indian Agent Michael Simmons met separately with the Quinault and Quileute in July 1855 and January 1856 to negotiate a new agreement, later known as the Treaty of Olympia, which established the Quinault Reservation within the territory of the Quinault on the Olympic Peninsula. In 1856, Congress ratified the treaty, and President Ulysses S. Grant expanded the original Quinault Reservation by executive order in 1873. The president's order provided for allotment of the reservation for the Quinault, Quileute, Queets, Hoh, and "other tribes of fish-eating Indians on the Pacific coast," such as the Chinook, and thereby extended to the Chinook the "benefits, rights, and privileges, and immunities of the Treaty of Olympia" (Beckham 1987:14; Marino 1990:171).

Two additional developments during the 1860s demonstrated the federal government's modest efforts to address the needs of the nontreaty Indians of western Washington Territory, including the Chinook. In 1864, Commissioner of Indian Affairs William Dole, in consultation with Secretary of the Interior John P. Usher, approved the creation of the Chehalis Reservation. Federal officials intended this tract of land, located within the territory of the Upper Chehalis, to serve as a reservation for the Upper Chehalis, the Cowlitz, and other nontreaty Indians of southwestern Washington Territory. Additionally, because some Lower Chehalis and the Willapa Chinook insisted on remaining in their aboriginal homelands, President Andrew Johnson created the small 640-acre Shoalwater Bay Reservation on Shoalwater Bay (now called Willapa Bay) in September 1866. Federal authorities intended this second reservation to serve Lower Chehalis and Chinook groups living in the surrounding areas (Beckham 1987:13; Hajda 1990:514–15; Marino 1990:171).

Throughout the remaining decades of the 19th century, the Chinook peoples of southwestern Washington experienced continued population decline, expropriation of their land and resources, and increasing pressure to assimilate into American society. From the 1880s through the 1920s, the US government subjected Indians to an intense program of religious instruction, educational training, and land reform designed to destroy their identities and absorb them into the dominant culture. Although most Chinook children lived off-reservation, beyond the reach of agency police, many attended distant federal boarding schools designed to stamp out indigenous languages and lifeways. Their families generally remained in Chinook territory, however, and authorities from the Office of Indian Affairs (renamed the BIA in 1949) continued to provide them with access to health care and other federal services despite their nontreaty status. From the 1850s through the early 1900s, Chinook bands had ongoing contacts with regional Indian agencies, including the Clatsop Plains Agency (1851–52); the Southern Indian District (1854–56); the Western (or Coast) District Agency (1856–62); the Chehalis Agency (1862–85); the Nisqually-Puyallup Agency (1874–88); the Puyallup Consolidated Agency (1888–1916); and the Taholah Agency, Western Washington Agency, Olympic Peninsula Agency, and Portland Area Office (1916 to the 1980s). The extensive documentary record, created by regional Indian agents and superintendents, provides substantial evidence of the federal government's recognition of the Chinook Tribe (Beckham 1987:15–37).

Nevertheless, the Chinooks, like many other landless Indian groups in western Washington, received inconsistent attention from Congress and federal authorities (Porter 1990:113–17). In 1899, members of the Lower Band of Chinook resolved to force the government into action and filed their first petition with the commissioner of Indian affairs to resolve their land claims under the Tansey Point Treaty and to receive compensation for wrongs they had suffered under US jurisdiction. Two years later, after receiving approval from Congress, the Lower Band of Chinook filed suit with the US Court of Claims. The Chinook petition, prepared by attorney Charles C. Lancaster, posed three main arguments: first, members of the Lower Band of Chinook were "legally and equably entitled to all monies received by the United States from sales of their lands amounting to not less than $625,000"; second, they "were legally and equitably entitled to be paid a fair compensation for the value of the land disposed of by the United States and the donation, preemption, and homestead acts at the time of their disposal"; and third, they were "legally and equitably entitled to be paid fair compensation for the value of their rights and privileges of fishing on the Columbia River within the limits of their lands bordering" the river (Beckham 1987:75–77).

In 1905, Congress included a provision in the Indian Appropriations Act directing the secretary of the Interior to draw up census lists for the "Lower Band of Chinook Indians of Washington, and the Kathlamet band Chinook of the state of Oregon," including the descendants of those who signed the 1851 Tansey Point treaties. Charles McChesney, former national supervisor of Indian schools, completed the required census and filed his report in December 1906. His "Rolls of Certain Indian Tribes of Oregon and Washington" lists the surviving signatories of some of the Tansey Point treaties and many of their descendants. (McChesney submitted supplementary census rolls of Chinook people, known as the "Supplemental McChesney Roll of Chinooks," in 1914.) In June 1906, Congress further instructed the secretary of the Interior to examine the claims of additional lower Columbia Chinookan bands, including the Waukikum Band and the Wheelappa Band of Washington and the Nue-que-clah-we-muck Band of Oregon (Beckham 1987:78–79).

The US Court of Claims submitted its findings to Congress regarding the *Lower Band of Chinook Indians v. United States* in 1907. The Tansey Point Treaty with the Lower Band of Chinook had been neither ratified nor rejected, the court found, and was therefore technically still pending in the Senate. The court also concluded that the total land claim for the Lower Band of Chinook under the Tansey Point Treaty was 232,814 acres, of which 217,036.26 acres had been appropriated by the US government for private land claims, homestead entries, railroad sections, state and local schools, military reserves, and lighthouse stations. Neither the signatories nor their descendants had been paid the $20,000 annuity payment amount specified in the Tansey Point Treaty (Beckham 1987:77–78).

Based on the Court of Claims findings, the McChesney census rolls, and Interior Department investigations, Congress made provisions to resolve several of the Tansey Point treaties. The Indian Appropriations Act of 1912 authorized the secretary of the Interior to pay the original sums outlined in the treaties to six Lower Chinookan bands, including the Clatsop Tribe ($15,000), the Nuc-que-clah-we-muck Tribe ($1,500), the Kathlamet Band of Chinook ($7,000), the Waukikum Band of Chinook ($7,000), the Wheelappa Band of Chinook ($5,000), and the Lower Band of Chinook ($20,000). The funds were to be apportioned among the living signatories of the treaties and the lineal descendants of those signatories who had died. The act also stipulated that the Lower Columbia Chinookan groups covered by the legislation should accept these monies in "full satisfaction of all demand of claims against the United States" for the lands described in the Tansey Point treaties (Beckham 1987:79).

Although federal officials may have believed that this legislation resolved Chinook land claims once and for all, the members of the Lower Band of Chinook had a different view. They found it unconscionable that the federal government had awarded them only $20,000 for nearly a quarter-million acres, a territory of immeasurable economic and spiritual value for the Chinook, and they pressed for a more equitable land claims settlement. Under the Oregon Donation Land Act of 1850, the Chinook argued, their aboriginal lands had a value of $1.25 per acre, a sharp contrast to the less than .20 cents per acre they had been awarded in 1912. Finally, in 1925, Congress allowed several landless Indian groups in western Washington, including the Chinook, to file compensation claims with the US Court of Claims. The tribes would have the right to appeal to the US Supreme Court (Beckham 1987:80–81, 271–72).

The Chinook bands, now collectively organized as the Chinook Indian Tribe, filed a land-claims suit with the US Court of Claims as part of a larger petition, *Duwamish et al. Indians v. United States*, spearheaded by the Northwestern Federation of Indians. The tribe claimed 822,000 acres, which encompassed the aboriginal territory of the Lower Columbia Chinookan bands of Washington State from the mouth of the Columbia River to the mouth of the Cowlitz. The court ultimately ruled against the Chinook Tribe in 1934. Basing its argument on a technicality, the court found that it lacked jurisdiction because, although Congress had passed legislation allowing suits by the landless Natives of Washington in 1925, the legislation did not give the Court of Claims jurisdiction to hear petitions from nontreaty Indians. In essence, the Court of Claims sided with the federal government's position, which held that because there was no ratified treaty between the Chinook and the US government, the government had never recognized the Chinooks' aboriginal title to the lands the tribe was claiming. Consequently, the court reasoned, they had no legal basis for compensation (Beckham 1987:80, 272–73).

This decision, while technically correct, overlooked several key historical developments, namely the extension of the Treaty of Olympia to the Chinook in 1873 and the payment of annuities in accordance with the Tansey Point treaties ordered by Congress in 1912. Further, according to Vine Deloria Jr. and Raymond J. DeMallie (1999), the creation of the McChesney census rolls by Congress "may be said to have reconstituted the tribes for the purpose of affirming and fulfilling the treaties. It can be said that following the appropriation act, both parties had ratified the treaties by performance. It is therefore logical to include these treaties with other treaties having legal force (207)."

Concomitant with issues of treaty rights and land claims under the Tansey Point agreements, Chinook tribal relations with the federal government turned on the question of land allotments on the Quinault Reservation during the early 1900s. In 1887, Congress had passed the General Allotment Act (or Dawes Severalty Act) with the intention of assimilating Indians into mainstream American society by turning them into farmers and property owners. Subsequent enabling acts, such as the Quinault Reservation Allotment Act of 1911, implemented the policy on targeted reservations. Eager to see the law applied in Oregon and Washington, the Northwest Federation of American Indians, under the leadership of Thomas G. Bishop, persuaded the Office of Indian Affairs to compile census rolls for nonreservation Natives in western Washington who might be eligible for allotment on the Quinault Reservation. Charles E. Roblin, the OIA enrollment officer charged with this task, noted in his 1919 report that both Bishop and H. H. Johnson, the superintendent responsible for the Quinault Reservation, agreed that the Quinault Allotment Act authorized allotments for the Hoh, Quileute, and other landless groups. Throughout the 1910s and 1920s, however, the Chinooks failed to secure allotments on the Quinault Reservation. Although Roblin had included the Chinook Tribe in his allotment census rolls, Chinook people either were unable to gain adoption by the Quinaults or to secure allotments through the Indian Office (Beckham 1987:83).

In 1925, faced with the need to secure legal counsel in order to press the issue further, the Chinook Tribe organized a Business Council to supersede the traditional, collective decision-making process practiced by village and family groups. At an April meeting in Bay Center, Washington, the Business Council discussed plans to pursue allotments on the Quinault Reservation through the courts and to initiate another claims case for a fair valuation of the aboriginal lands ceded by the Tansey Point treaties. To facilitate the allotment effort, tribal member Myrtle Woodcock began compiling and updating individual enrollment information to prove descent in the Chinook Indian Tribe. Her daughter, Oma (Woodcock) Singer, later recalled how "a very, very large number of the Chinooks who were enrolled in 1906 & still living in the 1920's came to our house [in South Bend, Washington] & re-enrolled & added children born subsequently to the 1906 enrollment." In the event of a legal victory, the tribe anticipated that these records would provide the Indian Office with a basis for distributing allotments at Quinault. Claiming rights on the reservation could cut both ways, however, as the Quinaults and Quileutes soon demonstrated by bringing their own suit to secure treaty fishing rights on the Columbia River (Beckham 1987:265).

The case of *US v. McGowan* developed from decades of conflict over fishing rights on the Lower Columbia, where the first of nearly three dozen salmon canneries had opened in 1866. As packing plants proliferated in the estuary, white-owned seining crews and fish traps usurped many of the traditional locations used by the Chinooks for centuries. By the 1920s, the intensive harvesting of salmon had seriously depleted the runs and invited state conservation laws that further impeded the Indians' ability to catch fish for ceremonial, subsistence, and commercial purposes. At the Chinook Business Council's meeting in April 1925, tribal leaders identified the protection of their fishing rights as a top priority. Two months later, the US Army ordered Chinook fishermen off Peacock Spit near Ilwaco, claiming that the area lay within the boundaries of the Fort Canby Military Reservation. That dispute had yet to be resolved when, in 1928, Washington State issued an exclusive lease to the Baker Bay Fish Company for seining grounds on the spit. The lease was quickly challenged by a group of more than 30 Indians, including many Chinooks from the Shoalwater Bay reservation and surrounding off-reservation communities. Because the Chinooks had no ratified treaty, however, federal attorneys tried to establish Peacock Spit as a reserved "usual and accustomed" fishing ground under the Treaty of Olympia. Most of the Indians who testified in the trial were actually Chinooks residing on Willapa Bay and the Columbia River. While individual Quinaults and Quileutes might have fishing rights on the Columbia through kinship ties, the estuary was not a traditional fishery for any of their villages. Consequently, in 1933 the US Ninth Circuit Court rejected their claim, leaving the Chinooks without a legal bulwark against non-Indian encroachment and state restrictions on their fishing (Beckham 1987:81–83, 270).

The Chinook Tribe fared better in its bid to obtain a land base on the Quinault Reservation. After compiling the necessary enrollment data, the Chinooks and two other local groups, the Cowlitz and the Chehalis, filed suit to gain allotments through the Dawes Act. After several years of litigation in which Chinook tribal members played an active role, the US Supreme Court decided the collective lawsuit, *Halbert v. United States*, in 1931. Individual members of the Chinook, Cowlitz, and Chehalis tribes, the court ruled, were affiliated with the tribes that had signed the 1856 Treaty of Olympia and were legally entitled to allotments on the Quinault Reservation. The justices cited both the Executive Order of 1873, which enlarged the reservation, and the Quinault Allotment Act of 1911 as evidence of legal jurisdiction. Because the Allotment Act did encompass Chinook tribal members, the Supreme Court concluded that new legislation was not necessary. It ordered the government to proceed with the allotment of lands for the Chinook, Cowlitz, and Chehalis tribes. The *Halbert* decision thereby formally recognized the post-treaty affiliation status of the Chinooks and enabled them to participate in the affairs of the Quinault Reservation (Beckham 1987:83–84).

The Chinooks secured their property interests just before the Indian Reorganization Act of 1934 ended the policy of allotment in severalty, which had severely eroded tribal landholdings across the West. Between 1932 and 1935, when the "Indian New Deal" ushered in an era of self-determination for Native Americans, several hundred Chinook tribal members received allotments on the Quinault Reservation. They soon held approximately 40 percent of the land on the reservation and the majority stake in the allotted lands, but they did not enroll in the Quinault Tribe. Most of the allottees retained their aboriginal identity and appeared in Indian Office records as "Chinooks" or "Quinault-Chinooks." At the same time, because they held land and "belonged" on the reservation, the Indian Office allowed 169 allottees of legal age to vote as Chinook tribal members in the Quinault Agency's referendum on the Indian Reorganization Act. Those Chinooks, most of whom were nonresidents and not enrolled by the Quinaults, helped carry the majority vote in favor of drafting a tribal constitution and organizing a confederated tribal government (Beckham 1987:42–45, 273–74).

Meanwhile, the Chinook Business Council continued to push for a conscionable settlement of its long-standing land claims. In the spring of 1940, the tribe hired a local attorney to force a final accounting of the payments made to tribal members under the 1912 Appropriation Act. At least 56 members had never received their shares, and many others still believed that the tribe was entitled to greater compensation for the loss of aboriginal territory. Congress once again enabled the Chinooks to renew their challenge to the government's valuation of the tribal homeland. At the end of World War II, in which many Chinooks and other Indians served, federal policy tilted back toward assimilation. As a first step toward ending the federal trust relationship with Native American nations and speeding their absorption into mainstream American society, Congress established the Indian Claims Commission (ICC) in 1946 to resolve all outstanding tribal claims against the United States. Some legislators balked at the projected cost of "cleaning the slate," but most welcomed the commission as a way to relieve the burden on the Court of Claims and rid the government of most fiduciary responsibilities to Native Americans. The tribes could not recover any land, and their financial awards would ostensibly end the need for further federal assistance. Although many Indians wanted land more than money, most tribes leaped at the chance to seek compensation for past injustices. In September 1951, the Chinook Indian Tribe filed Docket 234 with the ICC and began raising funds to cover the cost of litigation. The Bureau of Indian Affairs (BIA) approved the tribe's attorney contract in 1952, once again signaling that the Chinooks remained a group worthy of federal recognition (Fixico 1986:276–78; Beckham 1987:276–78).

Myrtle Woodcock, Claude Wain, and other Chinook leaders acted on that assumption by reorganizing the tribal government to more effectively address the challenges confronting their people. Approved in August 1951—a century after Chinook headmen had signed the Tansey Point treaties—the tribe's new governing document outlined a broad mandate:

> We, the members of the Chinook Tribes, Incorporated, in order to give our tribe a more complete organization; to establish a closer acquaintanceship among the members; to promote the study of the history of our ancestors; to investigate the present social, economic and legal problems affecting the Tribe; to establish and enforce our ancient rights and to prevent any encroachment upon those rights by any person whomsoever, do hereby adopt this Constitution and By-Laws. (Beckham 1987:277)

Unfortunately for the Chinooks, the constitution's ambitious declaration of sovereignty ran headlong into the juggernaut of federal termination policy. In 1951–52, federal officials held several meetings with the tribes of southwestern Washington to discuss the proposed closure of the Taholah Agency and the dissolution of the Quinault Reservation. Although the BIA invited Chinook participation in these discussions, it quickly became apparent that the government had plans for the tribe to disappear (Beckham 1987:278–79).

The Chinooks vigorously opposed termination as a direct threat to their tribal integrity and economic well-being. Dissolving the Quinault Reservation would cut off access to BIA services and potentially force the liquidation of tribal assets, including valuable timberlands and allotments held in trust for individual Chinooks. The Chinook Indian Tribe responded with intensified political activity aimed at raising its profile with the BIA, preventing state interference with tribal fishing rights, and defending its property interests against federal mismanagement. In May 1952, the Chinook Tribal Council issued a resolution protesting recent timber sales on the reservation. In June, Councilman Claude Wain subjected a visiting BIA official to a "tirade" in favor of "homerule and local jurisdiction, in other words, complete tribal authority and control." Without a ratified treaty to back up such demands, however, the Chinook Tribe remained vulnerable to the charge that it possessed no legal status or authority. In early 1953, the BIA's Portland Area Office insisted that "there was no Chinook tribal organization," even though Taholah Superintendent Raymond H. Bitney reported that the Chinook Tribal Council held regular meetings and governed some 516 adult members. The council promptly submitted copies of its constitution and bylaws and filed articles of incorporation with the State of Washington, only to have the papers returned by the BIA "for whatever disposition you may desire to make in the matter." Shortly thereafter, Bitney invited Chinook leaders to attend regional hearings on the subject of termination. Although Congress ultimately failed to pass legislation implementing that policy in southwestern Washington, the BIA unilaterally proceeded with the "administrative termination" of the Chinooks and other landless tribes in the region (Beckham 1987:278–81).

During the 1950s, the stress of termination precipitated a split within the tribe. One faction, based in Bay Center and South Bend, continued to operate as the Chinook Tribes Inc. under the constitution adopted in 1953. Led by Council Chairman Roland Charley and veteran officers such as Myrtle Woodcock and Claude Wain, the Bay Center group focused on monitoring Quinault timber sales and obtaining "Blue Cards" that exempted tribal members from Washington State hunting and fishing regulations. Chinook Tribe Inc. also successfully prosecuted a lawsuit against two non-Indians accused of looting Chinook graves. Its pursuit of the ICC claims case, however, was blocked by the rival Chinook Indian Nation. That faction, led by Chairman John Grant Elliott and Vice-Chairman Kent Elliott, primarily represented Chinooks who lived along the north bank of the Columbia River. From its headquarters in Skamakowa, Washington, the Chinook Indian Nation hired its own attorneys to handle Docket 234, sparking a dispute with the Bay Center faction over access to the tribal enrollment records maintained by Woodcock. Both factions recognized their mutual interests in the claim, however, and in 1957 they created a joint executive committee for "transacting business of the thereby unified groups of Chinook Indians." Although real unity eluded them for another 25 years, the Bay Center and Skamakowa Chinooks followed parallel but complementary paths toward their ultimate goal of federal recognition (Beckham 1987:280, 282–86).

The Bureau of Indian Affairs, while formally maintaining that an official Chinook Tribe no longer existed, continued to deal with both factions through the 1970s. In 1963, as termination slowly yielded to a revived policy of self-determination across Indian Country, BIA employee Jess Town advised the Chinook Indian Nation council concerning their ICC case. Seven years later, the Chinook Indian Tribe received an economic development grant from the BIA to study the feasibility of starting a charter boat operation in Ilwaco. Additional funds appeared to be forthcoming in 1971, when the ICC finally awarded the Chinooks an additional $48,692 for the loss of their aboriginal lands. Members of both factions participated in meetings to discuss a distribution plan, and the majority favored the tribal use of funds rather than the allocation of individual shares. In 1976, however, after several years of bureaucratic foot-dragging, the Department of the Interior informed the Chinook's joint executive committee that they would have to accept a per capita plan because the tribe was not federally recognized. Chinook leaders immediately and forcefully objected. "If that is the case," they fumed in a letter to Senator Henry M. Jackson, "then the Indian Judgment Funds Act is a farce." Refusing to take no for an answer, the Chinooks began gathering the historical documentation necessary to assemble a petition for federal recognition (Beckham 1987:284, 288–92).

The creation of the Federal Acknowledgment Program (FAP) in 1978 contributed to a sense of renewed hope and solidarity among the Chinooks. Working through the Small Tribes of Western Washington (STOWW), the Chinook Tribe successfully applied for federal grants to finance recognition research, tribal services, and economic development projects. The tribe also approached the Native American Rights Fund regarding a potential lawsuit to assert Chinook fishing rights on the Columbia River. Favorable decisions in *US v. Oregon* (1969) and *US v. Washington* (1974) had placed treaty fishing rights on firm legal footing, but the Quinault Tribal Council excluded off-reservation Chinooks from fishing under the Treaty of Olympia. The case of *Wahkiakum Band v. Bateman*, started in 1978 by fishermen from the Chinook Indian Nation, failed to win them a separate right when the US Ninth Circuit

Court dismissed their unratified treaty as a dead letter. If they could gain federal recognition, however, the Chinooks might still intervene in *US v. Washington*. To maximize their chances of success, the Bay Center and Skamakowa factions agreed in 1982 to set aside their differences and unite behind their FAP petition (Beckham 1987:290–91, 297).

Chinook leaders hoped that political reunification would answer any questions from the Branch of Acknowledgment and Research concerning the continuity and legitimacy of their tribal government. At a joint meeting on June 19, 1982, in Kelso, Washington, the councils of the Chinook Indian Tribe and the Chinook Indian Nation unanimously agreed to vest all political power in the former group. The resolution, which received an encouraging response from the federal government, declared: "the TRIBE should move forward with its petition for federal acknowledgment as the proper and lawful governing body of its members, and the NATION renounces any governmental authority it may ever appeared to have possessed over members of the TRIBE." Two years later, the Portland Area Office informed tribal chairman Donald E. Meachals that the BIA would seek congressional authorization for the release of the tribe's judgment fund in Docket 234. Bureau officials prepared the draft legislation without consulting the Chinooks, however, and tribal members were shocked to learn that the bill proposed giving their money to a nonprofit, state educational institution selected by the BIA. In an angry meeting, nearly a hundred tribal members strongly criticized both the process and the product of BIA planning. Tribal secretary Elmer Wilson spoke for many when he turned to John H. Weddell of the Tribal Operations Branch and said simply, "It stinks!" Shortly thereafter, the Chinooks notified the BIA that they wanted no further action taken on the judgment fund until the Branch of Acknowledgment and Research had completed its review of their petition (Beckham 1987:297–98).

The long process of applying for recognition put tribal members through an emotional wringer. In 1987, after nearly a decade of research, tribal attorney Dennis Whittlesey and historian Stephen Dow Beckham completed the tribe's voluminous petition. It was another 10 years before the BAR rendered a preliminary finding against Chinook recognition. Whittlesey and Beckham quickly submitted 150 new documents and highlighted others they insisted the BIA had ignored. While awaiting the final decision, tribal members sought media attention to publicize their story. "We want people to realize we're not extinct," said Midge Porter. "We have been here forever and we are staying [on] the Columbia." Finally, in January 2001, outgoing Assistant

Secretary of Indian Affairs Kevin Gover informed the Chinooks that they were once again a federally recognized tribe. Tribal members rejoiced but held their breath during the 90–day comment period, which allows other tribes and interested parties to challenge the proposed finding. On the 89th day, the Quinault Indian Nation requested reconsideration by the Interior Board of Indian Appeals (IBIA), claiming that the Chinooks had not followed the proper procedures in assembling their petition. The review passed through the Board of Appeals and the Interior Department to the new assistant secretary of Indian affairs, Neal McCaleb, who determined that the 2001 decision had either wrongly allowed or misinterpreted crucial evidence in favor of Chinook recognition. In his judgment, the remaining documentation did not satisfy three of the seven FAP criteria: they failed to demonstrate that the tribe has maintained political influence over its members from historical times to the present, that a predominant portion of its members comprise a distinct social community, and that outside observers have historically identified it as an Indian entity (Sanders 2005; Middlewood 2000; Thompson 2001).

The news of the reversal—and the manner in which it was delivered—sent shock waves through the Chinook Tribe. "To us, this is a very political decision," stated Chairman Gary Johnson. "We're just very frustrated and very angry. The thousands of pages that we have provided prove, beyond any doubt, the areas where they question tribal existence and tribal political authority" (Shaw 2002). Many Chinooks blamed the Quinault Indian Nation for scuttling the recognition bid in order to prevent the Chinooks from obtaining treaty fishing rights and managing their allotted lands on the reservation. They also lashed out at the Federal Acknowledgment Process for setting unrealistic standards and trapping petitioners in an evidentiary Catch-22. As Kevin Gover testified in defense of the Chinooks and other unrecognized tribes:

> The United States sought a final solution for the "Indian problem," and that solution was assimilation, a deliberate assault on Indian tribalism. The United States sought to withdraw from its responsibilities to Indian tribes in many circumstances; other tribes suffered from benign neglect or were simply left for the states to deal with. Still other tribes, I believe, adopted a strategy of anonymity, believing it better not to be noticed than to come to the attention of federal and state authorities. Small wonder, then, that documentary evidence of some tribes in this period is sparse. (Johnson 2005)

Federal assimilation programs hastened the death of the Chinook language and other elements of aboriginal culture, while intermarriage with neighboring non-Indians gradually diminished the physical attributes commonly associated with Indian identity. At the same time, economic pressures—most notably the decline of the aboriginal fishery—eroded Chinook communities by forcing people to move onto reservations or into cities for survival. Under such circumstances, said Johnson, "It's almost a miracle that the Chinook have maintained as well as they have" (Shaw 2002).

The Chinook tribal leadership is determined to continue the fight for recognition. Working as volunteers from a headquarters in the former home of hereditary chief Lewis Hawks in Bay Center, they have explored the legal and legislative options available to groups that fail to satisfy the Bureau of Acknowledgment and Recognition. A court case would avoid some political hurdles but might take as long as five years and $600,000 to conclude, with no guarantee of success in an increasingly hostile judicial climate. Until 2010, the legislative path looked more promising because the Chinooks had a strong ally in Washington State Representative Brian Baird. In July 2008, after a nearly unanimous vote by tribal members, Baird introduced HR 6689, the Chinook Nation Restoration Act, with bipartisan support. "While we can't change the past, we can change the future," he said. "This bill will ensure the Chinook are finally treated fairly. This is about fixing an injustice; it is simply the right thing to do" (Baird 2008).

HR 6689 would not have given the tribe everything some members wanted. To reduce the chances of opposition from recognized tribes and local non-Indians, the Chinooks agreed to forgo fishing and hunting rights except for limited, ceremonial purposes. They also renounced any residual claims they might have on private property, although the tribe would be free to acquire land from willing sellers. In exchange for these concessions, the Chinooks would have become eligible to establish a reservation, receive federal funding for health care and housing improvements, and access services through the Indian Health Services and Bureau of Indian Affairs. They would also have gained the option to build a casino after negotiating a compact with the state government. Representative Baird's bill was silent on that issue, however, and the Chinooks were divided. Although the erstwhile presence of a Chinook bingo hall in Ilwaco suggests that some members are not averse to gaming, Vice Chairman Sam Robinson and others have voted against it in previous council meetings. In any event, the tribe's 2,300 people resent the suggestion that their recognition bid is simply about money. For Tribal

Chairman Ray Gardner, it is about fulfilling the dreams of his grandmother: "We've waited a long time, we've come a long way, and while this is still only the end of the beginning, it's exciting to see the finish line in sight" (Baird 2008). Tribal members were bitterly disappointed when Congress repeatedly failed to act on Baird's bill, and his departure from the House of Representatives in 2010 has forced them to seek a new sponsor.

Many Chinooks see federal recognition as the key to preserving their identity and sense of community. Without access to BIA assistance, the tribal council holds rummage sales to fund its operations, and there is little money to support cultural preservation efforts. Tony Johnson, Gary Johnson's son, runs an immersion program in Chinuk Wawa. He worries that the language and stories will die out when the few remaining elders pass away, though, and he fears that the Lewis and Clark Bicentennial commemoration may have been the tribe's last, best chance to raise its profile and galvanize public support for recognition. On March 29, 2005, the Johnsons were among the Chinook delegates invited to attend the public dedication of the Cathlapotle Plankhouse, a reconstructed dwelling on the site of an ancient village located within the Ridgefield National Wildlife Refuge. The building's completion gave them reason to celebrate. Refuge officials and tribal leaders agreed that the Chinooks could have access to the plankhouse for cultural events and ceremonies, and tribal members helped ritually cleanse the house with cedar branches on the day it opened. They hope that visitors will come away with an appreciation of the tribe's culture and a favorable attitude toward their acknowledgment claim (Baker 2004a; Baker 2004b; Daehnke 2007).

Whether or not they receive federal recognition, the Chinooks are determined to preserve their heritage and sense of community, and they continue to be acknowledged in other ways. In September 2011, descendants of the explorer William Clark met with Chinook representatives to present a replica of the canoe that the Corps of Discovery stole in 1806. Named *Klmin*, the canoe took its maiden voyage in June 2012, traveling from the Ridgefield National Wildlife Refuge to Fort Columbia together with canoes from other Northwest tribes. As they moved downriver, Chinook families along the way hosted dinners and provided shelter to the crews in the manner of their ancestors. Two months later, the National Park Service honored Chinook representatives at the opening of the Middle Village and Station Camp Park on US Highway 101, just across the Columbia from Astoria, Oregon. The site features an unfinished plankhouse and three concrete canoe sculptures, and there are plans to install traditional Chinookan artwork. Chairman Gardner, who received the Washington State Historical Society's Peace and Friendship Award during the opening ceremony, took the opportunity to remind the audience that his people had been there to welcome "every new person who came into the area" and would continue to do so in the future. "I think we've got a place that's a good beginning," he said. "There's more stories to be told here and they will as time goes on" (NBC News 2011; Hazen 2012; Sedlak 2012).

FIFTEEN

HONORING OUR TILIXAM: CHINOOKAN PEOPLE OF GRAND RONDE

David G. Lewis, Eirik Thorsgard, and Chuck Williams

THE Confederated Tribes of the Grand Ronde comprises descendants of 30 western Oregon tribes, including the Middle Chinook tribes— the Cascades, Clackamas, Willamette Falls, and Multnomah—whose traditional homelands were on both sides of the Columbia River. Many families at Grand Ronde trace their lineage from Middle Chinookan chiefs such as Kiesno (Multnomah), LalBick (Willamette Falls), Wacheno (Clackamas), and Tumulth (Cascades). In the years since the Grand Ronde Reservation was established, tribal members have continued to visit Willamette Falls and the Columbia River to live and work in traditional ways, catching lamprey, erecting fishing platforms, and maintaining age-old fishing rights.

In January 1855, the Treaty with the Kalapuya Etc., also known as the Willamette Valley Treaty, ceded to the United States the entire Willamette River drainage, except the lands reserved for a permanent reservation, and all of what is now Multnomah, Clackamas, and Columbia Counties. At the time, Kalapuya and Molala peoples inhabited the Willamette Valley, and Middle Columbia Chinook lands encompassed all of Portland and the surrounding area south to Oregon City and Willamette Falls and north of the Columbia several miles inland. The specific part of the Columbia that the treaty addresses is between the rapids of The Cascades and Oak Point, but it also mentions an area north of the river, as yet undefined.

Most Middle Chinookan tribes came to the Grand Ronde Reservation in 1856, when the federal government removed people from their homelands without making efforts to keep families and tribes together. Some Cascades were removed to the Yakama Reservation in Washington and the Warm

Springs Reservation in Oregon. Between 1853 and 1855, most western Oregon tribes ceded through treaties the majority of their lands in exchange for reservations that were meant to be permanent. In 1887, Congress passed the General Allotment Act, which impressed individual landownership on tribal members and sold millions of acres of tribal land to the non-Indian public.

In the mid-20th century, the Grand Ronde Tribe was caught up in a new policy of the federal government to "terminate" tribes in the United States, which meant eliminating all services and reservations and extinguishing tribes' rights under law. The Bureau of Indian Affairs (BIA) designated Grand Ronde as an "assimilated" tribe, and in 1954 it was one of the first tribes to be terminated. Oregon has the distinction of being the state with the highest number of terminated tribes, 63 out of 109 nationally. The termination acts were the culmination of over a hundred years of efforts by the federal government to eliminate tribal claims to their lands. During those decades, the tribes of western Oregon went from owning all of their homelands to being dispossessed of them.

Elder stories of the period tell us that we did not agree to termination, although stories from other tribes and the federal government told us that we had agreed. It seems clear from archival documents that the superintendent of Indian affairs in Portland, E. Morgan Pryse, manipulated the tribes and Congress to get the termination bill approved. The tribal documents that Pryse submitted to Congress were not created in support of the 1954 termination bill but instead for the so-called Early Termination bill that had been submitted to the tribes in 1952. In reports to his superiors and to Congress, Pryse stated that the tribes would not be available to testify but that they had agreed in principle to termination. The tribes, which were not told about the hearings, said they would not support the bill. Nevertheless, Congress passed the Western Oregon Indian Termination Act (PL 588), which identified 60 Oregon tribes to be terminated and sold the majority of tribal lands remaining in western Oregon. When the act took effect in 1956, few tribal members had agreed to termination and all were forced to either buy their allotments or leave. Few members had the resources to purchase their allotments (Lewis 2009).

Termination was a terrible experience for the Grand Ronde people. Many tribal members lost hope and faith, and over the years they and their descendants suffered a loss of familial and cultural identities. In the generations following termination, cultural continuity was lost and descendants no longer learned tribal history and tradition. Many people, thrust into poverty, immigrated to the cities and disappeared among the many other wage laborers who were struggling to make a living. Tribal members lost contact with their extended families, and many moved to urban areas far from Oregon.

Some tribal members who had more resources and options purchased their land from the federal government and remained in the Grand Ronde area. This local community, along with others in the region, gradually worked toward restoration; and in the 1970s, a few tribal members began organizing to restore the tribe. They began by connecting with the surrounding community and with Oregon politicians to gain public support for restoration. Senator Mark Hatfield and Congressman Les AuCoin helped shepherd the bill through Congress because, as Kathryn Harrison (2006) said, "It was the right thing to do," and the federal government restored the tribe in 1983. The tribal government worked to re-establish its governing functions, and in 1988, 9,811 acres of former reservation lands were given to the tribe by Congress through the Grand Ronde Reservation Act.

In the 21st century, the Confederated Tribes of the Grand Ronde (CTGR) is working to restore significant sectors of its governance and to regain sovereign rights. Since restoration in 1983, CTGR has developed nearly all of the services it needs to serve its more than five thousand members. The tribe is making progress in becoming party to agreements that were made between other area tribes, the states, and the federal government during the years when it was terminated or engaged in restoration activities. The tribe is also working to restore selected rights to its ceded lands, the traditional homelands that were given up in signed treaties in exchange for a reservation and services.

Perhaps the most significant issue is the tribe's ceded lands along the Columbia River, a focal point for fish and power resources that many other tribes claim sections of as well. In the early 21st century, tribes must negotiate claims to the same area, either lands ceded through treaties or through usual and accustomed land-use rights. The Middle Chinook peoples have both types of claims for lands north and south of the Columbia River.

WILLAMETTE FALLS

Eirik Thorsgard (Tumwater Band of Clalliwalla, Cascade, Toppenish, Paiute, Klikatat)

W ILLAMETTE FALLS, located about 26 miles from the mouth of the Willamette River, is a unique geological and geographic feature with special cultural meaning to the peoples of the Grand Ronde Tribe. Due to its historical importance as a trade and fishing location, the falls is well known by most tribes across the Northwest, with some from as far away as Idaho claiming customary fishing rights. While the falls' status as a fishery is well enough established to earn nomination as a Traditional Cultural Property, its importance in a culturally based geography is less well known (Hajda et al. 2004).

Traditionally, the concentrated access to vast amounts of salmon and lamprey at Willamette Falls lent a metropolitan atmosphere to the area. Access was preferentially restricted to the Clowewalla and Clackamas Tribes (villages Charcowah *čaká·wa*, Clowewalla *(t)łáwiwala*, Walamt *wálamt*, Qau-wuhaipa *qawaháipa*? [Gladstone]) and was based on marriages and trade. People from neighboring and distant tribes who did not have local familial connections had to offer a gratuity for the right to fish there. The Tualatin Kalapuya and Northern Molala regularly intermarried with local indigenous peoples, which gave them fishing rights at Willamette Falls. The Shahala people at The Cascades and the Clowewalla people at Willamette Falls were related, and they regularly moved between these areas to access resources and visit relatives (Michelle n.d.; Kane 1971b; Boyd and Hajda 1987). Social inter-actions also included "Fun Dances," which were a way to display hospitality and wealth to visitors (Jacobs 1958–59).

Willamette Falls
Chinook Name: *ikíšačk* 'falls'
Chinook Wawa Name: *təmwáta*
    Alternate spelling: *dəmwáda*
    Alternate spelling: Tum-water
Clawewalla *(t)łáwiwala* Name: Kwgchyawhesuschk
Northern Kalapuya Name: *čadú·lik* 'falls-place'
Molalla Name: *čaká·wa*

The name Kwgchyawhesuschk appears in the original draft of "Just a Memo-randum," written on February 29, 1956, by Mary Anne Michelle, the grand-daughter of LalBick and the author's great aunt, and also in an unpublished letter by Mary Anne Michelle with an alternate spelling of Kwyshy awhe suschk. Most of these names are scattered throughout various linguistic notes and are being compiled into a document by the Grand Ronde Tribe under a Native Place Names Project.

Before white settlement, Willamette Falls was a major regional center of contact and commerce for tribes, much as The Dalles was. Today, many tribes—including the Nez Perce (Niimipu), Umatilla, Warm Springs, and Yakama—claim gathering rights at usual and accustomed places at the falls. The Grand Ronde tribe still maintains intimate connections to the area, where they regularly gather lamprey for cultural use. Grand Ronde's Natural Resources Division has begun to track lamprey so they can manage this cul-turally vital resource for future generations (CTGR 2006–12).

Several Willamette Falls people have been important to historians and anthropologists. Victoria Howard, a Clackamas-speaking Grand Ronde woman who lived in the Oregon City area when she was interviewed by Mel-ville Jacobs (1958–59) in 1930, was the source of the largest collection of Chi-nookan myths and tales, *Clackamas Chinook Texts*. John Wacheno, the son of treaty-signer Chief Wacheno, provided ethnographic information about the Clackamas people to anthropologist Philip Drucker in 1934. Mary Anne Michelle, a genealogist, was a granddaughter of treaty-signer LalBick, or John, chief of the Oregon City tribe at Grand Ronde. Descendants of these individuals are part of almost all of the larger families in the Grand Ronde Tribe today. Clackamas and Oregon City people were very successful in arrang-ing political marriages that were meant to create alliances between commu-nities, enabling access to other resources and creating good trade alliances. Descendants of the Apperson, Hoffer, and Wacheno families in the commu-nity of Grand Ronde, for example, are married into Molala and Kalapuya groups and into other reservation communities in the Northwest.

Legends of Willamette Falls contain a variety of culturally bound con-cepts of identity and place, whether related in oral traditions about how the world was set into order or based on cultural practices and taboos associated with place and identity. The oral traditions are intimately involved in the landscape, tying people to place.

Victoria Howard told Melville Jacobs some stories that involve Willamette Falls. "Tongue" describes how a young boy defeats a large monster, creates several depressions in the land with his tears, and later becomes Salmon (Jacobs 1958–59:369–75; Lyman 1900:185–87; Ramsay 1977:94–95). "Tongue" ties the local people to a major resource through explaining how, during the Myth Age, specific geologic features were created. Mrs. Howard also told a story called "Coyote Makes a Dance for his Daughter," which is not only a rich description of ceremonial practices at Willamette Falls but also a story of how a conflict between Mudfish and Coyote affected the landscape—again tying the oral tradition to place (Jacobs 1958–59:67–75).

Some stories discuss taboo locations—areas where dangerous beings lived. One identifies some specific marks on river rocks between present-day Lake Oswego and Oregon City, Oregon, as ribs of people who had died from starvation (Jacobs 1958–59:664). Rock Island, downriver from the falls, was the residence of the creature Tongue (Jacobs 1958–59:369, 635n315). Another story about the creation of Willamette Falls, related by several people, is used by the Grand Ronde tribe in its place-based Chinuk Wawa language program.

COYOTE AT THE WILLAMETTE FALLS

Now we will tell a short myth to you. The Clackamas Chinook people used to tell this story a long time ago.

Coyote was traveling over by Clackamas country. The people there were always hungry. They could not get salmon because the salmon stayed deep in the water. Coyote thought, "I should make a waterfall here. I should also make a salmon-trap here."

Then he arrived at the Pudding River, Kalapuya peoples' country. He thought, "I should make a waterfall here." He built it poorly. There is just a little gravel bar there in the river now.

Then he traveled down river. Soon he came to a little island that was all stone. He thought, "I should make a waterfall here." He built it poorly. There is just a strong rapid in the river there now where he broke up a lot of rock.

Then again he traveled down the river. Soon he came to a place that we call "Tumwata" (Oregon City) today. He thought, "I should make a waterfall here." Then he made a very good waterfall. People came right away to get salmon.

Then Coyote made a salmon-trap. He made it very well. He made it so that when it became full of salmon it would say "nosipsk."

After a while then Coyote became hungry. He fixed up his salmon-trap close to the waterfall. Then he was making a fire. He thought, "I'll roast salmon on sticks here." Before he could make a fire he was hearing "nosipsk! nosipsk!" Right away he ran to the salmon-trap. It was entirely full of salmon.

Then he got those salmon and he fixed up the salmon-trap. Again he was making a fire. Before he could make that fire, "nosipsk! nosipsk!" Right away he ran to the salmon trap. It was entirely full of salmon again.

Then he got those salmon and he fixed up the salmon-trap. Again he was making a fire. Before he could make that fire, "nosipsk! nosipsk!" Right away he ran to the salmon-trap. It was entirely full of salmon again.

Then he got those salmon and he fixed up the salmon-trap. Again he was making a fire. Before he could make that fire, "nosipsk! nospisk!" Right away he ran to the salmon-trap. It was entirely full of salmon again.

Then he got those salmon and he fixed up the salmon-trap. Again he was making a fire. Before he could make that fire, "nosipsk! nosipsk!" Right away he ran to the salmon-trap. It was entirely full of salmon again.

Then he got those salmon and he fixed up the salmon-trap. Again he was making a fire. Before he could make that fire, "nosipsk! nosipsk!" Right away he ran to the salmon-trap. It was entirely full of salmon again

Then Coyote scolded his salmon-trap, "Why don't you wait for my fire? I want you to wait!"

Then that salmon-trap became angry. It never caught salmon again. And never again have people been able to get salmon like that. Never again can you just sit around and get salmon. Now people who want salmon have a lot to be doing. It is like that for all time now because of what Coyote did a long time ago.

Another version of this story, also attributed to the Clackamas Chinook, was related to Horace Lyman by Louis LaBonte at the beginning of the 20th century (Lyman 1900b:185–87; Ramsay 1977:93).

Neighboring non-Chinookan tribal groups also had intimate connections with Willamette Falls through trade and intermarriage. Kalapuya oral traditions say that the falls were created by Coyote and Meadowlark when they stretched a rope across the river and it turned to stone. The Santiam Kalapuya story, "They Knew It before Coyote Came," reproduces a well-known incident from Coyote's travels. It explains the origin of a distinctive land feature and at the same time tells why dark secrets in the world of humans have a way of coming to light. We do not know the identity of the rock formation referred to but suspect that it was near Willamette Falls. This kind of dual message—attributing cultural meaning to a landscape feature while conveying a lesson in social morality—is typical of Lower Columbia myths. These myths are mnemonic devices that bind people to location and social practices and that create relationships with neighboring groups. The stories and landscape together weave a tapestry of self and group identification that enables people to have a sense of belonging and home.

THE CASCADE INDIANS

Chuck Williams (Cascade Chinook)

THE Cascade Indians, the Chinookan people who lived in proximity to the Great Cascades of the Columbia River, have suffered not only from exotic diseases, violent conflicts with newcomers, and the loss of fishing and home sites, but also from having their homeland divided by Euro-American boundaries established by the 1855 treaties and the creation of the states of Oregon and Washington. In addition, most of their lands on the north bank downriver from the Yakama Treaty boundary in Clark County, Washington, are not covered by ratified treaties with the United States, and title to them has never been ceded, although the Treaty with the Kalapuya Etc. acknowledges those lands, and some treaty tribes consider them "usual and accustomed" places for fishing and other traditional activities (Williams 1980).

Divided among confederated tribes on faraway reservations, Cascade Indians often became minorities among minorities, which has created many problems, including having their language become less prominent on the multitribal reservations. The goal of the US government and most settlers was to remove Native Americans from the Columbia and Willamette Rivers and to send them to reservations, thus opening up the rich bottomlands to Euro-American immigrants. But the Cascades and other Natives who lived along the Lower Columbia generally did not like life on the reservations, where they were far from their original homeland and fishing sites and where they were not always treated well. Cascade Indians traditionally controlled the portage around the rapids, a location that gave them considerable wealth and power.

So it is not surprising that it has been a constant struggle since the treaties were signed in 1855, with the US government removing the River people to reservations only to have them often return to the Columbia as soon as they could (Williams 1971).

At the time of contact, Chinookan-speaking peoples were the dominant population from the mouth of the Columbia up to the Narrows east of The Dalles, although they often shared villages with Sahaptin-speaking Klikatats on the north shore east of Vancouver, Washington. The Chinookans who were farthest upriver were the Wish-com people—the Wascos of the Confederated Tribes of the Warm Springs Reservation and the Wishrams of the Yakama Indian Nation. Since the Chinook villages were essentially autonomous and the Columbia River was not recognized as a political boundary, it is often difficult to determine which people are Cascade, Wasco, or Wishram (Chinook people living around the mouths of the Hood and White Salmon Rivers are sometimes considered part of these three groups or as separate tribes). Marriage further complicated matters, and which identity each Upper Chinook person has is often based on where he or she was raised and is enrolled (French and French 1998).

The leaders of the Cascade Indians living at and downriver from the rapids that gave them their present name signed the 1855 Willamette Valley Treaty in Dayton, Oregon, as the "Wah-lal-la band of Tumwaters" (Clahclel-lah). Because of the ease of canoe travel between The Cascades and Willamette Falls and Sauvie Island, where wapato was abundant, the Cascade Indians had close connections with the Chinookans living at those places and spoke the same language, Kiksht.

The Grand Ronde Reservation was established near the coast, a long distance from the Great Cascades, and many of the Cascade people who were removed from the river went instead to the Yakama and Warm Springs Reservations (Zucker et al. 1983). In 1856, a temporary reservation was established east of the White Salmon River for Indians native to eastern Clark and Skamania Counties. As a result of area battles in the mid-1850s, the Cascade Indians were among the tribes removed to this temporary reservation. At the end of the Yakama War, tribes scattered to escape settler retribution and had to endure ad hoc attempts by the US Army to remove them from the area of conflict. Most Cascade Indians, however, tried to stay on the river to be near their fishing sites and the graves of their ancestors; that was much easier to accomplish when they married non-Indians.

In January 1855, my father's great-grandfather Tumulth signed the Willamette Valley Treaty as the "first chief" of the remaining Cascade people. They were the survivors of those who had lived at the rapids and along the river and who had regrouped following the epidemics, which had ended only a few years earlier. The epidemics, mainly of the introduced diseases of small-pox, malaria, and measles, resulted in a devastating cumulative population loss of over 90 percent for the Portland Basin River peoples (Boyd 1999b).

One of the battles of the so-called Yakama War was at The Cascades in early 1856, and it was very destructive to the remaining disease-scarred Cas-cade people. Some Yakama and Klikatat Indians, angered by the increasing encroachment of Euro-American immigrants onto their lands, attacked the new blockhouses and houses at The Cascades portage. The strategy, if they were victorious, would have blocked the main trade route down the Colum-bia and into western Oregon. While the battle raged, Lt. Philip Sheridan and his army dragoons from Fort Vancouver, warned by settlers who had escaped the attack, came upriver, and the attacking Indians fled. Tumulth and many of the Cascades did not flee, however, since they were under treaty and were trying to live in peace with the immigrants. Nevertheless, Sheridan hanged Tumulth and eight other Cascades men. Their trials consisted of Sheridan putting his finger into the barrels of their guns and finding guilty the owners of the guns that had been fired recently. Following the battle, outraged set-tlers took justice into their own hands and murdered at least 13 more Cascade Indians along the portage. The murders included children being strangled, which appalled even Sheridan (Skamania County Pioneer 1977). Most histo-rians have relied on Sheridan's account of the incident, but descendants of the families have insisted that Tumulth did not participate in the attacks and was innocent. In 1910, Edward Curtis (1970) photographed Tumulth's oldest daughter Whylick Quiuck (Virginia Miller) and recorded her version of the battle. Some of Sheridan's soldiers felt so guilty that they took up a collection of gold and gave it to her.

After Tumulth was hanged, his daughter Kalliah ("Indian Mary" Stoo-quin), then a young child, was sent to the temporary reservation and then to the Yakama Reservation with her mother and enrolled there. When she grew up, she returned to the Great Cascades and traded horses to home-steaders to get back a piece of her original homeland. Because Indians could not own land, some immigrants tried to file homestead claims on her land. But Kalliah had a contract with the US government to meet the mailboat at the lower end of the rapids and to deliver the mail by horseback, and she was able to persuade the Indian agent in Vancouver to write a letter scaring off the settlers who were trying to take her land (US Land Office 1891). In 1891, the agent got a proclamation from President Grover Cleveland that put her land into trust. Her allotment remained in family ownership until the 1980s, when it became Franz Lake National Wildlife Refuge, where wapato has now returned, a great victory since our potato had earlier been wiped out in the Columbia Gorge, especially by cattle grazing.

The treatment of our other ancestors laid to rest has been no better. The main cemetery for Cascade Indians living at the rapids was on what is now known as Bradford Island. Most of our people who died were traditionally placed into above-ground cedar vaults, often on islands to protect them from animals. But this made them vulnerable to looting and vandalizing by non-Indian newcomers who fancied "Indian curios," to the point that Indian snipers would sometimes try to protect them. When Bonneville Dam was built straddling our cemetery (where the main visitor center now is), the US Army Corps of Engineers took all of the bodies and put them into a common grave in the Cascade Pioneer Cemetery near the town of North Bonneville. Many of the people buried in the cemetery, including Kalliah and most of my family, are Cascade Indians. The cemetery district changed the name to the Cascade Indian & Pioneer Cemetery when my father was buried there in 1992.

Many Cascade Indians lived on the south bank upriver and thus were in the ceded area of the 1855 Treaty with the Tribes of Middle Oregon, which established the Warm Springs Reservation. The boundary between the Grand Ronde and Warm Springs ceded areas is described in the treaties as along the summit of the Cascade Mountains south from the rapids, now the town of Cascade Locks, Oregon. These Cascades and residents of the Hood (Dog) River Valley were included in the Warm Springs Treaty as Wascos, and many were relocated to the Warm Springs Reservation, where the traditional Wasco chief serves on the tribal council. Many Warm Springs members are listed on their enrollment cards as both Cascade and Wasco, and Cascades have generally had acceptance at Warm Springs, where the Chinookans are one of only two language groups that signed the treaty (Aguilar 2005). In fact, the late Zane Jackson, the longest serving Warm Springs tribal chairman in recent times, was the son of a Wasco father and a Cascade mother (a granddaughter of Tumulth) raised at the mouth of the Wind River in Washington (Shaw 2004). The third tribe, the Paiutes, were removed to the reservation following the dissolution of the Malheur Reservation. The riverbank downriver of Cascade Rapids is within the boundaries of the Willamette Valley Treaty, and those Cascades and other Chinookan tribes were removed to the Grand Ronde Indian Reservation.

The western ceded-area boundary for the 1855 treaty with the 14 Confederated Tribes and Bands of the Yakama Indian Nation is east of Wind River, Washington, and thus included many Chinookan residents who considered themselves Cascade Indians (and ended up enrolled at Yakama). The small community of Underwood, Washington, for example, just west of the mouth of the White Salmon River, is named for the Euro-American husband of Ellen Chenowith, daughter of a Cascade leader hanged at the Cascade Rapids in 1856.

Nevertheless, the relationship between many Cascade Indians enrolled at Yakama and the tribal government at Toppenish, Washington, on the Yakama Reservation has often been strained. During the allotment period, the Yakamas enrolled many nonaffiliated Indians, including Cascades, in part because they would lose less land to non-Indians (Fisher 2010). A couple of generations ago, however, the Yakama stopped enrolling Cascades born outside their ceded area, and later they stopped enrolling most Cascades. As a result, for example, my oldest aunts and uncles were enrolled at Yakama, but my father Clyde Williams, the youngest of eleven children, and a sister Ida Altringer were not; they later enrolled at Grand Ronde. When my grandmother Amanda Williams passed on—she was enrolled at Yakama as "4/4 Cascade; 0/4 Yakama"—my father's generation was not allowed to inherit her reservation allotment, a place where they had spent part of the Depression. The land reverted back to the tribe (Williams 1977). Kalliah had given up her reservation allotment in favor of a Vancouver allotment just downriver from Beacon Rock, east of Washougal, Washington; it was inherited by her two daughters, my grandmother and her sister Abbie Estabrook.

In the 1980s and 1990s, a campaign began to get the Yakama Indian Nation to again enroll Cascades, since children of enrollees were being denied. Finally, the Yakama General Council voted to order the tribal council to resume enrolling Cascades, which led to some council members being suspended (Cleveland 1995). Meanwhile, the US Army Corps of Engineers sent the items from the excavation of Clahclellah, which was dug up for the second powerhouse at Bonneville Dam, to the Yakama tribal museum without any consultation with the Warm Springs or Grand Ronde Tribes.

Being part of three federally recognized confederated tribes often has not been good for the Cascade Indians, especially regarding fishing rights at our traditional fisheries. As a result of the treaties and legal cases on fishing rights, for example, Cascade Indians who are not enrolled at Yakama or Warm Springs do not have treaty-guaranteed fishing rights at The Cascades, but members of the upriver Umatilla and Nez Perce Tribes can live and fish there, a frustration for local Cascade Indians (CRTFC 1986). Unfortunately, this complaint is not new. In 1891, for example, Kalliah and 68 other Cascade Indians (using that identification) signed an agreement with a Washington, DC, attorney to try to have land on the north shore of the Columbia set aside for their fishing, plus financial compensation "in case they are permanently deprived of said fishing rights and lands of which they are now dispossessed by the encroachment of settlers and others" (Foote 1891). The north bank area is a part of the traditional Cascades homelands that was never ceded in treaties, from Beacon Rock (tidewater) upriver to the ridgetop between the Wind and Little White Salmon Rivers, the western boundary of the Yakama Treaty ceded area.

Despite the problems resulting from the epidemics that devastated our people, the political division of our home territory, and the dispersal of many people to distant reservations, Cascade Chinooks have held on and are probably better recognized today (although not in the legal sense) than we have been for decades. Unlike tribes that are returning to traditional names instead of the non-Indian ones they have become identified with, Cascade Indians have proudly embraced their name, which refers to the natural wonder that once defined our home and our way of life. Some of this is due to advances in Native pride and cultural resurgence, but it also has to do with a common identity for related people who are otherwise known by the autonomous villages they were from, people who have been split up and often have been at odds with distant tribal governments that are supposed to look out for their best interests.

The 1983 congressional restoration of the Confederated Tribes of Grand Ronde was a major victory for many Cascade Indians whose ancestors had signed the 1855 treaty and as a result are finally enrolled with a federally recognized tribe (although the official logo of the Confederated Grand Ronde Tribes, which includes five feathers—the Chinookan ritual number—for confederated groups, still doesn't have a feather representing Chinookan people, even though many of the treaty signers were Chinooks). The legal status of Cascade Indians was helped, but also made even more complex, by the federal recognition of the Cowlitz Tribe in 2000. Numerous Cascade Indians, especially younger people from Skamania County in Washington State, were not enrolled with the three treaty tribes (although their parents and grandparents often were Yakama members) but were also descended from Cowlitz people; they are now enrolled at Cowlitz. Regardless of where we are enrolled, our primary identification is as Cascade Indians, the Chinookan people from the western Columbia River Gorge, the spectacular landscape that created and enriched us.

CLACKAMAS AND CASCADES TREATIES

David G. Lewis (Chinook, Takelma, Santiam Kalapuya)

T HE tribes and bands of the Middle Chinook engaged in two rounds of treaty-making. The first, in 1851, began under the direction of Anson Dart, superintendent of Indian affairs for the Oregon Territory. Dart and his commissioners were ordered to begin negotiations in the Willamette Valley, the most thickly settled and coveted region of Oregon. The intent was to open up the best land for American settlers and to move western Oregon tribes east of the Cascade Range to live on a single reservation in the Umatilla area. The Umatilla tribes did not agree, however, and all of the western tribes refused to remove. The chiefs of the Santiam Kalapuya, for example, stated: "Our hearts are upon the land. . . . We do not wish to remove" (Lewis 2009; Beckham 2006). Their determination forced Dart to accept and write treaties that guaranteed each local tribe a permanent reservation within its traditional homelands.

Dart began treaty negotiations at Clackamas in August 1851 with a band living on a small reserve near the Oregon City ferry. The treaty included rights for the Clackamas to fish at their usual places, one of the few times this right was included in western Oregon treaties. With initial negotiations in Oregon City unsuccessful, Dart signed treaties with the Kalapuyan bands, negotiated 10 treaties at Tansey Point on the Lower Columbia with the Chinook and Tillamook Tribes, and then signed three treaties in southern Oregon. After negotiating 18 other treaties in western Oregon, Dart returned to Oregon City. The Clackamas treaty was signed in November 1851. Dart took the treaties to Congress; but because he had failed to remove the tribes and white settlers complained about having reservations near their homesteads, Congress tabled action on the treaties and they were never ratified.

In 1853, Joel Palmer was named the new superintendent of Indian affairs, and he too began working on a plan to remove Oregon tribes to one reservation east of the Cascade Range. When the proposal failed a second time, he decided on establishing a single reservation "for the Coast and Willamette Tribes" in western Oregon, later called the Coast Reservation. In the summer of 1855, however, the Rogue River War intervened, and Palmer's plan changed: he would create a second, temporary reservation in the Grand Ronde Valley, where he worked with the US Army to purchase land from white settlers.

From January 8 to January 22, 1855, at Dayton, Oregon (about 30 miles northeast of the town of Grand Ronde), leaders of Clackamas and Cascades tribes and bands and bands of the Kalapuya and Molala negotiated and signed the Willamette Valley Treaty. Three chiefs of the Clackamas tribes and "the Wah-lal-lah band of Tum-waters" (or Cascades) signed the treaty on January 10; the "chiefs and headmen of the Clow-we-wal-la, or Willamette Tum-water band of Indians" signed on January 18, 1855 (Boxberger 2009). Congress ratified the treaty in March 1855, and all of the signatory tribes were confederated as one tribe under one treaty for the Willamette Valley drainage.

Each tribe that was a party to the Willamette Valley Treaty was temporarily removed to a small reservation within their lands. In October 1855, the Willamette Falls people were brought together on a small reservation at Gladstone. Natives near St. Helens in Columbia County were placed on a temporary reserve at Milton. By November 9, 1855, almost a hundred Indians from between The Cascades and the mouth of the Willamette River had been removed to a reserve "three miles above Mt. Switzlers," near the east end of the present Portland International Airport (Boxberger 2009).

The 1855 treaty stipulates that the confederated tribes of the Willamette Valley ceded the region from the Calapooia Mountains in the south to the Columbia River in the north, to the crest of the Coast Range in the west and the Cascade Range in the east. In addition, Palmer stated that if "any of the tribes becoming parties to this treaty establish a legitimate claim to the country north of the Columbia river," they could negotiate for payment for those lands. In a letter that accompanied the treaty, he wrote:

> The permanent places of residence of the Wal-lal-la band, are on the southern bank of the Columbia River between the Willamette and Sandy, though they claim a considerable tract north of the Columbia, commensing [sic] a few miles above Fort Vancouver and extending to the cascade falls [Cascade

Rapids], the latter being their residence in the fishing season. . . . It was their desire to be embraced in this treaty; yet to permit this without securing in the general fund the purchase price of their lands north of the Columbia. Would be inequitable in regards to bands associated with them. I have learned that the Indians on Sauvies island claim a tract north of the river. (Kappler 1903(2):665–69)

In early 1856, Palmer ordered supplies and began construction on the reservation. In March, he hired wagons to take the tribes to the reservation; and on April 3, 1856, he reported that the Clackamas, Wah-lal-la, and Clowe-walla, numbering 160 people, had been transported to Grand Ronde (Box-berger 2009). Within about three months, some two thousand people had been removed to Grand Ronde Agency from the Columbia River, Willamette Valley, Cascade foothills, and upper Umpqua and Rogue Valleys. The tribes made the journey during the winter and spring, when weather conditions were wet and treacherous. From the Table Rock Reservation near Medford, in southern Oregon, people walked north for most of the month of March; during the trek, George Ambrose recorded in his diary. "8 people died and 8 babies were born" (Beckham 1996). Some of the journey from the Columbia River was up the Willamette River and into the Yamhill River as far as Dayton. The people then followed the wagon road into the Grand Ronde Valley.

Once at the reservation, each tribe camped in their own area along the Yamhill River, where most people remained for a year or two. Fort Yamhill was built in 1856, with a barracks, store, blacksmith, bakery, and other buildings. The fort overlooked a mountain pass and an Indian trail that enabled US Army dragoons to make certain the tribes stayed on the reservation. The troops were also charged with keeping settlers off the reservation because of their animosity toward the Indians at the time. Native people could not legally leave the reservation without a pass.

Grand Ronde became a permanent reservation in 1857 through a presidential executive order. Headmen and chiefs from most of the tribes, including the Clackamas Chinook, formed an intertribal council that later became the tribal government. Through the treaties, the federal government provided payments, established schools, and informally allotted lands for people to farm. The community was centered at first on the Yamhill River, then later around the agency properties on present-day Grand Ronde Road, called Old Grand Ronde. Under the direction of Belgian missionary Rev. Adrien Croquet, tribal people and army regulars built a Catholic church, St. Michaels, in 1860. Reverend Croquet also supervised the on-reservation boarding school. In 1889, eligible tribal members gained allotments through the General Allotment Act (1887); the remaining lands were surplused to the public for $1.10 per acre. By the 1940s, most tribal allotments had been sold or had passed from tribal hands.

The community of Grand Ronde assimilated well into rural Oregon. Tribal members lived and worked in jobs similar to those held by non-Indian rural Oregonians and most went to on- or off-reservation Indian schools where they learned a trade. Opportunities to make money on the reservation were scarce, so most families supplemented their meager incomes by working the harvest in the Willamette Valley. Families lived at farms and picked hops, berries, and beans throughout the summer, and migrant tribal farmworkers became part of Oregon's cultural landscape. Many men went into logging, beginning a long-standing tradition of tribal loggers. People regularly received passes to leave the reservation from the agents, and the pass program continued well into the 1920s. Tribal members returned to their ceded homelands annually for several weeks or months to fish and gather and to visit relatives who had refused to be removed. Passes allowed the Middle Chinook peoples to visit and fish at Oregon City (Willamette Falls) and the Columbia River (Grand Ronde Pass Book). Until at least 1950, an informal agreement was formed between Indian agents and state law enforcement to allow Oregon Indians to fish in their accustomed places regardless of whether their treaties mentioned these rights.

From 1857 to 1956, there were many marriages between the tribes. This was a natural outgrowth of being confined on a multitribal reservation, but the practice was also traditional, as intertribal marriages were encouraged in aboriginal times. By the 1950s, many tribal members had at least five tribal ancestries, and Chinookan ancestral bloodlines are now in nearly every Grand Ronde family.

The Confederated Tribes of the Grand Ronde continue to advocate for their rights within the ceded lands. Because there was no funded tribal government during termination (from 1956 to 1983), the tribe could not represent the interests of its members in projects, meetings, boards, and events. During those years, many federal laws were enacted and efforts were made to return sovereign rights to other tribes for fishing, hunting, water rights, cultural resource rights, and environmental health and sustainability. After restoration, the Grand Ronde Tribe spent a decade developing its government infrastructure. In the mid-1990s, the tribe began advocating for its rights, and conflicts arose over which tribes were the legitimate advisers and participants in the management of western Oregon environmental and cultural resources. The most contentious of these conflicts are between the Grand Ronde and the Cowlitz and the Warm Springs Tribes over the location of casinos. Both Cowlitz and Warm Springs wanted to locate their casinos on lands that are traditional homelands of the Middle Chinook or are within the boundaries of the Willamette Valley Treaty, which Grand Ronde claims.

Additionally, according to the Army Corps of Engineers, the Yakama, Warm Springs, and Cowlitz Tribes claim usual and accustomed rights in the Willamette Valley Treaty lands, which means that federal and state agencies must consult with them as well as with the Grand Ronde. In 1986, Congress passed the Columbia River Gorge National Scenic Area Act, and four tribes— Yakama, Nez Perce, Umatilla, and Warm Springs—have been consulted throughout its history. The Grand Ronde Tribe claims that because the Willamette Valley Treaty land base overlaps with the Columbia Gorge at The Cascades, the commission should consult with the Grand Ronde as well. Current tribal participants have opposed that change because the Willamette Valley Treaty does not grant fishing rights to the signatories. Any changes to the act would require congressional action.

Two focal areas of Middle Chinook settlement were Willamette Falls and The Cascades, both significant fisheries. The tribes and subtribes of these areas are interrelated, speaking close dialects of the Upper Chinook language, Kiksht. All peoples along the Columbia River also spoke Chinuk Wawa (also called Chinook Jargon) as a common language of intertribal relations. Chinookans of the region preferentially married outside their village or local group, normally with women going to the tribe of their husbands. These intertribal marriages helped keep trade and social relations good among all tribes in the region.

In many different ways, contemporary tribal people are reclaiming and embracing their Middle Chinookan ancestry. At Grand Ronde, members are working to restore carving traditions in the Chinookan Art Style, practicing canoe traditions by carving shovel-nosed river and Chinook styles of canoes, building a traditional plankhouse, and restoring traditional ceremonies. Chinuk Wawa is being taught through an immersion program with tribal youth and in cultural education programs for adults. Ancestry and culture are a big part of Grand Ronde's identity as it approaches 30 years of restoration.

The Grand Ronde tribe is working on projects to restore a historical consciousness to tribal members. Because of termination and as part of a progression of assimilation pressures placed on tribes for 160 years, many people have not learned their tribal history, genealogy, and kinship with other tribes. The tribe is addressing this issue with historical research and the development of archives. Tribal historians are also making history presentations at tribal meetings, and new findings are often published in *Smoke Signals*, the tribal newspaper.

These projects are helping the Grand Ronde Tribe continue its sovereignty within its ceded territory. These lands are vast, stretching from the California-Oregon state line to the Columbia River, but the tribe is also developing its capacity to educate its tribal community and restore their knowledge of where they came from. The colonization of western Oregon has gone on for over two hundred years, and it will take some time for the tribe to recover from its effects. The Middle Chinookan peoples of the Portland Basin are an integral part of the Grand Ronde Tribe's cultural fabric.

SIXTEEN

CHINOOKAN WRITINGS: ANTHROPOLOGICAL RESEARCH AND HISTORIOGRAPHY

Wayne Suttles and William L. Lang

THOUGH Chinookans have sometimes been treated in other kinds of writings (e.g., fiction and poetry), it is the books and articles penned by anthropologists and historians that have recorded the most basic data and been the most influential in presenting what is known about Chinookan culture and history to the reading public.

HISTORY OF ANTHROPOLOGICAL RESEARCH ON LOWER CHINOOKAN PEOPLES

Wayne Suttles

LINGUISTIC RESEARCH

Horatio Hale was the first professional linguist to work in the homeland of the Chinook people. At the age of 20, he was ethnologist and philologist with the US Exploring Expedition of 1838–42, which spent part of 1841 in the Oregon country. Hale collected ethnographic and especially linguistic data from Native people and from missionaries and Hudson's Bay Company (HBC) people. His interest was mainly in language, linguistic relations, and the possibilities both offer for the reconstruction of history. Hale (1846) defined and mapped language families and gave some grammatical data on several languages and comparative vocabularies. His treatment of the "Tshinuk Family" is brief, presenting a first glimpse of the complex morphology of Upper Chinook (562–61). Struck by the difficulty of the sounds and complexity of the grammar of Chinookan, he suggested that this accounted for the development of Chinuk Wawa (635–50; Hale 1890).

William Fraser Tolmie, an HBC officer, arrived at Fort Vancouver in 1833 and was soon sent to Fort Nisqually on Puget Sound. There he set about collecting vocabularies in Native languages, using an inadequate English-based spelling, which were later presented in a work edited by Canadian geologist George M. Dawson. The vocabularies include a short list of Lower Chinook words elicited from a Songhees woman in Victoria, who had been a slave of the Chinook, and a similar list of Wishram words "obtained from an Indian of that tribe" (Tolmie 1884:51–61, 121–22).

George Gibbs arrived in the region in 1849 and stayed until 1860, occupying several official positions that required research on Native peoples. His geographic orientation was largely north of the Columbia, but he recorded place-names in Chinookan country (1853–56), collected a Chinook vocabulary (1863b), and compiled a Chinook Jargon dictionary (1863a). In 1877, Albert Gatschet (1877a, 1877b) collected some Clackamas linguistic data, as well as 21 words of "Wacanessisi," spoken near Fort Vancouver and presumably representative of the Multnomah dialect. The Gibbs and Gatschet materials are in manuscript in the National Anthropological Archives at the Smithsonian.

Research on the Chinookans changed radically with the work of Franz Boas, the most influential American anthropologist of the early 20th century. A German with a degree in physics and experience in the Arctic, Boas began his research in the region with a trip to Vancouver Island in 1886, where he met W. F. Tolmie just before he died. Soon after, Boas moved to the United States. In 1888, he met Horatio Hale, who had been appointed to a committee (which included George M. Dawson) to do research in British Columbia. Poor health and age prevented Hale from going himself, and he invited Boas to undertake the research. For several years, Boas pursued work in British Columbia, getting instructions, which he did not always appreciate, from Hale. He soon also got support from the American institutions that enabled him to work south of the International Boundary, and before long he had done some research with nearly every people from the Tillamook to the Tlingit.

Boas's contribution was especially great in linguistics. The Native languages of the region use a great many sounds that do not occur in the languages of Western Europe. Tolmie and other early traders and missionaries tried to represent Native words with the Roman alphabet in an impressionistic and inconsistent fashion, representing different sounds with the same letters and sometimes representing the same sound with different letters and combinations of letters. Hale used a few other symbols, and his transcriptions are consistent; but he did not make several distinctions that make the difference between one word and another. Gibbs used a similar system. Boas seems to have been the first to grasp the necessity of distinguishing sounds that were meaningful in non-Western languages, for Chinookan the several lateral sounds, between velars and uvulars and between plain and glottalized stops and affricates. The method Boas developed was to find a good Native speaker, record texts, and work out the grammatical system with the speaker. His first volume of texts was in Chinook.

In June and July 1890, Boas was in northwestern Oregon and southwestern Washington. In the introduction to *Chinook Texts* (1894), he tells us that while studying the Salish languages he had learned that Lower Chinook was "on the verge of extinction" and decided to collect what he could. In Seaside, Oregon, he discovered that a small group of Native people of Clatsop descent had adopted the Nehalem Tillamook language. One middle-aged man and two old women remembered some of the Clatsop dialect of Lower Chinook, but Boas (1890) could get only words and sentences, no texts. They had evidently forgotten the history of their tribe, and they assured him that no other dialect of their language was spoken on the north side of the river, the whole country being occupied by the Chehalis. They did have a few Clatsop-speaking relatives on Shoalwater (now Willapa) Bay living among the Chehalis.

This led Boas to Bay Center, where he discovered the last survivors of the Chinook, who had largely adopted the (Lower) Chehalis language. Only two people spoke Chinook—Charles Cultee (*q̓ə́ltí* in modern orthography) and a woman named Catherine. Boas was unable to get anything from Catherine, but Mr. Cultee "proved to be a veritable storehouse of information." It turned out that he also spoke Kathlamet. Two other people also spoke Kathlamet—Sampson at Bay Center and Mrs. Wilson at Nemah, also on Willapa Bay—but Boas could not elicit any connected texts from either and so had to rely on Mr. Cultee for Kathlamet as well (Boas 1894:5–6, 1901:5–6).

Boas identified Charles Cultee's genealogy: his mother's mother was a Kathlamet, his mother's father a Qwilá'pax *q̓ʷilápax* (Willapa; that is, Shoalwater Salish), his father's mother a Clatsop, and his father's father a "Tinneh, from the interior" (Kwalhioqua Athapaskan). His wife was a Chehalis, and he used the Chehalis language with her and their children. He had lived in Cathlamet, his mother's town, and spoke that language (that is, Kathlamet Chinook) as well, but little English. Boas (1894) recorded texts in Chinook during the summers of 1890 and 1891 and Kathlamet texts then and in 1894. He wrote:

> My work of translating and explaining the texts was greatly facilitated by Cultee's remarkable intelligence. After he had once grasped what I wanted, he explained to me the grammatical structure of the sentences by means of examples, and elucidated the sense of difficult periods. This work was the more difficult as we conversed only by means of the Chinook jargon. (6)

The results were two short papers (1893a, 1893b); *Chinook Texts* (1894), consisting of 18 myths, 13 accounts and tales illustrating beliefs and practices, and 2 historical tales, all presented in Lower Chinook with interlinear translations and free translations; *Kathlamet Texts* (1901), consisting of 17 myths, 11 tales, and 5 historical narratives, all presented as in the Chinook volume; an article (1904) on the vocabulary of Chinook; a description of Chinook grammar (1911); and an article on Chinook verb morphology by John R. Swanton (1900). Boas also supplied information for Livingston Farrand's entries on Chinookan villages in the *Handbook of American Indians* (Hodge 1971). In his classes at Columbia University, where he taught nearly all of the first generation of American anthropologists, Boas used Cultee's Chinook texts in teaching linguistics (Kroeber 1943:15). Our knowledge of the Chinookan languages and the fields of linguistics and anthropology owe a great debt to the intelligence, imagination, and linguistic skills of Charles Cultee.

Volume 8 of E. S. Curtis's monumental *The North American Indian* (1970:180–83, 198–205) includes a Lower Columbia Chinookan village names list as well as short vocabularies of both Lower Chinook and Kathlamet Upper Chinook. A draft of the work preserved at the Natural History Museum of Los Angeles County (Curtis ca. 1910a) identifies Chinookan informants, including Sam Millett (also spelled Millet, Mallet, etc.), apparently the source of the Kathlamet vocabulary, and Catherine Hawks (also known as Catherine George), apparently the source of the Lower Chinook vocabulary (see McChesney et al. 1969:23–26, 28–30; Catherine Hawks may be the Catherine earlier encountered by Boas). Millett's name appears as informant on draft lists of Chinook, Clatsop, and Kathlamet village names, while a draft list of Cascades and lower Willamette names bears the name of a half-Cascades Métis riverboat captain, Michelle (Michel) Martineau (Table S16.1 on line). The work with these and other informants is probably to be credited to W. E. Myers, Curtis's field ethnographer and linguist (Gidley 2003:11–12). Myers worked outside the Boasian tradition and developed an independent phonetic notation. While exhibiting a more limited range of phonetic contrasts than Boas's transcriptions, Myers's are accurate as far as they go and provide the single most complete record of Chinookan village names extant.

In 1928, Melville Jacobs, a student of Boas, took a position at the University of Washington and began linguistic work in western Oregon. While working with a Santiam Kalapuya, Jacobs learned that there were two speakers of the Clackamas dialect of Kiksht still living, Victoria Howard of West Linn and John Wacheno of Grand Ronde. Mrs. Howard was originally from Grand Ronde, where she had been married to one of Wacheno's brothers. She possessed "a large store of information" and "exhibited fine humor, sharp intelligence, and excellent diction in both Clackamas and English." Jacobs worked for four months with Mrs. Howard in 1929 and 1930 and published two volumes of Clackamas texts (1958–59) and two volumes of analysis, *The Content and Style of an Oral Literature* (1959a) and *The People Are Coming Soon* (1960). The texts include myths and accounts of cultural activities, presented with the English at the top of the page and the Clackamas below, without any grammatical analysis. *Content and Style* discusses social relations, male and female personality traits, humor, ethics, and worldview as Jacobs infers them from the texts, as well as literary devices and features. *The People Are Coming Soon* outlines each myth in the texts and gives further interpretations of each. Jacobs (1936) also recorded Chinuk Wawa texts from Mrs. Howard.

In 1942, John P. Harrington (1942–43) attempted to elicit Curtis's Lower Chinook and Kathlamet vocabularies from Sam Millett's daughter, Emma Luscier, a resident of Bay Center, Washington. Mrs. Luscier was also Harrington's source for vocabularies in Chinuk Wawa, Lower Cowlitz Salishan, and Lower Chehalis Salishan, all languages that she spoke fluently, but she did not speak Chinookan. In most cases, she appears to have depended on her knowledge of Chinuk Wawa to recognize and reproduce Curtis's Chinookan models. Harrington's meticulous phonetic transcriptions of her Chinuk Wawa provide proof that she pronounced Chinuk Wawa words with a full array of indigenous phonetic features.

Although Lower Chinook, Kathlamet, and the Clackamas dialect of

Kiksht probably had no speakers after the 1930s, there were speakers of Cascades for a few more years, while Wishram-Wasco has survived to the present with a slowly diminishing pool of competent speakers. Thus linguists had materials recorded earlier on downriver Chinookan, and they could find speakers upriver. In 1950, David and Kathrine French began linguistic and ethnographic work with speakers of Kiksht from The Cascades rapids upriver. In 1955, Dell Hymes wrote his doctoral dissertation at Indiana University on Kathlamet and later worked with speakers of Wasco on the Warm Springs Reservation. In his treatment of oral literature, he used materials in several forms of Chinookan. In 1966, Michael Silverstein (1974) began work with speakers of Wishram on the Yakama Reservation and has done comparative work on Chinookan. More recently, Rob Moore, French, Hymes, and Silverstein worked on a dictionary of Chinookan, but the work was suspended after French's death in 1994.

LINGUISTIC HISTORY

The languages of the Chinookan family are, presumably, the products of changes in the speech of different groups of speakers of an earlier language, called Proto-Chinook. This language was most likely spoken where we find the oldest division within the family—its "center of gravity," as Edward Sapir (1949:455) called it. The center of gravity of the Chinookan family is not far above the mouth of the Columbia River.

Of course, the proto-language of any family must have started as an offshoot of a more remote proto-language. In 1929, Sapir proposed a classification of North American Indian languages north of Mexico, grouping them into six super-families on the basis of presumed common origin. One of these, Penutian, consisted of six subdivisions, one of which was Chinookan. Two others were Oregon Penutian, which included Kalapuya in the Willamette Valley, and Plateau Penutian, which included Sahaptin spoken all around Wishram and Wasco at The Dalles. If the Penutian grouping is more than theoretical, it must be in the order of several thousand years old. Dale Kinkade (Thompson and Kinkade 1990:45) has taken the "great diversity and remoteness of relationships among the northern Penutian languages" to suggest an Oregon homeland and has suggested that speakers of Proto-Penutian may have settled in the Willamette Valley. Proto-Chinookan, then, spread downriver from the Portland Basin.

Boas thought it unlikely that relationships of any great time depth could ever be established, because the evidence may have been obscured by the influence of one language on another. He was struck by "areal features" in the region, similarities among neighboring languages that belong to different families. The languages of the Northwest Coast and Plateau share sounds that are rare or absent in most of the rest of the world. Some features of grammar are also shared by adjacent languages of different families. The Chinookan and Salish languages on the coast (but not those in the interior) and Quileute have grammatical gender. These and British Columbia languages Kwakwala or Kwakiutl (but not the related Nuuchalhnulth or Nootka) have demonstrative systems (terms corresponding to *this* and *that*) that express visibility versus invisibility (Boas 1929). These and other features must have "diffused" from one language family to another, showing that the network of intermarriage and other contacts known from historic times must be very old. Because the other Penutian languages do not have gender while all Salish languages on the coast do, Proto-Chinookan probably developed gender as a result of contact with Salishan languages. This could mean that Salish territory extended continuously across the mouth of the Columbia before Chinookan arrived.

More recently, Silverstein (1974) showed that the verb in Lower Chinook distinguishes aspect but little in the way of tense, while upriver the elements indicating aspect are increasingly used in the development of a system of tenses. This development must be the result of the influence of Sahaptin, which distinguishes several tenses, and it implies Chinookan moved upriver into the Plateau (see Foster 1996:82–83).

Thus, we have a picture of Chinookan being first spoken in the Portland Basin, expanding downriver and being influenced by Salish, splitting into Lower and Upper Chinook, with the latter then expanding farther upriver and being increasingly influenced by Sahaptin. These expansions of the Chinookan languages need not imply great movements of people down and up the river; they may have been simply the result of speakers of other languages adopting Chinookan.

ETHNOGRAPHIC RESEARCH

The ethnographic report on northwestern America by Horatio Hale (1846:214–17) includes only a short description of the Chinookans and contains judgments about their intellects and morals. George Gibbs's ethnographic work (1855, 1877, 1955–56) contains scattered references to the Chinookans. One of

Gibbs's sources was James G. Swan, who settled in 1852 on Shoalwater Bay. A keen observer of the natural environment, the Natives, and the settlers, Swan's observations during his three years on Willapa Bay are embodied in a delightfully readable book, *Northwest Coast; or Three Years Residence in Washington Territory* (1972).

Toward the end of the 19th century, three men with Chinookan mothers and white fathers wrote short pieces on their mothers' people. Silas Smith was the son of Solomon Smith, a pioneer in Clatsop County, and Celiast, the daughter of the Clatsop chief Coboway. He contributed a list of Chinook salmon names (1882), two short pieces that included Native traditions of shipwrecks (1899, 1900), and an article describing Native culture in the region (1901). He also provided information to the historian Horace Lyman (1900, 1903, n.d.), and Celiast has been the subject of an article by David Peterson del Mar (1995). The other men were grandsons of the Chinook chief Concomly. William McKay was the son of Timmee and Thomas McKay, and Ranald McDonald (Lewis and Murakami 1923) was the son of Raven and Alexander McDonald.

Work by Franz Boas and Melville Jacobs was primarily linguistic, but the texts they recorded were also of ethnographic value and were used in later descriptions of Chinook culture. John Wacheno, the Clackamas contemporary of Victoria Howard, was interviewed at Grand Ronde in late July 1934 by Philip Drucker of the University of California. His field notes, though well known among local scholars, were never published.

The only standard ethnography of the Lower Chinook is Verne F. Ray's *Lower Chinook Ethnographic Notes* (1938). Ray began work in the Plateau as a student at the University of Washington and studied under Leslie Spier at Yale before he returned to teach at the UW. In 1930, he learned of Lower Chinook people still living in the Willapa Bay area, and he did research there between 1931 and 1936. His principal sources were Emma Millet Luscier and Isabel Bertrand. Ray (1938) wrote that Mrs. Luscier "proved to be an extremely intelligent woman and an excellent informant considering the remoteness of the culture." Mrs. Bertrand was much older, reportedly born in 1843. She spoke no English, and her daughter interpreted for her. She was less ready to give information, but her age made what she gave more valuable. Mrs. Luscier spoke two Salish languages—Cowlitz and Lower Chehalis—and Chinuk Wawa but used only a few words of Lower Chinook (29–30). Ray gives genealogies for "practically all" of the families at Bay Center with Chinook ancestry (63–67), and it is clear that all had Salish ancestry. Mrs. Luscier's father,

Sam Millett, was the son of a Wahkiakum *wáqaiqam* (Kathlamet-speaking) father and a Tokeland (Shoalwater Salish) mother, and Mrs. Luscier's mother was the daughter of a Cowlitz "chief" and a Kathlamet mother (McChesney 1969). Her father had been Edward Curtis's Shoalwater and Kathlamet source, and her mother was his Cowlitz source (Curtis ca. 1910, 1913:172–73; Silverstein 1990:546).

Ray's "Lower Chinook" includes not only the speakers of the Chinook proper and Clatsop but also Kathlamet, the most downriver speakers of Upper Chinook. In view of more recent research by Hajda (1984), however, it seems that Ray's "single ethnic unit" was not differentiated as such within the regional social network in which it participated. In addition to information from Mrs. Luscier and Mrs. Bertrand, Ray used all the historical sources available at the time, as well as Boas's *Chinook Texts*. His ethnography includes a description of the environment and chapters on the usual cultural categories, plus four myths told by Mrs. Luscier. In general, Mrs. Luscier and Mrs. Bertrand contributed more to the chapters on society and the guardian spirit complex, while the chapters on subsistence and material culture owe more to historical sources. Ray included his "Lower Chinook" in his contribution to the University of California's Culture Element Survey (a checklist of culture traits) for the Plateau (1942), and he published an article on the cultural position of the Lower Chinook within the larger region (1937).

ETHNOHISTORY

Ethnohistorical research involving the Chinookans began with the work of Albert Buell Lewis (1906), a student of Boas who combed the historical literature for a description of the Native peoples of the Columbia Basin and western Washington and Oregon. Also based on the early literature are two works on tribal distribution, one by Leslie Spier (1936), the other by Joel Berreman (1938). Both would have to be modified by more recent research. Verne F. Ray combined ethnohistorical with ethnographic work in his Lower Chinook study (1938), and two later articles (Ray and Lurie 1954; Ray 1975) are essentially ethnohistory. Adams (1958) combined ethnographic and ethnohistorical work on the Cascades people, and Becky Saleeby and Richard M. Pettigrew (1983) examined the historical record for a brief account of villages and seasonal movements on the Lower Columbia.

Robert T. Boyd used historical documents in a series of works on disease and demography, beginning with a study of the "Fever and Ague" (1975), a disease that greatly reduced the Chinookan population in 1830. Chapters on Chinookans are also included in his history of disease on the Northwest Coast (1999b). In 1987, Boyd and Yvonne Hajda reviewed Lewis and Clark's population estimates and related them to seasonal movements. Hajda (1984) described the social network that extended beyond the Chinookans themselves (see ch. 10 in this volume), documented a house style in the Wappato Valley that was different from that previously described (1994), and examined slavery in the Greater Lower Columbia (2005). Melissa Cole Darby (1996, 2005) researched the use of wapato in the Lower Columbia Valley.

HISTORICAL NARRATIVES ABOUT CHINOOKAN PEOPLES

William L. Lang

IT goes without saying that the written histories of any people reflect the interests and opinions of writers and their era. The historical literature on Chinookan peoples is a testament to this truism. The first published accounts were the work of Euro-American explorers and traders, and the earliest scholarship, written during the late 19th and early 20th centuries, tended to repeat the themes they laid down, with some attention paid to the consequences of Euro-American resettlement. By the end of the 20th century, however, scholars had directed their attention toward Native cultural traditions and history that contradicted characterizations of Chinookan people and key events. Chinookans became recognized as important agents of change, as wave upon wave of new people, industries, and institutions settled into their homelands. Modern historiography increasingly has presented a more complex understanding of the history of Chinookan people in the Columbia River region.

FIRST DESCRIPTIONS

The earliest description of Chinook people on the Columbia appeared in 1798 with publication of George Vancouver's *A Voyage of Discovery* (1984), which included descriptions of trading and general engagement between British explorers and Indian people and Lt. William Broughton's survey of the Lower Columbia in November 1792. Broughton's map of the lower 100 miles of the Columbia advertised to the world the river's commercial potential and described Chinook people as territorial and as vitally interested in trade. Broughton's descriptions portrayed Indian villagers near the mouth of the Willamette as threatening, but his depiction of Chinookan people farther upriver, near the mouth of the Sandy, cast them as hospitable and accommodating. Their interest in trade seemed to be the salient point.

A second published description appeared in summer 1807, when Patrick Gass, a member of the Lewis and Clark Expedition, published an abbreviated account of the great exploration across the continent to the Pacific. In a half-dozen brief references to Chinookan villages and culture, Gass reported on December 20, 1805, on the general collegiality of the interactions: "Some of the natives again came to see us, whom we suffered, contrary to out usual practice, to remain in the fort all night; the evening was so wet and stormy" (Lewis and Clark 1996:189).

A detailed account of the expedition's encounters with Chinookan people on the Lower Columbia during the winter of 1805–6 came with the publication in 1814 of Nicholas Biddle's two-volume *History of the Expedition under the Command of Captains Lewis and Clark*. The explorers characterized Indian people who frequented Fort Clatsop, the Corps' wintering encampment, as pleasant and agreeable but prone to pilfering goods and being "great higlers in trade" (Lewis and Clark 1990:164). Their commentaries on Chinookan personal appearance, styles of dress, living conditions, fishing technology, and especially their facility in boat building and canoe handling established the Indians' reputation as masters of their domain.

A careful reading of Lewis's and Clark's descriptions reveals a mixed appraisal of Chinookan groups, laudatory of their skills and tenacity in trade but also critical and disdainful of their personal habits and trustworthiness. In Clark's December 3, 1805, entry, for example, he portrayed Chinookan canoe skills: "The Indians proceeded on down through emence high waves maney times their Canoe was entirely out of Sight before they were $\frac{1}{2}$ a mile distance" (Lewis and Clark 1990:106). After an often tense winter at Fort Clatsop, Lewis wrote that he found the local Natives "treacherous" and untrustworthy:

we never suffer parties of such number to remain within the fort all night; for notwithstanding their apparent friendly disposition, their great avarice and hope of plunder might induce them to be treacherous. At all events we determined always to be on our guard as much as the nature of our situation will permit us, and never place our selves at the mercy of any savages. (330–31)

The explorers left Fort Clatsop and the Lower Columbia in early March 1806 and took back with them a generally negative impression of the river, the landscape, the climate, and the people. Their report to President Thomas Jefferson in September made clear that the Lower Columbia offered few benefits to the nation and that Chinookans were people to be avoided.

Three decades after Lewis and Clark said goodbye to the Lower Columbia, the first book on the 1811 establishment of Fort Astoria was published in New York in 1836. Washington Irving wrote *Astoria, or Anecdotes of an Enterprise beyond the Rocky Mountains* (1976), a romantic and fast-paced history of the Pacific Fur Company's three-year effort to establish a major fur post on the Columbia. His descriptions of Chinook, Clatsop, Wakaikum, and Kathlamet people parroted the views of Lewis and Clark, especially in his depictions of their physical stature, use of head-flattening, practice of polygyny, and religious ideas, which Irving characterized as "limited and confined." His images of Chinookan people became nearly indelible, partly because *Astoria* was widely read in the US and Europe and partly because it seemed to confirm an image of Lower Columbia River people as exotic and "inferior in many respects to the tribes east of the mountains."

During the 1830s, Pacific Northwest Indians drew attention from the Christian evangelical community. In addition to newspaper articles that mentioned Columbia River tribes, a popular account of a missionary exploring expedition by Rev. Samuel Parker (1936) in 1835–36 provided a view of Chinookan peoples. Parker's book, part travelogue and part journal, included personal observations meant for a broad reading audience and was couched to encourage support of missionary activities in the region. He contradicted the characterizations of Chinooks as intransigent and ungrateful and claimed that no Chinook or other Native should be considered inferior to Euro-Americans if they "imbibed principles of the Christian religion" (165). His overnight accommodation in a Chinook plankhouse was very "sociable," he wrote (167), even though his communication with his Chinook host was minimal. Aid from Cowlitz canoeists prompted Parker to write: "This act proved them to be susceptible of kindness, and increased my confidence in their integrity" (179). Nonetheless, his moralistic evaluations included the charge that the ultimate losers in gambling contests among Indians went "into perpetual slavery" as a consequence of their bad luck (247–48).

Ten Years in Oregon (1968), a memoir and history by missionaries Daniel Lee and John Frost, included descriptions and characterizations of Chinookan people that came directly from their missionary activities in the late 1830s and early 1840s. The authors took issue with Parker's relatively optimistic view of Chinookans. They disagreed about the Indians' supposed penchant for thievery and pilfering but emphasized the Chinookans' culturally degraded condition by highlighting their war-making and disputations. Lee and Frost focused on the institution of slavery, the practice of head flattening, and the missionaries' criticism of Chinookan treatment of women as "property" (97–98). Much of this commentary made their "history" an apology for the missionaries' failure to convert many Indians in the Lower Columbia region (100–103).

Four years later, Elijah White published his own *Ten Years in Oregon* (1850), a missionary history that had more to do with American nationalism than the missionary effort in the Pacific Northwest. His overview of Pacific Northwest history was laced with heavy criticism of the Hudson's Bay Company, and his discussion of missionary activities and Native people served primarily to expose what he considered the company's and other fur traders' degradation of Indians. The traders were nefarious, White argued, and the consequence was culturally destructive to Chinookans. In a longish discussion of the marriage of Chinook chief Concomly's daughter to a Pacific Fur Company functionary, White charged that Comcomly effectively made a deal with the Astorian enterprise that "infallibly" joined the Chinook "to the interests of the Astorians" (120–21). His characterization underscored an earlier stereotype of Chinookan trading prowess, making Comcomly not only a powerful aboriginal trade manager but also a clever diplomat who made a political and economic bargain with an untrustworthy business combine. White's descriptions of Chinook relationships with fur traders contrast markedly with William H. Gray's anti-HBC history, *The History of Oregon, 1792–1849* (1870), which portrayed the fur company as abusers of Native people, including Chinookans. Gray's depiction of Indian relationships with HBC traders, especially Chief Factor John McLoughlin, was more a product of his antipathy toward the fur trade behemoth than his empathy for the fate of the Chinook people (42–45, 55–56).

Alexander Ross's *Adventures of the First Settlers on the Oregon or Columbia River* (2000) became among the most widely read historical accounts of early Euro-American contact with Chinookan people on the Lower Columbia. Employed by the Pacific Fur Company (American) and the North West Company (Canadian), Ross wrote an account of the Astoria enterprise from his own experience. Although his account was published after Ross Cox's *The Columbia River* (1957), Ross wrote in a more engaging style and featured graphic descriptions of fur traders overcoming great odds in pursuit of their work. He tended to exaggerate conflicts between Chinooks and Astorians, although he affirmed the views of Lewis and Clark that the Chinook controlled trade on the lower river and were most remarkable for their abilities in making canoes and decorative items. Ross also repeated charges made by earlier authors that Chinookans "are crafty and intriguing, and have probably learned the arts of cheating, flattery, and dissimilation in the course of their traffic with the coasting traders." He described Chinookan men and women in unappealing terms, emphasizing the men's penchant for gambling, the women's "lewdness," and their "superstitious" beliefs. In all, Ross described Chinookan people as adept users of their environment but also as groups that were untrustworthy in trade. *The Columbia River* continued a strong descriptive line in Euro-American representations of Chinookans as crafty and accomplished yet somehow inferior peoples. It was a prejudicial viewpoint that had dominated nearly all Euro-American estimations of Native people in North America, where tribal groups rated higher or lower in Euro-Americans' evaluations relative to how pliant and unresistant they were in economic and social exchanges.

Gabriel Franchère, a veteran of the Pacific Fur Company and the author of *Journal of a Voyage on the North West Coast of North America* (1969), generally agreed with Ross, but he inquired more about Chinookan culture and appeared to understand more, including their generosity, sensible attitudes about warfare, and strong sense of justice. "I regard them," Franchère wrote, "as nearer to a state of civilization than any of the tribes who dwell east of the Rocky Mountains." Nonetheless, the Astorians rated Chinookans low on the trustworthy scale, in part because they were less pliant and more confident in trade.

In 1845, Charles Wilkes (1845) wrote his account of the United States Exploring Expedition, which had brought him and his flotilla to the mouth of the Columbia in the 1840s. Wilkes's purpose was exploration and survey, but he expanded knowledge about Chinookans in his references to their roles as river pilots, especially in his description of the wreck of one of his vessels, the *Peacock*. More detailed knowledge about Chinooks came from James Swan, who spent the better part of three years among Chinookan and Salish people on Willapa Bay. In *The Northwest Coast*, published in 1857, Swan (1972) portrayed the tribal fishing communities in a much different light than previous writers. His amateur but detailed ethnography emphasized the richness of Chinook culture and the certainty, in his mind, that Euro-Americans and Chinooks could live productively without conflict. His positive assessment of Chinook culture stood for decades as the only widely disseminated description that avoided detrimental assessments of Indian groups in the Greater Lower Columbia.

EARLY HISTORIES

A History of the Willamette Valley, edited by Herbert O. Lang and published by George Himes in 1885, was among the earliest histories of the region that went beyond memoir or firsthand accounts. From a late-19th-century vantage point, interactions between Native people and resettlers in the Willamette Valley seemed benign to the author, a history with "little thereof to chronicle." The explanation, Lang related, was the advent of disease and alcohol abuse, which together decimated the aboriginal population to "as few squalid and miserable survivors, especially where the country has been occupied thickly by whites, as in this valley" (482). He characterized the Chinooks as weak and small in stature because they were fish eaters, expressing a bias in favor of meat-eating groups east of the Cascades Mountains. He praised them for their craftsmanship, especially the construction of plankhouses and canoes, but Lang agreed with Parker that they "gambled as a steady habit, and sacrificed their property, their wives and children, and their own liberty in order to satisfy their devotion to that vice" (485).

The publications of Hubert Howe Bancroft were the first general histories of Oregon and the Pacific Northwest that attempted to cover political, economic, and social topics in an integrated way. Based in San Francisco, Bancroft constructed his histories by collecting primary information from participants in historical events and contracting with local authors to write the narratives. The volumes that included descriptions of Chinookan peoples were the work of Frances Fuller Victor, a Portland author who also wrote histories and biographies under her own name. In the *History of the Northwest Coast* (1886), Victor summarized the Lewis and Clark Expedition's encounters with Chinook Indians by repeating the explorers' characterizations. "The Chinooks," Victor wrote, "were most annoying from their thievish propensities, which at last resulted in their exclusion from the fort. When a Clatsop or Kathlamet approached he stopped a little way off, and shouted "No Chinook" (56).

The first volume of a popular subscription, or "mugbook," history, *An Illustrated History of the State of Oregon,* by Rev. Harvey K. Hines (1893), included limited references to Chinookan people. A Methodist missionary who taught religion at Willamette University, Hines had come to Oregon in 1853 and was unofficial historian of the missionary experience in the Pacific Northwest by the 1890s. His viewpoint reflected his strong belief that Christianity, common literacy, and a market economy were essential to modern civilization. Indian lives and activities could not be included because "without a written language of any kind, unless it was the use of the rudest and most barbarous symbols, they have passed away and left no recorded history; without architecture, except that which exhausts its genius in the construction of a skin wigwam or a bark lodge, they have died and left no monuments" (26). Hines could see no purpose in digging into their past, for there had been "no progress and being no progress [Chinookans] had no civilization." The climate had made them

> indolent and sluggish in movement; without alertness or perception of mind; indolent and inactive in all their habits; sleeping away nearly all but the little time that was requisite . . . they thus droned away their meaningless life, and the few additional moments required to boil or roast it sufficient to gratify their uncultured appetite. (26–28)

Hines epitomized the narrowest cultural perspective on Chinookan people. In some ways, his characterizations—along with similar ones written by journalists and other popular authors—put the harshest stamp on Chinookan culture, the image of a people with no history worth discovering. It is difficult to think of a more culturally dismissive view.

Horace S. Lyman's *History of Oregon* (1903), among the first traditional-style history textbooks, narrated resettlement in the region in broad terms. References to Chinook peoples were limited to contact with white explorers, and his depictions repeated earlier descriptions of Chinookans as troublesome people and impediments to easy resettlement. William Lyman, a history professor at Whitman College in Walla Walla and no relation to Horace Lyman, wrote the first comprehensive history of the Columbia River in 1909. He treated Chinookan people as part of a "discovered land," as if they were part of the environment, by focusing primarily on Indian stories. The "Bridge of the Gods" on the mid-Columbia, for example, was "perhaps the most perfect and beautiful of all Indian fire myths of the Columbia" (20–26). He considered the story a demonstration of the Chinookans' close relationships to landscape, climate, and natural history. In describing Tsagiglalal, the ancient petroglyph in Upper Chinook territory near The Dalles, Lyman emphasized a moralistic view of Chinookan culture. Its enormous human eyes were a "Witch's Head, near Old Wishram Village; the Indian superstition is that these Eyes will follow any unfaithful woman" (31). His interpretation varies substantially from modern analyses, and his appropriation of sexual references seems an intentional contradiction of Lewis and Clark's depiction of Chinookan women as lewd and promiscuous.

The Centennial History of Oregon, a popular subscription history written by Joseph Gaston in 1912 (in commemoration of Astor's founding of Astoria), reflected the Progressive Era's attention to the social characteristics of distinct populations in the nation. In the first volume, Gaston characterized the Chinook and other Indian peoples in the Pacific Northwest as examples of people who "divided the fruits of all his labors as a socialist, and died in conviction that the white man had robbed him of his God-given birthrights" (72). He criticized Chinookan lifestyle, arguing that they and other Columbia River Natives had rejected the missionaries' appeals and avoided learning; hence, they had lost their land and their position in the region because they could not compete and had not embraced the new culture of Euro-Americans. It was a simple matter of power overcoming weakness. In effect, Gaston wrote off Chinookan culture as a failed system and the people as doomed to pass from the scene (127–28).

MODERN HISTORIES

By the mid-20th century, state and regional histories had incorporated critical readings of primary documents and materials that directed attention away from filiopietistic and nationalistic narratives that had prevailed during the late 19th and early 20th centuries. Still, the most widely read general textbook on Pacific Northwest history, Dorothy O. Johansen and Charles M. Gates's *Empire of the Columbia* (1957), limited discussion of Chinookan people to a few sentences that emphasized canoe manufacture and proficiency in trading (11, 12, 75). The best scholarship, in other words, tended to present a very limited description of Native people on the Lower Columbia. By the early 1960s, however, some scholars began to realize that Native oral tradition provided a significant source of information that was absent from the written record. Beginning with Alvin Josephy's *The Nez Perce Indians and the Opening of the Northwest* (1965), historians began to revisit long-ignored topics and initiated a significant revision of the story of Native-white interaction.

Within a decade of Josephy's revisionist work, Robert M. Ruby and John A. Brown published *The Chinook Indians: Traders of the Lower Columbia River* (1976; see also Ruby and Brown 1965, 1972). At the heart of their text was an acknowledgement of Chinook cultural heritage and their centuries-long history on the Lower Columbia. Contrary to earlier historical depictions, Ruby and Brown portrayed relationships between Chinook and Euro-Americans as meetings of equally important cultures, with emphasis on the decisions Native leaders made. Their explanation of Chinook reactions to two white intruding groups, for example, created a much different storyline than those in earlier histories: "The Chinooks' welcome to their village of [Astorians in 1811] was in sharp contrast to their reception of the Winships [American traders] the previous year, possibly because the natives had learned of the [Astorians'] plan to establish a post among them near the mouth of the Columbia river and not at some distance away [as the Winships had proposed]" (1976:129).

The overall message of *The Chinook Indians* was the perseverance of Lower Columbia River people in the face of unremitting and destructive events, from onslaughts of infectious diseases to government perfidy and white economic control of the region. Ruby and Brown emphasized the Chinookan peoples' incomparable mastery of their environment, especially their control of aboriginal trade exchanges and their creative uses of natural resources. Nonetheless, their history was presented as a tragedy on a grand scale, for despite the Chinooks' most adept accommodations of the white intruders, their grasp on the lower river weakened, until by the dawn of the 20th century they were but a small percentage of their numbers at the time of contact. "We respect these people," Ruby and Brown (1976) wrote, "who made a mariner's peace with nature and a mercantile peace with men" (250).

After World War II, historians revisited the Lewis and Clark Expedition, and new interpretive work had an important effect on how scholars understood early contact between Chinookans and Euro-Americans. For the better part of the 20th century, the narrative of the expedition had been primarily an adventure story, but historians in the 1960s and 1970s began investigating important scientific, geographical, and social aspects of the exploration narrative (e.g., Cutright 1969; Allen 1975; Jackson 1978).

The most important study was James P. Ronda's *Lewis and Clark among the Indians* (1984), which completely recast the explorers' encounter with Lower Columbia River people. Ronda devoted a full chapter to the 1805–6 winter, which the explorers spent in the Chinook homeland. By focusing on this neglected portion of the voyage, he highlighted significant exchanges between the members of the Corps of Discovery and Chinook leaders, especially Concomly of the Chinook and Coboway of the Clatsop. The Chinooks became the important actors, the controllers of conditions around Fort Clatsop. Ronda underscored the Chinooks' long experience with international maritime traders and their resistance to the American explorers' entreaties to trade, noting that women played an important role in mercantile exchanges and that their sexual activities—often harshly criticized by observers—could best be understood in a socio-economic context. It was, in short, an expression of power (207–8).

Ronda followed his path-breaking interpretation of Lewis and Clark with an investigation of the origins and history of Astoria, John Jacob Astor's short-lived fur-trade post at the mouth of the Columbia. In *Astoria and Empire* (1990), he described the role that Chinook leaders—especially Concomly—played in the development of the international fur trade in the early 19th century. Concomly emerges as a smart politician and economic strategist who was able to measure his trading partner, Astor's Pacific Fur Company, with great success. The Astorians, Ronda concluded, grasped only a fraction of the Chinookan world, but what they recorded included enough detail to establish that the Chinooks were masters of their region and that their lives were characterized by political, economic, and social complexity (Ronda 1990:219–22, 227–28, 320–22; see also Ronda 1999).

RECENT SCHOLARSHIP

The most significant recent scholarship that bears on the history of Chinookan people on the Lower Columbia focuses on the Lewis and Clark Expedition. In 1983, the University of Nebraska Press embarked on a nearly 20-year project to publish a comprehensive edition of the *Journals of the Lewis and Clark Expedition*. Under the editorship of Gary Moulton, the new edition stretched to 13 volumes, including a facsimile atlas of manuscript maps and the journals of three enlisted corps members. Volume six (1990) covers the Corps of Discovery's winter at Fort Clatsop, while volumes five (1988) and seven (1991) include the explorers' contact with Chinookan people on the Columbia and Willamette Rivers. Moulton drew on experts in anthropology, meteorology, geology, cartography, and ornithology, along with specialists in Native studies and local history. The result is a compendium of detailed notation on hundreds of Chinook-related descriptions in the original journals of the expedition.

New research on fur-trading enterprises on the Lower Columbia have expanded knowledge about Chinookan participation in the trade and put it in a broader international context. Two primary-source volumes on Astor's Pacific Fur Company, *Astorian Adventure* (Seton 1993) and *Annals of Astoria* (McDougall 1999), include daily logs and journals from the post's first years. The editors' notations, especially in *Annals of Astoria*, provide important references to other primary sources about interactions between Chinook and Euro-American traders and details about exchanges between named Chinook headmen and white traders. The daily reports at Fort Astor reveal that Chinookan groups, from the mouth of the Columbia upriver to the Willamette, made their way to Astoria with a range of materials to trade, from beaver skins to wapato. Additional research on HBC operations at Fort Astoria (identified as Fort George after the War of 1812) has been collated and reframed best in Richard Mackie's *Trading beyond the Mountains* (1997), which sets the Chinookan trading relationships with the company within a regional context. As HBC increased its presence on the Columbia after 1821, Mackie makes clear, the less Chinookan people could control trade relationships and the more they became workers in the international fur trade.

Native historians have focused on inner histories of Chinookan people on the Columbia River. In *The Si'lailo* Way, Joseph Dupris, Kathleen Hill, and William Rodgers (2006) introduce small but important stories about individuals and small groups of Indian fishers who contested their marginalization at the hands of white fishing interests and the state. Their recounting of George Charley's physical and legal battle against white horse-seining fishing groups in the Columbia estuary in the 1920s and 1930s highlights not only the perseverance of Native fishers but also the legal limbo that "nonrecognized" Indians faced during the 20th century (see Aguilar 2005).

Historians continue to pursue new topics in the history of Chinookan relationships with Euro-American groups from the first contact to the 20th century. In addition to revisiting well-known events and personalities, they have begun to incorporate new social themes. In some ways, the most recent historical work is just beginning to probe the complexity of Chinookan history.

BIBLIOGRAPHY

Adams, Barbara. 1958. The Cascade Indians: Ethnographic notes and an analysis of early relations with whites. B.A. thesis, Reed College.

Adams, David. 1995. *Education for extinction: American Indians and the boarding school experience, 1875–1928*. Lawrence: University Press of Kansas.

Adamson, Thelma. 1934. *Folktales of the Coast Salish*. Memoirs of the American Folk-lore Society 27.

Aguilar, George. 2005. *When the river ran wild! Indian traditions on the mid-Columbia and the Warm Springs Reservation*. Portland: Oregon Historical Society Press.

Aikens, C. Melvin. 1993. *Archaeology of Oregon*. 3d ed. Portland: US Department of the Interior, Bureau of Land Management, Oregon State Office.

Allen, Cain. 2000. They called it progress: Indians, salmon, and the industrialization of the Columbia River. MA thesis, Portland State University.

Allen, John. 1975. *Passage through the garden: Lewis and Clark and the image of the American Northwest*. Urbana: University of Illinois Press.

Allen, Paul. 1814. *History of the expedition under the command of Captains Lewis and Clark*. Philadelphia: Bradford and Inskeep.

Ambrose, Stephen. 1996. *Undaunted courage: Meriwether Lewis, Thomas Jefferson, and the opening of the American West*. New York: Simon & Schuster.

Ames, Kenneth. 1994. The Northwest Coast: Complex hunter-gatherers, ecology, and social evolution. *Annual Review of Anthropology* 23:209–29.

———. 1995. Chiefly power and household production on the Northwest Coast. In *Foundations of social inequality*, ed. T. Douglas Price and Gary Feinman, 155–87. New York: Plenum.

———. 1996. Life in the big house: Household labor and dwelling size on the Northwest Coast. In *People who lived in big houses: Archaeological perspectives on large domestic structures*, ed. Gary Coupland and Edward Banning, 131–50. Madison, WI: Prehistory Press.

———. 1999. Myth of the hunter-gatherer. *Archaeology* 52(5):45–9.

———. 2002. Going by boat: The forager-collector continuum at sea. In *Beyond foraging and collecting: Evolutionary change in hunter-gatherer settlement systems*, ed. Ben Fitzhugh and Junko Habu, 17–50. New York: Kluwer/Plenum.

———. 2008. Slavery, household production, and demography on the southern Northwest Coast: Cables, tacking, and ropewalking. In *Invisible citizens: Captives and their consequences*, ed. Catherine Cameron, 138–58. Salt Lake City: University of Utah Press.

Ames, Kenneth, and Alan Marshall. 1981. Villages, demography, and subsistence intensification on the southern Columbia Plateau. *North American Archaeologist* 2(1):25–52.

Ames, Kenneth, and Herbert Maschner. 1999. *Peoples of the Northwest Coast: Their archaeology and prehistory*. London: Thames and Hudson.

Ames, Kenneth, and Cameron Smith. 2010. Ground stone, metallurgy and embedded specialization on the Southern Northwest Coast . Poster presented to the 75th Annual Society for American Archaeology Meetings, April 14–18, St. Louis.

Ames, Kenneth, and Elizabeth Sobel. 2009. Finding and dating Cathlapotle. *Archaeology in Washington* 15:5–32.

Ames, Kenneth, Cameron Smith, and Alexander Bourdeau. 2008. Large domestic pits on the Northwest Coast of North America. *Journal of Field Archaeology* 33(1):3–18.

Ames, Kenneth, Don D. Dumond, Jerry Galm, and Rick Minor. 1998. Prehistory of the Southern Plateau. In *Handbook of North American Indians*, vol. 12: *Plateau*, ed. Deward Walker, 103–19. Washington, DC: Smithsonian.

Ames, Kenneth, Doria F. Raetz, Stephen C. Hamilton, and Christine McAfee. 1992. Household archaeology of a southern Northwest Coast plank house. *Journal of Field Archaeology* 19(3):275–90.

Ames, Kenneth, Cameron Smith, Greg Baker, and William Gardner-O'Kearny. 2011. Chinookan households on the Lower Columbia River: Contact and complexity. Grant (RZ-50601–06). Report to the National Endowment for the Humanities, Washington, DC.

Ames, Kenneth, et al. 1999. Archaeological investigations at 45CL11 Cathlapotle (1991–1996), Ridgefield National Wildlife Refuge, Clark County, Washington: A preliminary report. Cultural Resource Series No. 13, US Fish and Wildlife Service, Region 1.

Anastasio, Angelo. 1972. The Southern Plateau: An ecological analysis of intergroup relations. *Northwest Anthropological Research Notes* 6(2):109–229.

Anderson, Eugene. 1996. *Ecologies of the heart: Emotion, belief, and the environment.* New York: Oxford University Press.

Anderson, M. Kat. 1997. From tillage to table: The indigenous cultivation of geophytes for food in California. *Journal of Ethnobiology* 17(2):149–69.

———. 2005. *Tending the wild: Native American knowledge and management of California's Native resources.* Berkeley: University of California Press.

Appadurai, Arjun. 1986. *The social life of things.* New York: Cambridge University Press.

Applied Archaeological Research. 2006. Fisher's Landing (45CL6): Report of test excavations at late period residential site in the eastern portion of the Portland Basin, Clark County, Washington. Applied Archaeological Research Report No. 464, prepared for CoreCar LLC, Vancouver.

Arnold, Jeanne, ed. 2001. *The origins of a Pacific Coast chiefdom: The Chumash of the Channel Islands.* Salt Lake City: University of Utah Press.

Atwater, Brian. 1987. Evidence for Great Holocene earthquakes along the outer coast of Washington State. *Science* 236:942–44.

———. 1992. Geological evidence for earthquakes during the past 2000 years along the Copalis River, southern coastal Washington. *Journal of Geophysical Research* 97:1901–19.

Atwater, Brian, and Eileen Hemphill-Haley. 1996. Preliminary estimates of recurrence intervals for great earthquakes of the past 3500 years at northeastern Willapa Bay, Washington. Open File Report 96-001. US Geological Survey.

Atwater, Brian, and David Yamaguchi. 1991. Sudden, probably coseismic submergence of Holocene trees and grass in coastal Washington State. *Geology* 19:706–9.

Atwater, Brian, et al. 2005. The orphan tsunami of 1700: Japanese clues to a parent earthquake in North America. Professional Paper 1707. US Geological Survey.

Avery, Mary. 1961. *Washington: A history of the Evergreen State.* Seattle: University of Washington Press.

Baird, Brian. 2008. Recognizing the Chinook Nation: Long-standing injustice about to be set right. Press release. July 31, 2008. www.house.gov/apps/list/press/wa03_baird/morenews1/ChinookBill.shtml.

Baker, Dean. 2004a. Tribal voices: Payback time on the Columbia. (Vancouver, WA) *Columbian,* March 22, 2004.

———. 2004b. Plankhouse progresses. (Vancouver, WA) *Columbian,* November 30, 2004.

Baker, R. Todd. 2007. Mammal and bird fauna from 35MU4. In *Evaluation of archaeological site 35MU4, the Sunken Village site, Multnomah County, Oregon,* ed. Dale Croes, John Fagan, and Maureen Zehendner, 121–22. Olympia, WA, and Portland, OR: South Puget Sound Community College and Archaeological Investigations Northwest.

Ball, John. 1835. Troy Lecture. John Ball Papers. Mss. 195. Oregon Historical Society Research Library, Portland.

———. 1925. *Autobiography of John Ball*, ed. Kate Powers, Flora Hopkins, and Lucy Ball. Grand Rapids, MI: Dean-Hicks.

Banach, Patricia. 2002. Copper on the Pacific Northwest Coast. MA thesis, Portland State University.

Barnett, Homer. 1937. Culture element distributions VII: Oregon Coast. *Anthropological Records* 1(3):155–203.

Barry, J. Neilson. 1932. Peter Corney's voyages, 1814–1817. *Oregon Historical Quarterly* 33(4):355–68.

Barth, Frederic. 1969. *Ethnic groups and boundaries: The social organization of culture difference*. Boston: Little, Brown.

Bar-Yosef, Ofer. 1998. The Natufian in the Levant, threshold to the origins of agriculture. *Evolutionary Anthropology* 6(5):159–77.

Baxter, Paul, Tom Connolly, and Craig Skinner. 2011. Obsidian use in the Willamette Valley and adjacent western Cascades of Oregon. Paper, annual meeting, Society for American Archaeology, Sacramento, CA.

Beckham, Stephen Dow. 1969. George Gibbs, 1815–1873: Historian and ethnologist. PhD diss., University of California, Los Angeles.

———. 1987. *Chinook Indian tribe: Petition for federal acknowledgement*. USA Research Technical Report No. 5, Lake Oswego, OR.

———. 1990. History of western Oregon since 1846. In *Handbook of North American Indians*, vol. 7: *Northwest Coast*, ed. Wayne Suttles, 180–88. Washington, DC: Smithsonian.

———. 1996. Trail of tears: 1856 diary of Indian Agent George Ambrose. *Southern Oregon Historical Society Magazine* 2(1):16–21.

———. 2006. *Oregon Indians: Voices from two centuries*. Corvallis: Oregon State University Press.

———. 2007. Federal-Indian relations. In *The First Oregonians*, ed. Laura Berg, 209–42. Portland: Oregon Council for the Humanities.

Befu, Harumi. 1977. Social exchange. *Annual Reviews in Anthropology* 6:255–81.

Belcher, Edward. 1843. *Narrative of a voyage round the world, performed in Her Majesty's ship* Sulphur, *during the years 1836–1842*. 2 vols. London: Henry Colburn.

———. 1979. *H.M.S.* Sulphur *on the Northwest and California Coasts*, ed. Richard Pierce and John Winslow. Kingston, ONT: Limestone.

Bell, Edward. 1932. Excerpt from Edward Bell's journal. In *Columbia River exploration, 1792*, ed. J. Neilson Barry. *Oregon Historical Quarterly* 33:31–42, 143–55.

Belshaw, Cyril. 1965. *Traditional exchange and modern markets*. Englewood Cliffs, NJ: Prentice-Hall.

Berkes, Fikret. 2008. *Sacred ecology*. 2d ed. New York: Routledge.

Berreman, Joel. 1934. Grand Ronde notes and reports, part 1: Field notes and various documents, research concerning cultural adjustment of the Grand Ronde Indian tribes, obtained during the summer of 1934; part 2: A preliminary report of the cultural adjustment of the Grand Ronde Indian tribes; part 3: History of the Grand Ronde Tribe. Duplicate of mss. in the Cultural Resources Archives, Confederated Tribes of Grand Ronde, Oregon.

———. 1938. *Tribal distribution in Oregon*. Memoirs of the American Anthropological Association No. 47.

Biological Review Team. 2008. Summary of scientific conclusions of the review of the status of eulachon (*Thaleichthys pacificus*) in Washington, Oregon, and California. Northwest Fisheries Science Center, National Marine Fisheries Service, Seattle. nwr.noaa.gov/Other-Marine-Species/upload/Eulachon -Review.pdf.

Bishop, Charles. 1967. *The journal and letters of Captain Charles Bishop on the Northwest Coast of America, 1794–1799*, ed. Michael Roe. Cambridge: Cambridge University Press.

Blackburn, Thomas, and M. Kat Anderson, eds. 1993. *Before the wilderness: Environmental management by Native Californians*. Menlo Park, CA: Ballena.

Blanchet, Francis Norbert. 1983 [1878]. *Historical sketches of the Catholic Church in Oregon*. Fairfield, WA: Ye Galleon Press.

Boas, Franz. 1890. Clatsop vocabulary. Ms. Pn 4b.6, Library of the American Philosophical Society, Philadelphia.

———. 1893a. The doctrine of souls and of disease among the Chinook. *Journal of American Folk-Lore* 6:39–43.

———. 1893b. Notes on the Chinook language. *American Anthropologist* 6:56–63.

———. 1894. *Chinook texts*. Bureau of American Ethnology Bulletin 20. Washington, DC.

———. ca. 1900–5. Information in entries on Chinookan groups and villages. In *Handbook of American Indians north of Mexico*, ed. Frederick Hodge. Bureau of American Ethnology Bulletin 30.

———. 1901. *Kathlamet texts.* Bureau of American Ethnology Bulletin 26.

———. 1904. The vocabulary of the Chinook language. *American Anthropologist* 6:118–47.

———. 1911. Introduction and Chinook. In *Handbook of American Indian languages,* ed. Frederick Hodge, Bureau of American Ethnology Bulletin 40(1):1–79, 563–677.

———. 1923. *Notes on the Tillamook.* University of California Publications in American Archaeology and Ethnology 20(1):3–16.

———. 1929. Classification of American Indian languages. *Language* 5(1):1–7.

———. 1966. *Kwakiutl ethnography,* ed. Helen Codere. Chicago: University of Chicago Press.

Bourdeau, Alex. 2001. Dating the landslide: End of an odyssey? *Current Archaeological Happenings in Oregon* 26(4):3–9.

Bovy, Kristine. 2007. Global impacts or climate change? Explaining the sooty shearwater decline at the Minard site, Washington State, USA. *Journal of Archaeological Science* 34(7):1087–97.

Bowen, William. 1975. The Oregon frontiersman: A demographic view. In *The western shore: Oregon Country essays honoring the American Revolution,* ed. Thomas Vaughan, 181–98. Portland: Oregon Historical Society Press.

Boxberger, Daniel. 2009. The heirs of succession of the Willamette Valley. Study conducted for the Confederated Tribes of Grand Ronde.

——— and Herbert Taylor. 1986. Charles Cultee and the father of American anthropology. *Journal of the Pacific County Historical Society* 21(1):3–7.

Boyd, Robert. 1975. Another look at the "fever and ague" of western Oregon. *Ethnohistory* 22(2):135–53.

———. 1985. The introduction of infectious diseases among the Indians of the Pacific Northwest, 1774–1874. PhD diss., University of Washington.

———. 1990. Demographic history, 1774–1874. In *Handbook of North American Indians,* vol. 7. *Northwest Coast,* ed. Wayne Suttles, 135–48. Washington, DC: Smithsonian.

———. 1996. *People of The Dalles: The Indians of Wascopam Mission.* Lincoln: University of Nebraska Press.

———. 1999a. Strategies of Indian burning in the Willamette Valley. In *Indians, fire, and the land in the Pacific Northwest,* ed. Robert Boyd, 94–138. Corvallis: Oregon State University Press.

———. 1999b. *The coming of the spirit of pestilence: Introduced infectious diseases and population decline among Northwest Coast Indians, 1774–1874.* Seattle: University of Washington Press.

————. 2011. *Cathlapotle and its inhabitants, 1792–1860.* US Fish and Wildlife Service, Region 1, Sherwood, OR.

————. n.d. The Columbia guide to the Indians of the Northwest. Ms. in the author's possession.

Boyd, Robert, and Yvonne Hajda. 1987. Seasonal population movement along the Lower Columbia River: The social and ecological context. *American Ethnologist* 14(2):309–26.

Bradley, Bruce. 1995. Clovis ivory and bone tools. In *Le travail et l'usage de l'ivoire au Paleolithique superieur,* ed. Joachim Hahn et al. Ravello, Italy: Centro Universitario Europeo per I Beni Culturali.

Brand-Miller, J., K. W. James, and P. M. A. Maggiore. 2010. Tables of composition of Australian Aboriginal Foods NUTTAB 2010—Nutrition Composition Tables: Food Standards Australia, New Zealand. University of New South Wales, Canberra.

Bright, William. 1987. The natural history of Old Man Coyote. In *Recovering the word: Essays on Native American literature,* ed. Brian Swann and Arnold Krupat, 339–87. Berkeley: University of California Press.

————. 1993. *A Coyote reader.* Berkeley: University of California Press.

Brodie, Neil, and David Gill. 2003. Looting: An international view. In *Ethical issues in archaeology,* ed. Larry Zimmerman, Karen Vitelli, and Julia Hallowell-Zimmer. Walnut Creek, CA: Altamira.

Brooks, Charles. 1876. Report of Japanese vessels wrecked in the North Pacific Ocean, from the earliest records to the present time. *Proceedings of the California Academy of Sciences* 6:50–66.

Broughton, Jack. 1994. Declines in mammalian foraging efficiency during the Late Holocene, San Francisco Bay, California. *Journal of Anthropological Archaeology* 13:371–401.

Brown, Steven. 1998. *Native visions: Evolution in Northwest Coast art from the eighteenth through the twentieth centuries.* Seattle: Seattle Art Museum and University of Washington Press.

Bryan, Alan. 1992. An appraisal of the archaeological resources of the Yale Reservoir on the Lewis River, Washington. *Archaeology in Washington* 4:61–69.

Bunnell, Clarence. 1933. *Legends of the Klickitats: A Klickitat version of the story of the Bridge of the Gods.* Portland: Metropolitan.

Burton, Carla, Nancy Turner, and Cecil Brown. 2007. Sharing innovation: Soapberry (*Shepherdia Canadensis*) indigenous use and cultural value in Northwestern North America. Paper, annual meeting, Society of Ethnobiology, Berkeley, CA.

Busch, Briton, and Barry Gough, eds. 1997. *Fur traders from New England: The Boston men in the North Pacific, 1787–1800.* Spokane, WA: Arthur H. Clark.

Bushnell, David. 1938. *Drawings by George Gibbs in the Far Northwest, 1849–1851.* Smithsonian Miscellaneous Collections 97(8).

Butler, B. Robert. 1957. Art of the Lower Columbia Valley. *Archaeology* 10:158–65.

———. 1959. Lower Columbia Valley archaeology: A survey and appraisal of some major archaeological sources. *Tebiwa* 2(2):6–24.

———. 1960. The physical stratigraphy of Wakemap Mound: A new interpretation. MA thesis, University of Washington.

———. 1965. Perspectives on the prehistory of the Lower Columbia Valley. *Tebiwa* 8(1):1–16.

Butler, Virginia. 1987. Fish remains. In *Duwamish No. 1 site: 1986 data recovery,* ed. URS Corporation and BOAS, 10.1–10.37. Contract No. CW/F2–82, Task 48.08. Seattle, WA.

———. 1992. Fish remains from the Meier Site. Data reporting results from excavation units S30–32/E30–32 and S12–14/E20–22. Unpublished.

———. 1993. Natural versus cultural salmonid remains: Origin of The Dalles Roadcut bones, Columbia River, Oregon, USA. *Journal of Archaeological Science* 20:1–24.

———. 1996. Fish remains from 35MU105. In *Data recovery excavations at the Columbia Slough site (35MU105), Multnomah County, Oregon,* Appendix B. Archaeological Investigations Northwest Report No. 121.

———. 1998. Fish remains from 35MU112. In *Cultural resource survey and archaeological test excavations for the proposed Pacific gateway storm sewer extension project, Portland, OR,* Appendix C. Archaeological Investigations Northwest Report No. 159.

———. 2000a. Resource depression on the Northwest Coast of North America. *Antiquity* 74:649–61.

———. 2000b. Faunal remains from 35MU117. In *Cultural resource survey for the proposed Wapato corrections facility and data recovery excavations at 35MU117,* Appendix B. Archaeological Investigations Northwest Report No. 205.

———. 2002a. Fish remains from Cathlapotle: Preliminary report. Available at the Department of Anthropology, Portland State University.

———. 2002b. Report on fish bone from 35MU119. In *Archaeological excavations at 35MU119, Portland, Oregon,* Appendix B. Archaeological Investigations Northwest Report No. 243.

———. 2004. Where have all the Native fish gone? The fate of the fish Lewis and

Clark encountered on the Lower Columbia River. *Oregon Historical Quarterly* 105(3):438–63.

———. 2005. Fish remains from the St. Johns site. In *Archaeological excavations at the St. Johns site (35MU44/46), Portland, Oregon*, ed. Richard Pettigrew, H1–H30. Seattle: Cascadia Archaeology.

———. 2007. Relic hunting, archaeology, and the loss of Native American heritage at The Dalles. *Oregon Historical Quarterly* 108(4):624–43.

———. 2009. White sturgeon (*Acipenser transmontanus*) fish comparative collection photographs. http://web.pdx.edu/~virginia/white_sturgeon//white_sturgeon.htm.

Butler, Virginia, and Sarah Campbell. 2004. Resource intensification and resource depression in the Pacific Northwest of North America: A zooarchaeological review. *Journal of World Prehistory* 18(4):327–405.

Butler, Virginia, and Michael Delacorte. 2004. Doing zooarchaeology as if it mattered: Use of faunal data to address current issues in fish conservation biology in Owens Valley, California. In *Zooarchaeology and conservation biology*, ed. R. Lee Lyman and Ken Cannon, 25–44. Salt Lake City: University of Utah Press.

Butler, Virginia, and Jim O'Conner. 2004. 9,000 years of fishing on the Columbia River. *Quaternary Research* 62(1):1–8.

Butler, Virginia, Kris Bovy, and R. Lee Lyman. 2009. Faunal remains from Station Camp (45PC105). In *Historical archaeology at the Middle Village: Station Camp/ McGowan site (45PC106), Station Camp unit Lewis and Clark National Park, Pacific County, Washington*. Northwest Cultural Resources Institute Report No. 1.

Byers, David, and Andrew Ugan. 2005. Should we expect large game specialization in the Late Pleistocene? An optimal foraging perspective on Early Paleoindian prey choice. *Journal of Archaeological Science* 32(11):1624–40.

Byram, Scott. 1998. Fishing weirs in Oregon Coast estuaries. In *Hidden dimensions: The cultural significance of wetland archaeology*, ed. Kathryn Bernick, 199–219. Vancouver: University of British Columbia Press.

Byram, Scott, and David G. Lewis. 2003. Ourigan: Wealth of the Northwest Coast, *Oregon Historical Quarterly* 102(2):126–57.

Campbell, Sarah. 1989. Postcolumbian culture history in the northern Columbia Plateau, AD 1500–1900. PhD diss., University of Washington.

Cannon, Michael, and David Meltzer. 2004. Early Paleoindian foraging: Examining the faunal evidence for large mammal specialization and regional variability in prey choice. *Quaternary Science Review* 23:1955–87.

Carlson, Keith, and Albert Jules McHalsie. 2001. *A Sto:lo–Coast Salish historical atlas.* Vancouver, BC, and Seattle: Douglas and McIntyre, Sto:lo Heritage Trust, University of Washington Press.

Carlson, Roy. 1982. *Indian art traditions of the Northwest Coast.* Burnaby, BC: Simon Fraser University.

———. 1994. Trade and exchange in prehistoric British Columbia. In *Prehistoric exchange systems in North America*, ed. Timothy Baugh and Jonathan Ericson, 307–36. New York: Plenum.

Carver, Deborah. 1998. *Native stories of earthquakes and tsunamis, Redwood National Park, California.* Report prepared for National Park Service, Redwood National and State Parks, Crescent City, CA.

Casteel, Richard. 1972. Some biases in the recovery of archaeological faunal remains. *Proceedings of the Prehistoric Society* 38:382–88.

———. 1976. Fish remains from Glenrose. In *The Glenrose Cannery site*, ed. R. G. Matson, 82–87. Mercury Series 52. Ottawa, ONT: National Museum of Man.

Chatters, James, and Kenneth Reid. 1997. Final report on archaeological investigations of the Camas Meadows and Camas Meadows east properties, Clark County, Washington. Project Report C-9, Applied Paleoscience, Bothell, Washington.

Chinuk Wawa Dictionary Project. 2012. *Chinuk Wawa kakwa nsayka ulmantilixam łaska munk-kəmtəks nsayka/Chinuk Wawa as our elders teach us to speak it.* Grand Ronde, OR: Confederated Tribes of the Grand Ronde Community of Oregon.

Clark, Ella. 1953. *Indian legends of the Pacific Northwest.* Berkeley: University of California Press.

Clark, Robert C. 1927. *History of the Willamette Valley, Oregon.* 3 vols. Chicago: S. J. Clarke.

Clark, Ross. 2005. Nootka jargon: Evidence from the earliest vocabularies. Unpublished ms. in possession of Ross Clark, Linguistics Department, University of Auckland, New Zealand.

Clarke, Samuel Asahel. 1905. *Pioneer days of Oregon history.* 2 vols. Portland: J. K. Gill.

Clayton, Daniel. 2000. *Islands of truth: The imperial fashioning of Vancouver Island.* Vancouver: University of British Columbia Press.

Cleveland, Greg. 1995. Letter to Yakama official, June 5.

Clewlow, C. William, Jr., Patrick Hallinan, and Richard Ambro. 1971. Crisis in archaeology. *American Antiquity* 36(4):472–73.

Close, David, et al. 2001. *Pacific lamprey research and restoration project.* Portland, OR: Bonneville Power Administration.

Close, David, Martin Fitzpatrick, and Hiram Li. 2002. The ecological and cultural importance of a species at risk of extinction, Pacific lamprey. *Fisheries* 27(7):19–25.

Close, David, et al. 2004. Traditional ecological knowledge of Pacific lamprey (*Entosphenus tridentatus*) in northeastern Oregon and southeastern Washington from indigenous peoples of the Confederated Tribes of the Umatilla Indian Reservation. *Journal of Northwest Anthropology* 28(2):141–62.

Coan, Charles. 1921. The first stage of federal Indian policy in the Pacific Northwest, 1849–1852. *Oregon Historical Quarterly* 22(1):46–89.

———. 1922. The adoption of the reservation policy in the Pacific Northwest, 1853–1855. *Oregon Historical Quarterly* 23(1):1–38.

Cohen, Faye. 1986. *Treaties on trial: The continuing controversy over Northwest Indian fishing rights.* Seattle: University of Washington Press.

Cohen, Mark. 1981. Pacific Coast foragers: Affluent or overcrowded? In *Affluent foragers: Pacific Coasts east and west*, ed. Shuzo Koyama and David Thomas, 275–95. Osaka, Japan: National Museum of Ethnology.

Cole, Douglas. 1999. *Franz Boas: The early years, 1858–1906.* Seattle: University of Washington Press.

Cole, Douglas, and David Darling. 1990. History of the early period. In *Handbook of North American Indians*, vol. 7: *Northwest Coast*, ed. Wayne Suttles, 119–34. Washington, DC: Smithsonian.

Collins, Michael. 2007. Discerning Clovis subsistence from stone artifacts and site distributions on the Southern Plains periphery. In *Foragers of the terminal Pleistocene in North America*, ed. Renee Walker and Boyce Driskell, 59–87. Lincoln: University of Nebraska Press.

Colton, Roger. 2002. Prehistoric mammal hunting in context. *International Journal of Osteoarchaeology* 12(1):12–22.

Columbia River Inter-Tribal Fish Commission (CRITFC). 1986. Columbia River treaty fishing: A special report to tribal members. *CRITFC News,* September–December.

Colwell-Chanthaphonh, Chip, and T. J. Ferguson, eds. 2007. *Collaboration in archaeological practice: Engaging descendant communities.* Walnut Creek, CA: Altamira.

Condon, Thomas. 1969. Geological notes from Oregon. *Overland Monthly* 3(4):355–60.

Confederated Tribes of the Grand Ronde (CTGR). 2006–12. Upstream migrating Pacific lamprey in the Willamette Basin.

Connolly, Thomas. 1992. *Human responses to change in coastal geomorphology and fauna on the southern Northwest Coast: Archaeological investigations at Seaside, Oregon.* University of Oregon Anthropological Paper 45.

———. 1995. Archaeological evidence for a former bay at Seaside, Oregon. *Quaternary Research* 43(3):362–69.

———. 1999. *Newberry Crater: A ten-thousand-year record of human occupation and environmental change in the Basin-Plateau borderlands.* University of Oregon Anthropological Paper 121.

———. 2000. Anthropological and archaeological perspectives on Native fire management in the Willamette Valley. Paper, annual meeting, American Association for the Advancement of Science, Pacific Division, Ashland, OR.

Connolly, Thomas J., Paul Baxter, Craig Skinner. 2011. Ancient obsidian trade routes in the Pacific Northwest. Paper presented at the 2011 Annual Meeting of the Society for American Archaeology in Sacramento, California.

Cook, Warren. 1973. *Flood tide of empire: Spain and the Pacific Northwest, 1543–1819.* New Haven, CN: Yale University Press.

Cooper, James, et al. 1859. *The natural history of Washington Territory.* New York: Bailliere Bros.

Corney, Peter. 1965. *Early voyages in the North Pacific, 1813–1818.* Fairfield, WA: Ye Galleon Press.

Cove, John. 1978. Survival or extinction: Reflections on the problem of famine in Tsimshian and Kaguru mythology. In *Extinction and survival in human populations,* ed. Charles Laughlin and Ivan Brady, 231–44. New York: Columbia University Press.

Cox, Ross. 1957 [1831]. *The Columbia River, or scenes and adventures,* ed. Edgar Stewart and Jane Stewart. Norman: University of Oklahoma Press.

Cramer, Renee. 2005. *Cash, color, and colonialism: The politics of tribal acknowledgement.* Norman: University of Oklahoma Press.

Crawford, Ailsa. 1983. Tillamook Indian basketry: Continuity and change as seen in the Adams collection. MA thesis, Portland State University.

Cressman, Luther, et al. 1960. Cultural sequences at The Dalles, Oregon: A contribution to Pacific Northwest prehistory. *Transactions of the American Philosophical Society* 50(10).

Cristancho, Sergio, and Joanne Vining. 2004. Culturally defined keystone species. *Human Ecology Review* 11(2):153–64.

Croes, Dale. *The Hoko River archaeological site complex: The wet/dry site (450a213), 3,000–1,700 BP.* Pullman: Washington State University Press.

Croes, Dale, John Fagan, and Maureen Zehendner, eds. 2007. *Evaluation of archae-*

ological site 35MU4, the Sunken Village site, Multnomah County, Oregon. Olympia and Portland: South Puget Sound Community College and Archaeological Investigations Northwest.

————. 2009. Sunken Village, Sauvie Island, Oregon USA: A report on the 2006–2007 investigations of National Historic Landmark wet site 35MU4. Special issue. *Journal of Wetland Archaeology* 9.

Cromwell, Robert J. 2010. *A typological analysis of the historic ceramic ware sherds recovered from the Cathlapotle (45CL1) site and the Meier (35CO5) site*. Report on File, Portland State University.

Crosby, Alfred. 1972. *The Columbian exchange: Biological and cultural consequences of 1492*. Westport, CN: Greenwood.

Cullis-Suzuki, Severn, et al. 2006. An ethnobotanical study of the Kwakwaka'wakw traditional harvesting of Ts'ats'ayen, the eelgrass *Zostera marina* L., Zosteraceae. Paper, annual conference, Society of Ethnobiology, University Park, PA.

Curtis, Edward. ca. 1910. The North American Indian. Mss., Vols. 8–9, GC 1143, Box 8, folder 8.15, Seaver Center for Western History Research, Natural History Museum of Los Angeles County.

————. 1970 [1911]. The Chinookan tribes, the Wishram, and Chinook and Kathlamet vocabularies. In *The North American Indian*, Vol. 8, 85–154, 172–83, 198–205. Norwood, MA: Plimpton.

————. 1913. Cowlitz villages. In *The North American Indian*, Vol. 9, 172–73. Norwood, MA: Plimpton.

Cutright, Paul. 1969. *Lewis and Clark: Pioneering naturalists*. Urbana: University of Illinois Press.

Daehnke, Jon. 2007. A "strange multiplicity" of voices: Heritage stewardship, contested sites and colonial legacies on the Columbia River. *Journal of Social Archaeology* 7:250–75.

————. 2008. Utilization of space and the politics of place: Changing pathways, persistent places and contested memory in the Portland Basin. PhD diss., University of California, Berkeley.

Daehnke, Jon, and Charles Funk. 2005. *Cathlapotle: Catching time's secrets*. Sherwood, OR: US Fish and Wildlife Service, Region 1.

Dalton, George. 1977. Aboriginal economies in stateless societies. In *Exchange systems in prehistory*, ed. Timothy Earle and Jonathon Ericson, 191–212. New York: Academic.

Darby, Melissa. 1996. Wapato for the people: An ecological approach to understanding the Native American use of *Sagittaria latifolia* on the Lower Columbia River. MA thesis, Portland State University.

———. 2005. The intensification of wapato (*Sagittaria latifolia*) by the Chinookan people of the Lower Columbia River. In *Keeping it living: Traditions of plant use and cultivation on the Northwest Coast of North America*, ed. Douglas Deur and Nancy Turner, 194–217. Seattle: University of Washington Press.

Darienzo, Mark, and Curt Peterson. 1990. Episodic tectonic subsidence of Late Holocene salt marshes, northern Oregon central Cascadia margin. *Tectonics* 9(1):1–22

———. 1995. Magnitude and frequency of subduction-zone earthquakes along the northern Oregon Coast in the past 3,000 years. *Oregon Geology* 57(1):3–12.

Davenport, T. W. 1885. Slavery question in Oregon. *The Nugget* (Chehalis, WA), November 14.

Deloria, Vine Jr., and Clifford Lytle. 1998. *The nations within: The past and future of American Indian sovereignty*. Austin: University of Texas Press.

Deloria, Vine Jr., and Raymond DeMallie, eds. 1999. *Documents of American Indian diplomacy: Treaties, agreements, and conventions, 1775–1979*. Vol. 1. Norman: University of Oklahoma Press.

Demers, Modeste, F. N. Blanchet, and L. N. St. Onge. 1871. Chinook dictionary, catechism, and hymns. Composed in 1838 & 1839 by Rt. Rev. Modeste Demers. Revised, corrected, and completed by Most Rev. F. N. Blanchet, with modifications and additions by Rev. L. N. St. Onge, missionary among the Yakamas and other Indian tribes. Montreal, QC.

DePuydt, Raymond. 1994. *Data recovery excavations from site 45PC101, Pacific County, Washington*. Eastern Washington University Reports in Archaeology and History 100–79. Archaeological and Historical Services, Cheney.

deSmet, Pierre. 1906. *Life, letters and travels of Father Pierre-Jean de Smet, S.J., 1801–1873*, ed. Hiram Chittenden. Vol. 2. New York: F. P. Harper.

Deur, Douglas. 2002. Rethinking precolonial plant cultivation on the Northwest Coast of North America. *The Professional Geographer* 54(2):140–57.

Deur, Douglas and Nancy Turner. 2005. *Keeping it living: Traditions of plant use and cultivation on the Northwest Coast of North America*. Seattle: University of Washington Press.

Diedrich, Melanie. 2007. Flora remains in 100% samples. In *Evaluation of archaeological site 35MU4, the Sunken Village site, Multnomah County, Oregon*, ed. Dale Croes, John Fagan, and Maureen Zehendner, 114–21. Olympia and Portland: South Puget Sound Community College and Archaeological Investigations Northwest.

———. 2008. Sunken Village, Sauvie's Island, flotation and screening samples from cores 5 and 6: Seed analysis. In *A U.S. National Landmark Wet Site,*

The Sunken Village site (35MU4), Portland, Oregon—The first explorations,
ed. Dale Croes, John Fagan, and Maureen Zehendner, 100–102. Olympia
and Portland: South Puget Sound Community College and Archaeological
Investigations Northwest.

Dietrich, William. 1995. *Northwest passage: The great Columbia River.* New York:
Simon and Schuster.

Dillehay, Thomas. 1997. *Monte Verde: A Late Pleistocene settlement in Chile,* vol. 2:
Paleo-environment and site context. Washington, DC: Smithsonian.

Disney, Beatrice. 2002. Interview. Chinook Nation Tribal Archives, Bay Center,
WA.

Dobyns, Henry. 1966. Estimating aboriginal American population, vol. 1: An
appraisal of techniques with a New Hemispheric estimate. *Current Anthropology* 7(4):395–416, 425–49.

Dodge, Midge. 2005. Immaculate conception and other methods for conceiving
life. Unpublished.

Dominis, John. 1827–30. Log of *Owyhee,* January 21, 1827, to October 1830. Ms 16.
California Historical Society, San Francisco.

Dongoske, Kurt, Mark Aldenderfer, and Karen Doehner, eds. 2000. *Working
together: Native Americans and archaeologists.* Washington, DC: Society for
American Archaeology.

Douglas, David. 1904. Sketch of a journey to the northwestern parts of the continent of North America. *Oregon Historical Quarterly* 5(3).

———. 1905. Sketch of a journey to the northwestern parts of the continent of
North America. *Oregon Historical Quarterly* 6(1).

———. 1959. *Journal kept by David Douglas during his travels in North America,
1823–1827.* New York: Antiquarian.

Douglas, Mary. 1967. Primitive rationing. In *Themes in economic anthropology,*
ed. Raymond Firth, 119–47. ASA Monograph No. 6. London: Tavistock.

Douglas, Mary, and Baron Isherwood. 1996. *The world of goods: Towards an anthropology of consumption.* Rev. ed. New York: Routledge.

Driver, Harold. 1961. *Indians of North America.* Chicago: University of Chicago Press.

Drucker, Philip. 1933–54. Phillip Drucker Papers, National Anthropological Archives,
Smithsonian, Washington, DC.

———. 1934. Clackamas notes from John Wacheno, July 25, 1934, Grand Ronde,
Oregon. Melville Jacobs Collection, Box 119.24, 66.24, University of Washington Library Special Collections, Seattle.

———. 1937. *The Tolowa and their southwest Oregon kin.* University of California
Publications in American Archaeology and Enthology, 26:221–99.

———. 1965. *Cultures of the North Pacific Coast*. San Francisco: Chandler.

Drury, Clifford. 1963. *First white women over the Rockies: Diaries, letters, and biographical sketches of the six women of the Oregon Mission*. Vol. 1. Glendale, CA: A. H. Clark.

DuBois, Cora. 1936. The wealth concept as an integrative factor in Tolowa-Tututni culture. *Essays in anthropology presented to A.L. Kroeber*, ed. Robert Lowie, 49–65. Berkeley: University of California Press.

———. 1938. *The Feather cult of the Middle Columbia*. General Series in Anthropology 7. Menasha, WI: George Banta.

Duff, Wilson. 1956. *Prehistoric stone sculpture of the Fraser River and Gulf of Georgia*. Anthropology in British Columbia 5. Victoria: British Columbia Provincial Museum.

———. 1985. *Images, stone, B.C: Thirty centuries of Northwest Coast Indian sculpture*. Saanichton, BC: Hancock House.

Duflot de Mofras, Eugene. 1937. Travels on the Pacific Coast, Marguerite Wilbur. Santa Ana, CA: Fine Arts Press.

Dunn, J. R. 1846. Journal on H.M.S. *Fisgard*. Public Record Office, Adm. 101/100.4 XC A/3930, Kew, Surrey, England.

Dunn, John. 1844. *History of the Oregon Territory and British North American Fur Trade*. London: Edwards and Hughes.

Dunnell, Robert, James C. Chatters, and Lawr Salo. 1973. *Archaeological survey of the Vancouver Lake–Lake River area, Clark County, Washington*. Report prepared for the US Army Corps of Engineers, Portland District, Department of Anthropology, University of Washington, Seattle.

Dunnell, Robert, and Charlotte Beck. 1979. *The Caples site, 45SA5, Skamania County, Washington*. University of Washington Reports in Archaeology No. 6, Seattle.

Dunnell, Robert, and Sarah Campbell. 1977. *History of aboriginal occupation of Hamilton Island, Washington*. University of Washington Reports in Archaeology No. 4, Seattle.

Dupris, Joseph, Kathleen Hill, and William Rodgers. 2006. *The Si'lailo way: Indians, salmon and law on the Columbia River*. Durham, NC: Carolina Academic Press

Ecotrust. 2001. Elakha Alliance. http://www.ecotrust.org/nativeprograms/elakha .html.

Eells, Myron. 1889. The Stone Age of Oregon. In *Annual report of the Smithsonian Institution for the year 1885*, 283–45, Washington, D.C.

———. 1893. A dictionary of the Chinook-Jargon language. Ms., Whitman College Library, Walla Walla, WA.

———. 1894. The Chinook Jargon. *American Anthropologist* 7:300–12.

Elliott, T. C., ed. 1914. Journal of David Thompson. *Oregon Historical Quarterly* 15:39–63.

Ellis, David. 1992. Data recovery excavations at 35MU29/32, Gresham, OR. Submitted to Scientific Resources. Copy on file US Army Corps of Engineers, Portland District.

———. 1996. *Data recovery excavations at the Columbia Slough site (35MU105), Multnomah County, Oregon*. Report No. 121, Archaeological Investigations Northwest, Portland.

———. 1998. *Cultural resource survey and archaeological test excavations for the proposed Pacific gateway storm sewer extension project, Portland, Oregon*. Report No. 159, Archaeological Investigations Northwest, Portland.

———. 2000. *Cultural resource survey for the proposed corrections facility and data recovery excavations at 35MU117, Portland, Oregon*. Report No. 205, Archaeological Investigations Northwest, Portland.

———. 2006. Of a more temporary cast: Household production at the Broken Tops site. In *Household archaeology on the Northwest Coast*, ed. Elizabeth Sobel, Ann Trieu Gahr, and Kenneth Ames, 120–39. Archaeological Series 16. Ann Arbor: International Monographs in Prehistory.

Ellis, David, and John Fagan. 1993. *Data recovery excavations at Broken Tops site (35MU57), Portland, Oregon*. Report No. 31, Archaeological Investigations Northwest, Portland.

Ellis, David, and Maureen Zehendner. 2002. *Archaeological excavations at 35MU119, Portland, Oregon*. Report No. 243, Archaeological Investigations Northwest, Portland.

Elmendorf, William. 1960. *The structure of Twana culture*. Monographic Supplement 2, Washington State University Research Studies, Pullman.

———. 1971. Coast Salish status ranking and intergroup ties. *Southwestern Journal of Anthropology* 27(4):353–80.

———. 1992. *Twana narratives*. Seattle: University of Washington Press.

Endzweig, Pamela. 1989. Of pots, pipes, and people: Prehistoric ceramics of Oregon. In *Contributions to the archaeology of Oregon, 1987–88*, ed. Rick Minor, 157–77. Association of Oregon Archaeologists Occasional Paper No. 4.

Erlandson, Jon, Robert Losey, and Neil Peterson. 2001. Early maritime contact on the northern Oregon Coast: Some notes on the 17th century Nehalem beeswax ship. In *Changing landscapes: Telling our stories*, ed. Jason Younker, Mark Tveskov, and David G. Lewis, 45–53. North Bend, OR: Coquille Indian Tribe.

Ermatinger, Francis. 1980. *Fur trade letters of Francis Ermatinger,* ed. Lois Halliday McDonald. Glendale, CA: Arthur H. Clark.

Eschmeyer, William N., and Earl S. Herald. 1983. *A field guide to Pacific Coast fishes: North America.* Boston: Houghton Mifflin.

Fagan, Brian. 2005. *Ancient North America: The archaeology of a continent.* 4th ed. New York: Thames and Hudson.

Farr, Ruth, and David Ward. 1993. Fishes of the lower Willamette River, near Portland, Oregon. *Northwest Science* 67(1):16–22.

Farrand, Livingston. ca. 1905. Chinook [group names in Franz Boas's hand]. Records of the Bureau of American Ethnology, Series 1, Correspondence, Letters Received, 1888–1906, Box 100. Ms. in National Anthropological Archives, Smithsonian, Washington, DC.

———. 1907. Articles on Chinook, Clatsop, Kathlamet, and Wahkiakum. In *Handbook of American Indians north of Mexico,* ed. Frederick Hodge. 2 vols. Bureau of American Ethnology Bulletin 30.

Fenn, Elizabeth. 2001. *Pox Americana: The great smallpox epidemic of 1775–82.* New York: Hill and Wang.

Fisher, Andrew. 2010. *Shadow tribe: The making of Columbia River Indian identity.* Seattle: University of Washington Press.

Fixico, Donald. 1986. *Termination and relocation: Federal Indian policy, 1945–1960.* Albuquerque: University of New Mexico Press.

Fladmark, Knut. 1975. *A Paleoecological model for Northwest Coast prehistory.* Mercury Series 43, Archaeological Survey of Canada Paper, Ottawa.

Foote, Oscar. 1891. Agreement between 69 Cascade Indians and attorney Oscar Foote, October 22. Copy in Chuck Williams's possession.

Ford, Richard. 2001. Ethnobiology at a crossroads. In *Ethnobiology at the millenium: Past promise and future prospects,* ed. Richard Ford, 1–9. Ann Arbor: University of Michigan Museum of Anthropology.

Foreman, Cam, and Dave Foreman. 1977. *Herzog (45CL11).* Publication 3, Oregon Archaeological Society, Portland.

Fortuine, Robert. 1989. *Chills and fever: Health and disease in the early history of Alaska.* Fairbanks: University of Alaska Press.

Foster, Michael. 1996. Language and the culture history of North America. In *Handbook of North American Indians,* vol. 17: *Languages,* ed. Ives Goddard, 64–110. Washington, DC: Smithsonian.

Fowler, Kay. 2010. What's in a name? Southern Paiute place names as keys to landscape perception. In *Landscape ethnoecology: Concepts of biotic and physical space,* ed. Leslie Johnson and Eugene Hunn, 241–51. Oxford, NY: Bergahn Books.

Frachtenberg, Leo. 1920. *Alsea texts and myths*. Bureau of American Ethnology Bulletin 67.

Franchère, Gabriel. 1967 [1820]. *Relation d'un voyage à la cote du Nord-ouest de L'Amerique Septentrionale, dans les années 1810, 11, 12, 13, et 14*. Montreal: C. B. Pasteur.

———. 1969 [1854]. *Journal of a voyage on the North West Coast of North America during the years 1811, 1812, 1813, and 1814*, ed. and trans. W. Kaye and Wessie Lamb. Toronto: Champlain Society.

Frederick, S. Gay. 2007. Report on the fish faunal remains from the Meier site, 35CO5, Oregon. On file, Laboratory of Archaeology and Anthropology, Portland State University.

———. 2009. Report on Meier (35CO5) and Cathlapotle (45CL1) archaeological bird remains. On file, Wapato Valley Archaeological Project, Portland State University.

French, David. 1961. Wasco-Wishram. In *Perspectives in American Indian culture change*, ed. Edward Spicer, 337–430. Chicago: University of Chicago Press.

———. 1999. Aboriginal control of huckleberry yield in the Northwest. In *Indians, fire, and the land in the Pacific Northwest*, ed. Robert Boyd, 31–35. Corvallis: Oregon State University Press.

French, David, and Kathrine French. 1998. Wasco, Wishram, and Cascades. In *Handbook of North American Indians*, vol. 12: *Plateau*, ed. Deward Walker, 360–77. Washington, DC: Smithsonian.

French, Kathrine. 1955. Culture segments and variation in contemporary social ceremonialism on the Warm Springs Reservation, Oregon. PhD diss., Columbia University.

Frey, Rodney. 1999. *Stories that make the world: Oral literature of the Indian peoples of the inland Northwest*. Norman: University of Oklahoma Press.

Frey, Rodney, and Dell Hymes. 1998. Mythology. In *Handbook of North American Indians*, vol. 12: *Plateau*, ed. Deward Walker, 584–99. Washington, DC: Smithsonian.

Friday, Chris. 2003. *Lelooska: The life of a Northwest Coast artist*. Seattle: University of Washington Press.

Fried, Morton. 1967. *The evolution of political society*. New York: Random House.

———. 1978. *The concept of tribe*. Menlo Park, CA: Cummings.

Froese, Rainer, and Daniel Pauly, eds. 2009. FishBase. www.fishbase.org.

Frost, Joseph. 1934. Journal of John [*sic*] H. Frost, 1840–43, ed. Nellie Pipes. *Oregon Historical Quarterly* 35:50–73, 139–67, 235–62, 348–75.

Fuld, Kristen. 2011. The technological role of bone and antler tools on the Lower

Columbia River: A comparison of two contact period sites. MA thesis, Portland State University.

Fulton, Leonard. 1968. *Spawning areas and abundance of chinook salmon* (Oncorhynchus tshawytscha) *in the Columbia River Basin—past and present.* US Fish and Wildlife Service Special Scientific Report—Fisheries No. 571, Washington, DC.

———. 1970. *Spawning areas and abundance of steelhead trout and coho, sockeye, and chum salmon in the Columbia River Basin—past and present.* National Marine Fisheries Service Special Scientific Report—Fisheries No. 618, Washington, DC.

Gairdner, Meredith. 1841. Notes on the geography of the Columbia River. *Journal of the Royal Geographical Society* 11:250–57.

Galm, Jerry. 1994. Prehistoric trade and exchange in the interior Plateau of northwestern North America. In *Prehistoric exchange systems in North America,* ed. Timothy Baugh and Jonathan Ericson, 275–306. New York: Plenum.

Gamble, Lynn. 2008. *The Chumash world at European contact: Power, trade, and feasting among complex hunter-gatherers.* Berkeley: University of California Press.

Garibaldi, Ann, and Nancy Turner. 2004. Cultural keystone species: Implications for ecological conservation and restoration. *Ecology and Society* 9(3):1.

Gardner-O'Kearny, William. 2010. Hearth features at the Meier and Cathlapotle archaeological sites. MA thesis, Portland State University.

Gardner, Ray. 2002. Interview. Chinook Nation Tribal Archives, Bay Center, WA.

Gary, George. 1923. Diary of Rev. George Gary, ed. Charles Carey. *Oregon Historical Quarterly* 24:68-105, 152-85, 269-333, 386-433.

Gaston, Joseph. 1912. *The centennial history of Oregon, 1811–1912.* Chicago: S. J. Clarke.

Gatschet, Albert. 1877a. Clackamas vocabulary. Ms. 268, National Anthropological Archives, Smithsonian, Washington, DC.

———. 1877b. Nestucca Tillamook vocabulary, with Wacanassisi Chinookan additions. Ms. 727, National Anthropological Archives, Smithsonian, Washington, DC.

Gibbs, George. 1851. January, census of the Chinook tribe of Indians and census of the Clatsop tribe of Indians. Records of the Oregon Superintendency of Indian Affairs, 1848–73, National Archives, Washington, DC.

———. 1853-56. Indian nomenclature of localities in Washington and Oregon territories. Ms. 714, National Anthropological Archives, Smithsonian, Washington, DC.

———. 1855. Report of Mr. George Gibbs to Captain McClellan, on the Indian tribes of the Territory of Washington. In *Reports of Exploration and Surveys . . . from the Mississippi River to the Pacific Ocean*. Vol. 1. 33d cong., 2d sess., H. Ex. Doc. 91, serial 736, 402–49, Washington, DC.

———. 1863a. A dictionary of the Chinook Jargon, or trade language of Oregon. Smithsonian Miscellaneous Collections 161, Washington, DC.

———. 1863b. *Alphabetical dictionary of the Chinook language*. New York: Cramoisy.

———. 1877. Tribes of western Washington and northwestern Oregon. *Contributions to North American Ethnology* 1:157–241.

———. 1955–56. George Gibbs' account of Indian mythology in Oregon and Washington territories, ed. Ella E. Clark. *Oregon Historical Quarterly* Part I: 56(4):293-325; Part II: 57(2):125-67.

Gibson, James. 1992. *Otter skins, Boston ships, and China goods: The maritime fur trade of the Northwest Coast, 1785–1841*. Seattle: University of Washington Press.

———. 1997. *The lifeline of the Oregon Country: The Fraser-Columbia brigade system, 1811–1847*. Vancouver: University of British Columbia Press.

Gidley, Mick. 2003. *Edward S. Curtis and the North American Indian project in the field*. Lincoln: University of Nebraska Press.

Gilbert, M. Thomas, et al. 2008. DNA from pre-Clovis human coprolites in Oregon, North America. *Science* 320(5877):786–89.

Gill, Steven. 1985. Indigenous food plants of the Lower Columbia River and Willapa Bay. Paper, annual meeting, Northwest Anthropological Association, Ellensburg, WA.

Goebel, Ted, Michael Waters, and Dennis O'Rourke. 2008. The Late Pleistocene dispersal of modern humans in the Americas. *Science* 319:1497–1502.

Gottesfeld, Leslie. 1994. Conservation, territory, and traditional beliefs: An analysis of Gitksan and Wet'suwet'en subsistence, Northwest British Columbia, Canada. *Human Ecology* 22(4):443–65.

Gould, Richard. 1966. The wealth quest among the Tolowa Indians of northwestern California. *Proceedings of the American Philosophical Society* 110(1):67–89.

Gramly, Robert. 1993. *The Richey Clovis cache: Earliest Americans along the Columbia River*. Buffalo: Persimmon.

Grant, Anthony. 1996. Chinook Jargon and its distribution in the Pacific Northwest and beyond. In *Atlas of intercultural communication in the Pacific, Asia, and the Americas*, ed. Stephen Wurm, Peter Muhlausler, and Darrel Tryon, 1185–1208. Amsterdam: Mouton de Gruyter.

Gray, William. 1870. *A history of Oregon, 1792–1849*. Portland: Harris and Holman.

Grayson, Donald. 1984. *Quantitative zooarchaeology: Topics in the analysis of archaeological faunas*. Orlando, FL: Academic Press.

Grier, Colin. 2006. Temporality in Northwest Coast households. In *Household archaeology on the Northwest Coast*, ed. Elizabeth Sobel, D. Ann Trieu Gahr, and Kenneth Ames, 97–119. Ann Arbor: International Monographs in Prehistory.

Griswold, Gillett. 1970 [1954]. Aboriginal patterns of trade between the Columbia Basin and the Northern Plains. *Archaeology in Montana* 11(2–3):1–96.

Gunther, Erna. 1928. A further analysis of the First Salmon ceremony. *University of Washington Publications in Anthropology* 2(5):129–73.

———. 1972. *Indian life on the Northwest Coast of North America*. Chicago: University of Chicago Press.

———. 1973 [1945]. *Ethnobotany of western Washington*. Rev. ed. Seattle: University of Washington Press.

Habu, Junko. 2004. *Ancient Jomon of Japan*. Cambridge: Cambridge University Press.

Haines, Francis. 1938. The northward spread of horses among the Plains Indians. *American Anthropologist* 40(3):429–37.

Hajda, Yvonne. 1977–80. Chinuk Wawa data from members of the Grand Ronde Community, Oregon. Duplicate in Cultural Resources archives, Confederated Tribes of Grand Ronde, Grand Ronde, Oregon.

———. 1984. Regional social organization in the Greater Lower Columbia, 1792–1830. PhD diss., University of Washington.

———. 1987. Exchange spheres on the Greater Lower Columbia. Paper, annual meeting, American Anthropological Association, Chicago.

———. 1990. Southwestern Coast Salish. In *Handbook of North American Indians*, vol. 7: *Northwest Coast*, ed. Wayne Suttles, 503–17. Washington, DC: Smithsonian.

———. 1994. Notes on Indian houses of the Wappato Valley. *Northwest Anthropological Research Notes* 28(2):177–88.

———. 2005. Slavery in the Greater Lower Columbia region. *Ethnohistory* 52(3):563–88.

Hajda, Yvonne, Kathrine French, and David Ellis. 2004. *Willamette Falls hydroelectric project FERC no. 2233*. Archaeological Investigations Northwest Report No. 249.

Hale, Horatio. 1846. *Ethnography and philology*, vol. 6: *Narrative of the US Exploring Expedition during the years 1838–42*, ed. Charles Wilkes. Philadelphia: Lea and Blanchard.

———. 1890. *An international idiom: A manual of the Oregon trade language, or "Chinook Jargon."* London: Whittaker.

Hall, Roberta, Robert Morrow, and J. Henry Clarke. 1986. Dental pathology of prehistoric residents of Oregon. *American Journal of Physical Anthropology* 69(3):325–34.

Hannah, John. 1996. Seated human figure bowls: An investigation of a prehistoric stone carving tradition from the Northwest Coast. MA thesis, Simon Fraser University.

Harmon, Alexandra. 1998. *Indians in the making: Ethnic relations and Indian identities around Puget Sound.* Berkeley: University of California Press.

———. 2008. *The power of promises: Rethinking Indian treaties in the Pacific Northwest.* Seattle: University of Washington Press.

Harpole, Judith L. 2006. Dead deer do tell tales: Mammalian systematic paleontology and temporal variation at Cathlapotle, 45CL1, southwestern Washington. MA thesis, University of Missouri, Columbia.

Harrington, John. 1942–43. Oregon Coast. Ms. 4360, mf., vol. 2, National Anthropological Archives, Smithsonian, Washington, DC.

Harris, Barbara. 1994. Chinook Jargon: Arguments for a pre-contact origin. *Pacific Coast Philology* 29(1):28–36.

Harris, R. Cole. 1994. "Voices of disaster": Smallpox around the Gulf of Georgia in 1782. *Ethnohistory* 41(4):591–626.

———. 1997. *The resettlement of British Columbia: Essays on colonialism and geographical change.* Vancouver: University of British Columbia Press.

Harrison, Kathryn. 2006. Interview with David Lewis, Grand Ronde, OR.

Hawes, Kathleen. 2007. *Woodworking debitage: Woodchip analysis of TU4. In Evaluation of archaeological site 35MU4, the Sunken Village site, Multnomah County, Oregon,* ed. Dale Croes, John Fagan, and Maureen Zehendner, 90–100. Olympia and Portland: South Puget Sound Community College and Archaeological Investigations Northwest.

———. 2008. Sunken Village National Heritage Landmark site (35MU4): Artifact plant material identification and archaeological charcoal identification and distribution-cellular analysis. In *A U.S. National Landmark Wet Site, The Sunken Village site (35MU4), Portland, Oregon—The first explorations,* ed. Dale Croes, Croes, John Fagan, and Maureen Zehendner, 77–83. Olympia and Portland: South Puget Sound Community College and Archaeological Investigations Northwest.

Hayden, Brian, and Rick Schulting. 1997 The Plateau interaction sphere and late prehistoric cultural complexity. *American Antiquity* 62(1):52–85.

Hayes, Derek. 1999. *Historical atlas of the Pacific Northwest: Maps of exploration and discovery.* Seattle: Sasquatch Books.

Hazen, Deborah Steele. 2012. Chinook Nation stops at Mayger during ceremonial voyage. *Clatskanie (OR) Chief,* June 21.

Heaney, Seamus. 2000. *Beowulf.* New York: Farrar, Straus and Giroux.

Henry, Alexander. 1992 [1814]. *The journal of Alexander Henry the Younger,* vol. 2: *The Saskatchewan and Columbia Rivers,* ed. Barry Gough. Toronto: Champlain Society.

Hewes, Gordon. 1998. Fishing. In *Handbook of North American Indians,* vol. 12: *Plateau,* ed. Deward Walker, 620–40. Washington, DC: Smithsonian.

Hinds, Richard Brinsley. 1836–42. Journal. Mss. 1524. Oregon Historical Society Research Library, Portland.

Hines, Donald. 1991. *The forgotten tribes: Oral tales of the Teninos and adjacent mid-Columbia River Indian nations.* Issaquah, WA: Great Eagle.

———. 1996. *Celilo tales: Myths, legends, tales of magic and the marvelous.* Issaquah, WA: Great Eagle.

———. 1998. *Where the river roared: The Wishom tales.* Issaquah, WA: Great Eagle.

Hines, Gustavus. 1850. *A voyage around the world with a history of the Oregon Mission.* Buffalo: George H. Derby.

Hines, Harvey. 1893. *An illustrated history of the State of Oregon.* Chicago: Lewis Publishing.

Hinrichsen, Richard. 1998. The ghost run of the Cowlitz. *Cowlitz Historical Quarterly* 40(2):5–21.

Hinton, Susan, George McCabe, and Robert Emmett. 1990. *Fishes, benthic invertebrates, and sediment characteristics in intertidal and subtidal habitats at five areas in the Columbia River estuary.* Report to the US Army Corps of Engineers, Portland District.

Hockett, Bryan, and Jonathan Haws. 2003. Nutritional ecology and diachronic trends in Paleolithic diet and health. *Evolutionary Anthropology* 12(5):211–16.

Hodge, Frederick. 1971 [1912]. *Handbook of American Indians north of Mexico.* 2 vols. New York: Rowman and Littlefield.

Hoffman, Brian, Jessica Czederpiltz, and Megan Partlow. 2000. Heads or tails: The zooarchaeology of Aleut salmon storage on Unimak Island, Alaska. *Journal of Archaeological Science* 27:699–708.

Hoffman, J. J., and Lester Ross. 1974. Fort Vancouver excavations VIII: Fur store. Report for the Fort Vancouver National Historic Site.

Hollowell-Zimmer, Julie. 2003. Digging in the dirt: Ethics and "low-end looting."

In *Ethical issues in archaeology*, ed. Larry Zimmerman, Karen Vitelli, and Julia Hallowell-Zimmer, 45-56. Walnut Creek, CA: Altamira.

Holm, Bill. 1965. *Northwest Coast Indian art: An analysis of form*. Seattle: University of Washington Press.

———. 1982. Objects of unique artistry. In *Soft gold: The fur trade and cultural exchange on the Northwest Coast of America*, ed. Thomas Vaughan and Bill Holm, 31-167. Portland: Oregon Historical Society Press.

———. 1987. The Lower Columbia people. In *Spirit and ancestor: A century of Northwest Coast Indian art at the Burke Museum*, 25-31. Seattle: Burke Museum and University of Washington Press.

Horrocks, Mark, et al. 2004. Starch grains and xylem cells of sweet potato (*Ipomoea batatas*) and bracken (*Pteridium esculentum*) in archaeological deposits from northern New Zealand. *Journal of Archaeological Science* 31(3):251-58.

Howay, Frederic. 1927. Early followers of Captain Gray. *Washington Historical Quarterly* 18(1):11-20.

———. 1933. The *Resolution* on the Oregon Coast, 1793-94. *Oregon Historical Quarterly* 34(3):207-15.

———. 1990 [1941]. *Voyages of the "Columbia" to the Northwest Coast, 1787-1790 and 1790-1793*. Portland: Oregon Historical Society Press.

———. 1943. Origin of the Chinook Jargon on the North West Coast. *Oregon Historical Quarterly* 44(1):27-55.

Howay, Frederic, and T. C. Elliott. 1929. Voyages of the "Jenny" to Oregon, 1792-94. *Oregon Historical Quarterly* 30(3):197-206.

Howison, Neil. 1913. Report of Lieutenant Neil M. Howison on Oregon, 1846. *Oregon Historical Quarterly* 14(1):1-60.

Hudson, William. 1841. Log, 1840-42. Ms., University of North Carolina Library, Chapel Hill.

Huelsbeck, David. 1994. Mammals and fish in the subsistence economy of Ozette. In *Ozette archaeological project research reports, fauna*, ed. Stephen Samuels, 17-92. Reports of Investigations 66, Department of Anthropology, Washington State University, Pullman.

Hunn, Eugene. 1980. Sahaptin fish classification. *Northwest Anthropological Research Notes* 14(1):1-19.

———. 1990. *Nch'i-wana, "the big river": Mid-Columbia Indians and their land*. Seattle: University of Washington Press.

———. 2007. Ethnobiology in four phases. *Journal of Ethnobiology* 27(1):1-10.

———. 2010. Place names as cultural artifacts. Keynote address, annual meeting, Northwest Anthropological Association, Ellensburg, WA.

Hunn, Eugene, and Brien Meilleur. 2010. Toward a theory of landscape ethno-ecological classification. In *Landscape ethnoecology: Concepts of biotic and physical space*, ed. Leslie Johnson and Eugene Hunn, 15–26. Oxford, NY: Bergahn Books.

Hunn, Eugene, et al. Forthcoming. *Chaw pawa laakni: Sahaptian place-names atlas of the Cayuse, Umatilla, and Walla Walla.* Pendleton, OR: Tamastslikt Cultural Institute.

Hunn, Eugene, Nancy Turner, and David French. 1998. Ethnobiology and sub-sistence. In *Handbook of North American Indians*, vol. 12: *Plateau*, ed. Deward Walker, 525–45. Washington, DC: Smithsonian.

Hussey, John. 1967. *Champoeg: Place of transition.* Portland: Oregon Historical Society Press.

Hutchinson, Ian, and Alan McMillan. 1997. Archaeological evidence for village abandonment associated with late Holocene earthquakes at the northern Cascadia Subduction Zone. *Quaternary Research* 48:79–87.

Hymes, Dell. 1955. The language of the Kathlamet Chinook. PhD diss., University of Indiana.

———. 1955–57. Wasco-Wishram linguistic slip-files. Ms., Archives of the American Philosophical Society, Philadelphia.

———. 1975. Folklore's nature and the Sun Myth. *Journal of American Folklore* 8:345–68.

———. 2004 [1981]. *"In vain I tried to tell you": Essays in Native American ethno-poetics.* Lincoln: University of Nebraska Press.

———. 1990. Mythology. In *Handbook of North American Indians*, vol. 7: *North-west Coast*, ed. Wayne Suttles, 593–601. Washington, DC: Smithsonian.

———. 1994. The Sun's Myth. In *Coming to light: Contemporary translations of the Native literatures of North America*, ed. Brian Swann, 273–85. New York: Random House.

———. 2003. *"Now I know only so far": Essays in ethnopoetics.* Lincoln: University of Nebraska Press.

Hymes, Dell, and Henry Zenk. 1987. Narrative structure in Chinook Jargon. In *Pidgin and Creole languages: Essays in memory of John E. Reinecke*, ed. Glen Gilbert, 445–65. Honolulu: University of Hawaii Press.

Irving, Washington. 1976 [1836]. *Astoria: Or, anecdotes of an enterprise beyond the Rocky Mountains*, ed. Richard Rust. Boston: Twayne.

Jackson, Donald, ed. 1978. *Letters of the Lewis and Clark Expedition with related documents, 1783–1854.* 2 vols. 2d ed. Urbana: University of Illinois Press.

Jacobs, Elizabeth Derr. 1933–34. Field notebook nos. 107, 113. Ms., Melville Jacobs Collection, University of Washington Special Collections, Seattle.

———. 1990 [1959]. *Nehalem Tillamook tales*. Corvallis: Oregon State University Press.

———. 2003. *The Nehalem Tillamook: An ethnography*, ed. William Seaburg. Corvallis: Oregon State University Press.

Jacobs, Melville. 1929–30. Clackamas Chinook field notebooks, based on fieldwork with Victoria Howard, West Linn, OR. Melville Jacobs Collection, University of Washington Libraries Special Collections, Seattle.

———. 1936. Texts in Chinook Jargon. *University of Washington Publications in Anthropology* 7(1):1–27.

———. 1945. Kalapuya texts. *University of Washington Publications in Anthropology* 11.

———. 1958–59. *Clackamas Chinook texts*. Part 1: Folklore and Linguistics Publication 8; Part 2: Folklore and Linguistics Publication 11. Indiana University, Bloomington.

———. 1959a. *The content and style of an oral literature: Clackamas Chinook myths and tales*. Chicago: University of Chicago Press.

———. 1959b. Folklore. In *The anthropology of Franz Boas*, ed. Walter Goldschmidt, 119–38. Memoirs of the American Anthropological Association 89.

———. 1960. *The people are coming soon: Analyses of Clackamas Chinook myths and tales*. Seattle: University of Washington Press.

———. ca. 1971. Spread of features of style in Indian oral genres in the Northwest states. Ms., Melville Jacobs Collection, University of Washington Libraries Special Collections, Seattle.

———. 1972. Areal spread of Indian oral genre features in the Northwest states. *Journal of the Folklore Institute* 9(1):1–10.

Jacoby, Gordon, Daniel Bunker, and Boyd Benson. 1997. Tree-ring evidence for an AD 1700 Cascadia earthquake in Washington and northern Oregon. *Geology* 25(11):999–1002.

Jennings, Berryman. 1855. Letter of January 30 to Joel Palmer. Oregon superintendency of Indian affairs, 1848–1873, mf reel 5:139–40, National Archives, Washington, DC.

Jermann, Jerry, Dennis Lewarch, and Sarah Campbell. 1975. Salvage excavations at the Kersting site (45CL21): A preliminary report. Reports in Highway Archaeology 2, Office of Public Archaeology, Institute for Environmental Studies, University of Washington, Seattle.

Jerzyk, Anna. 1940. Winship settlement in 1810 was Oregon's Jamestown. *Oregon Historical Quarterly* 41(3):175–81.

Johansen, Dorothy. 1957. The role of land laws in the settlement of Oregon. In *Genealogical Material in Oregon Donation Land Claims*, iii–viii. Portland, OR: Genealogical Forum of Portland.

Johansen, Dorothy, and Charles Gates. 1957. *Empire of the Columbia: A history of the Pacific Northwest*. New York: Harper Brothers.

Johnson, Jean. 2005. Chinook Nation against the wall. *Indian Country Today*, March 14.

Johnson, Leslie. 2010a. *Trail of story, traveller's path: Reflections on ethnoecology and landscape*. Edmonton, AB: Athabasca University Press.

———. 2010b. Visions of the land: Kaska ethnoecology, "kinds of place," and "cultural landscape." In *Landscape ethnoecology: Concepts of biotic and physical space*, ed. Leslie Johnson and Eugene Hunn, 203–21. Oxford, NY: Bergahn Books.

Johnson, Leslie, and Eugene Hunn, ed. 2010. *Landscape ethnoecology: Concepts of biotic and physical space*. Oxford, NY: Bergahn Books.

Johnson, Tony. 1998. Chinuk Wawa data from members of the Grand Ronde Community. Duplicates in Cultural Resources archives, Confederated Tribes of Grand Ronde, Grand Ronde, Oregon.

Jones, A. 2006. *Iqaluich Nibieaqtuat, fish that we eat*. Final Report No. FIS502–023, US Fish and Wildlife Service, Office of Subsistence Management, Fisheries Resource Monitoring Program, Anchorage, AK.

Jones, Roy. 1972. *Wappato Indians of the Lower Columbia River Valley*. Portland, OR, privately printed.

Jorgensen, Joseph. 1980. *Western Indians: Comparative environments, languages, and cultures of 172 western American Indian tribes*. San Francisco: W. H. Freeman.

Josephy, Alvin. 1965. *The Nez Perce Indians and the opening of the Northwest*. New Haven, CN: Yale University Press.

Kane, Paul. 1971a. *Paul Kane, Columbia wanderer, 1846-7*, ed. Thomas Vaughan. Portland: Oregon Historical Society Press.

———. 1971b. *Paul Kane's frontier*, ed. J. Russell Harper. Austin: University of Texas Press.

Kappler, Charles. 1903ff. *Indian affairs, laws, and treaties*. Washington, DC: Government Printing Office.

Kaufman, Terrence. 1971. A report on Chinook Jargon. In *Pidginization and Creolization of languages*, ed. Dell Hymes, 275–78. Cambridge: Cambridge University Press.

Keely, Patrick, et al. 1982. Composition of Native American fruits in the Pacific Northwest. *Journal of the Dietetic Association* 81(5):568–72.

Keith, H. Lloyd. 2008. Voyage of the *Isaac Todd*. *Oregon Historical Quarterly* 109:27–40.

Kennedy, Alexander. 1824–25. Report, Fort George District, Columbia Department. Ms. B. 76/e, Hudson's Bay Company Archives, Winnipeg.

Keyser, James. 1992. *Indian rock art of the Columbia Plateau*. Seattle: University of Washington Press.

Keyser, James, et al. 2006. The beaver bowl: Ethnographic evidence for a Northwest Coast shaman's petroglyph. In *Talking with the past: The ethnography of rock art*, ed. James Keyser, George Poetschat, and Michael Taylor, 158–75. Portland: Oregon Archaeological Society.

Kidd, Robert. 1967. The Martin site, southwest Washington. *Tebiwa* 10(2):13–38.

King, Thomas. 2004. *Cultural resource laws and practice: An introductory guide.* Walnut Creek, CA: Altamira Press.

Kinkade, M. Dale. 1991. *Upper Chehalis dictionary.* Occasional Paper in Linguistics No. 7, University of Montana, Missoula.

Kinkade, M. Dale, and Jay Powell. 2005. And now, finally, the last word on the Lower Chehalis loanwords into Chinook Jargon. Paper, Chinuk lu?lu? (Chinook Gathering), University of Victoria, BC, June 5–7.

Knutzen, John, and Rick Cardwell. 1984. *Final report for fisheries monitoring program, Vancouver Lake restoration project.* Rev. draft. Envirosphere Company for Cooper Consultants, Portland.

Koenninger, Tom. 2008. Recognition for Chinook overdue. (Vancouver, WA) *Columbian,* August 21.

Koppel, Tom. 1995. *Kanaka: The untold story of Hawaiian pioneers in British Columbia and the Pacific Northwest.* Vancouver, BC: Whitecap Books.

Kornfeld, Marcel. 2007. Are Paleoindians of the Great Plains and Rockies subsistence specialists? In *Foragers of the terminal Pleistocene in North America*, ed. Renee Walker and Boyce Driskell, 32–58. Lincoln: University of Nebraska Press.

Kroeber, Alfred. 1939. *Cultural and natural areas of Native North America.* University of California Publications in American Archaeology and Enthology 38.

———. 1943. *Franz Boas, 1858–1942.* Memoirs of the American Anthropological Association 61.

———. 1976. *Yurok myths.* Berkeley: University of California Press.

Kuhnlein, Harriet. 1989. Nutrient values in indigenous wild berries used by the Nuxalk people of Bella Coola, British Columbia. *Journal of Food Composition and Analysis* 2:28–36.

———. 1990. Nutrient values in indigenous wild green plants and roots used by the Nuxalk people of Bella Coola, British Columbia. *Journal of Food Composition and Analysis* 3:38–46.

Kuhnlein, Harriet, and Nancy Turner. 1991. *Traditional plant foods of Canadian indigenous peoples: Nutrition, botany and use.* Philadelphia: Gordon and Breach Science Publishers.

Kukla, Jon. 2003. *A wilderness so immense: The Louisiana Purchase and the destiny of America.* New York: Alfred Knoph.

Kuykendall, George. 1889. A graphic account of the religions or mythology of the Indians of the Pacific Northwest. In *History of the Pacific Northwest: Oregon and Washington*, ed. Elwood Evant, 60–95. Vol. 2. Portland: North Pacific History.

LaBelle, Jason. 2003. Coffee cans and Folsom points: Why we cannot continue to ignore the artifact collectors. In *Ethical issues in archaeology*, ed. Larry Zimmerman, Karen Vitelli, and Julia Hallowell-Zimmer, 115–28. Walnut Creek, CA: Altamira.

Lagergren, George. 2002. Interview. Chinook Nation Tribal Archives, Bay Center, WA.

Laliberte, Andrea, and William Ripple. 2003. Wildlife encounters by Lewis and Clark: A spatial analysis of interactions between Native Americans and wildlife. *Bioscience* 53(10):994–1003.

Lamson, E. F. 1891. Annual report of the commissioner of Indian affairs for the year 1891, 340–42, Washington, DC.

Landerholm, Carl, trans. and ed. 1956. *Notices and voyages of the famed Quebec mission to the Pacific Northwest.* Portland: Oregon Historical Society Press.

Lane, Barbara, and Robert Lane. 1986. *The treaty council that failed: A commentary on the proceedings of the Chehalis River treaty council.* Vienna, VA: Institute for the Development of Indian Law.

Lang, George. 2008. *Making Wawa: The founding of Chinook Jargon.* Vancouver: University of British Columbia Press.

Lang, Herbert O. 1885. *A history of the Willamette Valley.* Portland, OR: Geo. Himes.

Lang, William L. 1992. The encounter on the Columbia: An inner history of trade and its consequences. *Columbia* 6:4–9.

———. 1996. Lewis and Clark on the Columbia: Power and landscape in exploration. *Pacific Northwest Quarterly* 87:141–48.

Langdon, Steve. 2006. Tidal pulse fishing: Selective traditional Tlingit salmon fishing techniques on the West Coast of the Prince of Wales archipelago. In *Tradi-*

tional ecological knowledge and natural resource management, ed. Charles Menzies, 21–46. Lincoln: University of Nebraska Press.

Lantz, Trevor, and Nancy Turner. 2003. Traditional phenological knowledge of aboriginal peoples in British Columbia. *Journal of Ethnobiology* 23(2):263–86.

Lassuy, Dennis, and David Moran. 1989. Species profiles: Life histories and environmental requirements of coastal fishes and invertebrates (Pacific Northwest)—Pacific herring. *US Fish and Wildlife Service Biological Report* 82(11):126.

Lattie, Alexander. 1963. Fort George journal, 1846, ed. Thomas Vaughan. *Oregon Historical Quarterly* 64(2):197–245.

Layton, Thomas. 1981. Traders and raiders: Aspects of trans-basin and California-Plateau commerce, 1800–1830. *Journal of California and Great Basin Anthropology* 3(1):127–37.

Leach, Edmund. 1964. *Political systems of Highland Burma*. Monographs in Social Anthropology No. 44. London: Athlone Press.

Lee, Daniel, and Joseph Frost. 1968 [1844]. *Ten years in Oregon*. Fairfield, WA: Ye Galleon Press.

Lee, David, et al. 1980. *Atlas of North American freshwater fishes*. Raleigh: North Carolina State Museum of Natural History.

Leopold, Estella, and Robert Boyd. 1999. An ecological history of Old Prairie areas in southwestern Washington. In *Indians, fire, and the land in the Pacific Northwest*, ed. Robert Boyd, 139–63. Corvallis: Oregon State University Press.

Lepofsky, Dana. 2004. Paleoethnobotany in the Northwest. In *People and plants in ancient western North America*, ed. Paul Minnis, 367–464. Washington, DC: Smithsonian.

Lepofsky, Dana, et al. 2005. Documenting precontact plant management on the Northwest Coast. In *Keeping it living: Traditions of plant use and cultivation on the Northwest Coast of North America*, ed. Douglas Deur and Nancy Turner, 218–39. Seattle: University of Washington Press.

Lewis, Albert Buell. 1906. Tribes of the Columbia Valley and the coast of Washington and Oregon. *Memoirs of the American Anthropological Association* 1(2):147–209.

Lewis, David G. 2009. Termination of the Confederated Tribes of Grand Ronde: History, politics, identity. PhD diss., University of Oregon.

Lewis, Meriwether, and William Clark. 1988–97. *The journals of the Lewis and Clark Expedition*, ed. Gary Moulton. Vols. 5–11. Lincoln: University of Nebraska Press.

Lewis, William, and Naojiro Murakami, eds. 1923. *Ranald McDonald*. Spokane: Eastern Washington Historical Society.

Lichatowich, James. 1999. *Salmon without rivers: A history of the Pacific salmon crisis*. Washington, DC: Island Press.

Limp, W. Frederick, and Van Reidhead. 1979. An economic evaluation of the potential of fish utilization in riverine environments. *American Antiquity* 44:70–77.

Livingston, Vaughn. 1969. Geologic history and rocks and minerals of Washington. Washington Department of Natural Resources Division of Mines and Geology, Information Circular 45.

Lockley, Frederic. 1928. *History of the Columbia River Valley from The Dalles to the sea*. Vol. 1. Chicago: S.J. Clarke.

Loewenberg, Robert. 1976. *Equality on the Oregon frontier: Jason Lee and the Methodist mission, 1834–43*. Seattle: University of Washington Press.

Long, Colin, Cathy Whitlock, and Patrick Bartlein. 2007. Holocene vegetation and fire history of the Coast Range, western Oregon, USA. *Holocene* 17(7):917–26.

Loring, J. Malcolm, and Louise Loring. 1982. *Pictographs and petroglyphs of the Oregon country*, part 1: *Columbia River and northern Oregon*. Monograph 21, Institute of Archaeology, UCLA.

Losey, Robert. 2002. *Communities and catastrophe: Tillamook response to the AD 1700 earthquake and tsunami, northern Oregon Coast*. PhD diss., University of Oregon.

———. 2003. Sea-level history and the archaeology of the northern Oregon Coast: A case study from Netarts Bay. *Journal of Northwest Anthropology* 37(2):101–16.

———. 2005. Earthquakes and tsunamis as elements of environmental disturbance on the Northwest Coast of North America. *Journal of Anthropological Archaeology* 24(2):101–16.

———. 2007. Native American vulnerability and resiliency to great Cascadia earthquakes. *Oregon Historical Quarterly* 108(2):201–14.

———, ed. In prep. Recent research on the archaeology of Seaside, Oregon: The Smithsonian collections from Palmrose, Par-Tee, and Avenue Q.

Losey, Robert, and Eleanor Power. 2005. Shellfish remains from the Par-Tee site (35-CLT-20), Seaside, Oregon: Making sense of a biased sample. *Journal of Northwest Anthropology* 39(1):1–20.

Losey, Robert, and Dongya Yang. 2007. Opportunistic whale hunting on the southern Northwest Coast: Ancient DNA, artifacts, and ethnographic evidence. *American Antiquity* 72(4):657–76.

Losey, Robert, Jon Erlandson, and Madonna Moss. 2000. Assessing the impacts of Cascadia Subduction Zone earthquakes on the people and landscapes of the Northwest Coast. In *Changing landscapes: Telling our stories,* ed. Jason Younker, Mark Tveskov, and David Lewis, 124–42. North Bend, OR: Coquille Indian Tribe.

Losey, Robert, N. Stenholm, P. Whereat-Phillips, and H. Vallianatos. 2003. Exploring the use of red elderberry (*Sambucus racemosa*) fruit on the southern North-west Coast of North America. *Journal of Archaeological Science* 30(6):695–707.

Lourandos, Harry. 1997. *Continent of hunter-gatherers: New perspectives in Austra-lian prehistory.* Cambridge: Cambridge University Press.

Ludwin, Ruth, et al. 2005. Dating the AD 1700 Cascadia earthquake: Great coastal earthquakes in Native stories. *Seismological Research Letter* 76(2):140–48.

Lyman, Horace S. 1900. Indian names. *Oregon Historical Quarterly* 1(3):316–26.

———. 1900. Reminiscences of Louis LaBonte. *Oregon Historical Quarterly* 1(2):169–88.

———. 1903. *History of Oregon: The growth of an American state.* Vol. 1. New York: North Pacific Publishing Society.

———. n.d. Indian legends, Horace Lyman Papers, Mss. 722, folder 2, Oregon Historical Society Research Library, Portland.

Lyman, R. Lee. 1994a. *Vertebrate taphonomy.* New York: Cambridge University Press.

———. 1994b. Mammalian zooarchaeology of the Meier site (35CO5), Department of Anthropology, Portland State University.

———. 2003a. Mammalian zooarchaeology of Cathlapotle (45CL1): Descriptive paleontology and taphonomic analyses, Department of Anthropology, Portland State University.

———. 2003b. Pinniped behavior, foraging theory, and the depression of meta-populations and nondepression of a local population on the southern North-west Coast of North America. *Journal of Anthropological Archaeology* 22(4):376–88.

———. 2005. Descriptive mammalian, avian and reptilian zooarchaeology of 35MU44/46. In *Archaeological investigations at the St. John's site (35MU44/46), Portland, Oregon,* ed. Richard Pettigrew, Appendix. Seattle: Cascadia Archaeology.

———. 2006. Late prehistoric and early historical abundance of Columbia white-tailed deer, Portland Basin, Washington and Oregon, USA. *Journal of Wildlife Management* 70(1):278–82.

———. 2008. Quantitative paleozoology. New York: Cambridge University Press.

Lyman, R. Lee, and Michael O'Brien. 1987. Plow-zone zooarchaeology: Fragmenta-tion and identifiability. *Journal of Field Archaeology* 13:493–98.

Lyman, R. Lee, and Steve Wolverton. 2002. The late prehistoric–early historic game sink in the northwestern United States. *Conservation Biology* 16(1):73–85.

Lyman, R. Lee, and Jamey Zehr. 2003. Archaeological evidence of mountain beaver (*Aplodontia rufa*) mandibles as chisels and engravers on the Northwest Coast. *Journal of Northwest Anthropology* 22(1):35–60.

Lyman, R. Lee, J. L. Harpole, C. Darwent, and R. Church. 2002. Prehistoric occurrence of pinnipeds in the Lower Columbia River. *Northwest Naturalist* 83(1):1–6.

Lyman, William. 1909. *The Columbia River: Its history, its myths, its scenery, its commerce.* New York: G. P. Putnam.

———. 1915. Indian myths of the Northwest. *Proceedings of the American Antiquarian Society* 25:375–95.

Lynch, Vera. 1973. *Free land for free men: A story of Clackamas County.* Portland, OR: Artline Print.

MacDonald, George. 1983. *Haida monumental art: Villages of the Queen Charlotte Islands.* Vancouver: University of British Columbia Press.

Mack, Cheryl, and Rick McClure. 2002. *Vaccinium* processing in the Washington Cascades. *Journal of Ethnobiology* 22(1):35–60.

Mackey, Harold. 1968. Siuslaw head flattening. *Oregon Historical Quarterly* 69(2):171–73.

Mackie, Richard. 1997. *Trading beyond the mountains: The British fur trade on the Pacific, 1793–1843.* Vancouver: University of British Columbia Press.

Maclachlan, Morag, ed. 1998. *The Fort Langley journals.* Vancouver: University of British Columbia Press.

Malinowski, Bronislaw. 1948. *Magic, science and religion, and other essays.* New York: Anchor.

Malloy, Mary. 2007. Passing the hats: On discovering Lewis & Clark. http://lewis-clark.org/content/content-article.asp?ArticleID=2981.

Manby, Thomas. 1992. *Journal of the voyages of the H.M.S. Discovery and Chatham.* Fairfield, WA: Ye Galleon Press.

Marino, Cesare. 1990. History of western Washington since 1846. In *Handbook of North American Indians*, vol. 7: *Northwest Coast*, ed. Wayne Suttles, 169–79. Washington, DC: Smithsonian.

Marquardt, William. 2001. The emergence and demise of the Calusa. In *Societies in eclipse: Archaeology of the eastern woodlands*, ed. David Brose, C. Wesley Cowan, and Robert Mainfort, 157–71. Washington, DC: Smithsonian.

Marr, John. 1941. NAA sound recordings nos. 682–696, National Anthropological Archives, Smithsonian, Washington, DC.

Martin, Douglas. 1986. Indian-white relations on the Pacific Slope, 1850–1890. PhD diss., University of Washington.

Martin, Irene. 1994. *Legacy and testament: The story of Columbia River gillnetters.* Pullman: Washington State University Press.

Martin, Michael. 2006. The fisheries of the Lower Columbia River, 1792 to 1850, based on Euroamerican explorer and fur company accounts. MA thesis, Portland State University.

Martin, Paul, and Christine Szuter. 1999a. War zones and game sinks in Lewis and Clark's West. *Conservation Biology* 13(1):36–45.

———. 1999b. Game parks before and after Lewis and Clark: Reply to Lyman and Wolverton. *Conservation Biology* 16(11):244–47.

Mathews, Bethany. 2007. Acorns and acorn leaching pits. In *Evaluation of archaeological site 35MU4, the Sunken Village site, Multnomah County, Oregon*, ed. Dale Croes, John Fagan, and Maureen Zehendner, 100–112. Olympia and Portland: South Puget Sound Community College and Archaeological Investigations Northwest.

———. 2009. Acorns and acorn leaching pits. *Journal of Wetland Archaeology* 9:85–95.

Matson, R.G. 1992. The evolution of Northwest Coast subsistence. In *Evaluation of archaeological site 35MU4, the Sunken Village site, Multnomah County, Oregon*, ed. Dale Croes, John Fagan, and Maureen Zehendner, 367–430. Olympia and Portland: South Puget Sound Community College and Archaeological Investigations Northwest.

Matson, R. G., and Gary Coupland. 1995. *The prehistory of the Northwest Coast.* Orlando, FL: Academic Press.

Matsui, Akira. 2009. Foreword. Special issue on Sunken Village. *Journal of Wetland Archaeology* 9:2–3.

Mauss, Marcel. 1972. *The Gift.* New York: Aldine.

May, James. 2002. Chinook status denied. *Indian Country Today*, July 12.

McChesney, Charles, et al. 1969. *Rolls of certain Indian tribes in Washington and Oregon.* Fairfield, WA: Ye Galleon Press.

McClure, Rick. 1978. The Tsagiglalal motif in rock art of the Lower Columbia River. In *American Indian Rock Art*, 173–89. Vol. 5. El Toro, CA: American Rock Art Research Association.

———. 2011. Elk Pass obsidian and precontact band territory in the southern Washington Cascades. Paper, annual meeting, Society for American Archaeology, Sacramento, CA.

McDonnell, Janet. 1991. *The dispossession of the American Indian, 1887–1934.* Bloomington: Indiana University Press.

McDougall, Duncan. 1999. *Annals of Astoria: The headquarters log of the Pacific Fur Company on the Columbia River, 1811–1813*, ed. Robert Jones. New York: Fordham University Press.

McGlone, Matt, Janet Wilmshurst, and Helen Leach. 2005. An ecological and historical review of bracken (*Pteridium esculentum*) in New Zealand, and its cultural significance. *New Zealand Journal of Ecology* 29(2):165–84.

McKelvey, Susan. 1991 [1955]. *Botanical exploration of the trans-Mississippi West, 1790–1850*. Corvallis: Oregon State University Press.

McLoughlin, John. 1941. *The letters of John McLoughlin from Fort Vancouver to the governor and committee: First series, 1825–38*, ed. E. E. Rich. Toronto: Champlain Society.

———. 1948. *Letters of Dr. John McLoughlin, written at Fort Vancouver 1829–1832*, ed. Burt Brown Barker. Portland, OR: Binfords & Mort.

McMillan, Alan, and Ian Hutchinson. 2002. When the mountain dwarfs danced: Aboriginal traditions of paleoseismic events along the Cascadia subduction zone of western North America. *Ethnohistory* 49(1):41–68.

McMillan, Alan, Iain McKechnie, Denis St. Claire, and Gay Frederick. 2008. Exploring variability in maritime resource use on the Northwest Coast: A case study from Barkley Sound, western Vancouver Island. *Canadian Journal of Archaeology* 32:214–38.

McNeill, William. 1976. *Plagues and peoples*. Garden City, NY: Anchor.

McWhorter, Lucullus. n.d. McWhorter collection. Holland Library, Washington State University, Pullman.

Meany, Edmund S. 1907. *Vancouver's discovery of Puget Sound*. New York: Macmillan.

Meeker, Jerry. n.d. Jerry Meeker/Minter notebooks, collected by Alfred Smith, acc. #4815-1, University of Washington Libraries Special Collections, Seattle.

Mercer, Bill. 2005. *People of the river: Native arts of the Oregon territory*. Seattle: University of Washington Press.

Michelle, Mary Anne. n.d. Documents on family history, unpublished.

Middlewood, Erin. 2000. 80 Chinook gather at park in rally for recognition from government. (Portland) *Oregonian*, June 17.

Miller, Jay. 1989. An overview of Northwest Coast mythology. *Northwest Anthropological Research Notes* 23(2):125–41.

———. 1999. *Lushootseed culture and the shamanic odyssey: An anchored radiance*. Lincoln: University of Nebraska Press.

Miller, Mark. 2004. *Forgotten tribes: Unrecognized Indians and the federal acknowledgement process*. Lincoln: University of Nebraska Press.

Minor, Rick. 1983. Aboriginal settlement and subsistence at the mouth of the Columbia River. PhD diss., University of Oregon.

———. 1984. An early complex at the mouth of the Columbia River. *Northwest Anthropological Research Notes* 18(1):1–22.

———. 1991. *Yaquina Head: A middle archaic settlement on the north-central Oregon Coast*. Cultural Resource Series No. 6. Portland: Oregon State Office, Bureau of Land Management.

Minor, Rick, and Laurie Burgess. 2009. Chinookan survival and persistence on the Lower Columbia: The view from the Kathlamat village. *Historical Archaeology* 43(4):97–114.

Minor, Rick, Ruth Greenspan, and Debra Barner. 2008. Chinookan resource exploitation in the Columbia River estuary. In *Dunes, headlands, estuaries, and rivers: Current archaeological research on the Oregon Coast*, ed. Guy Tasa and Brian O'Neill, 37–55. Association of Oregon Archaeologists Occasional Paper No. 8, Eugene, OR.

Minor, Rick, and Wendy Grant. 1996. Earthquake-induced subsidence and burial of late Holocene archaeological sites, northern Oregon Coast. *American Antiquity* 61(4):772–81.

Minor, Rick, Christine Pickett, and Ruth Greenspan. 1985. *Archaeological investigations at the Ede site, Columbia County, Oregon*. Heritage Research Associates Report 38.

Minor, Rick, and Kathryn Toepel. 1985. *Archaeological investigations at 45CL4, Ridgefield National Wildlife Refuge, Clark County, Washington*. Heritage Research Associates Report 37.

Minor, Rick, Kathryn Toepel, and Stephen Beckham. 1989. *An overview of investigations at 45SA11, archaeology of the Columbia River Gorge*. Rev. ed. Heritage Research Associates Report 83.

Minto, John. 1895. The Indians of Oregon fifty years ago. (Portland) *Oregonian*, November 7.

———. 1900. The number and condition of the Native race in Oregon when first seen by white men. *Oregon Historical Quarterly* 1(3):296–315.

———. 1915. *Rhymes of early life in Oregon*. Salem: Statesman.

Mithun, Marianne. 1999. *The languages of Native North America*. New York: Cambridge University Press.

Monaco, Mark, et al. 1990. *Distribution and abundance of fishes and invertebrates in West Coast estuaries*. 2 vols. ELMR Rep No. 4 NOAA/NOS Strategic Environmental Assessments Division, Silver Springs, MD.

Monks, Gregory. 2007. The fauna from Ma'acoah (DfSi-5), Vancouver Island, British Columbia: An interpretive summary. *Canadian Journal of Archaeology* 30:272–301.

Mooney, James. 1928. *The aboriginal population of America north of Mexico*. Smithsonian Miscellaneous Collections 80(7).

Moore, Robert. 1988. Lexicalization versus lexical loss in Wasco-Wishram language obsolescence. *International Journal of American Linguistics* 54(4):453–68.

Morison, Samuel Eliot. 1927. New England and the opening of the Columbia River salmon trade, 1830. *Oregon Historical Quarterly* 28:111–32.

Moses, Israel. 1855. On the medical topography of Astoria, Oregon Territory. *American Journal of Medical Science* 29:32–46.

Moss, Madonna. 1989. Archaeology and cultural ecology of the prehistoric Angoon Tlingit. PhD diss., University of California, Santa Barbara.

———. 1993. Shellfish, gender, and status on the Northwest Coast: Reconciling archaeological, ethnographic, and ethnohistorical records of the Tlingit. *American Anthropologist* 93:631–52.

———. 2007. The Killisnoo picnic midden (49-SIT-124) revisited: Assessing archaeological recovery of vertebrate faunal remains from Northwest Coast middens. *Journal of Northwest Anthropology* 41:1–17.

———. 2012. Fishing traps and weirs on the Northwest Coast of North America: New approaches and new insights. In *Oxford Handbook of Wetland Archaeology*, ed. Francesco Menotti and Aidan O'Sullivan, 323–38. Oxford: Oxford University Press.

Moulton, Gary. 1983. *Atlas of the Lewis and Clark Expedition.* Lincoln: University of Nebraska Press.

Munnick, Harriet, ed. 1972. *Catholic Church records of the Pacific Northwest: Vancouver,* 2 vols, and *Stellamaris Mission.* St. Paul, OR: French Prairie Press.

Murdock, George. 1968. The current status of the world's hunting and gathering peoples. In *Man the hunter,* ed. Richard Lee and Irven DeVore, 13–20. Chicago: Aldine.

Nagaoka, Lisa. 2005. Differential recovery of Pacific island fish remains. *Journal of Archaeological Science* 32:941–55.

NBCNews. 2011. Clark's descendants replace stolen tribal canoe. September 25. http://www.msnbc.msn.com/id/44658752/ns/us_news/t/clarks-descendants -replace-stolen-tribal-canoe.

Neusius, Sarah, and Timothy Gross. 2007. *Seeking our past: An introduction to North American archaeology.* New York: Oxford University Press.

Nisbet, Jack. 1994. *Sources of the river: Tracking David Thompson across western North America.* Seattle: Sasquatch Books.

Nokes, J. Richard. 1991. *Columbia's river: The voyages of Robert Gray, 1787–1793.* Tacoma: Washington State Historical Society.

Norman, Stephanie, et al. 2004. Cetacean strandings in Oregon and Washington between 1930 and 2002. *Journal of Cetacean Research and Management* 6(1):87–99.

Norton, Helen. 1979a. The association between anthropogenic prairies and important food plants in western Washington. *Northwest Anthropological Research
Notes* 12(2):175–200.

———. 1979b. Evidence for bracken fern as a food for aboriginal peoples of western
Washington. *Economic Botany* 33(4):384–96.

Norton, Helen, Robert Boyd, and Eugene Hunn. 1999. The Klikitat trail of south
central Washington: Reconstruction of seasonally used resource sites. In
Indians, fire, and the land in the Pacific Northwest, ed. Robert Boyd, 65–93.
Corvallis: Oregon State University Press.

NWPPC. 1986. Compilation of information on salmon and steelhead losses in the
Columbia River Basin, Portland, Oregon. Northwest Power Planning Council,
Portland, Oregon. http://www.nwcouncil.org/library/1986/Compilation.htm.

O'Conner, Jim. 2004. The evolving landscape of the Columbia River Gorge: Lewis
and Clark and cataclysms on the Columbia. *Oregon Historical Quarterly*
105(3):390–421.

O'Donnell, Terence. 1991. *An arrow in the earth: General Joel Palmer and the Indians
of Oregon*. Portland: Oregon Historical Society Press.

Ogden, Peter. 1933 [1853]. *Traits of American-Indian life and character*. San Francisco:
Grabhorn Press.

Olson, Diane. 1993. Analysis of faunal remains from 35MU57. In *Data recovery at
Broken Tops, site 35MU57*, ed. David Ellis and John Fagan, Appendix G. Report
for Scientific Resources, Portland, submitted to Portland District, US Army
Corps of Engineers.

Olson, Ronald. 1936. The Quinault Indians. *University of Washington Publications
in Anthropology* 6(1).

Oregon Archaeological Society. 1966. Multnomah Village. *Screenings* 15(1):1–3.

Oregon Territory. 1821–68. Territorial Papers of the United States. Micro 979.7
Un33IT, Washington State Library, Olympia.

O'Rourke, Leslie. 2005. The Wapato Valley predictive model: Prehistoric archaeological site location on the floodplain of the Columbia River in the Portland
Basin. MA thesis, Portland State University.

Orr, Elizabeth, William Orr, and Ewart Baldwin. 1992. *Geology of Oregon*. Dubuque:
Kendal Hunt.

Ozbun, Terry. 2008. Applying traditional knapping technologies to manufactured
glass during the contact period in the Lower Columbia River Valley. Paper,
annual meeting, Society for American Archaeology, Vancouver, BC.

Parker, Samuel. 1967 [1838]. *Journal of an exploring tour beyond the Rocky Mountains
under the direction of the ABCFM*. Minneapolis: Ross and Haines.

————. 1936. The report of Rev. Saml. Parker: Tour west of the Rocky Mountains in 1835-7. In *Overland to the Pacific*, vol. 6: *Marcus Whitman, crusader*, ed. Archer Hulbert and Dorothy Hulbert, 90-135. Denver: Denver Public Library.

Parsley, Michael, Lance Beckman, and George McCabe. 1993. Spawning and rearing habitat use by white sturgeons in the Columbia River downstream from McNary Dam. *Transactions of the American Fisheries Society* 122:217-27.

Partlow, Megan. 2006. Sampling fish bones: A consideration of the importance of screen size and disposal context in the Pacific Northwest. *Arctic Anthropology* 43:67-79.

Peacock, Sandra, and Nancy Turner. 2000. "Just like a garden": Traditional resource management and biodiversity conservation on the interior plateau of British Columbia. In *Biodiversity and Native America*, ed. Paul Minnis, 133-79. Norman: University of Oklahoma Press.

Peterson, Curt, Debra Doyle, and Elson Barnett. 2000. Coastal flooding and beach retreat from coseismic subsidence in the central Cascadia margin, USA. *Environmental and Engineering Geoscience* 6(3):255-69.

Peterson, Curt D., et al. 2011. Pre- and post-Missoula Flood geomorphology of the pre-Holocene ancestral Columbia River Valley in the Portland forearc basin, Oregon and Washington, USA. *Geomorphology* 129(3):276-93.

Peterson, Marilyn Sargent. 1978. Prehistoric mobile stone sculpture of the Lower Columbia River Valley. MA thesis, Portland State University.

Peterson, Robin. 2006. The role of traditional ecological knowledge in understanding a species and river system at risk: Pacific lamprey in the Lower Klamath Basin. MA thesis, Oregon State University.

Peterson del Mar, David. 1995. Intermarriage and agency: A Chinookan case study. *Ethnohistory* 42(1):1-30.

Pethick, Derek. 1979. *First approaches to the Northwest Coast*. Seattle: University of Washington Press.

Pettigrew, Richard. 1981. *A prehistoric culture sequence in the Portland Basin of the Lower Columbia Valley*. University of Oregon Anthropological Papers 22.

————. 1990. Prehistory of the Lower Columbia and Willamette Valley. In *Handbook of North American Indians*, vol. 7: *Northwest Coast*, ed. Wayne Suttles, 518-29. Washington, DC: Smithsonian.

————. 2005. Archaeological excavations at the St. Johns site (35MU44/46), Portland, Oregon. Report prepared for CH2M Hill, Cascadia Archaeology, Seattle.

Phebus, George, and Robert Drucker. 1979. Archaeological investigations at Seaside, Oregon. Seaside Museum and History Society, Seaside, OR.

Philip, Kenneth. 1977. *John Collier's crusade for Indian reform, 1920–1954*. Tucson: University of Arizona Press.

Pilling, James. 1893. *Bibliography of the Chinookan languages*. Bureau of American Ethnology Bulletin 15.

Porter, Frank. 1990. In search of recognition: Federal Indian policy and the landless tribes of western Washington. *American Indian Quarterly* 14(2):113–32.

Post, Richard. 1938. The subsistence quest. In *The Sinkaietk or Southern Okanagon of Washington*, ed. Leslie Spier, 11–34. Menasha, WI: George Banta.

Powell, Jay. 1991. *Our world—our ways: T'aat'aaqsapa cultural dictionary*. Port Alberni, BC: Nuuchahnulth Tribal Council.

Prentiss, William, and Ian Kuijt, eds. 2004. *Complex hunter-gatherers: Evolution and organization of prehistoric communities on the Plateau of northwestern North America*. Salt Lake City: University of Utah Press.

Price, T. Douglas, and James Brown, eds. 1985. *Prehistoric hunter-gatherers: The emergence of cultural complexity*. Orlando, FL: Academic Press.

Pringle, Patrick, et al. 2002. Tree-ring analysis of subfossil trees from the Bonneville Landslide deposit and the "Submerged Forest of the Columbia River Gorge" described by Lewis and Clark. Paper, annual meeting, Geological Society of America, Corvallis, OR.

Pryor, Frederick. 1977. *The origins of the economy*. New York: Academic Press.

Quinn, William. 1990. Federal acknowledgement of American Indian tribes: The historical development of a legal concept. *American Journal of Legal History* 34:331–64.

Ramsay, Jarold. 1977. *Coyote was going there: Indian literature of the Oregon Country*. Seattle: University of Washington Press.

Ray, Verne. 1937. The historical position of the Lower Chinook in the Native culture of the Northwest. *Pacific Northwest Quarterly* 28(4):363–72.

———. 1938. Lower Chinook ethnographic notes. *University of Washington Publications in Anthropology* 7(2):29–165.

———. 1942. Culture element distributions 22, Plateau. *University of California Anthropological Records* 8:99–262.

———. 1975. The Chinook Indians in the early 1800s. In *The western shore*, ed. Thomas Vaughan, 120–50. Portland: Oregon Historical Society Press.

Ray, Verne, and Nancy Lurie. 1954. The contributions of Lewis and Clark to ethnography. *Journal of the Washington Academy of Sciences* 44(11):358–70.

Reimchen, Tom. 1994. Predators and morphological evolution in threespine stickleback. In *The evolutionary biology of the threespine stickleback*, ed. Michael Bell and Susan Foster, 240–76. New York: Oxford University Press.

Rieman, Bruce, and Richard Beamesderfer. 1990. White sturgeon in the Lower Columbia River: Is the stock overexploited? *North American Journal of Fisheries Management* 10:388–96.

Roberge, Earl. 1985. *Columbia, great river of the West*. San Francisco: Chronicle Books.

Roberts, George. 1962. The round hand of George B. Roberts: The Cowlitz farm journal, 1847–1851, ed. Priscilla Knuth. *Oregon Historical Quarterly* 63(2–3):101–74.

Robertson, David D. 2003. What there is to C in Kamloops Wawa shorthand. In *Papers for ICSNL XXVIII: The thirty-eighth international conference on Salish and neighboring languages,* ed. J. C. Brown and Michele Kalmer, 185–206. Vancouver: University of British Columbia.

———. 2005. Louis-Napoleon St. Onge. History of the Old Testament: Age I. Ms. in possession of Department of Cultural Resources Archives, Confederated Tribes of Grand Ronde, OR.

———. 2011. Kamloops Chinúk Wawa, Chinuk pipa, and the vitality of pidgins. PhD diss., University of Victoria.

Rohner, Ronald, ed. 1969. *The ethnography of Franz Boas*. Chicago: University of Chicago Press.

Ronda, James. 1984. *Lewis and Clark among the Indians*. Lincoln: University of Nebraska Press.

———. 1990. *Astoria and empire*. Lincoln: University of Nebraska Press.

———. 1999. Coboway's tale: A story of power and place along the Columbia. In *Power and place in the North American West*, ed. Richard White and John Findlay, 3–22. Seattle: University of Washington Press.

Roosevelt, Anna. 2000. Who's on first? *Natural History* July/August:76–9.

Roosevelt, Anna, et al. 1996. Paleoindian cave dwellers in the Amazon: The peopling of the Americas. *Science* 272:373–84.

Ross, Alexander. 2000 [1849]. *Adventures of the first settlers on the Oregon or Columbia River*. Corvallis: Oregon State University Press.

———. 1956 [1855]. *The fur hunters of the Far West*, ed. Kenneth Spaulding. Norman: University of Oklahoma Press.

———. 1974 [1821]. Map of Columbia. Friends of the Ellensburg Public Library, Ellensburg, WA.

Roth, Christopher. 1994. Towards an early social history of Chinook Jargon. *Northwest Anthropological Research Notes* 28(1):157–75.

Ruby, Robert, and John Brown. 1965. *Half-Sun on the Columbia: A biography of Chief Moses*. Norman: University of Oklahoma Press.

———. 1972. *The Cayuse Indians: Imperial tribesmen of old Oregon*. Norman: University of Oklahoma Press.

———. 1976. *The Chinook Indians: Traders of the Lower Columbia River*. Norman: University of Oklahoma Press.

Sahlins, Marshall. 1965. On the sociology of primitive exchange. In *The relevance of models for social anthropology*, ed. Michael Banton, 139–236. London: Tavistock.

———. 1968. *Tribesmen*. Englewood Cliffs, NJ: Prentice-Hall.

———. 1972. *Stone Age economics*. Chicago: Aldine-Atherton.

Saleeby, Becky. 1983. Prehistoric settlement patterns in the Portland Basin of the Lower Columbia River: Ethnohistoric, archaeological, biogeographic perspectives. PhD diss., University of Oregon.

Saleeby, Becky, and Richard Pettigrew. 1983. Seasonality of occupation of ethnohistorically documented villages on the Lower Columbia River. In *Prehistoric places on the southern Northwest Coast*, ed. Robert Greengo, 169–93. Thomas Burke Memorial Washington State Museum Research Report 4, Seattle.

Samarin, William. 1986. Chinook Jargon and pidgin historiography. *Canadian Journal of Anthropology* 5(1):23–34.

———. 1988. Jargonization before Chinook Jargon. *Northwest Anthropological Research Notes* 22(2):219–38.

———. 1996. Arctic origin and domestic development of Chinook Jargon. In *Language contact in the Arctic: Northern pidgins and contact languages*, ed. Ernst Jahr and Ingvild Broch, 321–39. Berlin: Mouton de Gruyter.

Sanders, Angela. 2005. The Chinook Nation. *Portland* 24(4):16–21.

Sapir, Edward. 1907. Preliminary report on the language and mythology of the upper Chinook. *American Anthropologist* 9(2):251–75.

———. 1909a. *Takelma texts*. University of Pennsylvania, University Museum Anthropological Publications 2(1).

———. 1909b. *Wishram texts*. Leyden, The Netherlands: E.J. Brill.

———. 1949 [1916]. The social organization of the West Coast tribes. In *Selected writings of Edward Sapir in language, culture and personality*, ed. David Mandelbaum, 468–87. Berkeley: University of California Press.

Sassaman, Kenneth. 2004. Complex hunter-gatherers in evolution and history: A North American perspective. *Journal of Archaeological Research* 12(3):227–79.

Satake, Kenji, et al. 1996. Time and size of a giant earthquake in Cascadia inferred from Japanese tsunami records of January 1700. *Nature* 379:246–51.

Schaeffer, Claude. 1963. William Brooks. *Oregon Historical Quarterly* 64(1):41–54.

Schaepe, David. 2009. Pre-colonial Sto:lo–Coast Salish community organization: An archaeological study. PhD diss. University of British Columbia.

Schafer, Joseph, ed. 1909. Documents relative to Warre and Vavasour's military reconnaissance in Oregon, 1845–46. *Oregon Historical Quarterly* 10(1).

Schalk, Randall. 1981. Land use and organizational complexity among foragers of northwestern North America. In *Affluent foragers: Pacific Coasts east and west*, ed. Shuzo Koyama and David Thomas, 53–76. Osaka, Japan: National Museum of Ethnology.

———. 1986. Estimating salmon and steelhead usage in the Columbia Basin before 1850: The anthropological perspective. *Northwest Environmental Journal* 2(2):1–29.

Scheinsohn, Vivian. 2003. Hunter-gatherer archaeology in South America. *Annual Review of Anthropology* 32:339–61.

Schlick, Mary Dodds. 1994. *Columbia River basketry: Gift of the ancestors, gift of the Earth*. Seattle: University of Washington Press.

Schulting, Rick. 1995. *Mortuary variability and status differentiation on the Columbia-Fraser Plateau*. Burnaby, BC: Archaeology Press, Simon Fraser University.

Schulz, Peter, and Dwight Simons. 1973. Fish species diversity in a prehistoric central California Indian midden. *California Fish and Game* 59(2):107–13.

Schurz, William. 1939. *The Manila galleon*. New York: E. P. Dutton.

Schuster, Robert, and Patrick Pringle. 2002. Engineering history and impacts of the Bonneville Landslide, Columbia River Gorge, Washington-Oregon, USA. In *Landslides: Proceedings of the 1st European conference on landslides*, ed. Jan Rybar, Joseph Stemberk, and Peter Wagner, 689–99. Rotterdam: A. A. Balkema.

Schwantes, Carlos. 1989. *The Pacific Northwest: An interpretive history*. Lincoln: University of Nebraska Press.

Schwartz, Glenn, and Peter Akkermans. 2003. *The archaeology of Syria: From complex hunter-gatherers to early urban societies*. New York: Cambridge University Press.

Scouler, John. 1848. On the Indian tribes inhabiting the North-West Coast of America. *Journal of the Ethnological Society of London* 1:228–52.

———. 1905. Journal of a voyage to Northwest America. *Oregon Historical Quarterly* 6:54–75, 159–205, 276–87.

Seaburg, William, and Pamela Amoss. 2000. *Badger and Coyote were neighbors: Melville Jacobs on Northwest Indian myths and tales*. Corvallis: Oregon State University Press.

Sedlak, Rebecca. 2012. Chinooks honored with opening of newest national park. *Chinook Observer*, August 21.

Senier, Siobhan. 2001. *Voices of American Indian assimilation and resistance: Helen Hunt Jackson, Sarah Winnemucca, and Victoria Howard.* Norman: University of Oklahoma Press.

Senos, Rene, et al., eds. 2006. *Restoring the Pacific Northwest: The art and science of ecological restoration in Cascadia.* Washington, DC: Island Press.

Seton, Alfred. 1993. *Astorian adventure: The journal of Alfred Seton, 1811–1815*, ed. Robert Jones. New York: Fordham University Press.

Shaw, Linda. 2002. Chinooks at White House party, then lose their federal recognition. *Seattle Times*, July 8.

Shaw, Robert. 1977. *Report of excavations: The Martin site (45PC7), 1974.* Washington Archaeological Society Occasional Paper No. 5.

———. 2004. Jackson's resignation marks end of era. *Spilyay Tymoo* (Warm Springs, OR), February 5.

Shebitz, Daniela. 2005. Weaving traditional knowledge into restoration. *Journal of Ecological Anthropology* 9:51–68.

Sheets, Payson. 1973. Pillage of prehistory. *American Antiquity* 38(3):317–20.

Shennan, Ian, et al. 1996. Tidal marsh stratigraphy, sea-level change and large earthquakes—I: A 5000 year record of large earthquakes in Washington, USA. *Quaternary Science Reviews* 15:1023–59.

———. 1998. Tidal marsh stratigraphy, sea-level change and large earthquakes—II: Submergence events during the last 3500 years at Netarts Bay, Oregon, USA. *Quaternary Science Reviews* 17:365–93.

Shepard, Cyrus. 1935. Letter of September 28, 1835. In *Overland to the Pacific*, vol. 6: *Marcus Whitman, crusader*, ed. Archer Hulbert and Dorothy Hulbert, 193–98. Denver: Denver Public Library.

Shimkin, Demitri. 1986. Introduction of the horse. In *Handbook of North American Indians,* vol. 11: *Great Basin,* ed. Warren D'Azevedo, 517–24. Washington, DC: Smithsonian.

Shortess, Robert. 1851. Letter of February 5 to Anson Dart. Records of the Oregon Superintendency of Indian Affairs, National Archives, Washington, DC.

Silverstein, Michael. 1972. Chinook Jargon: Language contact and the problem of multi-level generative systems. *Language* 48:378–406, 596–625.

———. 1974. *Dialectical developments in Chinookan tense-aspect systems: An areal-historical sketch.* International Journal of American Linguistics Memoir 29.

———. 1990. Chinookans of the Lower Columbia. In *Handbook of North Ameri-*

can Indians, vol. 7: *Northwest Coast*, ed. Wayne Suttles, 533–46. Washington, DC: Smithsonian.

———. 1996. Chinook Jargon. In *Handbook of North American Indians*, vol. 17: *Languages*, ed. Ives Goddard, 127–30. Washington, DC: Smithsonian.

Simpson, George. 1968. *Fur trade and empire: George Simpson's journal*, ed. Frederick Merk. Cambridge, MA: Harvard University Press.

———. 1847. *An overland journey round the world during the years 1841 and 1842.* 2 vols. Philadelphia: Lea and Blanchard.

Skamania County Pioneer. 1977 [1935]. First Bonneville project inspired account of sailor's marriage to chief's daughter, May 6.

Skinner, S. Alan. 1981. *Clah-cleh-lah: An archaeological site at Bonneville Dam, Washington*. Dallas: Environment Consultants.

Slacum, William. 1972 [1837]. Memorial of William Slacum. Fairfield, WA: Ye Galleon Press.

Slocum, Robert, and Kenneth Matsen. 1968. *Shoto Clay: A description of clay artifacts from the Herzog site (45CL4) in the Lower Columbia region*. Portland, OR: Binfords & Mort.

Smith, Bruce. 2005. Low-level food production and the Northwest Coast. In *Keeping it living: Traditions of plant use and cultivation on the Northwest Coast of North America*, ed. Douglas Deur and Nancy Turner, 37–66. Seattle: University of Washington Press.

Smith, Cameron. 2006. Formation processes of a Lower Columbia protohistoric Chinookan plankhouse. In *Household archaeology on the Northwest Coast*, ed. Elizabeth Sobel, Ann Trieu Gahr, and Kenneth Ames, 233–69. Archaeological Series 16. Ann Arbor: International Monographs in Prehistory.

———. 2008. The organization of production among sedentary hunter-gatherers of the southern Pacific Northwest Coast. British Archaeological Reports International Series 1741. Oxford, England: Archaeopress.

Smith, Harlan. 1906. Noteworthy archaeological specimens from the Lower Columbia Valley. *American Anthropologist* 8:298–307.

———. 1907. Archaeology of the Gulf of Georgia and Puget Sound. *American Museum of Natural History Memoir* 4(6).

Smith, Marian. 1943. Columbia Valley art style. *American Anthropologist* 45:158–60.

———. 1952. Basketry design and the Columbia Valley art style. *Southwestern Journal of Anthropology* 8(3):336–41.

Smith, Ross, and Virginia Butler. 2008. Towards the identification of lamprey (*Lampetra* spp.) in archaeological contexts. *Journal of Northwest Anthropology* 42(2):131–42.

Smith, Ross, Virginia Butler, Shelia Orwoll, and Catherine Wilson-Skogen. 2011. Pacific cod and salmon structural bone density: Implications for interpreting butchering patterns in North Pacific archaeofaunas. In *The Archaeology of North Pacific Fisheries,* ed. Madonna Moss and Aubrey Cannon. Submitted to University of Alaska Press.

Smith, Silas. 1882. On the Chinnook names of the salmon in the Columbia River. *Proceedings of the US National Museum, SMC,* Vol. 4, 1881, 391–92.

———. 1899. Mr. Smith's address, newspaper clipping (unknown source), September 18 Scrapbook 35:30–31, Oregon Historical Society Research Library, Portland.

———. 1900. Tales of early wrecks on the Oregon Coast. *Oregon Native Son* 1(8):443–46.

———. 1901. Primitive customs and religious beliefs of the Indians of the Pacific Northwest Coast. *Oregon Historical Quarterly* 2(3):255–65.

———. n.d. Stories of Tallupus. Horace Lyman Papers. Mss. 722, Oregon Historical Society. Portland.

Smith, Wendell, and Robert Saalfeld. 1955. Studies on Columbia River smelt, *Thaleichthys Pacificus. Washington Fisheries Research Papers* 1(3):3–26.

Snow, Charles. 1969. A lower Chehalis phonology. MA thesis, University of Kansas.

Sobel, Elizabeth. 2004. Social complexity and corporate households on the southern Northwest Coast, A D 1400–1840. PhD diss., University of Michigan.

———. 2006. Household prestige and exchange in Northwest Coast societies: A case study from the Lower Columbia River Valley. In *Household archaeology on the Northwest Coast,* ed. Elizabeth Sobel, Ann Trieu Gahr, and Kenneth Ames, 159–99. Archaeological Series 16. Ann Arbor: International Monographs in Prehistory.

———. 2009. The Meier and Clahclellah sites. In *Archaeology in America: An Encyclopedia,* vol. 4: *West Coast and Arctic/Subarctic,* ed. Francis McManamon, 203–6. Westport, CT: Greenwood Press.

———. 2012. An archaeological test of the "Exchange Expansion Model" of contact era change on the Northwest Coast. *Journal of Anthropological Archaeology* 31(1):1–21.

Sobel, Elizabeth, and Chris Cotter. 2008. The evolving role of Long Island, WA, in Chinookan identity and culture. Paper, annual meeting, Society for American Archaeology, Vancouver, BC.

Spencer, Omar. 1933. Chief Cassino. *Oregon Historical Quarterly* 34(1):19–30.

Spier, Leslie. 1930. *Klamath ethnography.* University of California Publications in American Archaeology and Ethnology 30.

————. 1935. *The Prophet Dance of the Northwest and its derivatives: The source of the Ghost Dance.* Menasha, WI: George Banta.

————. 1936. *Tribal distribution in Washington.* General Series in Anthropology No. 3. Menasha, WI.

Spier, Leslie, and Edward Sapir. 1930. Wishram ethnography. *University of Washington Publications in Anthropology* 3(3):151–300.

Sprague, Roderick. 1980. Carved stone heads of the Columbia River and Sasquatch. In *Manlike monsters on trial,* ed. Marjorie Halpin and Michael Ames, 229–33. Vancouver: University of British Columbia Press.

Stapp, Darby. 1984. Late protohistoric burials with copper artifacts in the Pacific Northwest. MA thesis, University of Idaho.

Steele, Harvey. 1980. *Bachelor Island.* Oregon Archaeological Society Report No. 8.

Stenger, Alison. 2009. *A vanished people: The Lake River ceramic makers.* Portland: Institute for Archaeological Studies.

Stenholm, Nancy. 1999. Botanical analysis of floral samples. In *Archaeological Investigations (1991–1994) at 45CL1 (Cathlapotle), Clark County, Washington: A Preliminary Report,* ed. Kenneth M. Ames, William L. Cornett, and Stephen C. Hamilton, Appendix B. Wapato Valley Archaeological Project Report No. 5, Department of Anthropology, Portland State University, US Fish and Wildlife Service.

Stern, Theodore. 1998. Columbia River trade network. In *Handbook of North American Indians,* vol. 12: *Plateau,* ed. Deward Walker, 1641–52. Washington, DC: Smithsonian.

Steward, Julian. 1927. A new type of carving from the Columbia Valley. *American Anthropologist* 29:255–61.

Stiner, Mary, et al. 1995. Differential burning, recrystallization, and fragmentation of archaeological bone. *Journal of Archaeological Science* 22:223–37.

Stone, Richard. 2003. Late date for Siberian site challenges Bering pathway. *Science* 301:450–51.

Strong, Emory. 1959. *Stone age on the Columbia.* Portland: Binfords & Mort.

————. 1961. Prehistoric sculpture from the Columbia River. *Archaeology* 14:131–37.

————. 1995. *Seeking western waters: The Lewis and Clark trail from the Rockies to the Pacific,* ed. Herb Beals. Portland: Oregon Historical Society Press.

Strong, Thomas. 1906. *Cathlamet on the Columbia: Recollections of the Indian people and short stories of early pioneer days in the valley of the Lower Columbia River.* Portland, OR: Metropolitan Press.

Strong, William. 1945. The occurrence and wider implications of a "ghost cult" on the Columbia River suggested by carvings in wood, bone and stone. *American Anthropologist* 47:244–61.

Stuart, Robert. 1935. *The discovery of the Oregon Trail: Robert Stuart's narratives of his overland trip eastward from Astoria, 1812–13*, ed. Phillip Rollins. New York: Scribner's.

Suckley, George. 1860. Report upon the fishes collected on the survey. In *The natural history of Washington Territory, with much relating to Minnesota, Nebraska, Kansas, Oregon, and California*, ed. J.G. Cooper and G. Suckley, 307–68. New York: Balliere Brothers.

Suttles, Wayne. 1968. Coping with abundance: Subsistence on the Northwest Coast. In *Man the hunter*, ed. Richard Lee and Irven DeVore, 56–68. Chicago: Aldine.

———. 1987. Cultural diversity within the Coast Salish continuum. In *Ethnicity and culture*, ed. Reginald Auger et al., 243–49. Calgary, AB: University of Calgary.

———, ed. 1990. *Handbook of North American Indians*, vol. 7: *Northwest Coast*. Washington, DC: Smithsonian.

———. 2005 Coast Salish resource management. In *Keeping it living: Traditions of plant use and cultivation on the Northwest Coast of North America*, ed. Douglas Deur and Nancy Turner, 181–93. Seattle: University of Washington Press.

Suttles, Wayne, and Barbara Lane. 1990. Southern Coast Salish. In *Handbook of North American Indians*, vol. 7: *Northwest Coast*, ed. Wayne Suttles, 485–502. Washington, DC: Smithsonian.

Suttles, Wayne, and Cameron Suttles. 1985 *Native languages of the Northwest Coast*. Map. Portland: Western Imprints, Oregon Historical Society Press.

Swan, James. 1972 [1857]. *The Northwest Coast; or, three years residence in Washington Territory*. Seattle: University of Washington Press.

———. 1880. The eulachon or candlefish of the Northwest Coast. *Proceedings of the United States National Museum* 8:257–64.

Swanton, John. 1900. Morphology of the Chinook verb. *American Anthropologist* 2(2):199–237.

Swidler, Nina, et al., eds. 1997. *Native Americans and archaeologists: Stepping stones to common ground*. Walnut Creek, CA: Altamira.

Tappan, William. 1854. Annual report, Southern Indian District, Washington Territory. Records of the Washington superintendency of Indian affairs, 1853–75, No. 5, roll 17, Letters from employees assigned to the Columbia River or Southern District, May 1, 1854–July 20, 1861. RG 75, National Archives, Washington, DC.

Thomason, Sarah. 1981. Chinook Jargon in a real and historical context [Collated

Chinuk Wawa phonetic forms, draft, 378–92]. Working papers of the International Conference of Salish and Neighboring Languages. University of Montana Occasional Papers in Linguistics 2.

———. 1983. Chinook Jargon in areal and historical context. *Language* 59(4):820–70.

Thompson, Courtenay. 2001. Chinook tribe wins struggle for federal recognition. (Portland) *Oregonian*, January 4.

Thompson, David. 1962. *David Thompson's narrative, 1784–1812*, ed. David Glover. Toronto: Champlain Society.

———. 1994. *Columbia journals*, ed. Barbara Belyea. Montreal: McGill–Queen's University Press.

Thompson, Laurence, and Dale Kinkade. 1990. Languages. In *Handbook of North American Indians*, vol. 7: *Northwest Coast*, ed. Wayne Suttles, 30–51. Washington, DC: Smithsonian.

Thompson, M. Terry, and Steven Egesdal, eds. 2008. *Salish myths and legends: One people's stories.* Lincoln: University of Nebraska Press.

Thompson, Sally, ed. 2004. *Native homelands along the Lewis and Clark trail.* Regional Learning Project, Center for Continuing Education, University of Montana, Missoula.

———. 2005. *Contemporary voices along the Lewis and Clark trail.* Regional Learning Project, Center for Continuing Education, University of Montana, Missoula.

———. 2007. Lower Chinook and Clatsop. Regional Learning Project, Center for Continuing Education, University of Montana, Missoula. www.trailtribes .org./fortclatsop/home.htm.

Thornton, Jessy. 1849. *Oregon and California in 1848.* New York: Harper.

Thornton, Thomas. 1998. Structure of Tlingit edible fruit resources at Glacier Bay, Alaska. *Journal of Ethnobiology* 19(1):27–48.

———. 2008. *Being and place among the Tlingit.* Seattle: University of Washington Press.

Thrush, Coll. 2007. *Native Seattle: Histories from the crossing-over place.* Seattle: University of Washington Press.

Tilling, Robert, Lyn Topinka, and Donald Swanson. 1990. *Eruptions of Mount St. Helens: Past, present, and future.* US Geological Survey Special Interest Publication. vulcan.wr.usgs.gov/volcanoes/MSH/Publications/MSHPPF/MSH _past_present_future.html.

Tolmie, William. 1963. *The journals of William Fraser Tolmie: Physician and fur trader.* Vancouver, BC: Mitchell Press.

———. 1884. *Comparative vocabularies of the Indian tribes of British Columbia*, ed. George Dawson. Montreal, QC: Dawson Brothers.

Townsend, John. 1999 [1839]. *Narrative of a journey across the Rocky Mountains to the Columbia River.* Corvallis: Oregon State University Press.

Trafzer, Clifford, ed. 1986. *Indians, superintendents, and councils: Northwest Indian policy, 1850-1855.* Lanham, NY: University Press of America.

Trieu, D. Ann. 1997. *Archaeobotanical analysis of carbonized wood remains, Bachelor Island (45CL105), Ridgefield Wildlife Refuge, Ridgefield, Washington.* Sherwood, OR: US Fish and Wildlife Service.

———. 2000. Analysis of plant remains from Meier (35CO5), Scappoose, Oregon. Lab notes, in possession of the author.

———. 2003. *Analysis of plant remains from Beacon 6 Cutbank, Sauvie Island, Columbia River.* Sherwood, OR: US Fish and Wildlife Service.

———. 2004a. *Analysis of archaeological plant remains from St. Johns site (35MU44/46), Portland, Oregon.* Seattle: Cascadia Archaeology.

———. 2004b. Chinookan fuelwood selection revealed by charcoal, myth and history. Paper, Northwest Anthropological Conference, Eugene, OR.

———. 2005. Analysis of archaeological plant remains from the St. Johns site (35MU44/46). In *Archaeological excavations at the St. John site (35MU44/46), Portland, Oregon*, ed. Richard Pettigrew, Appendix D. Seattle: Cascadia Archaeology.

Turner, Nancy. 1979. *Plants in British Columbia Indian technology.* Handbook No. 38. Victoria: British Columbia Provincial Museum.

———. 1992. Edible woodfern rootstocks of western North America: Solving an ethnobotanical puzzle. *Journal of Ethnobiology* 12(1):1-34.

———. 1996. Traditional ecological knowledge. In *The rainforests of home: Profile of a North American bioregion*, ed. Peter Schoonmaker, Bettina von Haggen, and Edward Wolf, 275-98. Washington, DC: Island Press.

———. 1999. "Time to Burn": Traditional use of fire to enhance resource production by aboriginal peoples in British Columbia. In *Indians, fire, and the land in the Pacific Northwest*, ed. Robert Boyd, 185-218. Corvallis: Oregon State University Press.

———. 2003. The ethnobotany of "edible seaweed" (*Porphyra abbottiae* and related species; Rhodophyta: Bangiales) and its use by First Nations on the Pacific Coast of Canada. *Canadian Journal of Botany* 81(4):283-93.

———. 2005. *The Earth's blanket: Traditional teachings for sustainable living.* Seattle: University of Washington Press.

Turner, Nancy, and Fikret Berkes. 2006. Coming to understanding: Developing conservation through incremental learning in the Pacific Northwest. *Human Ecology* 34:495–513.

Turner, Nancy, and Alison Davis. 1993. "When everything was scarce": The roles of plants as famine foods in northwestern North America. *Journal of Ethnobiology* 13(2):1–28.

Turner, Nancy, and Harriet Kuhnlein. 1982. Two important "root" foods of the Northwest Coast Indians: Springbank clover (*Trifolium wormskioldii*) and Pacific silverweed (*Potentilla anserine*, spp. pacifica). *Economic Botany* 36(4):411–32.

————. 1983. Camas and riceroot—two lileaceous root foods used by British Columbia Indians. *Ecology of Food and Nutrition* 13(4):199–219.

Turner, Nancy, and Keith Egger. 1987. The cottonwood mushroom (*Tricholoma populinum* Lange): A food resource of the interior Salish peoples of British Columbia. *Canadian Journal of Botany* 6:921–27.

Turner, Nancy, and Dawn Loewen. 1998. The original "free trade": Exchange of botanical products and associated plant knowledge in northwestern North America. *Anthropologica* 60:49–70.

Turner, Nancy, and Sandra Peacock. 2005. Solving the perennial paradox: Ethnobotanical evidence for plant resource management on the Northwest Coast. In *Keeping it living: Traditions of plant use and cultivation on the Northwest Coast of North America*, ed. Douglas Deur and Nancy Turner, 101–50. Seattle: University of Washington Press.

Turner, Nancy, Robin Smith, and James Jones. 2005. "A fine line between two nations": Ownership patterns for plant resources among Northwest Coast indigenous peoples. In *Keeping it living: Traditions of plant use and cultivation on the Northwest Coast of North America*, ed. Douglas Deur and Nancy Turner, 151–78. Seattle: University of Washington Press.

Turner, Victor. 1969. *The ritual process: Structure and anti-structure*. Chicago: Aldine.

Ugan, Andrew. 2005. Does size matter? Body size, mass collecting, and their implications for understanding prehistoric foraging behavior. *American Antiquity* 70(1):75–89.

Underhill, Ruth. 1944. *Indians of the Pacific Northwest*. Washington, DC: Bureau of Indian Affairs.

US Court of Claims. 1902. *The lower band of Chinook Indians of the State of Washington vs. the United States*, testimony. Mss. 5, Oregon Historical Society Research Library, Portland.

US Department of Agriculture (USDA), Agricultural Research Service. 2012. USDA national nutrient database for standard reference, release 25. http://www.ars.usda.gov/ba/bhnrc/nd/.

US Geological Survey (USGS). 2008. Geological history of the Columbia Gorge. http://vulcan.wr.usgs.gov/volcanoes/Washington/ColumbiaRiver/geo_history_gorge.html.

US Land Office (Vancouver, WA). 1891. Letter and presidential proclamation, signed by President Grover Cleveland, May 12.

Vancouver, George. 1984 [1798]. *A voyage of discovery to the North Pacific and round the world*, ed. W. Kaye Lamb. Vol. 2. London: The Haklupt Society.

van Gennep, Arnold. 1960. *The rites of passage*. Chicago: University of Chicago Press.

Verano, John, and Douglas Ubelaker. 1992. *Disease and demography in the Americas*. Washington, DC: Smithsonian.

Vibert, Elizabeth. 1997. *Traders' tales: Narratives of cultural encounters in the Columbia Plateau, 1807–1846*. Norman: University of Oklahoma Press.

[Victor, Frances Fuller]. 1886. *The works of Hubert Howe Bancroft*, vol. 28: *History of the Northwest Coast*. San Francisco: The History Company.

Vrzić, Zvjezdana. 1999. Modeling pidgin/creole genesis: Universals and contact influence in Chinook Jargon syntax. PhD diss., New York University.

Waitt, Richard. 1980. About forty last-glacial Lake Missoula jokulhlaups through southern Washington. *Journal of Geology* 88(6):653–79.

Walker, Deward. 1997. The Yakama system of trade and exchange. *Northwest Anthropological Research Notes* 31(1):71–94.

Walker, Deward, and Roderick Sprague. 1998. History until 1846. In *Handbook of North American Indians*, vol. 12: *Plateau*, ed. Deward Walker, 138–48. Washington, DC: Smithsonian.

Walsh, Megan. 2008. Natural and anthropogenic influences on the Holocene fire and vegetation history of the Willamette Valley, northwest Oregon and southwest Washington. PhD diss., University of Oregon.

Walsh, Megan, Cathy Whitlock, and Patrick Bartlein. 2008. A 14,300-year-long record of fire-vegetation-climate linkages at Battle Ground Lake, southwestern Washington. *Quaternary Research* 70(2):251–64.

Walter, M. Susan. 2006. Polygyny, rank, and resources in Northwest Coast foraging societies. *Ethnology* 45(1):41–52.

Warre, Henry. 1845–46. Journal. MG 24, F71, vols. 1–3, Public Archives of Canada, Ottawa.

———. 1976. *Overland to Oregon in 1845: Impressions of a journey across North America*, ed. Madeleine Major-Fregeau. Ottawa: Public Archives of Canada.

Warren, Claude. 1958. A Re-evaluation of southwest Washington archaeology. *Tebiwa* 2(1):9–26.

———. 1960. Housepits and village patterns in the Columbia Plateau and southwest Washington. *Tebiwa* 3:25–28.

Waterman, Thomas. 2001 [1920]. *Puget Sound geography*, ed. Vi Hilbert, Jay Miller, and Zalmai Zahir. Federal Way, WA: Lushootseed Press.

Waters, Michael, and Thomas Stafford. 2007. Redefining the age of Clovis: Implications for the peopling of the Americas. *Science* 315:1122–26.

Watkins, Joe. 2000. *Indigenous archaeology: American values and scientific practice.* Walnut Creek, CA: Altamira.

Webber, Burt. 1984. *Wrecked Japanese junks adrift in the North Pacific Ocean.* Fairfield, WA: Ye Galleon Press.

Wessen, Gary, and Richard Daugherty. 1983. *Archaeological investigations at Vancouver Lake, Washington.* Olympia, WA: Western Heritage.

Whaley, Gray. 2007. Complete liberty? Gender, sexuality, race, and social change on the Lower Columbia River, 1805–1838. *Ethnohistory* 54(4):677–78.

White, Elijah. 1850. *Ten years in Oregon: Travels and adventures of Dr. E. White and lady, west of the Rocky Mountains*, comp. A. J. Allen. Ithaca, NY: Press of Andrus, Guantlett.

Whitlock, Cathy, and Margaret Knox. 2002. Prehistoric burning in the Pacific Northwest: Human versus climate influences. In *Fire, Native peoples, and the natural landscape*, ed. Thomas Vale, 195–231. Washington, DC: Island Press.

Widmer, Randolph. 1988. *The evolution of the Calusa: A nonagricultural chiefdom on the southwest Florida Coast.* Tuscaloosa: University of Alabama Press.

Wiegardt Perrow, Anna. 1971. My girlhood days in Bruceport. *The Sou'wester* 1971(2):31.

Wigen, Rebecca. 2009. Synthesis and summary of Sunken Village fauna, 2006–2007 excavations. In *Sunken Village, Sauvie Island, Oregon USA*, ed. Dale Croes, John Fagan, and Maureen Zehendner. Special issue. *Journal of Wetland Archaeology* 9:104–13.

Wilbert, Claire Thomas. 2010. Confronting unprovenanced collections: A case study of Lake River ceramics from the Columbia River region of the Northwest Coast. BA thesis, Scripps College.

Wilkes, Charles. 1845. *Narrative of the United States Exploring Expedition during the years 1838, 1839, 1841, 1842.* Vols. 4 and 5. Philadelphia: Lea and Blanchard.

———. 1851. *Voyage round the world, embracing the principal events of the narrative of the United States Exploring Expedition.* New York: G. P. Putnam.

————. 1925. Diary of Wilkes in the Northwest, ed. Edmond S. Meany. *Washington Historical Quarterly* 16:56–58, 140–45, 297–98.

Williams, A. Clyde, comp. 1977. Family ancestry chart and affidavit (February 18, 1958) for Amanda Stooquin Williams' estate, Yakama Agency Files, Toppenish, WA.

Williams, Chuck. 1980. *Bridge of the Gods, mountains of fire: A return to the Columbia Gorge.* New York: Friends of the Earth.

Williams, Marsha. 1971. First white descriptions of the Shahala (Cascade) Indians. Unpublished.

Wilson, Douglas. 1999. *Archaeological excavations at Fort Vancouver National Historic Site 1999: New office, waterline, and stockade investigations.* Archaeological Consulting Report No. 12. Seattle: National Park Service, Columbia Cascades Support Office.

————. 2008. Exploring Chinook cultural contact at Station Camp at the mouth of the Columbia River. Paper, annual meeting, Society for American Archaeology, Vancouver, BC.

Wilson, Douglas, et al. 2009. *Historical archaeology at the Middle Village: Station Camp/McGowan archaeological site (45CPC106), Station Camp unit, Lewis and Clark National Park, Pacific County, Washington.* Northwest Cultural Resources Institute Report No. 1.

Wingert, Paul. 1949. *American Indian sculpture: A study of the Northwest Coast.* New York: J. J. Augustin.

————. 1952. *Prehistoric stone sculpture of the Pacific Northwest.* Portland, OR: Portland Art Museum.

Wissler, Clark. 1917. *The American Indian.* New York: Douglas McMurtrie.

Woodward, John. 1986. Prehistoric shipwrecks on the Oregon Coast? Archaeological evidence. In *Contributions to the Archaeology of Oregon, 1983–1986,* ed. Kenneth Ames, 219–64. Association of Oregon Archaeologists Occasional Paper No. 3, Portland.

Work, John. 1824. Journal, April 15–November 25, 1824. Ms. 219, Oregon Historical Society Research Library, Portland.

Wright, Robin. 1991. Masterworks of Washington Native art. In *A time of gathering: Native heritage in Washington State,* ed. Robin Wright, 43–152. Seattle: Burke Museum and University of Washington Press.

Wydoski, Richard, and Richard Whitney. 2003. *Inland fishes of Washington.* 3d ed. Seattle: University of Washington Press.

Wyeth, Nathaniel. 1973 [1899]. *The correspondence and journals of Captain Nathaniel J. Wyeth, 1831–6,* ed. Frederick Young. New York: Arno Press.

Yamaguchi, David, et al. 1997. Tree-ring dating the 1700 Cascadia earthquake. *Nature* 389:922–23.

Yang, Dongya, Aubrey Cannon, and Shelley Saunders. 2004. DNA species identification of archaeological salmon bone from the Pacific Northwest Coast of North America. *Journal of Archaeological Science* 31:619–31.

Zehr, Jamey. 2002. A study of a sample of mammalian remains from Cathlapotle (45CL1), southwestern Washington. MA thesis, University of Missouri, Columbia.

Zenk, Henry. 1976. Contributions to Tualatin ethnography: Subsistence and ethnobiology. MA thesis, Portland State University.

———. 1978–83. Chinuk Wawa data from members of the Grand Ronde Community, Oregon, tapes and tape transcripts. Copies in the cultural resources archives of the Confederated Tribes of the Grand Ronde.

———. 1988. Chinook Jargon in the speech community of Grand Ronde Reservation, Oregon: An ethnography-of-speaking approach to an historical case of creolization in process. *International Journal of the Sociology of Language* 71.

———. 1999. Dr. McKay's Chinook address, May 11, 1892: A commemoration in Chinook Jargon of the first Columbia River centennial. In *Great River of the West: Essays on the Columbia River*, ed. William L. Lang and Robert Carriker. Seattle: University of Washington Press.

———. 2008. Notes on Native American place-names of the Willamette Valley region. *Oregon Historical Quarterly* 109(1):6–33.

Zenk, Henry, and Tony Johnson. 2003. Chinuk Wawa translations by Joe Peter, 1941: Glimpses of a "Chinuk man" in action. In *Papers for ICSNL XXXVIII*, 323–31. Vol. 11. Vancouver: University of British Columbia Working Papers in Linguistics.

———. 2005. Chinookan word classes and Chinuk Wawa etymologies. In *Papers for ICSNL XL*, 331–55. Vol. 16. University of British Columbia Working Papers in Linguistics.

Zucker, Jeff, Kay Hummell, and Bob Hogfoss. 1983. *Oregon Indians: Culture, history and current affairs*. Portland: Oregon Historical Society Press.

CONTRIBUTORS

KENNETH M. AMES is professor emeritus of anthropology at Portland State University and past president of the Society for American Archaeology. He has conducted archaeological field research in western North American since 1968 and along the Lower Columbia River since 1984. The coauthor of *Peoples of the Northwest Coast, their Archaeology and Prehistory* and coeditor of *Household Archaeology on the Northwest Coast*, his work has appeared in *American Antiquity, Antiquity, Journal of Archaeological Science, Evolutionary Anthropology,* and *Journal of Field Archaeology.*

ROBERT T. BOYD is affiliated associate professor in the Anthropology Department at Portland State University. His research specialty is Native American ethnohistory of the Pacific Northwest, and his books include *People of The Dalles, The Coming of the Spirit of Pestilence,* and *Indians, Fire, and the Land in the Pacific Northwest* (editor). He has published articles in *Ethnohistory, American Ethnologist, BC Studies,* and *Oregon Historical Quarterly* and is currently researching a book on Native Portland before the mid-1850s removals.

VIRGINIA L. BUTLER is a professor in the Department of Anthropology, Portland State University. A specialist in zooarchaeology, she studies the relationship between people and animals using archaeological fish remains, with a focus on western North America. Her papers include "Resource Intensification and Resource Depression in the Pacific Northwest of North America" and "Where Have All the Native Fish Gone? The Fate of the Fish that Lewis and Clark Encountered on the Lower Columbia River," and she has published articles in *American Antiquity, Journal of World Prehistory, Journal of Archaeological Science,* and *Quaternary Research.*

DAVID V. ELLIS has done archaeological, historical, and ethnohistorical research on the Lower Columbia River area for over 30 years. His research includes archival research and field studies at numerous archaeological sites, and he has worked with many tribal elders and other tribal representatives. He is the author of dozens of technical reports and conference papers. He was appointed to the Oregon Heritage Commission in 1995, serving as commission chair from 2000 to 2006, and was president of the Association of Oregon Archaeologists. Since 2007, he has been principal archaeologist with Willamette Cultural Resources Associates, Ltd.

ANDREW FISHER, associate professor of history at William & Mary College, received his PhD from Arizona State University. His research and teaching interests focus on modern Native American history, environmental history, and the American West. He is the author of *Shadow Tribe: The Making of Columbia River Indian Identity*, which examines off-reservation communities and processes of tribal ethnogenesis on the mid-Columbia River. His work has appeared in several journals, including *Oregon Historical Quarterly* and *Western Historical Quarterly*.

D. ANN TRIEU GAHR, a paleoethnobotanist and doctoral candidate in anthropology at Southern Illinois University at Carbondale, is coeditor of *Household Archaeology on the Northwest Coast*. Her work has ranged from archaeological projects in Georgia to the Aleutian Islands but has focused on the Northwest. She has worked on many projects, from wood remains at Fort Vancouver, Washington, to fiber and plant remains from Paisley Caves in Oregon's High Desert.

YVONNE HAJDA is a cultural anthropologist, linguist, and ethnohistorian who worked for several years with Native informants on the Warm Springs Reservation. Her 1984 dissertation "Social Organization on the Greater Lower Columbia" at the University of Washington is the fundamental source on the social organization of the Lower Columbia Chinookans. Her publications include "Southwest Washington Salishans" in volume 7 of the *Handbook of North American Indians* and journal articles "Seasonal Population Movement on the Lower Columbia River" (with Robert T. Boyd) and "Slavery in the Greater Lower Columbia Region."

DELL HYMES (1927–2009) was emeritus professor at the University of Virginia and president of the American Anthropological Society and the American Folklore Society. He was a sociolinguist, a pioneer in the study of ethnopoetics, and an expert in Chinookan languages. His dissertation was on the Kathlamet language, and his fieldwork was primarily with Kiksht (Upper Chinook) speakers on the Warm Springs Reservation. His major works include *Foundations in Sociolinguistics* and *"In vain I tried to tell you": Essays in Native American Ethnopoetics*.

MELINDA MARIE JETTÉ, assistant professor of history at Franklin Pierce University in New Hampshire, received a PhD from the University of British Columbia. She has published several articles on the history of the Pacific Northwest in the 19th century and has completed a book-length manuscript on the history of French Prairie, Oregon, in the early 1800s. As a descendent of French Canadians and Natives (Walla Walla) who resettled the Willamette Valley, she has a primary research interest in the role of French-speaking peoples in the American West during the 19th century.

TONY A. JOHNSON, a member of the Chinook Indian Nation, is chair of the Chinook Tribal Cultural Committee. He was cultural education coordinator for the Confederated Tribes of Grand Ronde, where he worked to revitalize and teach Chinuk Wawa (Chinook Jargon). He holds Oregon's first license to teach Chinuk Wawa. As an artist, he is working to revive the Chinookan Art Style, often collaborating with Adam McIsaac, as at the Ridgefield Plankhouse, and he carves canoes in traditional styles—all in the service of revitalizing Chinook culture and heritage.

WILLIAM L. LANG is professor emeritus of history at Portland State University and author or editor of several books on Pacific Northwest history, including *Two Centuries of Lewis and Clark* and *Great River of the West: Essays on the Columbia River*. He is the founder of the Center for Columbia River History, serving as its director from 1990 to 2003, and the *Oregon Encyclopedia of History and Culture*, where he was executive editor and now serves on the editorial advisory board.

DAVID LEWIS is an enrolled member of the Confederated Tribes of Grande Ronde, with ancestral ties to the Santiam Kalapuya, Chinook, Takelma, and

Yoncalla Kalapuya peoples. He was manager of the Grand Ronde Cultural Resources Department and is Tribal Historian and manager of the Cultural Exhibits and Archives Program. Lewis completed his PhD in anthropology at the University of Oregon, where he was director of the Southwest Oregon Research Project. His dissertation was on the termination of the Confederated Tribes of Grand Ronde. A descendant of Santiam treaty-signer Alquema and great-great-grandson of John (Mose) Hudson, the last fluent Kalapuya speaker, Lewis lives in Salem with wife Donna and sons Saghaley and Inatye.

ROBERT LOSEY is an associate professor in the Department of Anthropology at the University of Alberta. His research interests are in human-animal relations, zooarchaeology, the Northwest Coast of North America, and the Lake Baikal region of Siberia. He received his PhD from the University of Oregon, where he studied the Tillamook response to the earthquake and tsunami on the Oregon Coast in 1700. His work has appeared in several journals, including *Journal of Anthropological Archaeology, Journal of Archaeological Science,* and *Oregon Historical Quarterly.*

MICHAEL A. MARTIN has worked as a staff archaeologist with the Portland District Army Corps of Engineers since the mid-1980s. He is interested in federal historic preservation work, and his MA describes the traditional tribal fisheries of the Lower Columbia River as reported in historical documents.

ADAM MCISAAC has dedicated almost 20 years of his life to the preservation of the art and living skills of the Northwest Coast indigenous cultures, studying art with Duane Pasco and living skills with Jim Riggs. He was the head carver for both the Cathlapotle Plankhouse at the Ridgefield National Wildlife Refuge Project and the Confederated Tribes of Grand Ronde carving program and a teacher of Columbia River Chinookan art. He has also collaborated with other artists on various commercial projects throughout the Pacific Northwest.

WILLIAM R. SEABURG is professor of anthropology in the Interdisciplinary Arts and Sciences Program at the University of Washington at Bothell. He has conducted linguistic fieldwork on the Lummi (Salish) and Smith River (Athabaskan) languages. His primary research interests include ethnohistory, the history of anthropological fieldwork in the Pacific Northwest, and Native American oral traditions. He is coauthor of *Coquelle Thompson, Atha-*

baskan Witness: A Cultural Biography, editor and annotator of *The Nehalem Tillamook: An Ethnography*, by Elizabeth D. Jacobs, and editor and annotator of *Pitch Woman and Other Stories: The Oral Traditions of Coquelle Thompson, Upper Coquille Athabaskan Indians*.

ELIZABETH A. SOBEL is assistant professor of anthropology at Missouri State University. She earned her PhD at the University of Michigan in 2004. She has conducted archaeological field research in western North America since 1988 and began focusing on the Lower Columbia River in 1994. She has worked as an archaeologist for federal and tribal agencies, including the Bureau of Land Management, US Fish and Wildlife Service, and the Yakama Nation. She is coeditor of *Household Archaeology on the Northwest Coast* and has published in the *Journal of Anthropological Archaeology*, *Journal of California and Great Basin Anthropology*, and *Archaeology in Washington*.

WAYNE SUTTLES (1918–2005) was professor emeritus at Portland State University. He was an anthropological linguist and ethnographer and an authority on Northwest Coast ethnography in the last half of the 20th century, although his own work was primarily with Coast Salish. He was editor of volume 7, *Northwest Coast*, of the *Handbook of North American Indians* and the authoritative *Musqueam Reference Grammar*. In the 1960s, he published a series of seminal papers on Northwest Coast social organization and environment, which were compiled in *Coast Salish Essays* (1987).

EIRIK THORSGARD is an enrolled member of the Confederated Tribes of Grand Ronde and a direct descendant of the people at Willamette Falls. He works in the tribe's Cultural Resources Department as the cultural protection coordinator and tribal historic preservation officer and is a PhD candidate at Flinders University in Adelaide, South Australia. He regularly participates in cultural events and is active in national and international archaeology conferences. He is the father of four children and the husband of Misty Thorsgard.

CHUCK WILLIAMS is a photographer and owner of the Columbia Gorge Gallery and American West Archives in The Dalles, a writer, and the former publications editor for the Columbia River Inter-Tribal Fish Commission. His photographs have been featured in several exhibits, and he is the author of *Bridge of the Gods, Mountains of Fire: A Return to the Columbia River Gorge* and two books on Mount St. Helens. He is a member of the Confederated Tribes of Grand Ronde and great-great grandson of Tumaulth, Cascades signer of the Willamette Valley Treaty, who was hanged by Lt. Philip Sheridan after the Cascades Incident of 1856.

HENRY ZENK received his PhD in anthropology from the University of Oregon in 1984. His dissertation was based on original field research with some of Oregon's last fluent speakers of Chinuk Wawa (Chinook Jargon), all elders of the Grand Ronde Indian Community. Since 1998 he has been working as a linguistic consultant with the Chinuk Wawa language program of the Confederated Tribes of Grand Ronde. In addition to contributing to scholarly series and symposia, he compiled and edited *Chinuk Wawa kakwa nsayka ulman-tilixam łaska munk-kəmtəks nsayka /Chinuk Wawa as Our Elders Teach Us to Speak It*, a Chinuk Wawa dictionary published in 2012 by the Confederated Tribes of Grand Ronde.

INDEX

McDougall, Duncan, 116–18, 157, 237–38, 264

McKay, William, 287, 333

McLoughlin, John, 239, 245, 266–67

measles. *See* disease

Meier (35CO5), 34, 67, 69–73, 96, 110, 130–31, 136–45, 223

menstruation, 46, 56, 140, 184–86, 198

metal, 110–11, 250, 252, 255

Metís, 285–87

miasmatic theory, 241

Michelle, Marianne, 311

migration hypotheses, 29

Millet, Sam, 5, 77, 189, 329, 334

minnows (*Cyprinidae*), 90–93, 96

minnow-sucker group, 92, 97, 99, 103

Minor, Rick, 58–59

Minto, John, 72, 236

missionaries, 161, 181, 245, 269–71, 273, 283, 285, 337–38, 341

Molala (people, language), 44, 275, 307, 310–11, 321

"monsters" (mythology), 45–46, 167, 172, 218, 250, 311

morticians, 193

mosquitoes (*Anopheles freeborni*), 104, 241

Mount Coffin, 57, 195–96

mourning, 121–22, 193–94, 196

Multnomah (people, dialect), x, xvi, 18, 33, 112, 148, 239, 243, 307, 321–22, 327

Multnomah Period, 26, 33, 93, 100–1

Myers, W. E., 330

Myth Age, 12, 42, 44, 46, 164, 184–86, 188, 312

mythology, 12–13, 163–70, 238; actors, 165–67; definition of, 164; motifs, 167; opening and closing of, 165–66; projection theory of, 164–65; story-telling, etiquette for, 171; tale-types and plots, 168–70

naming, 5, 13

Naselle, 7, 85, 190

Nechacolee, 149, 235

Neerchokioo, 56, 152, 255, 261

Nehalem. *See* Tillamook

Nemah, 12, 14, 247

Nemalquinner, 152–53, 260

nephrite, 107

nets, 11, 53, 83–84, 86, 91–92, 137, 184–85, 270, 297

Nez Perce, 118, 311, 319, 324

Nootka Jargon, 277–78, 281–82

Northern Art Style, ix, xii

North West Company, 264–66

Northwest Coast (culture area), ix, xi–xii, 31, 76, 80, 84, 125–26, 182, 185

Oak Point, 51, 56, 92, 130, 152, 307

oak savanna, 24, 27–28, 37, 77

object intrusion, 233

obsidian, 67, 106–08, 111, 113–14, 122, 138

olivella shells, 107–08

oral literature, ix, 163–80; performance of, 170–71

Oregon City, 307, 311

Oregon Donation Land Act, 290, 295

O'Rourke, Leslie, 59

overfishing, 38, 73, 81, 86, 186

overharvest, 38, 73, 81, 86, 186

Owl (spirit), 72, 188–89, 211, 223

ownership, of resources, 49, 68–69, 72

Owyhee (ship), 238, 241

oysters, 11, 14, 53

Ozette, 137

Pacific Fur Company, 118–21, 148, 150, 155–59, 183, 185, 229, 237, 262–64, 337, 339, 344–45

Pacific Period, 31, 33, 36

Paisley Cave, 26, 28

Paleoindian Period, 29